STUDIO GHIBLI
DREAM ARTISTS

TRANSLATED BY BETH SMITH

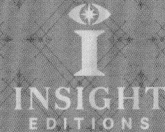

INSIGHT
EDITIONS

SAN RAFAEL · LOS ANGELES · LONDON

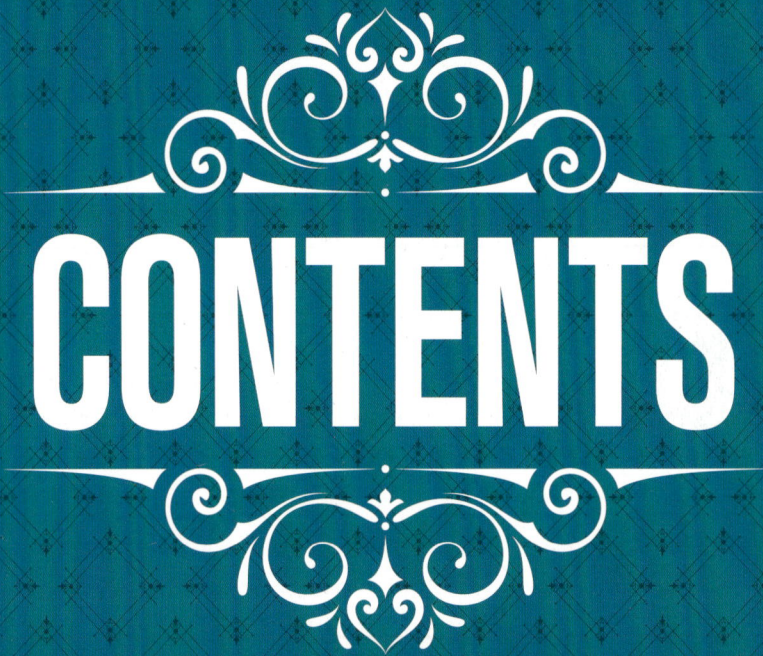

CONTENTS

INTRODUCTION

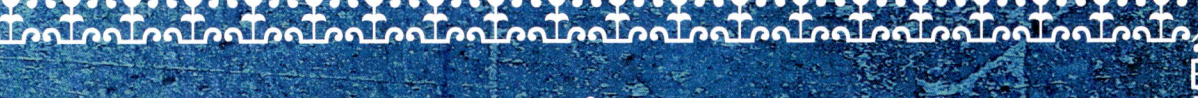

GHIBLI: THE HOLY MONSTER

After several months in the making, this tribute to Ghibli was published in 2018. Six years later, it was updated to keep up with the legendary studio's latest developments. Nearly forty years after its creation, its productions haven't aged a bit, and despite the constant evolution of animation techniques, the Ghibli style remains intact.

Ghibli is all about worlds, characters, strong emotions, and, of course, music. Ghibli films are renowned worldwide, sometimes reaching unexpected viewers who are moved by both the simplicity of a story and the explosion of color, a unique aesthetic that has never been equaled. Although a new generation of young filmmakers is making a mark on Japanese animation, Ghibli remains the *monstre sacré* (the holy monster), lending its prestige to a sometimes disparaged art form.

This book chronicles the journey of a studio that has captured our hearts for many years with its powerful messages and subtle poetry. Talented French artists have been enlisted to pay tribute to those who still inspire us.

GLOSSARY

Anime: Pronounced "animay." Term used to designate comics in Japan.
Character designer: Person in charge of creating the graphic (and even psychological) charter for a project's characters.
Fan service: Behavior intended to fuel fans' fantasies.
Kanji: Chinese characters used in the Japanese language.
Kawaii: A Japanese cultural style that emphasizes childlike imagery and bright pastels, its name literally meaning "cute."
Mangaka: Manga author.
OAV: Abbreviation for "original animated video," the equivalent of today's direct-to-video (DTV).
Otaku: An obsessive fan (a pejorative term in Japan). In some countries, it is often incorrectly used to describe someone who loves manga and anime.
Shōjo (manga): Manga for girls, ages 12–18.
Shōnen (manga): Manga for boys, ages 12–18.
Seinen (manga): Manga for adults.

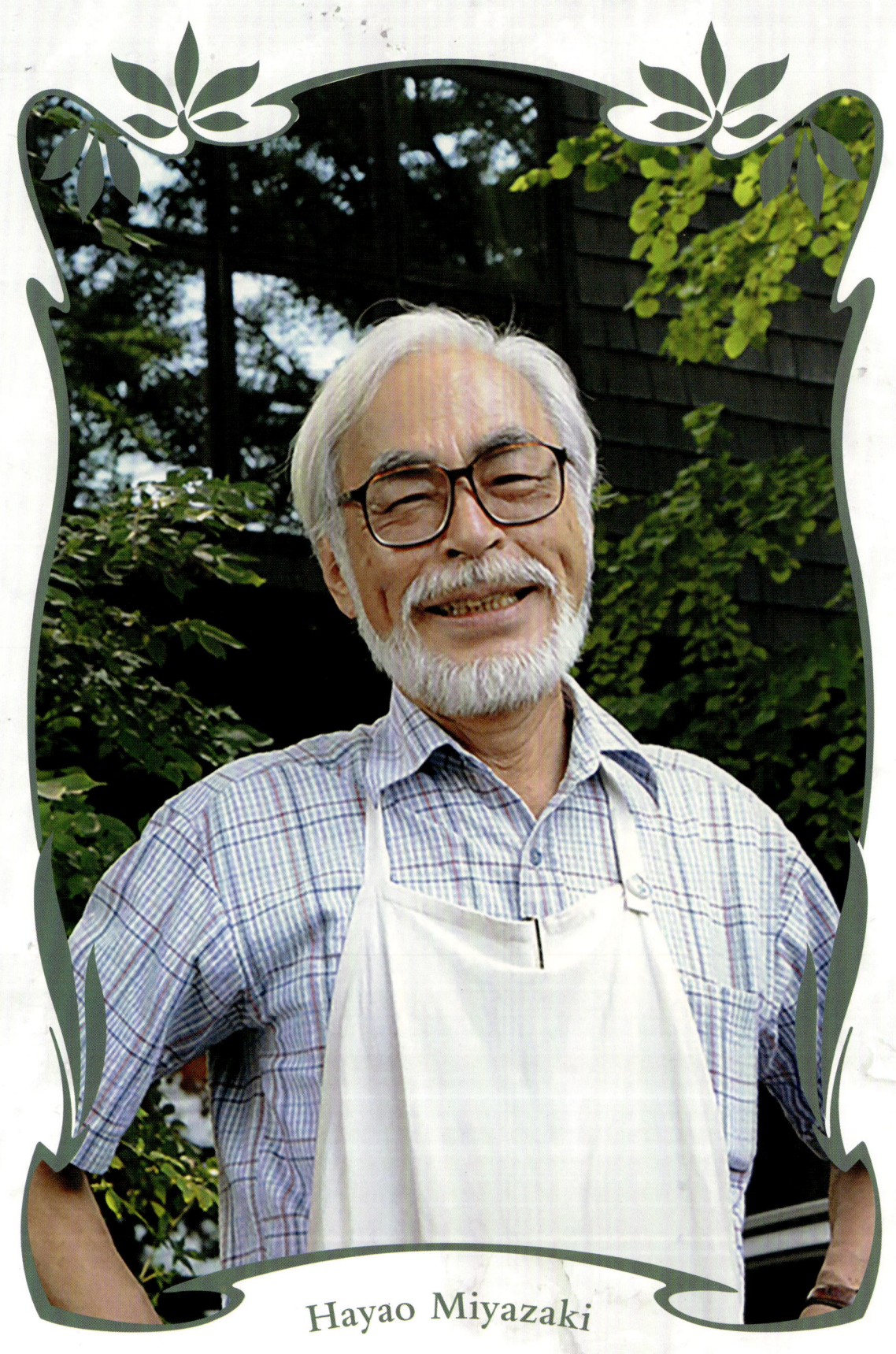

Hayao Miyazaki

HAYAO MIYAZAKI

Although *Nausicaä* was the film that allowed Miyazaki to make enough money to go independent and found Ghibli, his films for younger viewers such as *My Neighbor Totoro* made him a household name and won him an Oscar (*Spirited Away*). Ironically, Miyazaki began his career wanting to make animated works that were not just for children.

By Bounthavy Suvilay

When Miyazaki joined Toei, he dreamed of feature films like Paul Grimault's *The Curious Adventures of Mr. Wonderbird* (1953) and *The Snow Queen* (1957) by Lev Atamanov. His goal was to one day work on a major motion picture like *The Legend of the White Snake* (Hakujaden, 1958), which the studio had produced. He trained with Toei veterans but rebelled against the producers' narrow vision and contributed to the *Horus: Prince of the Sun* project, on which he developed his vision of animation for an adult audience.

A FRUSTRATED REBEL

The film's box office failure prevented its team from repeating the experience, but the idea of a feature film not geared to children continued to take shape. In the meantime, Miyazaki joined his mentor, Ôtsuka, at the rival animation studio A Production, where he also worked with Takahata. They were involved in the creation of a series not intended for a young audience: *Lupin III*. This adaptation of a successful *seinen* manga featured lots of chases and curvaceous female characters. But above all, it allowed the *Horus* team to continue to explore non-Manichaean characters and complex plots. Tight deadlines meant the teams worked on several episodes simultaneously, benefiting from the combined influence of several directors rather than a single person. It was in this setting that Miyazaki no doubt tried directing. Unfortunately, commercial success was

once again elusive. It seemed that the public at the time wasn't ready for this type of series, even though today, this first anime version of *Lupin III* is the most popular with the Japanese.

After that, Miyazaki continued to work on television series, but this time, he and his colleagues targeted a children's audience, most notably with animated adaptations of major novels from world children's literature for Nippon Animation. Takahata directed *Heidi* (1974) and *Anne of Green Gables* (1979), while Miyazaki was in charge of the layout. His return to series was more a matter of circumstance than of choice for this particular format. It followed the failure to adapt *Pippi Longstocking* into a film after the author refused. Miyazaki and Takahata then made *Panda! Go Panda!* and its sequel (1972, 1973), short films that revived elements of

the suspended feature-length project and held the seeds of the future *Totoro*. Although series were not Miyazaki's preferred format, he made his directorial debut in this medium. In 1978, he created *Future Boy Conan* for NHK, with Ôtsuka as animation director. It was an enormous success that helped him establish himself in the director's chair, and the following year, he direc-

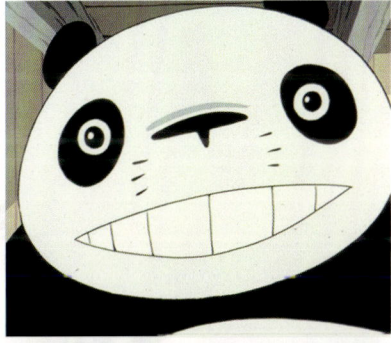

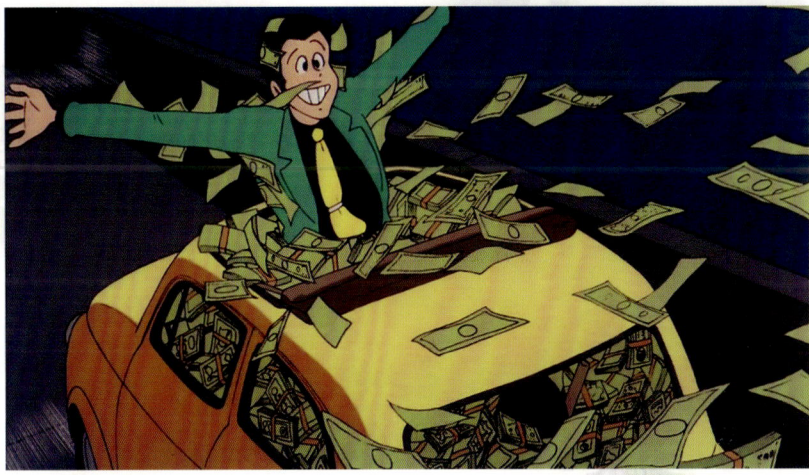

ted the feature film *Lupin III: The Castle of Cagliostro* (1979). From then on, he primarily worked on films as a director, as this gave him control over the entire chain of production and ensured that the final product reached the high standards he required.

A DRAWING FANATIC

Of course, being a director didn't keep him from drawing and correcting some or all of other people's work on his projects; Miyazaki has always been a workaholic. On Takahata's series, he handled layout on his own, doing what was usually a three-person job. On *Conan* and his early works, he took on almost every task: character design, script, storyboard, layout, and so on. Takahata stated in an interview that Miyazaki wanted to control everything, and that if he could have cloned himself, he would have. When it came to using new technologies like 3D, Miyazaki maintained his desire for control and checked everything relentlessly. On *Princess Mononoke*, for example, he is said to have redrawn 80,000 key poses. He used those exacting standards to create stunning action scenes in which everything (characters, objects, and clothing) moves, with variations in framing to better create the illusion of depth in the scenery.

When he wasn't drawing to correct others on his films, Miyazaki was making manga. In addition to *Nausicaä*, a major work that ran from 1982 to 1994, he regularly published stories in *Model Graphix*, a monthly magazine on model-building. This gave him the opportunity to illustrate his other obsessions: airplanes, tanks, and various other machinery. His short stories, usually in watercolor, were then collected and often adapted for feature films; these included *Hikoutei Jidai* (*The Age of the Flying Boat*, 1989), *Zassô Nôtu* (*Daydream Data Notes*, 1990), *Hansu no kikan* (*The Return of Hans*, 1994), *Doromamire no Tora* (*Mud-covered Tigers*, 1999), and *The Wind Rises* (2009–2010).

These manga provided a kind of safety valve for the busy film studio co-founder. But they were also the precursors of *Porco Rosso* and *The Wind Rises*. Miyazaki's many other manga include *Shuna no Tabi* (*Shuna's Journey*, 1983) and *Princess Mononoke* (1993), a hundred-page book of sketches dating back to 1980. In these pages, we also find the seeds of many of his future creations, such as *Nausicaä*, *Totoro*, and *Princess Mononoke*. When Miyazaki wasn't sketching for his films, he was illustrating stories that almost always ended up as feature-length films. His need to draw no doubt explains why he has announced his retirement so many times only to return to work.

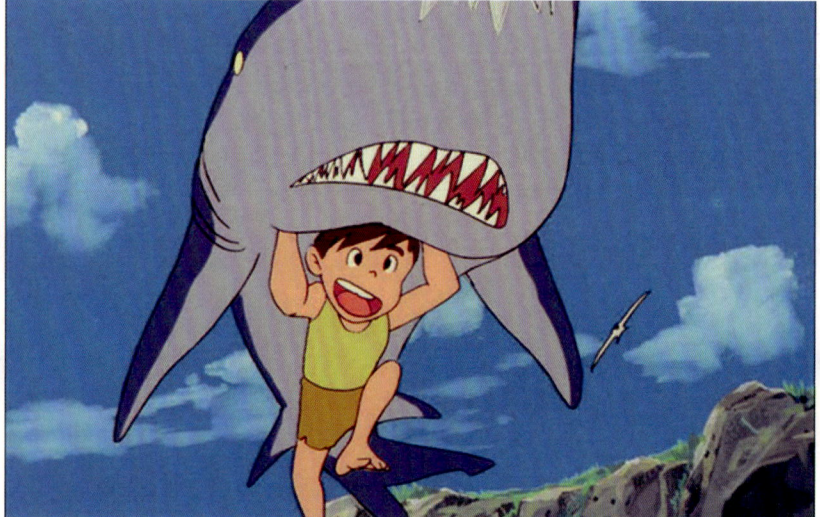

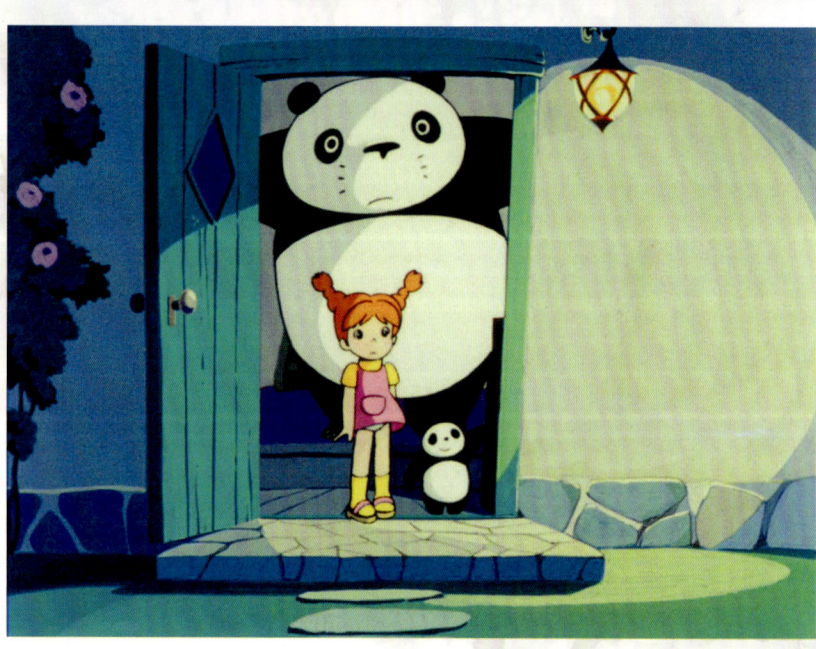

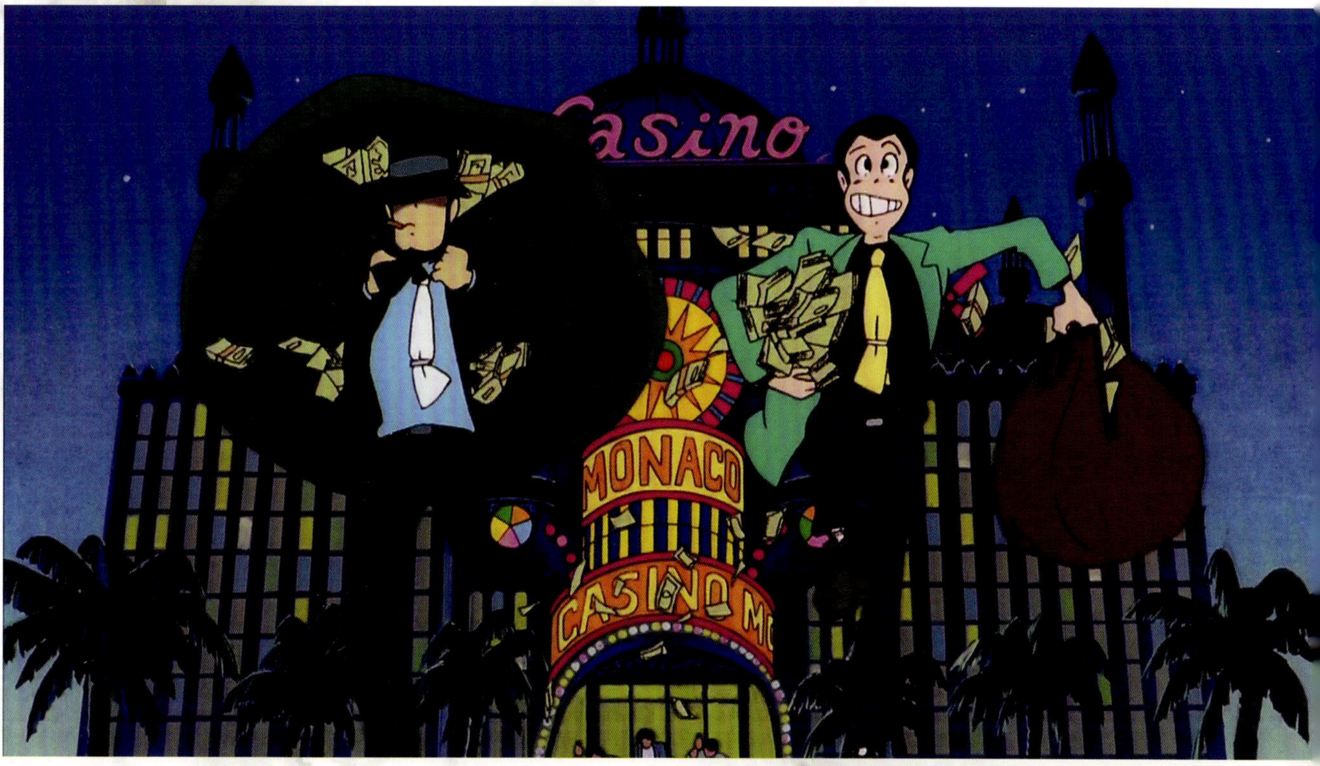

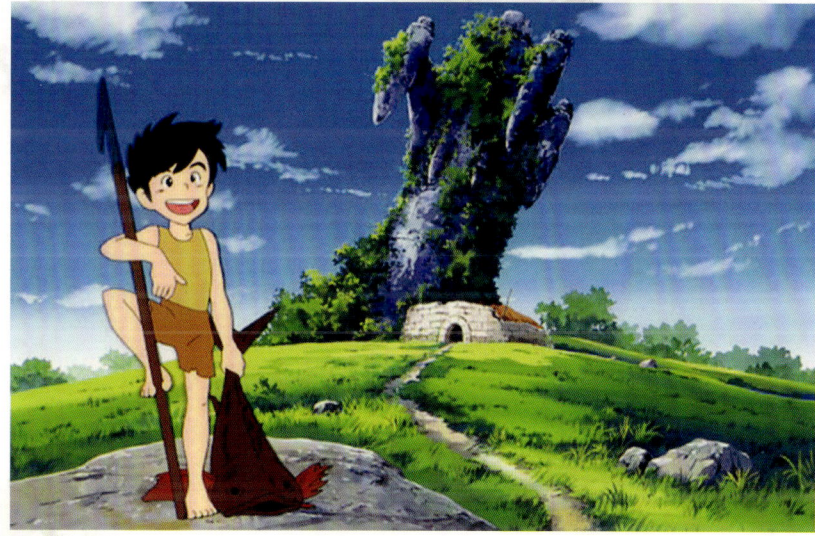

AN ACTIVE PESSIMIST

Although he is best known as the creator of the benevolent and smiling Totoro, Miyazaki is first and foremost a pessimist interested in war and its ravages. While he admires the technological achievements that may have been facilitated during times of war, he is a constant, fervent denouncer of the absurdity of war. Born in 1941, he was too young to really understand the Second World War.

Nevertheless, he has long been resentful of his country's involvement in an absurd conflict. More recently, he openly opposed a change in the constitution allowing Japan to rebuild its army. He is relatively pessimistic when it comes to humans, and prefers to represent himself as a pig, especially in stories about war machines. His manga *Nausicaä* ends with a bitter conclusion about the foresight of scientists and politicians. In an interview with novelist Ryu Murakami, Miyazaki explained that today's problems are too complicated for a male hero to solve through simple, epic action, like in an Indiana Jones movie. This is one of the factors that led him to draw female characters as heroines. They are more complex and reasonable, and bet-

ter able to reflect the evolution of the modern world.

This pessimism regarding humanity no doubt explains his attachment to nature, which is glorified in all his films. He was also determined to set up Studio Ghibli in a location surrounded by greenery, and he provides financial support for ecological associations. He is aware of his rather negative outlook and doesn't seek to impose it on future generations. His children's films tend to perpetuate

a sense of wonder for the natural world. Let's hope that *Totoro* will succeed in guiding mankind where *Nausicaä*'s scientists failed.

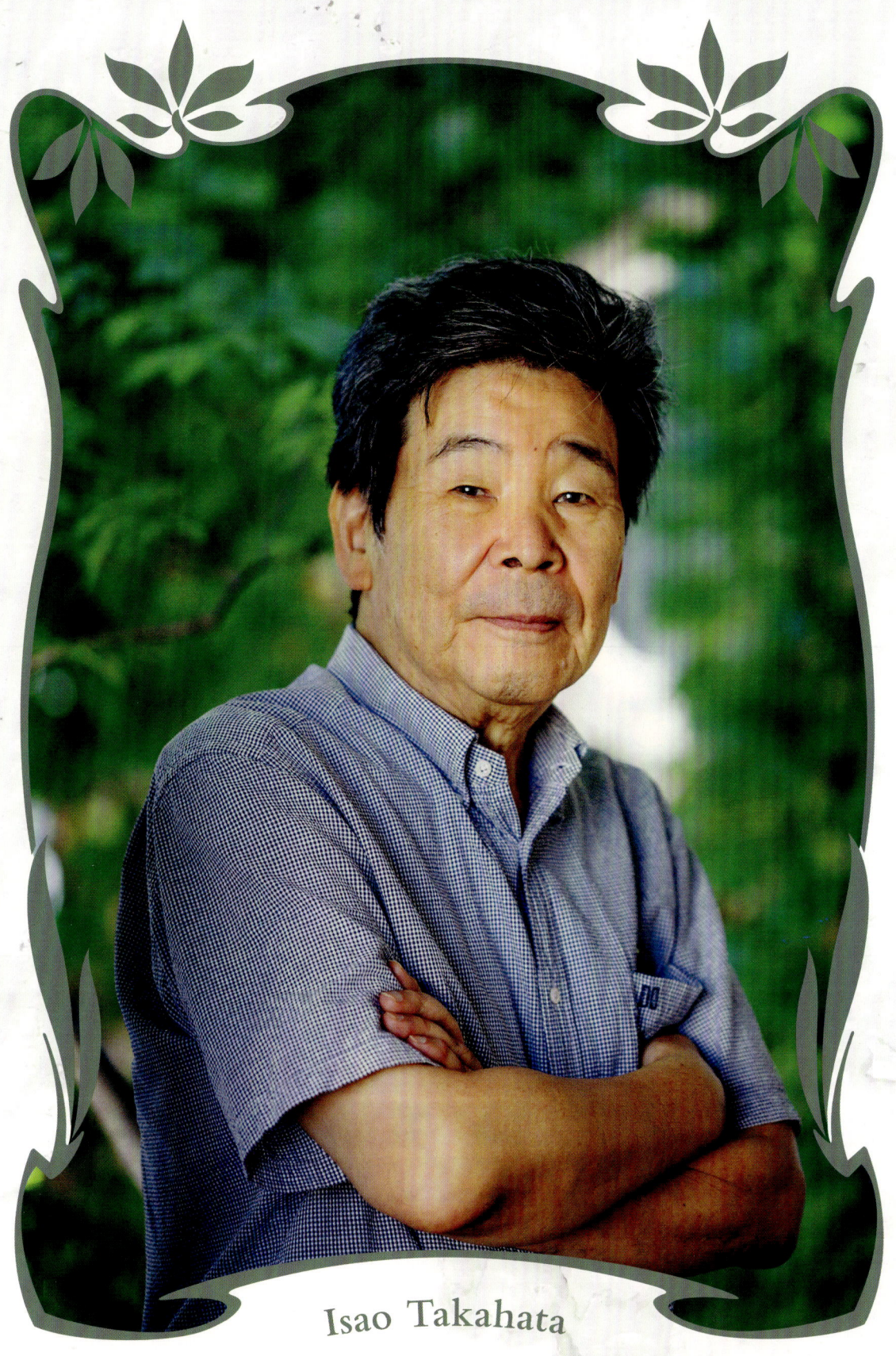

Isao Takahata

ISAO TAKAHATA

Unlike Miyazaki, Isao Takahata didn't draw (initially, he was exclusively a director), and he directed a lot of anime before Studio Ghibli was founded. The failure of his first feature film, *Horus: Prince of the Sun*, left a lasting impression on him. However, he maintained his ideal of aesthetic perfection and his desire to create "realistic" films to the very end.

By Bounthavy Suvilay

Isao Takahata—who died on April 5, 2018, at the age of eighty-two—was Hayao Miyazaki's mentor before becoming the other founding pillar of Studio Ghibli. His conception of animated films differed from that of his colleague, being less fantastic and more realistic. Of course, it wasn't a question of redrawing what could be done with live-action images; Takahata sought to capture the essence of characters and situations and translate them to the screen. He was interested in the intimate, not the heroic. This is undoubtedly why he was considered more "Japanese" than Miyazaki.

A SCHOLAR AND MUSIC LOVER

While Miyazaki directed his own scripts, Takahata seemed to prefer to start from existing works and adapt them to the medium of animation. He was behind Nippon Animation's series of children's literature classics, including *Heidi: A Girl of the Alps* (1974), *3000 Leagues in Search of Mother* (1976), and *Anne of Green Gables* (1979). He also adapted short stories by Japanese novelists, such as Akiyuki Nosaka's *Grave of the Fireflies* (1988) and Kenji Miyazawa's *Gauche the Cellist* (1982). He also managed to re-create the world of the *mangaka* in a coherent film with a combination of comics with gags and personal memories, even though it had no unifying structure or storyline. That was the case with the sketches in *Chie the Brat* (1981), *Only Yesterday* (1991), and *My Neighbors the Yamadas* (1999). The only work in which

he played an active role in creating the original story was *Pom Poko* (1994), an ecological fable about the destruction of the forests. Nevertheless, Takahata made the works he adapted his own, modifying them in line with the medium and his personal convictions.

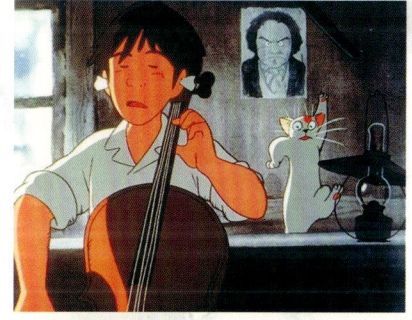

Was his respect for texts related to his studies in French literature? Perhaps. In any case, after his university studies, Takahata was hired by Toei Animation to equal the esteemed French animator Grimault. There's no doubt that he was as captivated by poet Jacques Prévert's dialogues as he was by the directing. His fascination with the medium led him to publish books spotlighting the animated films he loved, such as *Tale of Tales* (1979) by the Russian Yuri Norstein and *The Man Who Planted Trees* (1987) by the Canadian Frédéric Back, adapted from a story by Jean Giono. He also organized exhibitions and took part in conferences to demonstrate the importance of twelfth-century *emakimono*. He considered the Japanese drawing scrolls to be the

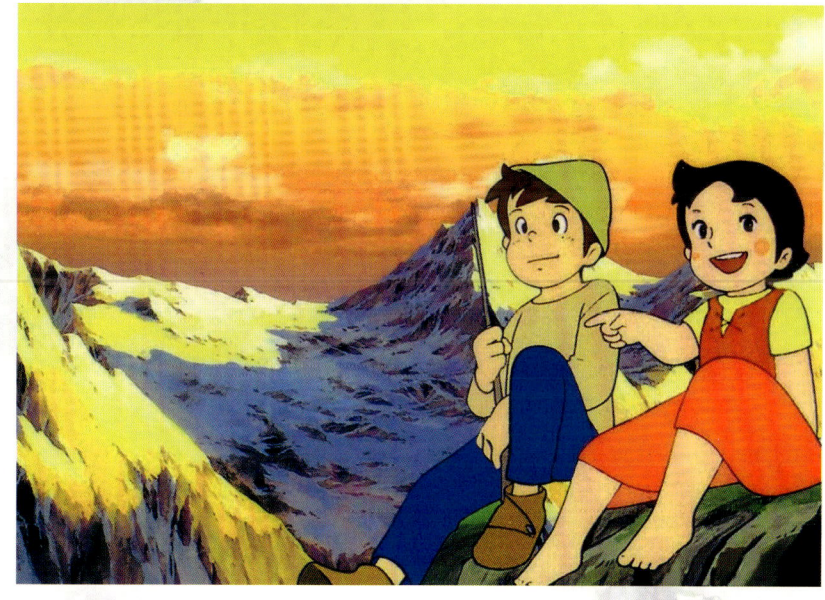

precursors of animation and devoted a book to them. In addition to his efforts to raise awareness of animation as a specific medium with its own history and artists, Takahata also devoted a great deal of time to music, which he loved. He dedicated an entire film to musical apprenticeship (*Gauche the Cellist*, 1982) to introduce classical music to the Japanese public. For that film, he even had the benefit of an almost entirely recorded soundtrack before creating the corresponding animation. He subsequently supervised the musical direction of several Ghibli films, including Miyazaki's 1989 feature *Kiki's Delivery Service*.

A METICULOUS DIRECTOR

Unlike directors who focus on the script or storyboard and neglect the other stages of production, Takahata was meticulous when it came to animation and art direction. On *Horus*, he asked the animators to justify the characters' behavior with feelings, rather than drawing poses because they seemed interesting to portray. He was able to impose an artistic coherence that had never been seen before in Japanese studios. A stickler for technical details, he hesitated to make *Grave of the Fireflies* because he felt that the celluloid used for animation at the time was not the best way to convey what he had in mind. He later used a unique computer colorization technique to achieve watercolor-like rendering on *My Neighbors the Yamadas*, and in his last film, 2013's *The Tale of the Princess Kaguya*, he wanted to push the limits of animation even further, with greater cohesion between characters and scenery, as well as images containing a lot of white, like in traditional prints, where emptiness is more suggestive than painted elements. A new studio was set up just a few minutes by train from Ghibli's premises to make it possible to produce the film.

In addition to this attention to technical detail, Takahata was also painstaking in his depiction of reality. To make the Alps in *Heidi* believable, he and his team traveled to Switzerland to scout out locations, which was not a common practice for animated series at the time. Takahata's desire for an almost documentary-like portrayal can be seen in the only film he made that is mostly live action: *The Story of Yanagawa's Canals*. His goal was to show the interaction between people and the environment, a relationship threatened by intensive urbanization and a lifestyle with no connection to natural cycles.

This attention to detail explains the requirement to constantly stay close to Takahata to be able to work with him. For example, when Yoshiaki Nishimura was appointed producer of *Princess Kaguya*, he was told that he would practically have to live with the master.

Takahata's commitment to control and perfectionism contrasted with his libertarian streak. He was a trade unionist at Toei and introduced a system of voluntary work for the film *Horus*. On *Gauche the Cellist*, participants were almost all volunteers, working in their spare time for six years. But after founding Ghibli, he had to focus more specifically on the budget needed to finance films and on marketing to ensure sufficient revenue to pay employee salaries. Nevertheless, he seemed to free himself from these concerns when making *Princess Kaguya*.

INTIMIST AND DISENCHANTED

In each of his works, Takahata sought to depict everyday elements as accurately as possible so that viewers could better identify with the characters. He explained how important it was to portray activities in the village that Horus later defends, so that the audience sympathizes with the

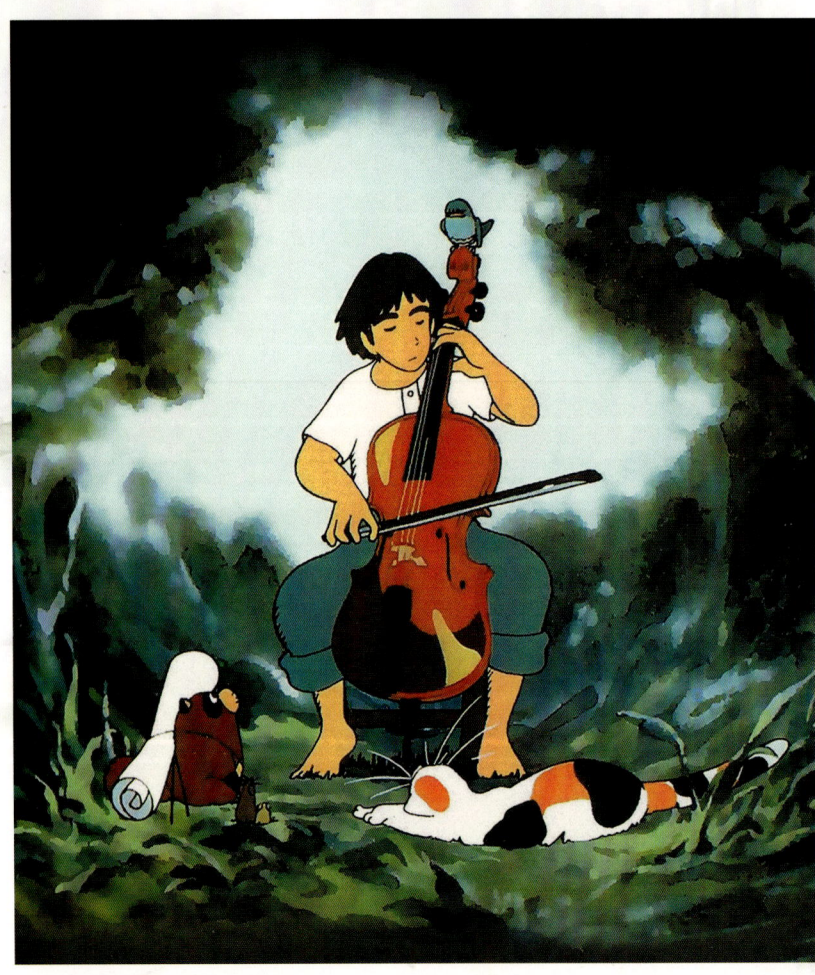

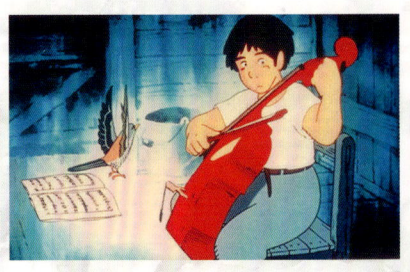

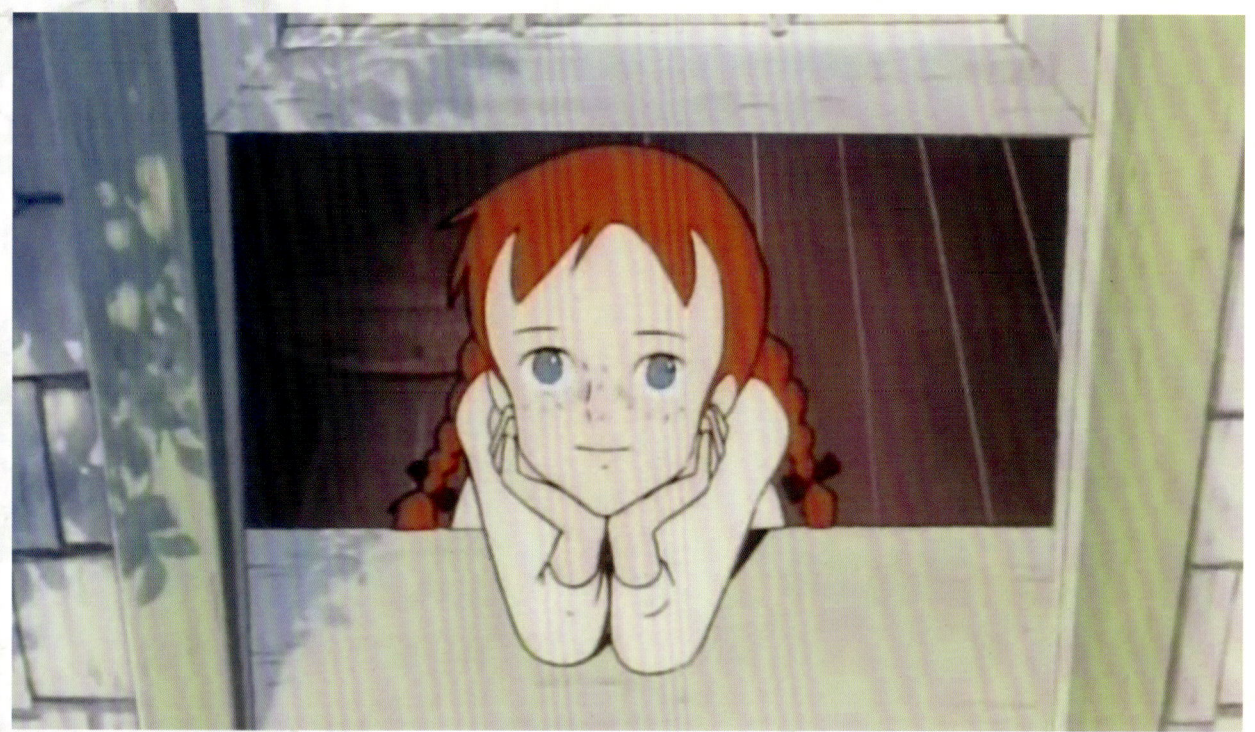

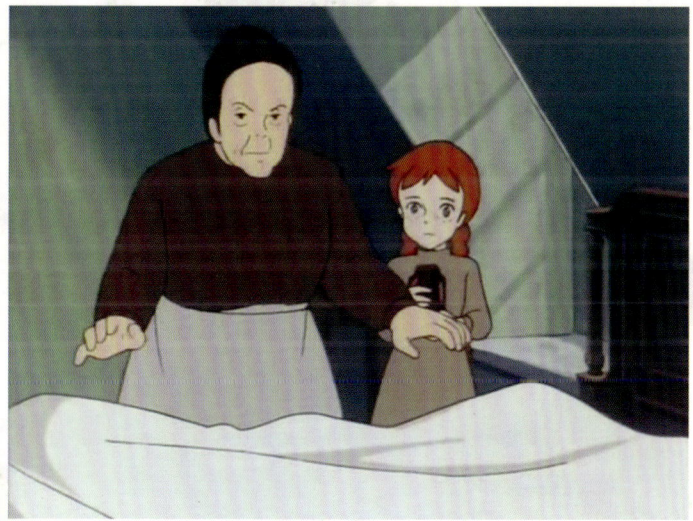

villagers' cause. We learn how to live in the mountains along with Heidi, or how to eat a pineapple (an exotic fruit in Japan at the time) with Taeko's family in *Only Yesterday*. These mundane details of everyday life are transformed into emotionally charged symbolic episodes, such as the holidays that the tanuki (raccoon dogs) no longer celebrate at the end of *Pom Poko* and, in *Grave of the Fireflies*, the empty candy tin that holds Setsuko's ashes.

The realism of everyday scenes is offset by a more poetic approach that allows the story to touch us. For example, the ghosts of *Fireflies* protagonists Seita and Setsuko rub shoulders with surviving children to convey the fragility of their existence. To show the family's unity despite their petty quarrels in *My Neighbors the Yamadas*, they transform into a bobsled team to overcome the obstacles of everyday life, finally soaring through the air in a fireworks display at the end of the film.

As he grew older, the scenes of metamorphosis took on greater scope—like in *Pom Poko*, *The Yamadas*, and *Princess Kaguya*—as a desire to transcend a disenchanted reality where the best is always in the past, whether it's a brief moment of joy with the fireflies before they die in the morning, walks with the children in the mountains before Kaguya and Heidi are forced to move to the city, or a Japan that no longer exists except in Taeko's memories.

Both realistic and poetic, Takahata's films bear witness to a society that is losing touch with its environment, its history, and its traditions. Undoubtedly as pessimistic as Miyazaki, the artist failed to make his creations as lighthearted as those of his colleague in a way that would have invited audiences to appreciate his work during his lifetime.

YASUO ÔTSUKA

THE *SENPAI* OF HAYAO MIYAZAKI AND ISAO TAKAHATA

Yasuo Ôtsuka, who died in March 2021 at the age of eighty-nine, was a pioneer in Japanese animation. He was so important to Studio Ghibli that even though he didn't work there, the studio dedicated a documentary to him in 2004: *Yasuo Ôtsuka's Joy of Motion*. He was considered the mentor of the Takahata-Miyazaki duo.

❧ By Bruno de la Cruz ☙

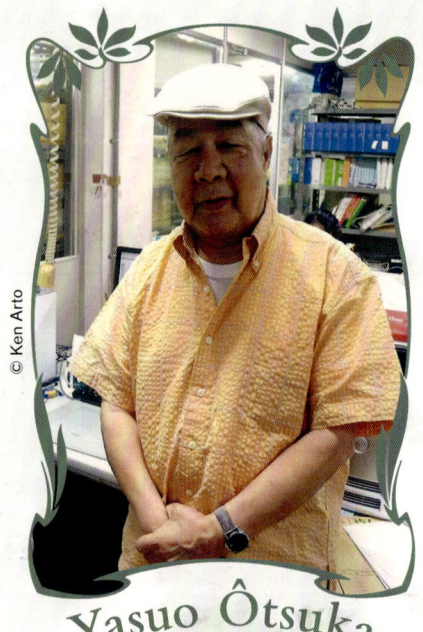

© Ken Arto

Yasuo Ôtsuka

"I first met Ôtsuka-san almost twenty years ago. For me, he's an excellent mentor." When Hayao Miyazaki talked about Yasuo Ôtsuka's importance to him in his book *Starting Point 1979–1996*, the director was full of praise. "Ôtsuka-san was the one who taught me the pleasure of work. He was always ready to discuss things with younger people on equal terms. I remember very vividly those days when, preparing for *Horus: Prince of the Sun* (1968), we used to get together at Paku-san's [Ôtsuka's] place and talk all night long. We were all young, and bursting with ambition and hope." The same was true for Takahata: "Ôtsuka influenced me from the start. I don't

draw, so I had to learn by watching animators. He was always happy to answer my stupid questions. I consider him one of my greatest teachers."[1]

A LITTLE HISTORY

To understand the two illustrious men's admiration for Yasuo Ôtsuka, we should look back at his unusual career, which began with a stint in the department of drug trafficking within the Ministry of Health, Labor, and Social Affairs. A fan of military vehicles, Ôtsuka was already an excellent illustrator when he joined Toei Animation in 1956. He quickly became a key animator and tried to break away from the constraints of limited animation (a practice that uses fewer frames than full animation and repeats illustration elements) with a more demonstrative style. Ôtsuka's exuberant realism, under the

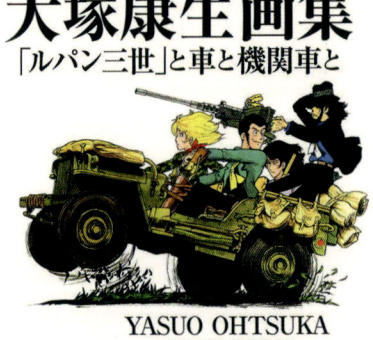

大塚康生画集
「ルパン三世」と車と機関車と

YASUO OHTSUKA
MECHANICAL ARTWORKS

guidance of his mentors Akira Daikubara and Yasuji Mori (two artists who had developed the *e-konte*, the Japanese equivalent of the storyboard), established him as a reliable key animator. He met the young Miyazaki (who was an inbetweener at the time) and Takahata at Toei Animation. With a crisis brewing at the studio, Ôtsuka was put in charge of the *Horus: Prince of the Sun* project (1968).

Ôtsuka threatened Toei that he would not take part in the film unless they appointed Takahata as director; it would be his first time directing a feature-length film. "*Horus: Prince of the Sun* must be the first feature film where directing took over the creative process. It could be said that the work changed history."[2] Ôtsuka assumed the crucial role of animation director. It's a unique position in Japanese animation, with huge responsibilities, as he himself explained. "The most important job is to make sure that the characters' faces are consistent throughout the film. The senior member of the team is the animation director. There are always new recruits entering the world of animation, and you need someone who can lead them. They need to guide the new recruits."[3]

[1] Hayao Miyazaki, *Starting Point 1979–1996*, Viz LLC.
[2] Studio Ghibli, Hayao Miyazaki, and Isao Takahata, *Studio Ghibli Layout Designs: Understanding the Secrets of Takahata-Miyazaki Animation*, published for the *Studio Ghibli Layout Designs Exhibition*.
[3] *Lupin III: The Castle of Cagliostro*, video extras on the French DVD, IDP, 2006.

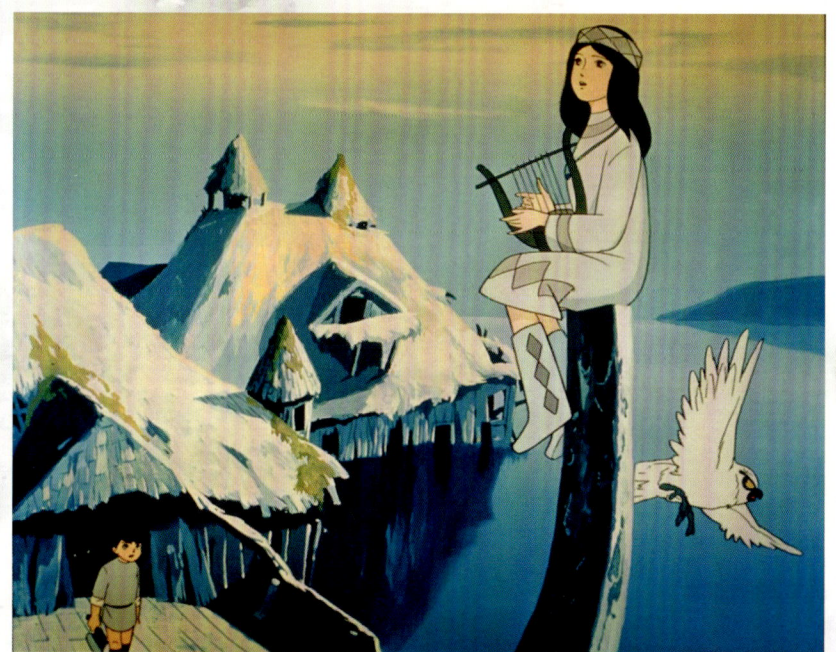

mation director, Ôtsuka would impress on Takahata's *Chie the Brat*.

In the documentary *Yasuo Ôtsuka's Joy of Motion*, Miyazaki talked about the infectious delight that emanated from Ôtsuka's work. The animation world being a field of emulation and influence, the energy of Ôtsuka's creations rubbed off on those around him. As a frequent animation director, Ôtsuka was able to let his great teaching spirit shine through. He trained many young people—including Yoshiyuki Sadamoto, the character designer on *Neon Genesis Evangelion*—at a time when studios no longer had the time to nurture new talent. Toshio Suzuki, former president of Studio Ghibli, announced his death at the Tokyo Anime Award Festival (TAAF) ceremony in 2021.

Ôtsuka is no longer with us, but his legacy remains eternal.

Despite its box office failure, this ambitious film produced by volunteers served as a laboratory of ideas. A trio was born, united by a vision: to offer daring, unconventional works, modernizing the animation industry's most important tool, after the pencil: the layout (a drawing on a sheet of paper representing a storyboard plan). Yasuo Ôtsuka contributed five pages to the inexhaustible bible of information that is *Studio Ghibli Layout Designs: Understanding the Secrets of Takahata-Miyazaki Animation*. He talked about the importance of layout in *Horus*, a film for which he was animation director: " 'It was a radical change in the creative process,' mused Yasuo Ôtsuka, then he continued. 'Until then, storyboards were under the direction of the animators [one scene = one animator; editor's note]. [...] What was special about the film was that the ideas presented on the imageboard weren't given to the artists as they were. We put everything into the storyboard, and then the work was completed according to its instructions. Paku [as Ôtsuka was affectionately known] gave me detailed instructions, and together we drew the storyboards for all the scenes, [...] established a storyboard as a basis for our work, then made a layout for each shot, and drew the key

images and backgrounds. I think we had just created Ghibli style.' "

TECHNICIAN AND TEACHER

Ôtsuka's next move was to join A Production (renamed Shin-Ei Animation, or Shin'ei Dôga, in 1976). The young Miyazaki and Takahata were quick to follow Ôtsuka's lead: proof, if any were needed, of the guiding role he played in their lives. The trio went on to work on the (abandoned) *Pippi Longstocking* project and, above all, the 1971 *Lupin the Third* series. It was a joy for Ôtsuka: "Since animation was mainly intended for children, it was rare for me to be able to draw vehicles, weapons, and watches with such realism and detail." Ôtsuka's next departure took him to Nippon Animation, where Hayao Miyazaki headed the *Future Boy Conan* series (1978). The director insisted that Ôtsuka join him. He was to be a character designer. "At the time, I was working at Shin'ei Dôga," Ôtsuka recalled in a bonus feature with *Lupin III: The Castle of Cagliostro* (1979). "So, I resigned to join him on *Conan*. Miyazaki owed me in a way, so when I asked him to come and do *Cagliostro* [Ôtsuka had joined the TMS studio by then], he kind of felt obliged [laughs]." Still in his role as ani-

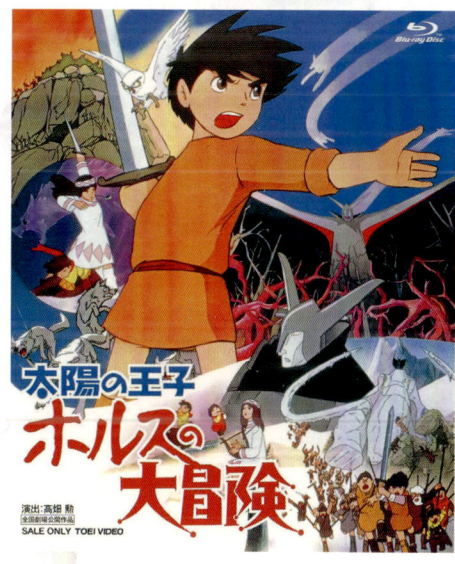

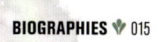

IN THE BEGINNING

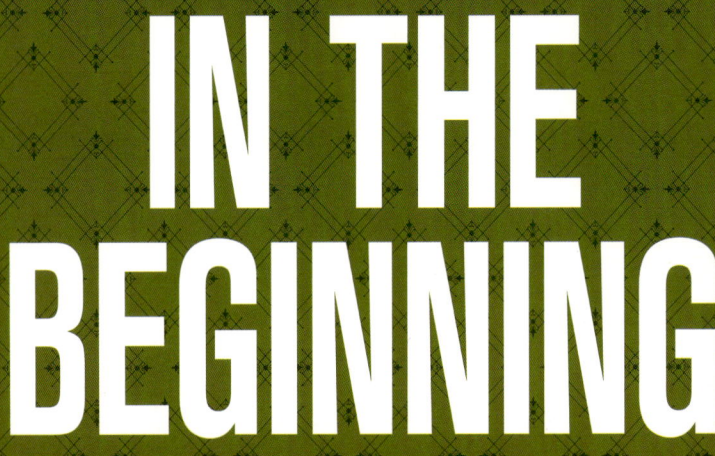

Life Before Ghibli

Studio Ghibli

Nausicaä of the Valley of the Wind

Castle in the Sky

LIFE BEFORE GHIBLI

By Bounthavy Suvilay

When Miyazaki joined Toei in 1963, the studio was making films and an increasing number of TV series, stretching its teams to the limit. Employees clashed with management over working conditions and the quality of the work produced. To keep up with the pace of a weekly series imposed by the revered animator Osamu Tezuka, teams had to adopt a system of limited animation (like that used for Hanna-Barbera's series). However, Toei was first and foremost made up of artists who had chosen the profession out of a love of movement and animation. It was within this atmosphere of conflict that Miyazaki met two union leaders who would become his two mentors: Yasuo Ôtsuka and Isao Takahata.

To calm things down, Toei asked Ôtsuka to direct a film on his terms. To this end, the team was assembled on a voluntary basis, creating an unprecedented dynamic. Among the participants were Takahata as director and Miyazaki as set designer and key animator. Ôtsuka served as animation director. Decisions were made by the community, which explains the numerous delays and the fact that it took three years to complete the film. Everyone could give their opinion, and the feature film progressed only with the consensus of the entire team. And the whole team was made up of perfectionists.

On this project, Ôtsuka, Takahata, and Miyazaki got to know each other and work together. They invented staging techniques, focused on themes that were important to them, and launched a manifesto for an animated film aimed at adult audiences. Their feature took a pacifistic stance, denouncing the Vietnam War as absurd. Given that producers had no say in the matter, this was essentially one of the first independent films of the era. Of course, *Horus: Prince of the Sun* (1968) was a commercial failure. Nevertheless, the freedom they experienced on the project laid the foundations for many changes in Japanese animation and gave the three men a taste for independence; they would go on to work on many TV series and feature films before the creation of Ghibli. When Ôtsuka left Toei Animation to join A Production in 1969, he set an example for Miyazaki and Takahata, who also, in 1971, left the company where they'd started.

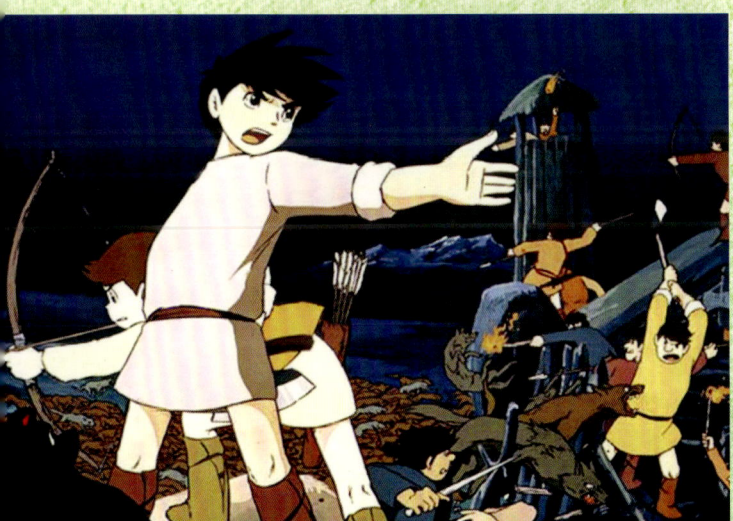

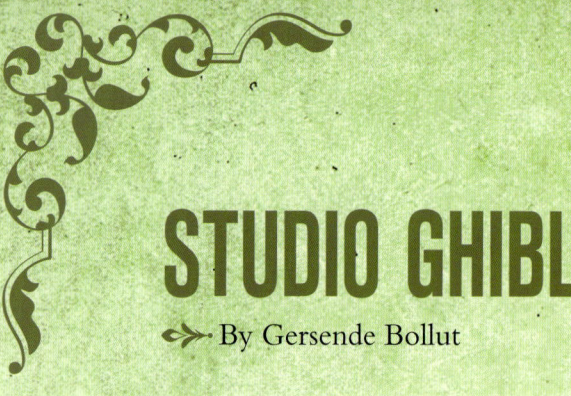

STUDIO GHIBLI

➣ By Gersende Bollut

Driven primarily by the desires and aspirations of Hayao Miyazaki and Isao Takahata, Studio Ghibli's artistic policies evoke the early spirit of United Artists, the renowned American company founded in 1919, on the eve of the 1920s, by Charlie Chaplin, Douglas Fairbanks, Mary Pickford, and D. W. Griffith. For the first time, independent artists seized power that had previously been monopolized by the major Hollywood studios, aiming to make more personal films. Sixty years later, Steven Spielberg continued in that vein with the creation of Amblin Entertainment, the embryo of the future DreamWorks studio. Even more strikingly, over the past four decades, Ghibli has never ceased to foster conditions conducive to the artistic development of its creators, setting itself apart from the unbridled productivity of its competitors, raising worldwide awareness of ecological and philanthropic themes, and shattering many preconceived ideas about Japanese animation.

FIRST STEPS

The origins of Studio Ghibli can be traced back to the early 1980s, when a wave of science fiction–infused animated films for mature audiences, such as *Galaxy Express 999*, *Space Adventure Cobra*, *Macross: Do You Remember Love?*, and *Arcadia of My Youth*, took Japanese movie theaters by storm.

Eager to capture the market by producing artistically ambitious works on a regular basis, publisher Tokuma commissioned Hayao Miyazaki to direct a feature film. The young filmmaker had already worked on several TV series, and was brimming with ideas, including a rough draft of a script that eventually led to *Princess Mononoke* in the late 1990s. However, investors were cautious or reluctant, opting instead for *Nausicaä of the Valley of the Wind*, a Miyazaki manga then being published in the monthly magazine *Animage* whose themes resonated with the public at the time.

Promoted to producer despite having no experience in production, his friend Isao Takahata went in search of a studio and set his sights on Topcraft

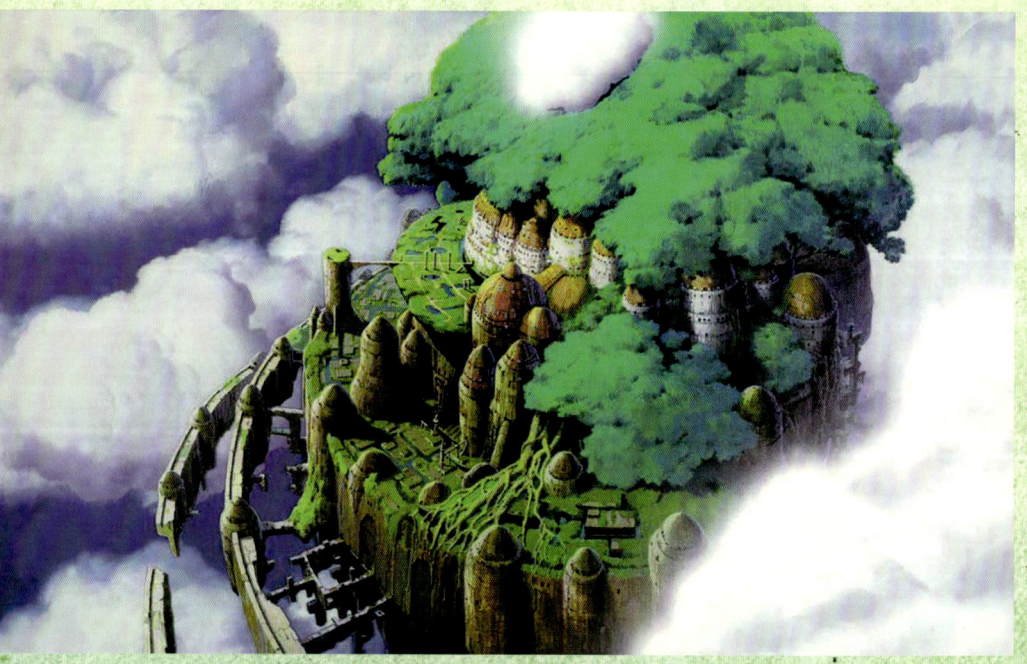

(*The Last Unicorn*), which was founded in the early 1970s by a Toei Animation defector. The film immerses us in a world that has become toxic, in which a princess risks everything to protect her valley from outside forces. Miyazaki wanted to make viewers aware of the unjust, unjustified, unjustifiable ravages that humankind inflicts on the environment, and the heroine's goal is to protect it by ensuring its continued existence, which is often in jeopardy. Far from being a closed-minded idealist, she travels through a forest that has become unbreathable, trying to penetrate the logic of an ecosystem that has become lethal to her fellow creatures. Her communion with nature gives her an almost mystical connection with living beings. A symbol of the fierce defense and preservation of an environment beset by human greed, she is the radiant embodiment of naturally altruistic, caring youth. By highlighting the discrepancy between the insignificant reasons that drive some people to destroy nature and the irreversible consequences of their actions, Miyazaki also encourages us to reflect on the very process of destruction itself. Begun in the summer of 1983, the adaptation of *Nausicaä* was released in theaters in March 1984, attracting almost a million Japanese viewers.

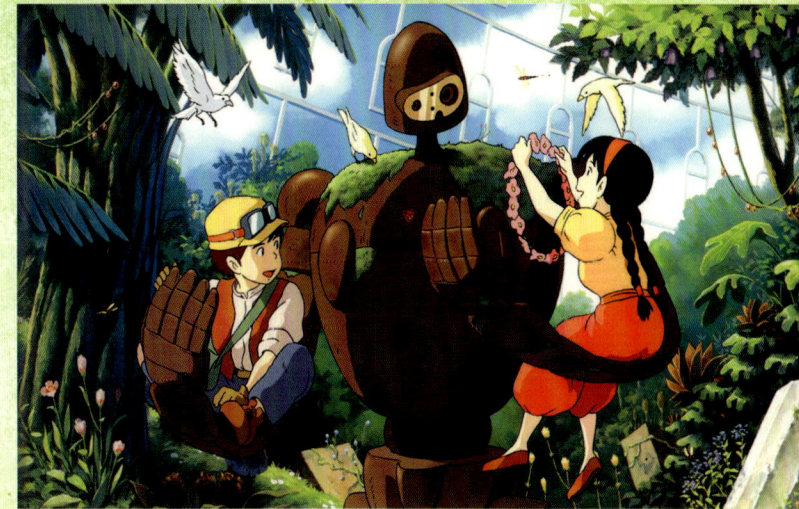

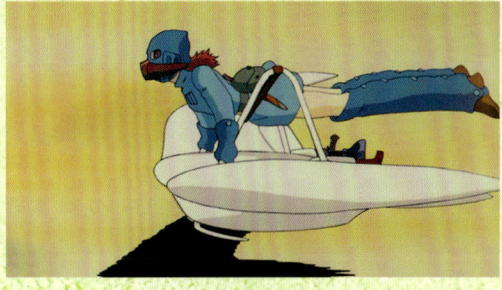

> *"Ghibli fosters conditions conducive to the artistic development of its creators."*

Bolstered by critical and public acclaim, Tokuma wanted to launch immediately into a new project, but disastrous personnel management brought the Topcraft studio to the brink of bankruptcy. Miyazaki and Takahata suggested that the publisher give himself the means to achieve his goals by founding an independent studio; Studio Ghibli was created in June 1985, when *Castle in the Sky* was already in production. The Arabic word *gibli* refers to a Saharan wind also known as a "sirocco"; Italian pilots used the term *ghibli* to describe a particular type of reconnaissance aircraft during World War II. A longtime aviation buff, Miyazaki was determined to bring a breath of fresh air to animation, while Takahata wanted a Japanese-sounding name (Musashino Studio), which was ultimately rejected.

A humanist fable that Miyazaki described as "a science fiction novel written at the end of the nineteenth century," *Castle in the Sky* drew inspiration from the filmmaker's adolescence, when he was fascinated by Jonathan Swift's literary classic *Gulliver's Travels*, in which an island appears in the sky, and by Tetsuji Fukushima's manga *Devil of the Desert*, published in the early 1950s, where a precious stone bestows the ability to fly through the air. The aim of this funny, action-packed film—which changed titles several times during production (from *Pazu and the Mystery of the Flying Stone* to *Pazu and the Flying Empire*) and took twice as long to develop as *Nausicaä*—was to bring together all generations of viewers around a universal theme devoid of cynicism.

Nausicaä of the Valley of the Wind
© 1984 Nibariki – GH
Castle in the Sky
© 1986 Nibariki – Tokuma Shoten

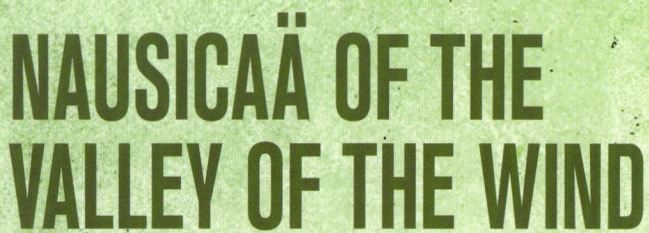

NAUSICAÄ OF THE VALLEY OF THE WIND

1984 - HAYAO MIYAZAKI

Nausicaä is a cornerstone of animation, inviting us to reflect on the process of destruction through the devastating spectacle of a natural world that is in turn bruised, rebellious, and reconciled. It emphasizes the discrepancy between the insignificant reasons that drive humans to destroy nature, and the irreversible results of their actions. A timeless classic.

— By Gersende Bollut

Hayao Miyazaki's entire oeuvre is encapsulated in *Nausicaä*. It contains the key themes that would drive the director throughout his career (protecting the environment, the barbaric madness of human beings, the rejection of Manichaeism) and the motifs that would characterize his filmography (charismatic young heroines, aerial sequences, and a sense of wonder). It's an essential feature film that some consider too watered down when compared with the original manga by the same author, forgetting that the film's production began when only two volumes had been published. In all, seven volumes were published in *Animage* magazine between 1982 and 1994, developing an ambitious narrative arc. Although it predates the founding of Studio Ghibli, *Nausicaä* certainly warrants inclusion in these pages, as its phenomenal success in Japan (a million viewers) led directly to the studio's creation, and, above all, because it's the first truly personal cinematic project from an auteur who, until then, had directed only one commissioned work for the big screen, the hectic *Lupin III: The Castle of Cagliostro*. Miyazaki's touch is present on all fronts: original work, character design, screenplay, direction, and production.

CREATIVE CONTEXT

It would be impossible to fully understand the filmmaker's personality if we omitted this deeply moving film, released in 1984, which expanded on the plot, characters, and environmental obsessions of the gripping *Future Boy Conan* series produced six years earlier and foreshadowed the equally masterful *Princess Mononoke* by thirteen years. The idea for *Nausicaä* came from a resounding public health problem that struck fear in the world's population. On the eve of the 1910s, the flourishing Chisso petrochemical plant decided to set up in Minamata, a coastal town on the island of Kyushu, and unabashedly discharged tons of heavy metals, including mercury, into the ocean. The consequences were disastrous: almost 900 deaths, thousands of poisonings, severe neurological symptoms from fish consumption, and many stillborn babies and babies with birth defects. The scandal was of such proportions that the government publicly apologized and (belatedly) compensated the victims, and in 2009, the UN adopted the Minamata Convention to limit human releases of mercury into the environment. Miyazaki was struck by the adaptability of the fish, who, when faced with the suspension of fishing in the polluted bay, saw their population grow spectacularly in the space of a few years. Set in a toxic forest populated by giant insects that have overtaken human civilization, *Nausicaä*'s plot is unsettling in this respect. To imagine the courageous heroine determined to protect her valley and understand the wrath of the animals, the director drew inspiration from the traditional Japanese tale "The Princess

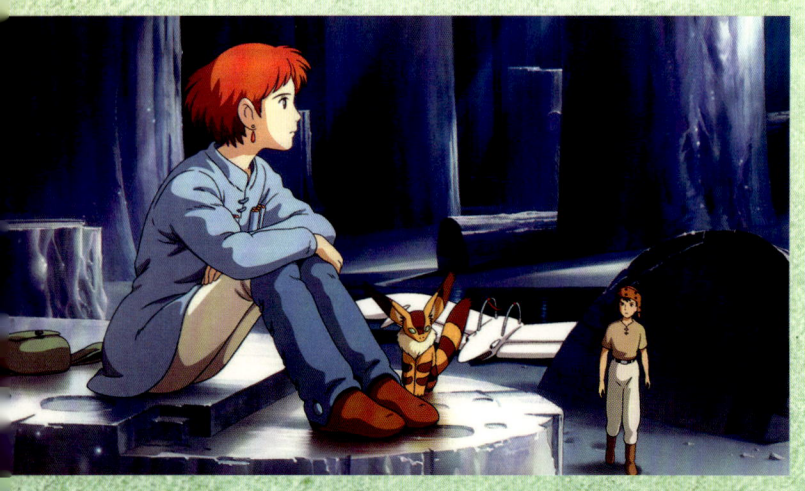

Who Loved Insects," in which a young woman of royal blood is fascinated by living creatures, particularly insects. The name Nausicaä comes from the Phoenician princess who helps Odysseus in Homer's *Odyssey*. Unlike future films such as *Spirited Away* and *Howl's Moving Castle*, which are heavily steeped in Japanese folklore, *Nausicaä* draws on a more universal imagination.

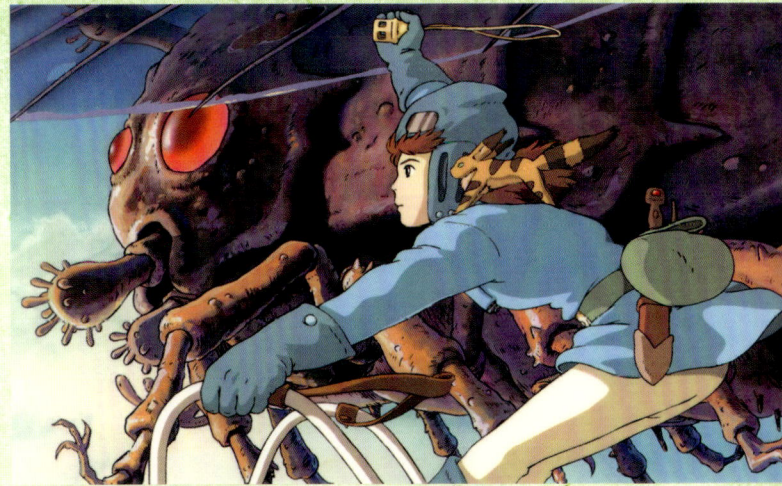

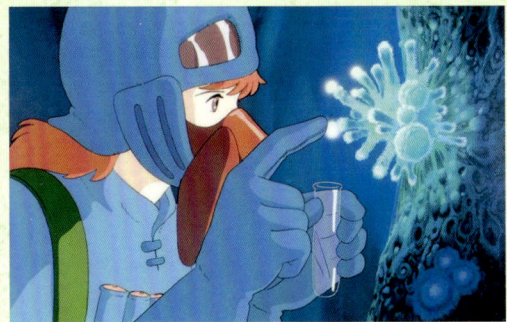

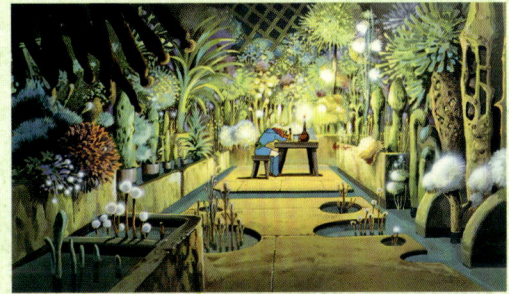

Swept along on an epic breeze, the adventure has lost none of the power of its message, and forty years after its release, it remains the most beautiful environmental manifesto imaginable. The film was a hit with audiences who were lucky enough to see it in theaters (prompting the late comics writer Moebius to name his daughter Nausicaä in direct reference to the film), and its reach and influence remain intact. Though at one point its reputation was, if not tarnished, at least clouded by the infamous American cut released in the 1980s under the title *Warriors of the Wind* (which cut no less than half an hour of footage), *Nausicaä* remains a jewel that invites us

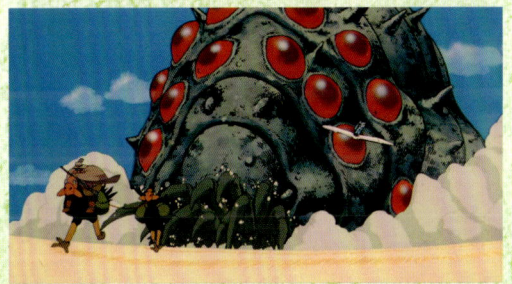

"The most beautiful environmental manifesto imaginable"

to protect the environment and establish (or reestablish) a dialogue among human beings. However, humankind doesn't escape a severe indictment, as weapons amplify the disruption of a natural world beset by a multitude of worrying phenomena, and which, in a devastated state, owes its salvation to its own inexhaustible resources. Composed of an infinite number of elements, plant and animal, tangible and volatile, nature is gradually being weakened by the actions of a handful of human beings who are quick to advance their own interests. This conflictual relationship allows for no compromise, precipitating both sides toward

a dramatic outcome. Yet *Nausicaä* is far from being a work of despair. In addition to poetic and uplifting interludes, it elegantly and sincerely hints at the hope of a peaceful outcome, thanks to the heroine, who symbolizes a new generation committed to the environmental cause.

CASTLE IN THE SKY

1986 - HAYAO MIYAZAKI

Nausicaä's success in 1984 positively impacted Tokuma company policy, particularly regarding the production of animated films. With the creation of a subsidiary that was to become Studio Ghibli, one of Hayao Miyazaki's most significant feature films, *Castle in the Sky*, was released in Japan in the summer of 1986.

By Romain Dasnoy

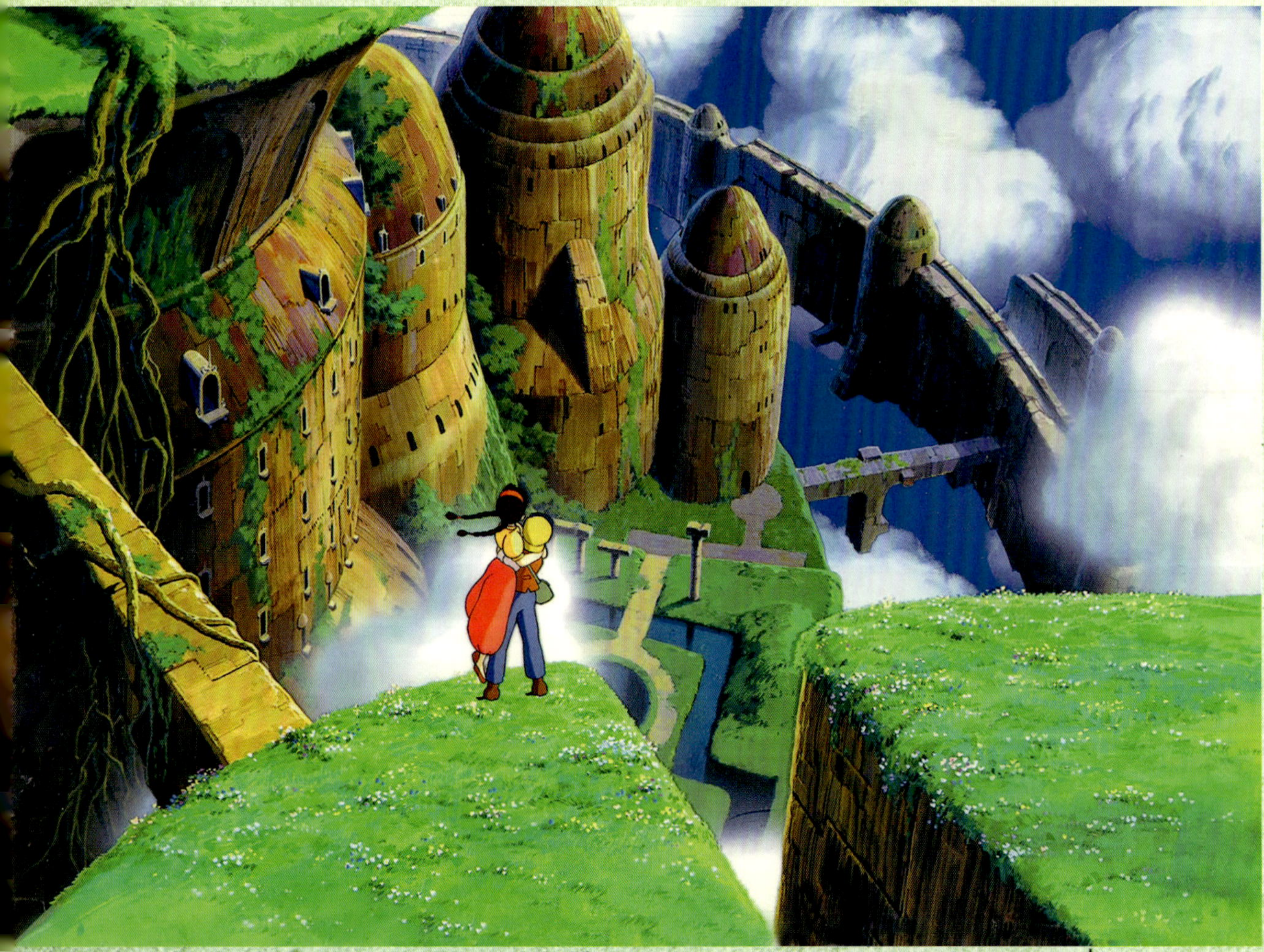

The story behind *Castle in the Sky* (*Tenkû no shiro Laputa*) began in Hayao Miyazaki's teenage years, when he was fascinated by exotic reading material, from *Gulliver's Travels* to *Sabaku no Maô*, a manga by Tetsuji Fukushima set in fantastical African lands. Miyazaki's literary experiences made a lasting impression, leading to the idea of a floating city and a medallion with magical powers. He was very receptive to Western-style stories featuring steam engines, fabulous heroes, and grandiose settings, and developed projects with script ideas

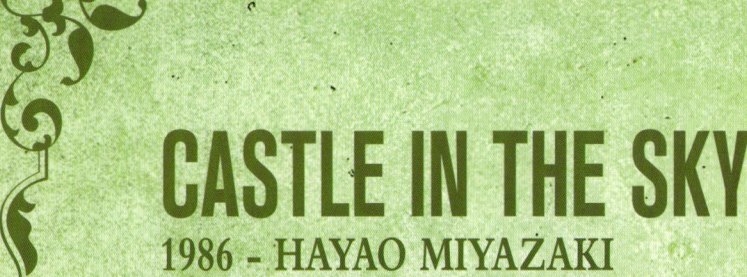

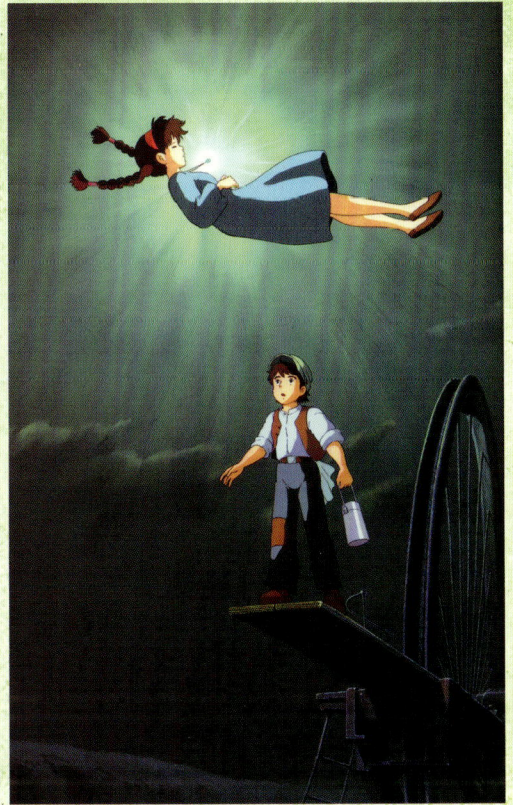

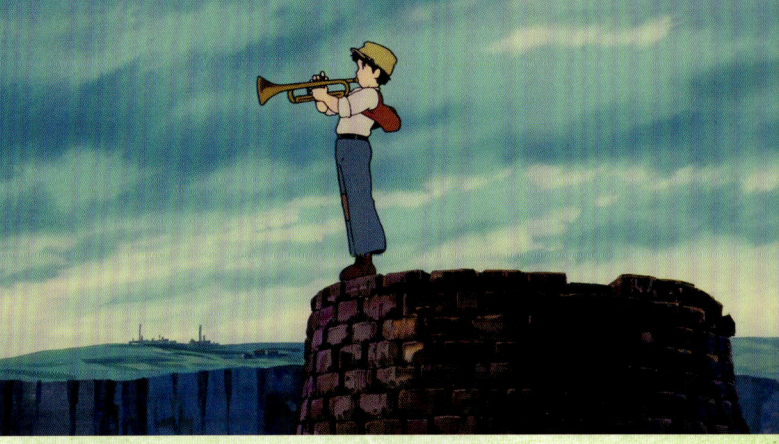

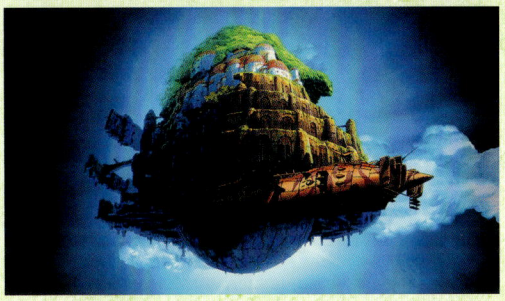

reminiscent of the aesthetics of the avant-garde classics of nineteenth- and twentieth-century literature, particularly those by Jules Verne and Arthur Conan Doyle. It's difficult not to compare *Castle in the Sky* with the *Conan* and *Sherlock Hound* series, both visually and narratively. This fascination with the West, already reflected in *Nausicaä*, was even more pronounced in this first production to be officially stamped "Studio Ghibli."

> *"A great family adventure filled*
> *with humor and surprises."*

With its diverse inspirations and highly recognizable character design, *Castle in the Sky* was made to appeal to the widest possible audience. Besides the quality approach initiated by producer Isao Takahata, who sent the team to the Welsh mining town of Rhondda (where Miyazaki found union tensions running high at the time), the film's primary role was to broaden *Nausicaä*'s target audience; its narrative was much more complicated and, though epic, more intellectual. By centering the plot on two children and setting the action in the

air and in locations that were as mysterious as they were enchanting, Hayao Miyazaki created a great family adventure filled with humor and surprises.

As for the music, Joe Hisaishi returned for a second collaboration, using the same ingredients as in *Nausicaä*: music that is not particularly present, but extremely striking, with beautiful melodies and children's choirs as a finale. For its US release almost fifteen years later, the score was completely reworked at the request of the distributor, who felt the film contained too many silences. Joe Hisaishi agreed, on one condition: that he would completely rewrite the orchestration, adding what turned out to be almost 50 percent more music. Purists may decry it, but it's still one of the most beautiful soundtracks in a Ghibli film.

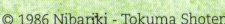

© 1986 Nibariki - Tokuma Shoten

ANIMATION GENIUSES

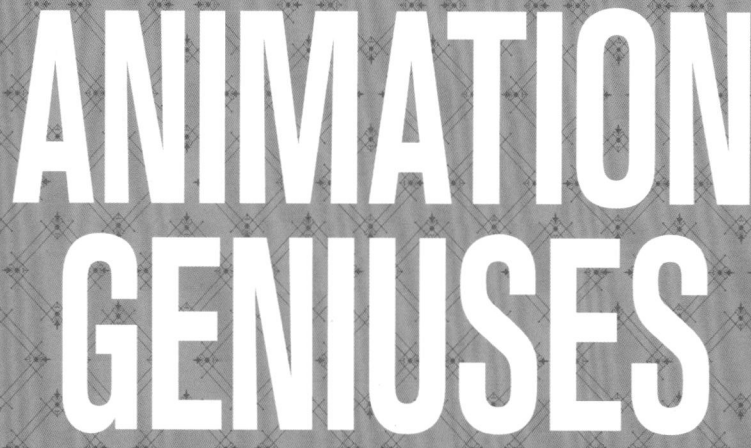

Challenges and Early Successes
Grave of the Fireflies
My Neighbor Totoro
Kiki's Delivery Service

CHALLENGES AND EARLY SUCCESSES

  ➤ By Gersende Bollut

The first Ghibli film, *Castle in the Sky*, was an instant success when released in Japan in August 1986 and gained cult status over the years, to the point where the studio was unsure of what to do next. Miyazaki suggested a story about a family living on the edge of a forest inhabited by a fantastic creature, which the producers rejected in favor of a short film before gradually returning to the long format.

Takahata suggested an adaptation of a short story published in the late 1960s, in which two children try to survive in a Kobe that has been devastated by World War II bombings. It was decided to produce the two films simultaneously: *My Neighbor Totoro*, directed by Miyazaki, and *Grave of the Fireflies*, with Takahata at the helm. On the one hand, an ode to childhood and the environment, transporting viewers into a fantastical world of poetic interludes where time seems suspended in a dreamy 1950s countryside; on the other, a fiercely anti-militaristic work that is both a visceral, distressing experience and a vibrant manifesto of indignation against injustice. Both were instant classics, indicative of the fledgling company's bold approach.

The risk was twofold, since the profits generated up to that point were at stake, while the team had to work on the films simultaneously; they were released together in April 1988, with a single admission ticket for both. Although audiences failed to turn out in force, the studio's reputation was established through several awards, and *Totoro* generated substantial revenue from the sale of tie-in merchandise. Its star creature was instantly adopted as Studio Ghibli's mascot, appearing as a prelude to every production, just like *Luxo Jr.*'s mischievous lamp before every Pixar production.

The studio's first commercial success came with *Kiki's Delivery Service,* which drew 2.6 million viewers in Japan in the summer of 1989.

Initially intended for a first-time director, Sunao Katabuchi (*Mai Mai Miracle*), the direction of this adaptation of a children's book by Eiko Kadono fell to Miyazaki, whose growing reputation

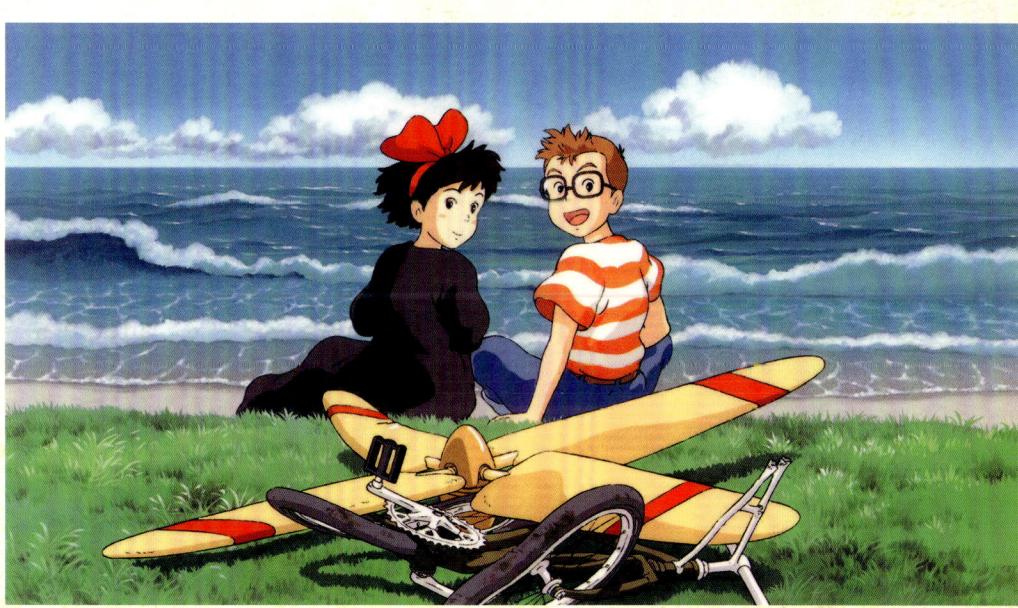

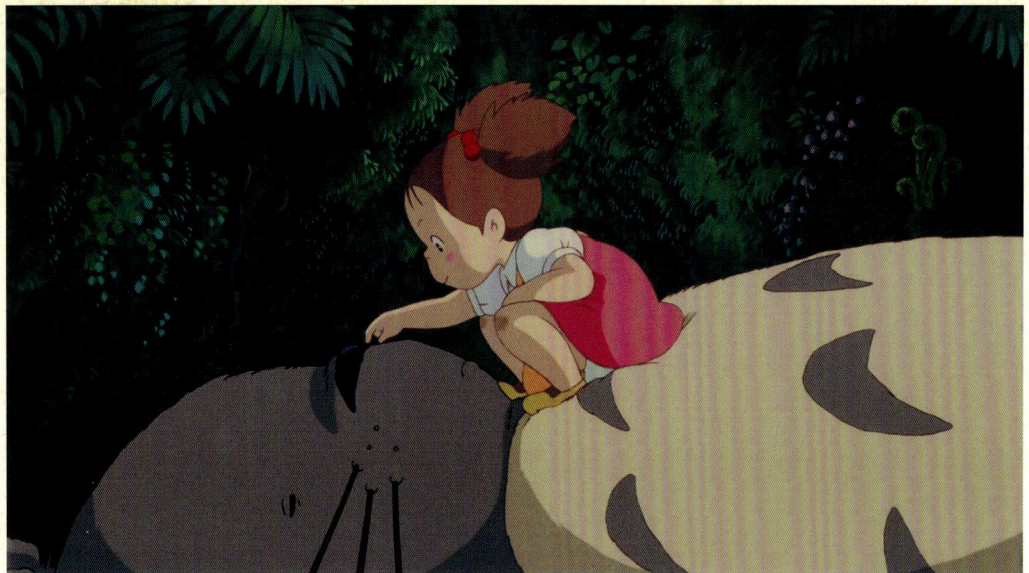

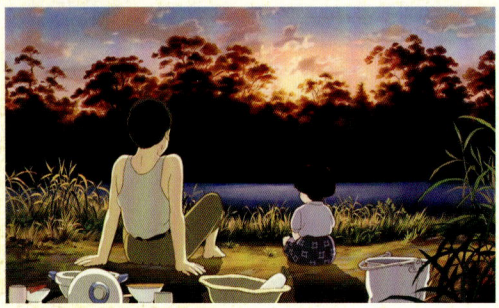

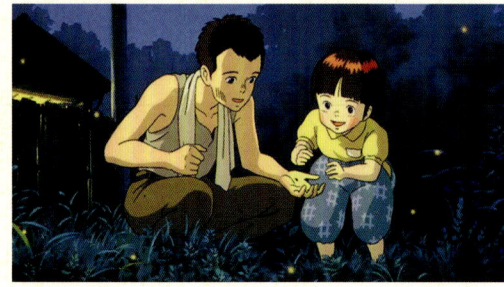

encouraged investor confidence. Keeping Katabuchi on as assistant director, the *Totoro* director's tale of an apprentice witch's empowerment is a charming chronicle that evokes the challenges young Japanese women face in their quest for independence.

Despite the tensions that arose with the book's irate author—who threatened to have the film project canceled after the filmmakers changed elements of her story's plot, even though the project was only at the storyboard stage—*Kiki* allowed the the studio didn't want to lose to the competition. A training department was also set up to foster new talent, and Toshio Suzuki, the former editor-in-chief of *Animage*, joined the company as a producer. He would later serve as president of Studio Ghibli, from 1991 to 2008. It should be noted that *Kiki* was the subject of another film adaptation in 2014, this time a live-action version directed by Shimizu Takashi (*The Grudge*).

> *"Totoro was instantly adopted as Studio Ghibli's mascot."*

studio to make significant advances. It moved into brand-new premises designed by Miyazaki himself (nearly 12,000 square feet, compared to around 3,000 previously), increased staff salaries, and above all, proceeded with a wave of hiring among the animators who had been loyal to the studio from the outset. These were artists who had been working on a temporary basis, by necessity, and whose skills

GRAVE OF THE FIREFLIES
1988 - ISAO TAKAHATA

Grave of the Fireflies is the most adult Ghibli film: human and harshly realistic. At the very beginning, the hero coldly states, "September 21, 1945; that was the night I died,"—an introduction that sounds like a conclusion. The film instantly touches the viewer.

By Gwenaël Jacquet

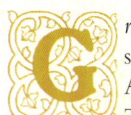Grave of the Fireflies was originally a semi-autobiographical short story by Akiyuki Nosaka, published in 1967. The big difference between fact and fiction is that, unlike in the film, the author was still alive to bear witness to the horrors of war. In 1945 Japan, the mother of Seita, age fourteen, and his four-year-old sister, Setsuko, dies in the bombing of Kobe, and their father no longer responds to letters sent to him on his ship. Living with an aunt who already has two children, the siblings find themselves in an unbearable situation during this period of food shortages. Once again abandoned to their fate, the children go to live in a makeshift shelter near a river. Big brother Seita makes it a point of honor to stand tall and look after his little sister who, despite the circumstances, has the carefree attitude of a young child, even though the viewer can see that she understands the situation. Despite her brother's best efforts, she doesn't get enough to eat and, heartbreakingly, slowly wastes away without ever complaining.

The film's title refers to the scene in which the two children take trapped fireflies into their cave for light. Setsuko finds them dead the next day. Shocked, she makes a grave for them and confesses to her brother that her aunt told her that their mother has also died, a fact that Seita has kept from his little sister.

Before Takahata approached him, Akiyuki Nosaka had refused all requests for a live-action adaptation of his story. He felt it was impossible for a little girl to play such a difficult role in a natural way. Nor was he convinced that it would be possible to faithfully depict Sannomiya, the Kobe

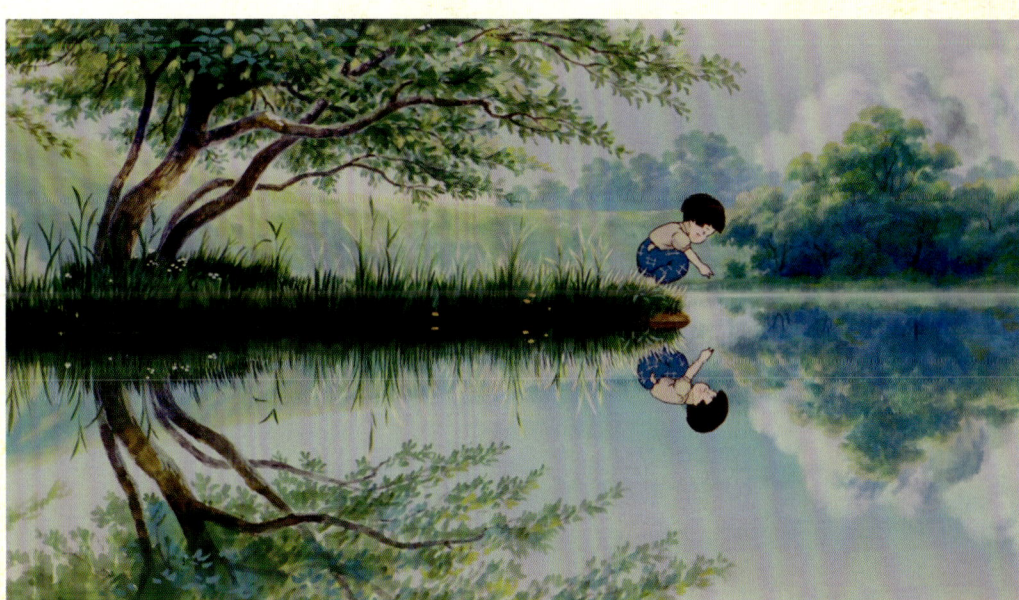

district where the story takes place. His fears gradually faded, especially concerning Setsuko's body language.

Isao Takahata himself admitted that, having never animated a person under the age of five, he wasn't sure he was up to the task. The on-screen result proves otherwise, and the fluidity of the animation shows that the director's choices paid off. Takahata also insisted that the film's protagonists should be voiced by actors of the same age as them, which was an added challenge. Since the action takes place in Kobe, it was also necessary to limit the search to children from the Kansai region to ensure the right dialect. Because Ayano Shiraishi (who plays Setsuko) was too young and inexperienced to deliver her lines within an ensemble performance, Takahata did things in reverse order, recording the child's part first. It was up to the animators to match the dubbing as closely as possible, which was highly unusual and fairly challenging for them.

A TITLE WITH SEVERAL MEANINGS

In the Japanese title, *Hotaru no haka*, spelled 火垂る の墓, the term *hotaru* (firefly) is symbolized by two kanji instead of the single symbol usually used to designate this insect (蛍). The first (火, *hi*) symbolizes fire and the second (垂, *tareru*) symbolizes decline. This choice can be explained by the cremation of one of the main characters, who thus disappears in smoke, but it also reflects the ephemeral nature of fireflies, which are represented as drops of light. The quantity is not indicated, suggesting that this could just as easily refer to one firefly as many of them, evoking the precariousness of life in wartime, and conveying the profusion of light the insects provide the two children in their shelter.

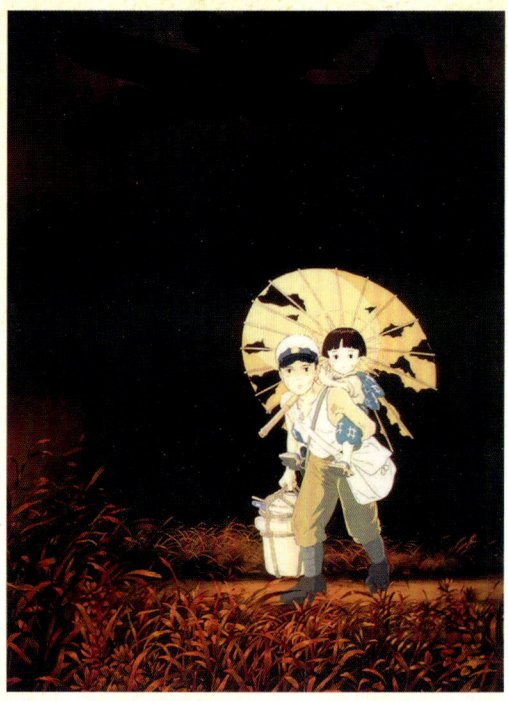

> *"This is more than an anti-war manifesto; it's a story of survival and family support."*

BEHIND THE SCENES

Several anecdotes about the film are worth mentioning, such as the one about Setsuko's candy and its now-iconic box, which wasn't produced by confectioner Sakuma until 1949. This object is essentially the third most important character in the story, and Sakuma chose to remarket the original design after the film's release, as well as a version adorned with a picture of Setsuko. The Setsuko version was still available until recently. As for the film's original release, it experienced some problems. Produced and screened at the same time as *Totoro, Grave of the Fireflies* didn't immediately find its audience. At the time, viewers were mainly parents with their children, and they often left the theater before the second film was shown. It took time for this production to become profitable.

Like any film about war, *Grave of the Fireflies* was not without controversy. The film was never released in theaters in South Korea, where the government believed it would justify Japan's entry into the war. The story is often seen as an anti-war manifesto, and Takahata defended his desire to make a film about this tragedy. He saw *Grave of the Fireflies* as a story of survival and family support.

MY NEIGHBOR TOTORO

1988 - HAYAO MIYAZAKI

Before it became the symbol of Studio Ghibli, *My Neighbor Totoro* was Miyazaki's most profitable film. Yet when it was released, it was rejected by audiences who couldn't understand why a children's film would be shown on a double feature with the more adult *Grave of the Fireflies*. It's now widely broadcast on television, and its theme song is a favorite in school music classes.

By Gwenaël Jacquet

Driving over bumpy roads in a van carrying all their belongings, Mr. Kusakabe and his two daughters, Mei and Satsuki (ages four and ten, respectively), move to a pretty Japanese country house to be closer to the girls' mother, who is bedridden in a nearby hospital. While playing in the garden, Mei discovers a small, semitransparent creature with pointed ears, chases it through bushes and shrubs, and ends up in front of a giant camphor tree that is the home of a forest spirit.

THE IMPORTANCE OF EVERYDAY LIFE

Hayao Miyazaki wanted to emphasize the pastoral aspect of this simple life that he himself experienced in the 1950s, while giving it a timeless quality so that it would be suitable for younger generations. In the film, the young girls know how to entertain themselves without necessarily needing a television or video games, and marvel at their surroundings. In *Totoro*, Miyazaki showcased the magic of everyday life and the carefree spirit of childhood. He distilled reassuringly familiar elements of Japanese life (such as Buddhism and the Shinto religion) and gave nature a prominent role.

This ecological fable also shares a hint of autobiography with Miyazaki, whose mother was bedridden for nine years because of spinal tuberculosis. Although this illness is never explicitly mentioned in the film, it could explain Mrs. Kusakabe's hospitalization.

TOTORO AND THE FIREFLIES

The most difficult thing about *Totoro* wasn't its production, but rather its financing: When Miyazaki presented his project for a children's tale featuring a lovable forest monster and a seven-year-old girl as his friend, nobody was willing to risk a penny

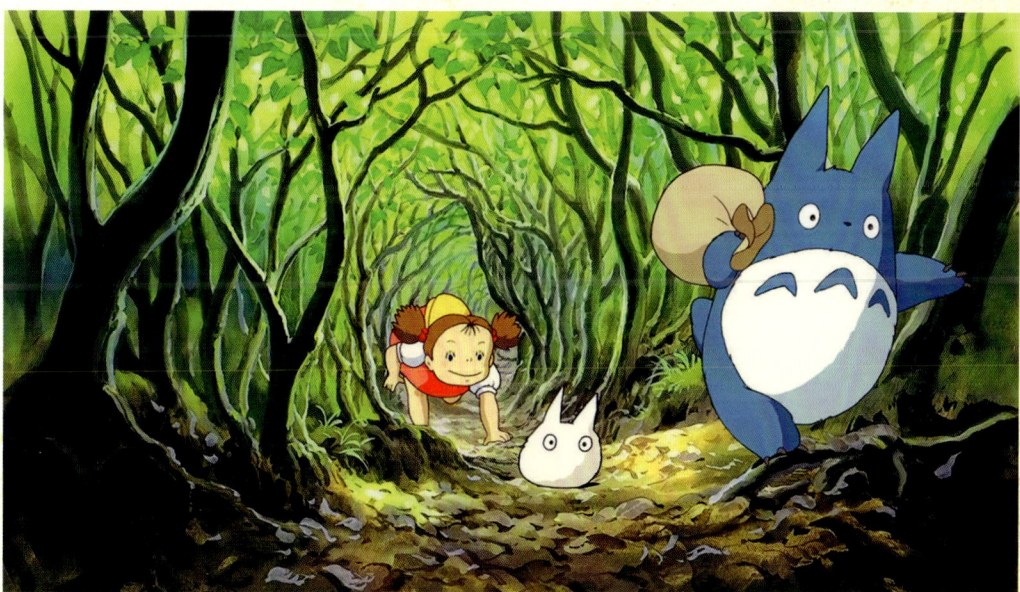

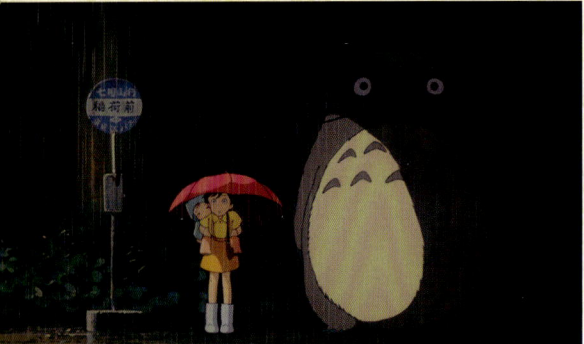
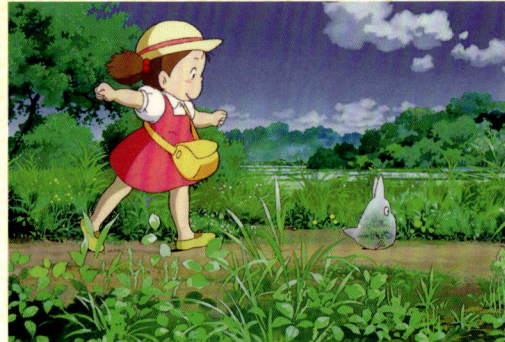

on it. Today, it's obvious that the film's charm lies in its direction and the quality of its animation, but back then, financiers had no way of knowing this. Miyazaki had not yet achieved his filmmaking reputation, and given that his idea was original, there were no best-selling manga or novels as source material to reassure bankers. Toshio Suzuki, who had the daunting task of finding investors, came up with the idea of playing up the educational aspect by offering not just one film, but two. *Totoro* was produced at the same time as *Grave of the Fireflies*. The latter, which was based on a famous semi-autobiographical short story by Akiyuki Nosaka, was touted as having pedagogical qualities that could encourage schools to bring children to the movies, where they could also enjoy a second, more entertaining film. But the reality was very different. In the end, the two films, screened back-to-back, managed only 800,000 admissions in their five-week run, which was still respectable for animated features at the time.

THE ARTISTS' ENTRANCE

The studio team split up to work on the two projects simultaneously: one in the former Ghibli premises, the other in the studio located thirty feet away, in a building still under construction that wasn't available until April 1, 1987. In the meantime, production began, with the two teams working together in the first studio. The *Totoro* part of the team took up only three tables: one for Miyazaki (the director), one for Yoshiharu Sato (the animation director), and one for Kazuo Oga (the art director). It was decided to transform the single seven-year-old child into two young girls, ages four and ten, to open up more storytelling possibilities. To sell the project, Suzuki presented it as a short film of just under an hour, but in the end, it was made into a ninety-minute feature. The film was divided into four major parts and distributed among different teams, with the fourth added at the last minute, in June 1987, at Miyazaki's insis-

tence. The tight production schedule (less than a year) forced the studio to hire subcontractors.

Until then, Studio Ghibli had been reluctant to fall into the trap of merchandising products that only served to finance the films. However, in 1990, a company succeeded in getting a license from Miyazaki to produce Totoro plush toys. Since then, the management of related products has been

"In Totoro, Miyazaki showcased the magic of everyday life and the carefree spirit of childhood."

tightly controlled; they must not misrepresent the films, as the aim is to satisfy the public without seeking to advertise through inappropriate media.

Totoro has left its mark on several generations of children (and adults!) thanks to its knack for realism that avoids overkill. While the film features imaginary creatures, Totoro isn't there to magically save the girls' mother: He's there to give Mei and Satsuki hope.

In short, *Totoro* is an ode to nature.

© 1988 Nibariki - G

KIKI'S DELIVERY SERVICE

1989 - HAYAO MIYAZAKI

Released shortly after *My Neighbor Totoro*, *Kiki's Delivery Service* was a transitional work for Studio Ghibli. Despite its simplistic, light-hearted themes, it was a high-quality affair with historic repercussions for the studio, which was still struggling to expand at the time.

➤ By Romain Dasnoy

In the early 1990s, the very young Studio Ghibli and its two founders were certainly brimming with ideas, but the two previous films, *Grave of the Fireflies* and *My Neighbor Totoro*, had only enjoyed critical success. Although they would become established over the years, building on the foundations already laid by past experience, it wasn't until 1989 and *Kiki's Delivery Service* that Studio Ghibli really took off. With over two and a half million box office admissions in Japan, the film established the company's reputation and, above all, its financial stability, enabling it to move to new premises and hire employees who had previously worked as freelancers. Toshio Suzuki, who had produced Hayao Miyazaki's films at Tokuma Shoten and had made *Nausicaä* possible, was then hired to fully integrate Studio Ghibli, becoming its director in 1990.

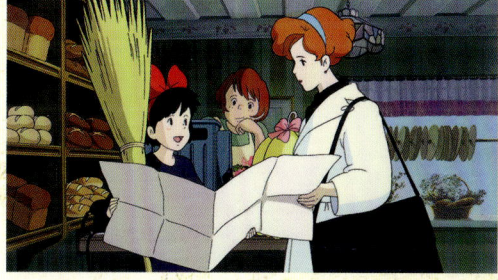

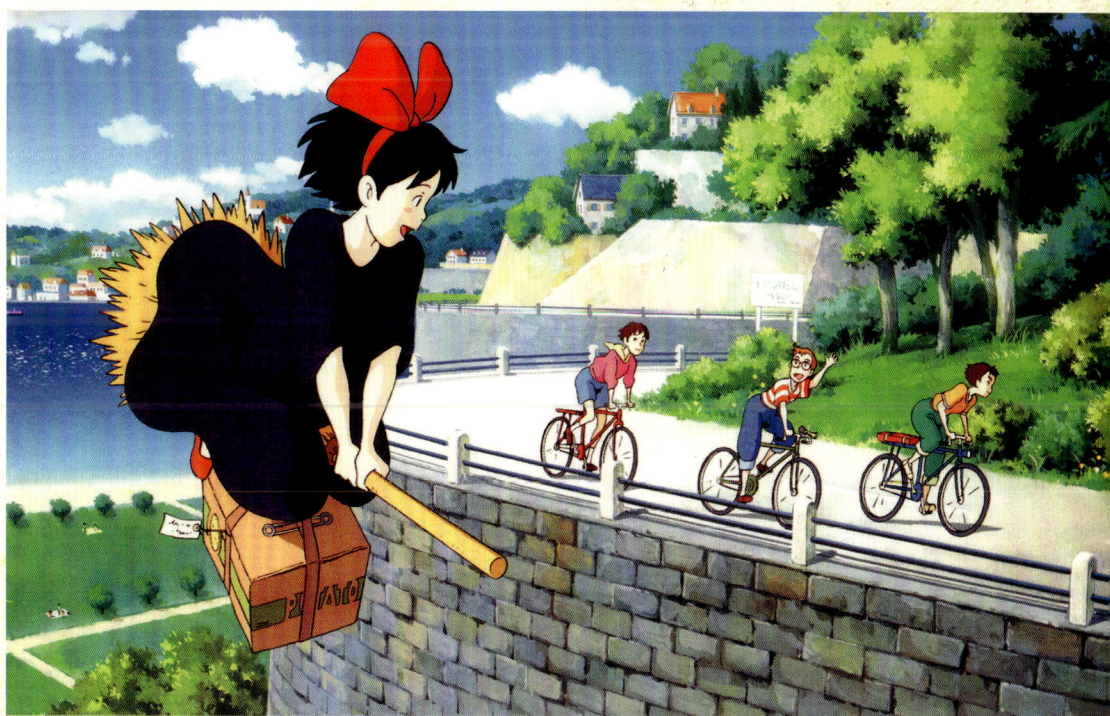

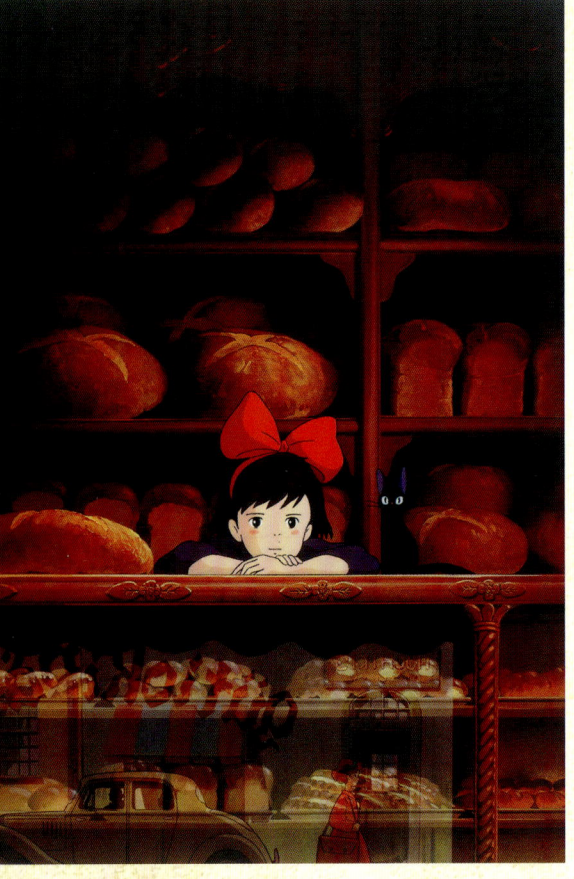

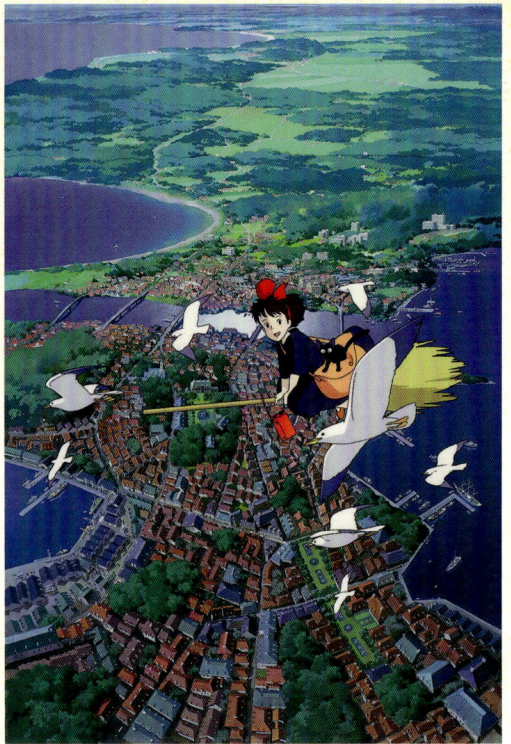

Despite its importance as a transitional work, *Kiki* is still perceived as a minor film. Adapted from a best seller in Japanese children's literature by Eiko Kadono,[1] this new feature film was initially to be directed by Sunao Katabuchi, who was later replaced by Miyazaki himself due to political reasons and other commitments. The result was a film that was fresh and light-hearted in its development that featured the master's key themes: the omnipresent motif of flight, coming of age, and the very Western aesthetic of the backdrop. Musically, it also marked a deliberate turnaround for Joe Hisaishi, who adopted an entirely orchestral approach, in stark contrast to his work in previous Miyazaki films and in many ways foreshadowing *Porco Rosso*.

Kiki, which was butchered like few other films for its video release in the US, was also one of the cornerstones of the agreement between Tokuma and Disney for the distribution of Studio Ghibli's works abroad. Released in France in 2004, fifteen years after its Japanese release, the film scored well and gradually established itself in the hearts of fans. Although *Kiki's Delivery Service* remains one of the studio's least popular films, its DNA contains everything that has contributed to Ghibli's success, with the lightness that is missing from so many more ambitious productions.

[1] Published, as were its sequels, by Ynnis Éditions.

THE STUDIO'S HEYDAY

›-•-‹

A Time of Recognition

Only Yesterday

Porco Rosso

Princess Mononoke

Ocean Waves

Pom Poko

Whisper of the Heart

A TIME OF RECOGNITION

By Gersende Bollut

At this point, the studio's reputation had been established, and its leaders were able to tackle one project after another at a steady pace, with Miyazaki or Takahata at the helm. *Only Yesterday*, a nostalgic chronicle of a young single woman recalling childhood memories—which was also adapted from a manga and directed by Takahata—topped the Japanese box office in July 1991. It was followed the next year by the triumphant *Porco Rosso*, which allowed Miyazaki to indulge and share his passion for seaplanes, just as his friend John Lasseter's affection for automobiles was expressed in *Cars* a few years later. *Porco Rosso* was followed by *Pom Poko* (after *Porco Rosso*'s pig, this time it was tanuki!), which topped the Japanese box office in the summer of 1994 and was the studio's first film to feature computer-generated images. Next came the *On Your Mark* video, intended to promote a song by the rock duo Chage and Aska in 1995, and finally, the masterful *Princess Mononoke* two years later.

This epic tale of a prince cursed by a boar demon was inspired by a 1983 collection of unfinished film projects, one of which was a script by Miyazaki featuring a princess living in the forest with a wild beast. The story was tinged with Japanese folklore and echoed the "Beauty and the Beast" fairy tale, but it was shelved for being too dark. Ten years later, Miyazaki returned to the project, reworking it after the release of Walt Disney Pictures' Oscar-winning musical *Beauty and the Beast*. Originally a simple story, the plot became a mythological tale, and the hero a cursed young man on a quest to find a cure.

Production began in the summer of 1995 and was completed two years later; a Studio Ghibli film had never taken so long and cost so much to produce. The excessively ambitious *Princess Mononoke* is the perfect synthesis of the director's favorite themes: bravery, altruism, and the need to protect the environment. While the story is reminiscent of *Nausicaä*, this time the action takes place in the past, during the Muromachi period (1338–1573), when Japan was undergoing great economic and social upheaval. With its lyrical composition, virtuoso fighting, strikingly credible mythical tribes, and enchanting forest setting, the film is also a portrait of two young people caught up in a disastrous imbroglio.

In Japan, the film's release was the event of the decade. It topped the box office with 13.6 mil-

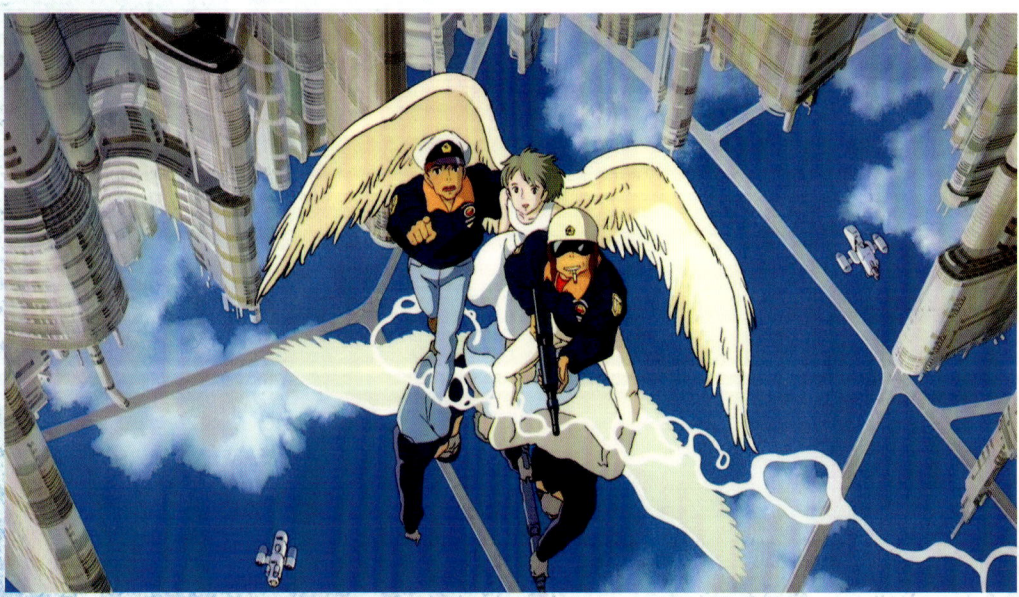

lion viewers (i.e., more than one in ten Japanese citizens!), dethroned *E.T. the Extra-Terrestrial* as the national box office champ until that point, and sold 4 million units on video.

Little by little, the styles of Studio Ghibli's two leading filmmakers became more distinct, diverging in their themes, treatment, and outlook on the world. Miyazaki is often described as a contrarian optimist, while his friend Takahata, whose films are darker and more intimate, is labeled a pragmatic pessimist. At the same time, two productions enabled up-and-coming directors to make their debuts: Tomomi Mochizuki with the little-known *Ocean Waves* (1993)—the studio's first TV movie— and Yoshifumi Kondô with the sensitive *Whisper of the Heart* (1995), a moving chronicle of adolescent first love.

With a promising future ahead of him, Yoshifumi Kondô, Miyazaki's longtime friend and co-animator of *Princess Mononoke*, was expected to eventually take over for his mentor. Studio Ghibli had deliberately pinned its hopes on this animator, to the point that Miyazaki was considering retirement. But on January 21, 1998, at the age of just forty-seven, Kondô died suddenly of a ruptured aneurysm. Miyazaki was devastated by his death, and decided not to leave the world of animation, nor to train a new director, knowing that he had lost his designated successor as well as someone who had meant a great deal to him.

To make matters worse, shareholder Tokuma, owner of Studio Ghibli, was heavily in debt. Some of the profits generated by the films were used solely to pay off the debt, and the studio was under pres-

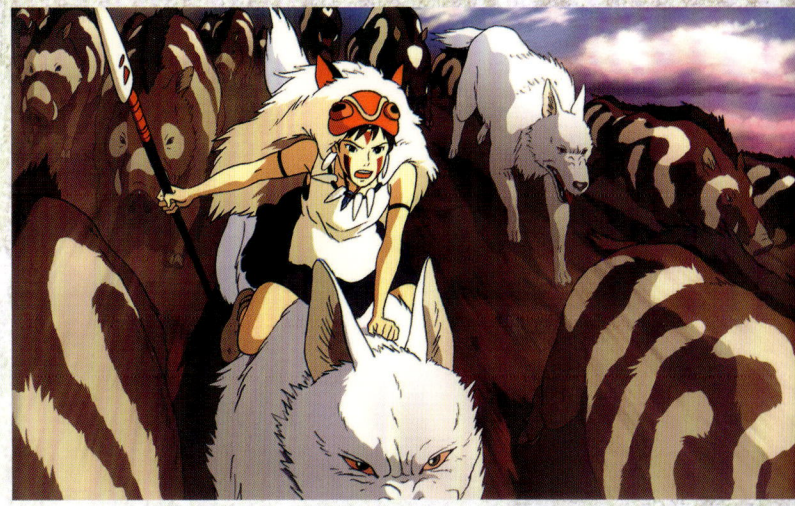

"Princess Mononoke revealed a true genius to the general public."

sure to make one success after another, with each project financed by the revenue from the previous one. The situation was hardly tenable, making each new project a gamble, with the threat of permanent bankruptcy looming. Then, a certain Disney stepped in.

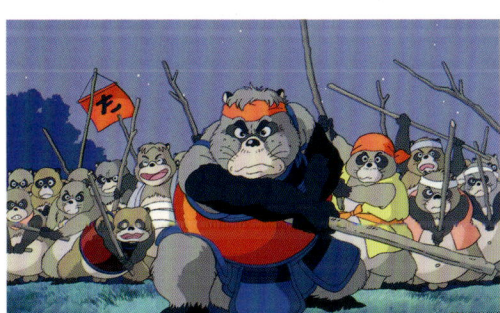

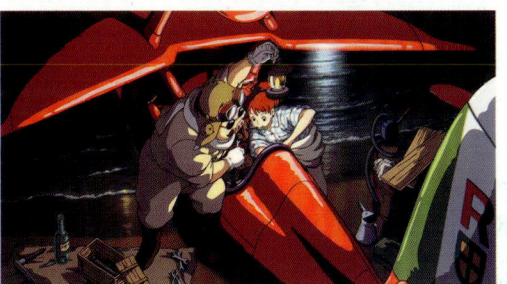

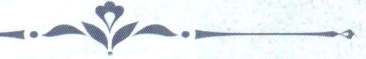

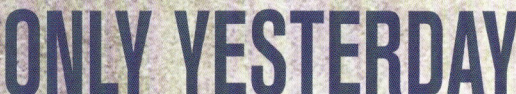

ONLY YESTERDAY
1991 - ISAO TAKAHATA

Literally meaning "native region," the Japanese term *furusato* refers to intimate memories of the place where one spent one's childhood. It's a feeling that is both universal and personal, prompting almost every Japanese person to return to their roots once in their life, especially when making a crucial choice, and it's at the heart of *Only Yesterday*.

 By Matthieu Pinon

The year is 1982, and Taeko has passed the quarter-century mark. An archetypal office lady, the twenty-seven-year-old single woman, who has only ever known Tokyo, escapes to the countryside for the summer: For the second year in a row, she goes to help distant relatives with the harvest. Taeko confesses that she has found in this remote region the *furusato* she never knew when growing up in the capital. As she travels by night train, her memories of being a city schoolgirl in 1966 come flooding back, intertwining with her stay on the farm. Perfectly acclimated to the Yamagata way of life, Taeko eventually asks herself a crucial question: Should she return to Tokyo or settle down in the country for good, along with Toshio, a young man with whom she feels a true connection?

Thanks to the success of *Kiki's Delivery Service* (see page 31), Ghibli was able to invest in larger projects, and the first to benefit was *Only Yesterday*, released in 1991. However, production didn't go smoothly; the team faced many challenges, starting with the hyperrealistic look Takahata demanded.

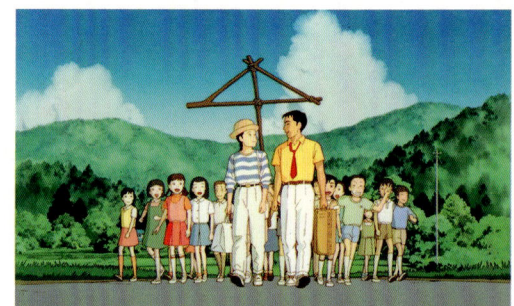

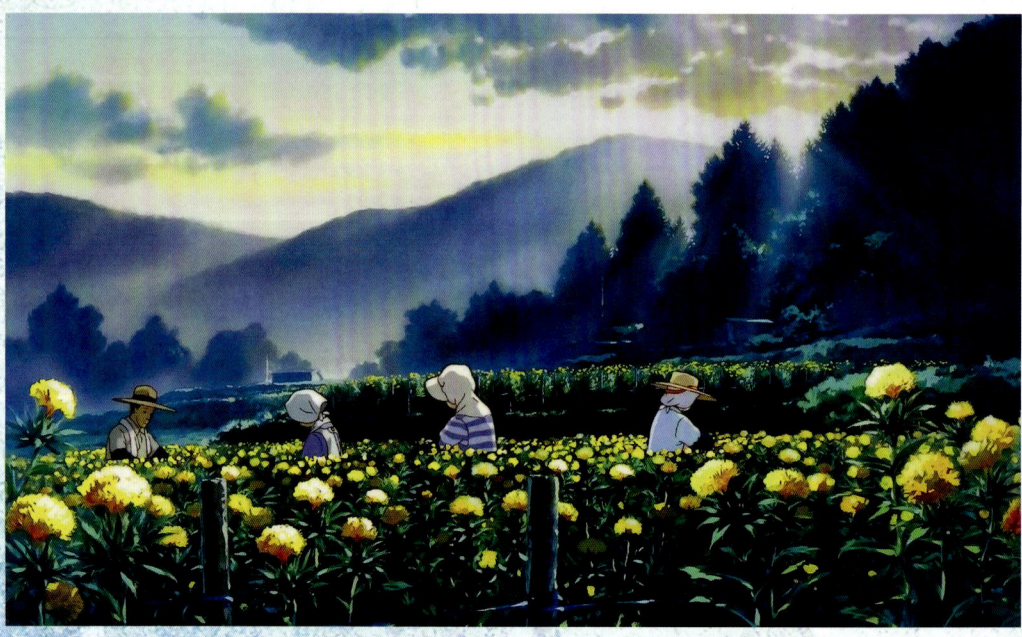

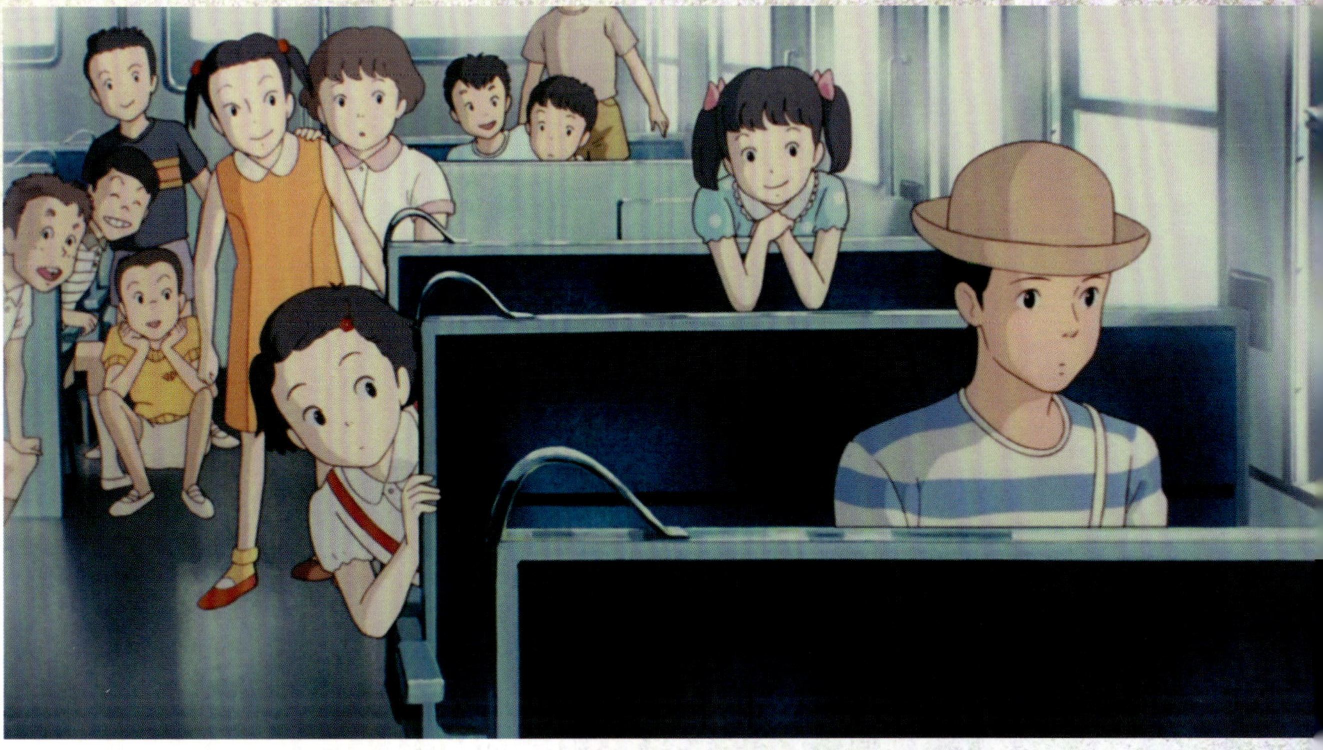

Character designer and animation director Yoshifumi Kondô built on the success of the facial expressions in *Grave of the Fireflies* (see page 27), particularly with Taeko's smile.

The heroine's childhood memories received a more stylized treatment. This was especially true of the backgrounds, whose wash drawings were treated with the utmost care: For certain scenes, Takahata chose from several hundred hues suggested by the art department. The contrast among the various settings was intended to capture Taeko's evolution over the course of fifteen years, as well as that of Japan as a whole.

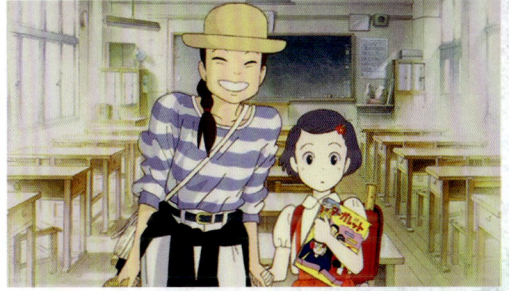

> *"Thanks to the success of Kiki's Delivery Service, Ghibli was able to invest in larger projects."*

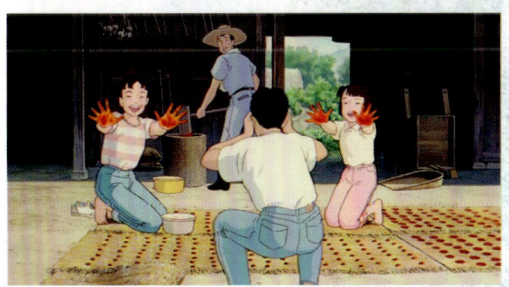

While the original manga offered only a succession of vignettes, Takahata invented the entire contemporary arc of *Only Yesterday*, the essence of the film, and a storyline conclusion whose impact depended on the viewer's investment. The film's final shots are contradicted by the sumptuous end credits. Many Japanese viewers were invested, echoing their own *furusato*: 2.2 million of them saw the film when it was released, placing it at the top of the 1991 box office charts.

PORCO ROSSO
1992 - HAYAO MIYAZAKI

It was originally a diversion for the Studio Ghibli employees, an unambitious project. In the end, *Porco Rosso*, which was released in Japan in 1992, proved to be Hayao Miyazaki's most mature and adult film to date.

By Matthieu Pinon

t's the Adriatic, in the late 1920s. Vacations are long for some World War I pilots, who have banded together as pirates in a gang called Mamma Aiuto. Tourists can rest assured that Marco Pagot's red seaplane is always just in time! The solitary knight owes his nickname, Porco Rosso, to his (literal) pig's head, the mark of his survival during the conflict that decimated his entire squadron during the war, starting with his friend Berlini.

Pursued by the Fascists, who want to get their hands on his plane, and hunted by the ace pilot Donald Curtis, who has been hired by Mamma Aiuto, Porco can only count on the owner of the Hotel Adriano, who is also Berlini's widow: his friend Gina, who is secretly in love with him. Then

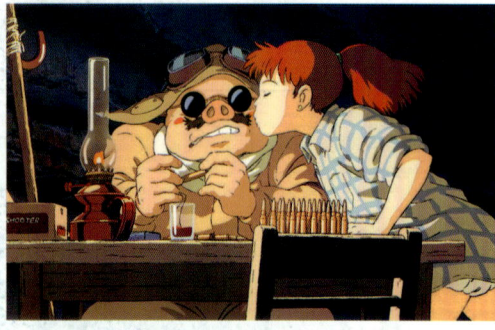

Fio, the granddaughter of his loyal aircraft manufacturer Piccolo, arrives on the scene. Not content with merely rebuilding his seaplane, she will go along on his adventures as his mechanic.

AIR TRAVEL

It was late 1990. *Only Yesterday* had exhausted the Studio Ghibli team. Miyazaki accepted a light project on a modest scale: a medium-length film to be shown on Japan Airlines (JAL) flights. This exclusive project, aimed primarily at tired *salarymen*—a Japanese term for a company's nonexecutive managers or employees—would require far less work than a feature-length film. The director saw this as an opportunity to combine two personal projects that had previously been published as short manga: the story of a soldier–pig who conquers all but the heart of the woman he loves, and that of a seaplane pilot.

During production in 1991, tensions in Yugoslavia, the last remaining symbol of communism, erupted into open conflict. Miyazaki, who had led the union at Toei alongside Takahata thirty years earlier, took great interest in the announced end of the political movement and the rise of war, themes he decided to inject into *Porco Rosso*. Ultimately, the project became so big that it was turned into

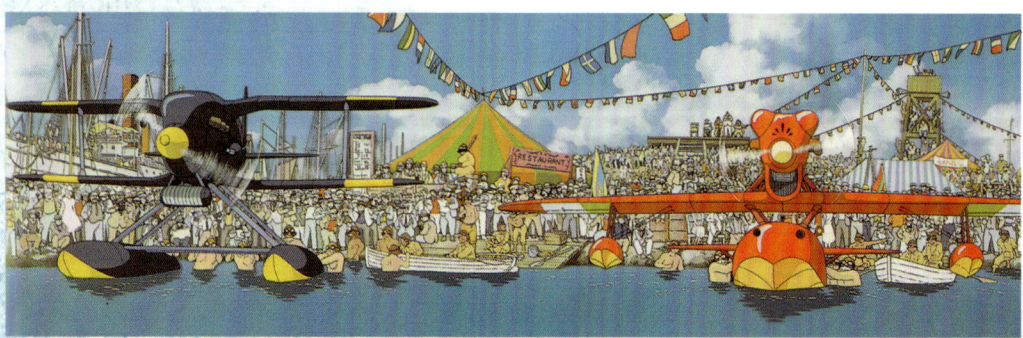

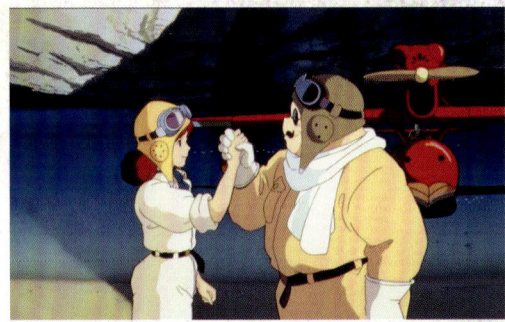

a feature-length film, which was released on JAL flights as promised from July 1 to 31, 1992, and in Japanese movie theaters on July 18.

SERIOUS, WITH A DASH OF FANTASY

For the first time, Miyazaki established a well-defined temporal and geographical window, a backdrop for the already-clashing rising fascism and militant communism. The scenery is strikingly realistic, despite a touch of the picturesque, offering a splendid panorama for the aerial duels; these were the last to be entirely hand-drawn at Ghibli, which subsequently embraced computer technology. Joe Hisaishi's soundtrack completes the immersive experience, evoking period ambience with mandolin and piano bar, along with harmoniously adapted melodies.

> *"Porco Rosso is a wonderful action comedy, achieving the feat of being accessible to every generation."*

The rare forays into fantasy have an even greater impact in this film, which is surprisingly realistic for Miyazaki. The incredible scene in the aerial cemetery will long be remembered, but it's above all the deliberately open-ended ending that raises lingering questions. After the stolen kiss (a Miyazaki first!), does Marco regain his human face? Where romantics may wonder at this retelling of the tale of the princess and the frog, the disillusioned follow the quest for redemption of a miraculous survivor of World War I. A fast-paced rhythm links two perspectives.

Porco Rosso achieves the considerable feat of being accessible to every generation by being, above all, a wonderful action comedy. Miyazaki's love of airplanes provides jaw-dropping moments of aerobatics that work hand in hand with funny supporting roles and situations, such as Mamma Aiuto's brigands looking after Fio. The director even reminds us of the absurdity of "manly" conflicts (the pathetic final duel between Porco and Curtis) and his admiration for women. After all, doesn't Porco fly a seaplane designed entirely by women?

PRINCESS MONONOKE

1997 - HAYAO MIYAZAKI

The longest of Miyazaki's award-winning films, *Princess Mononoke* is an exception in the director's career. It's full of sound and fury, and nearly twenty years after its release, it reminds us that behind the poet there lies an angry man.

By Matthieu Pinon

 little history: At the end of World War II, defeated Japan was devastated. Over the next thirty-odd years, a succession of stimulus packages propelled the country to the forefront of the international economy. The best known was the "Izanagi boom," which began shortly after the 1964 Olympic Games and saw the country's GNP grow by more than 10 percent a year between 1965 and 1970.

PROTECT NATURE!

This economic miracle was the result of galloping industrialization, which undermined Japanese ecology—and nobody intervened. It wasn't until the early 1970s that Japan discovered the scandal involving the city of Minamata, where tens of thousands of inhabitants had been suffering for decades from mercury poisoning caused by a petrochemical plant, resulting in fatal leukemia.

This scandal, combined with the horrors of a not-so-distant armed conflict, formed the basis of *Nausicaä of the Valley of the Wind* in the early 1980s (see page 20). After that blast of rage, Miyazaki abandoned his vindictive resentment in favor of

poetry, hoping that future generations would not repeat the mistakes of their elders. The resounding success of 1988's *My Neighbor Totoro* (see page 29) made it seem like the message had sunk in with the younger generation, but Japanese industries continued to expand to the detriment of the country's natural resources (which were already limited). By this point, Miyazaki had become a national star; he decided to use his fame to once again sound the alarm and issue a new warning in 1997: *Princess Mononoke*.

> "Hayao Miyazaki decided to use his fame to issue a new warning: Princess Mononoke."

TAKING ECO-FRIENDLINESS BACK SEVEN CENTURIES

Set in the Muromachi era (1338–1573), the film makes concrete the metaphorical struggle between the future-oriented Japanese and their ancestral roots, a simmering conflict that claims another victim in the hero Ashitaka; when he kills a bewitched boar god, his arm becomes strangely infected. The young archer may now possess supernatural strength, but his life is at stake. Determined to learn more, Ashitaka sets off on a quest to discover the origins of the evil that is consuming him.

He then discovers a long-running war between the forest spirits—led by the giant she-wolf Moro and her adopted daughter (San, the human wild child)—and the village metalworkers who exploit the local iron resources to make the firearms that protect them from woodland attacks.

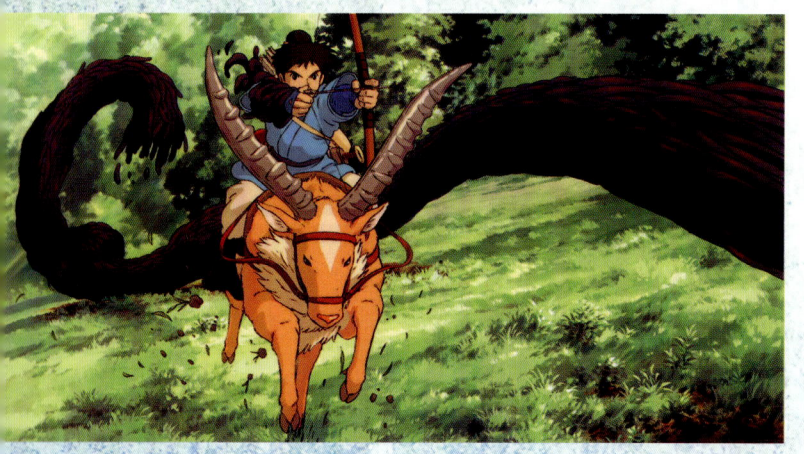

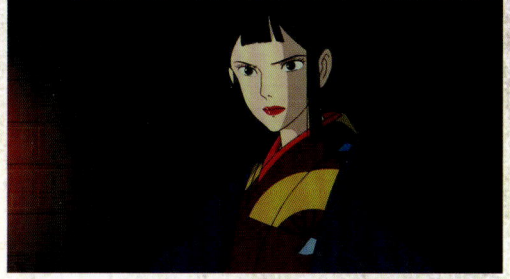

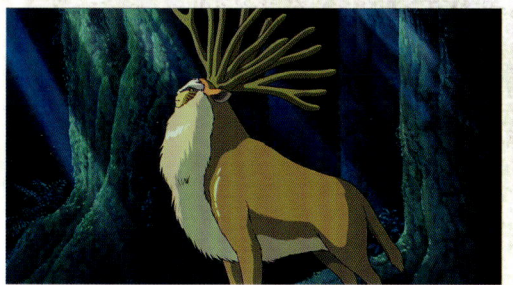

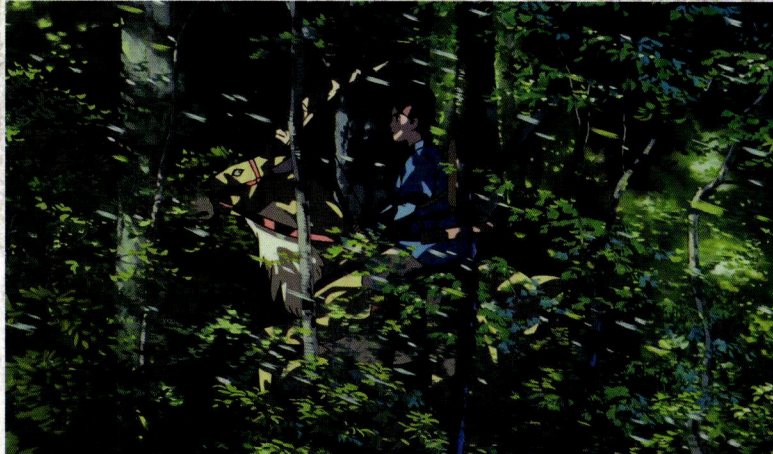

Sent by the emperor, the monk Jiko intends to take advantage of the ongoing chaos to carry out an important mission: collecting the head of the Deer God, which will bring immortality to its possessor.

Unlike *Nausicaä of the Valley of the Wind*, which sometimes verged on Manichaeism, *Princess Mononoke* doesn't pit "nice forest creatures" against "evil humans." Lady Eboshi, the leader of the fortress, isn't interested in destroying the forest for her own pleasure; the survival of her fellow citizens is at stake. Stripping metal mines and uprooting trees are the only ways to feed the forge where firearms are produced, and to get the money to feed her constituents. These include lepers, pariahs of conventional society who are a direct reference to the victims of the Minamata poisonings. Miyazaki's aim is laudable as he repeats his sermon: The end doesn't justify the means.

The situation is far from rosy on the other side, too. A world away from the anthropomorphic animals usually found in animated productions, the forest creatures are guided solely by their instinct for survival and self-preservation. While Lady Eboshi and her troops seek to establish themselves over the course of several generations, the animals see no further than their natural needs, starting with their territory. When humans encroach on their land, their fury overrides all else: a dark anger that literally consumes them. Gone are the hopes of peaceful cohabitation from *My Neighbor Totoro*; there is no room for both clans in this wooded territory. In this respect, *Princess Mononoke* can be compared to John Ford's Westerns: It's not a battle between the civilized and the uncivilized, but between invaders and natives ready to do anything to protect their native habitat.

AN UNAVOIDABLE WAR?

The *kodama*, translucent imps embodying the soul of the forest, sum up this dilemma. Although they're seemingly harmless, their blank stares and constant bone-rattling noises cause distress among humans, who are no longer capable of surviving in the wild after their taste of industrial comfort.

It's when they discover a common enemy that Ashitaka and San come together to fight. Human and animal alike are at risk of suffering an unfortunate fate if the Deer God doesn't get his head back. Once a source of life, the supernatural being has become a destructive entity, crystallizing the ambiguity that permeates the film. Abandoning their personal quests (extermination of the village for San, regeneration of his contaminated body for Ashitaka), the two teenagers fight for the common good. This alliance is the only way for the rival factions to find a way forward and to finally learn to coexist.

Japan has come to understand this lesson: The country exploited 1.92 million tons of natural resources in 2000, but the figure dropped to 1.33 million tons in 2011. That same year, the devastating tsunami (reminiscent of the near-drowning sequence in *Princess Mononoke*) finally generated the solidarity needed to return to a life that is more in tune with nature.

OCEAN WAVES

1993 - TOMOMI MOCHIZUKI

Ocean Waves is probably the least popular of all Ghibli productions. It's a departure from the rest of the studio's filmography in its format, story, and atmosphere, which makes it especially interesting.

By Matthieu Pinon

y 1992, Ghibli had already been in business for six years, with just as many films to its credit. For the first time in its history, the studio launched a production without the participation of Miyazaki or Takahata, who were working on *Princess Mononoke* and *Pom Poko*, respectively. However, taking too many risks was out of the question: Produced for their partner channel Nippon Telebi[1] from the outset, the TV movie had a lower budget than usual.

MAKING WAY FOR THE NEXT GENERATION

Ghibli's real aim in accepting this project was to let its young animators express themselves freely. The producers' decision to adapt Saeko Himuro's best-selling serial novel gave the team a helping hand: Katsuya Kondô, who had illustrated every chapter of the novel since its monthly publication began in 1990, served as character designer for the TV movie. It was directed by Tomomi Mochizuki, who was recruited based on his work on *Maison Ikkoku* and *Kimagure Orange Road*, animated series revolving around young characters. Who could be more qualified to deal with this teenage romance?

Taku and Yutaka's long-standing friendship is tested when a new student arrives at their high school in Kôchi, on the island of Shikoku. While Taku can't stand the snobbish Tokyoite, Yutaka falls head over heels for beautiful Rikako, who is as brilliant in class as she is in sports. The daughter of divorced parents whose mother dragged her to this small town, Rikako has only one dream: to get back to her father in Tokyo. Constantly studying so she can earn a place at a university in the capital, she's willing to do anything to achieve her goal.

"A portrait of youth in the 1990s"

A UNIQUE DEPARTURE

Made over a period of six months, the TV movie, which debuted on the small screen May 5, 1993, and received a theatrical release a few months later, on December 25, stands out from the studio's previous productions in that it makes no use of fantasy elements. Told in flashback, *Ocean Waves* portrays youth in the 1990s, with the rise of divorce and the emancipation of women (as seen in Rikako's memorable bender scene). The two sexes are usually seen in contrast in conventional productions but are treated on an equal footing here, particularly in a slapping scene whose raw violence stands in stark contrast to Ghibli's typical fare.

The studio's usual high technical and artistic standards are maintained, even though the film is a departure from its predecessors. It's an essential reminder of Ghibli's versatility; the studio is often dismissed as a producer of fairy tales. *Ocean Waves* suffers from its uniqueness—it remained unreleased in many parts of the world for several years.

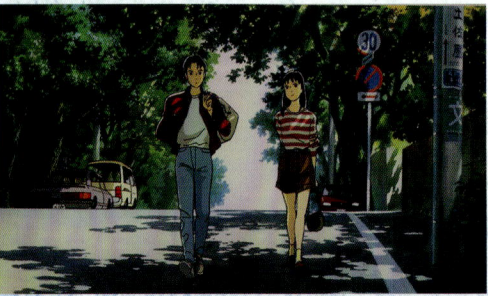

---

[1] A clock designed by Miyazaki stands at the foot of the network's building.

© 1993 SAEKO HIMURO - GN

POM POKO

1994 - ISAO TAKAHATA

A symbol of good fortune, the tanuki, a canine subspecies that somewhat resembles a raccoon, remains an immensely popular animal in Japan, where restaurant storefronts are adorned with carved wooden statues in its likeness. Six years after *Grave of the Fireflies*, Isao Takahata decided to devote an entire film to the animal.

By Gersende Bollut

 lthough the idea of a feature-length film centered on tanuki originated with Hayao Miyazaki, who suggested to the studio in the wake of *Porco Rosso* that it pay homage to these typical Japanese animals that are said to have fabulous virtues, the resulting movie has Takahata's fingerprints all over it. After abandoning the idea of setting the story in feudal Japan because of the parallel development of *Princess Mononoke*, the future director of *The Tale of the Princess Kaguya* decided to spread the story over several years and to choose the humorous title *Pom Poko*, which is supposedly the sound made by a tanuki's belly when it hits it like a drum. Despite Miyazaki's disapproval and attempts to involve himself in production decisions, Takahata held firm on the title and prevailed.

The film is packed with highly entertaining ideas and zany scenes, alternating between cartoonish, anthropomorphic, and realistic graphics for the heroes. Writer-director Takahata uses the art of disguise for an animal supposedly capable of taking human form to blend in with the general population, and exploits one of its physical characteristics (enlarged testicles).

But *Pom Poko* is first and foremost a resigned, even fatalistic, environmentalist manifesto. The carefree daily routine of the tanuki is shattered when they realize that humans are relentlessly chipping away at their living space, until the day a vast urbanization plan threatens to turn their mountain into a concrete suburb of Tokyo. The resistance is

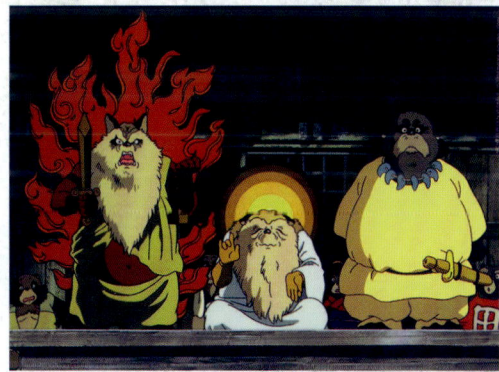

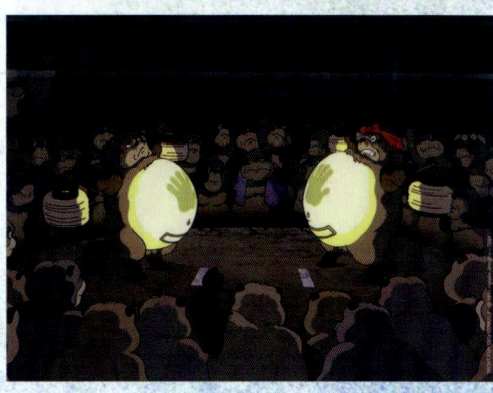

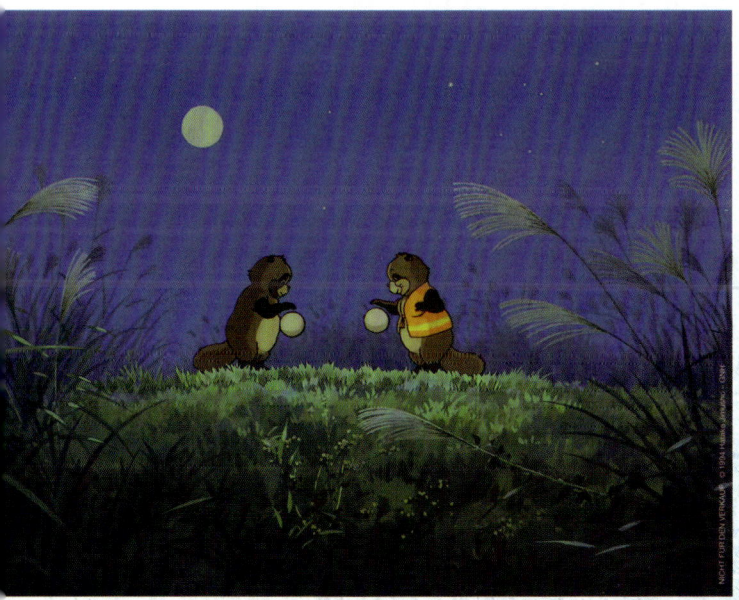

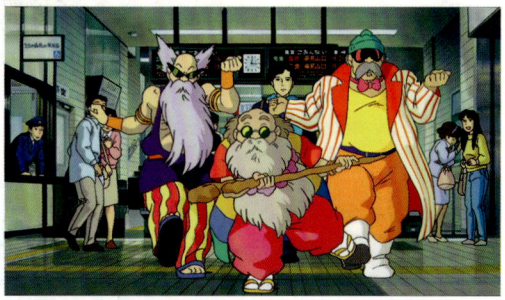

organized, replaying the eternal battle of David against Goliath. Despite a few lulls in the action, the film provides a mischievous and stirring illustration of an issue that is still relevant today: rampant deforestation with no regard for the survival of our precious ecosystem.

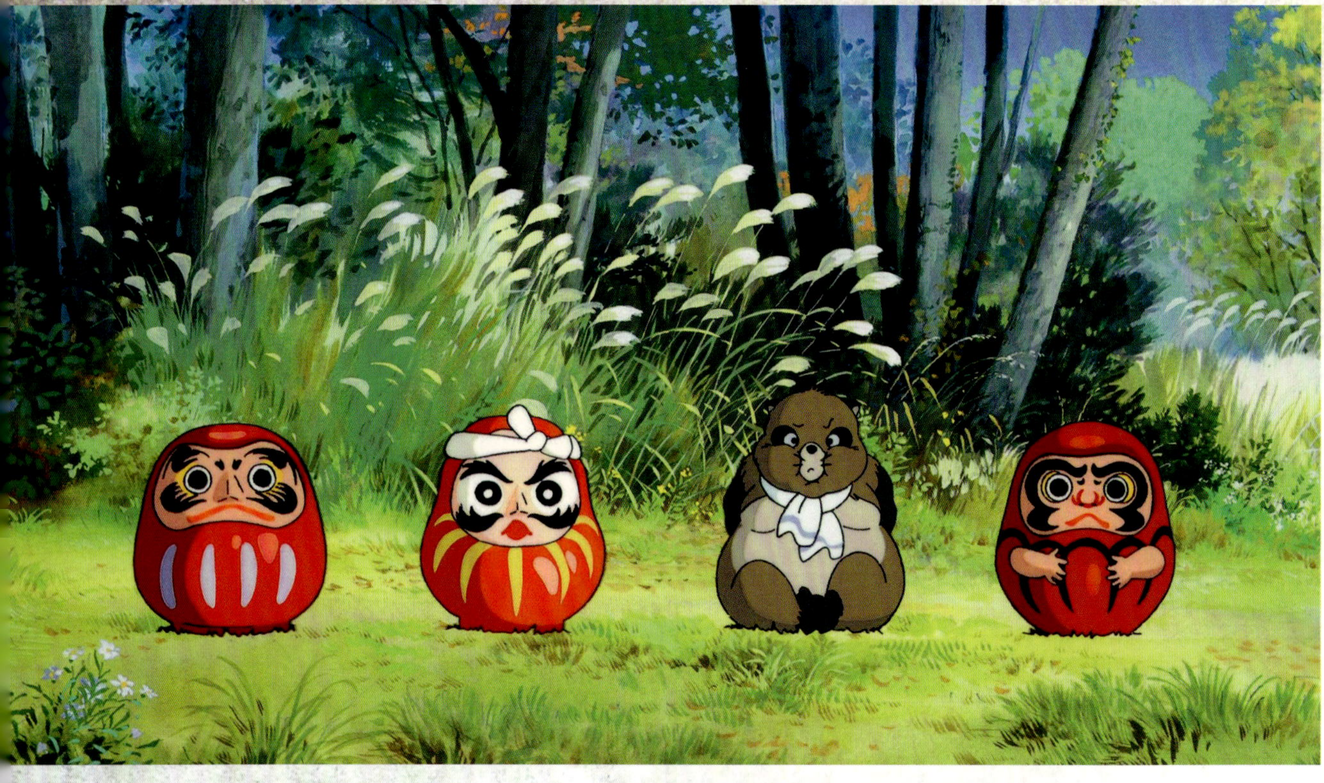

> *"The film provides a mischievous and stirring illustration of an issue that is still relevant today."*

Takahata's sharp eye hits the mark, with an inventiveness, a playfulness, and a vulnerability to the tanuki that inspires deep empathy in the viewer. When it was released in 1994, *Pom Poko* enjoyed a triumphant reception in Japan, even beating out *The Lion King* at the local box office. The film won the Feature Film Award at the Annecy International Animation Film Festival, but it remains less well known in many countries compared to the great classics.

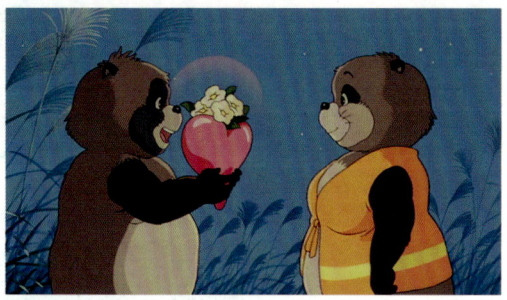

WHISPER OF THE HEART

1995 - YOSHIFUMI KONDÔ

Yoshifumi Kondô was expected to be a worthy successor to the great Miyazaki, but died far too young of an aneurysm, leaving behind only one animated film: *Whisper of the Heart*. Released by Studio Ghibli in 1995, this poetic coming-of-age tale filled with common sense will remain the ultimate tribute to the great director.

➤ By Yasmine Baouche

he plot revolves around young Shizuku Tsukishima, a junior high school student on the outskirts of Tokyo with a passion for literature who takes full advantage of her good relationship with the school nurse and her father's work as a librarian to borrow as many books as possible. In her spare time, she also tries to adapt the song "Country Roads" into Japanese, including a parody version, "Concrete Roads," which makes fun of the city where she lives. In the course of her readings, she notices that a person by the name of Seiji Amasawa has borrowed them before her. One day, after showing her two songs to her friend Yuko Harada, she forgets her book and lyrics on a bench. Fate then decides to play a trick on her: Seiji Amasawa is the one who finds Shizuku's things, and he is quick to tease her about her writings. Shortly thereafter, Shizuku encounters a big cat on a train who appears to know his way around public transportation perfectly. She decides to follow him and comes across an incredible shop full of objects that seem to have sprung from poems or stories. She is warmly welcomed by an old antique dealer, but as she is leaving, she comes face-to-face with Seiji. Who is this boy? And when will she be able to return to this unusual store?

THE 1990S GENERATION

Shizuku and Seiji soon get to know each other, and while the girl is carried away by her desire to write without really knowing how to go about it, the boy shows amazing determination about his future. His self-assurance intimidates Shizuku as much as it motivates her to achieve her dreams. This duality is indicative not just of a generation, but also of a period in life: an agonizing adolescence that wants to find a place in the adult world. But

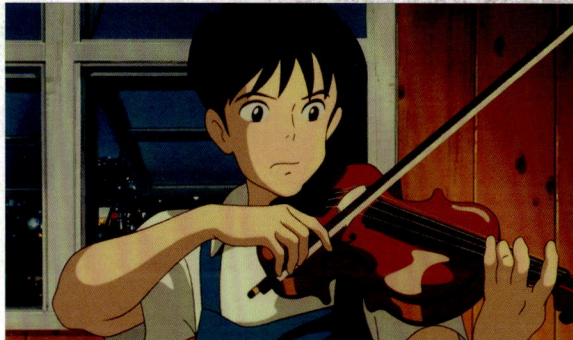

"Whisper of the Heart is an ode to adolescence and a true life lesson."

this is a frightening world that seems to leave little room for imagination and dreams. But in the magical store, Shizuku has found friends, music, and fantastical objects that seem to tell the story of their past when you look at them. In the guise of a love story, *Whisper of the Heart* is an ode to adolescence, as well as proof that perseverance and patience go hand in hand for anyone who wants to make their dreams come true. It's more than just a story; it's a true life lesson.

AN UNCERTAIN FUTURE

❯-•-❮

The Contentious Agreement
My Neighbors the Yamadas

THE CONTENTIOUS AGREEMENT

By Gersende Bollut

After categorically declining offers from the Warner Bros. and Fox studios to distribute Ghibli films in the US, both of which had expressed the heretical intention of making cuts, modifying the music, and even reediting Ghibli's works, Miyazaki avoided the majors like the plague; they were attracted by the films' growing success with Asian audiences. But, in the summer of 1996, in the middle of production on *Princess Mononoke* (with a budget twice that of previous productions), a deal was struck with Buena Vista Home Entertainment, a unit of the Walt Disney Company. This was an unexpected opportunity for Tokuma to get out of a tricky financial situation. The entire Ghibli catalog was handed over to Disney for theatrical and video release worldwide, except in Asia. The creator of *Totoro* took a dim view of this agreement and remained on his guard, still bitter about the odious 1985 American cut of his *Nausicaä*, which removed more than twenty minutes, primarily from the ecological sequences, and was renamed *Warriors of the Wind* (with the princess herself renamed Zandra!). Many illegal copies of this film circulated with impunity for a long time, particularly on VHS and DVD under the New World Video label.

While Disney's contract in no way impacted the artistic independence of Ghibli's creators, its announcement mobilized the animation fan community, which was concerned about the fate of their beloved studio. Fears included a takeover motivated by a desire to undercut the competition. In any case, Disney agreed not to interfere with editing or music, with the exception of dubbing, of course. Certain subtle but effective modifications were nevertheless denounced, such as a "Westernized" handwritten letter, the addition of music to fill silent scenes for the video release of *Kiki's Delivery Service*, and the rerecording of the title song in English for the end of *Princess Mononoke*.

In any case, the film became a headache for Disney, which was convinced that Studio Ghibli would stick to "inoffensive" works such as *My Neighbor Totoro*. The violence of Ashitaka's

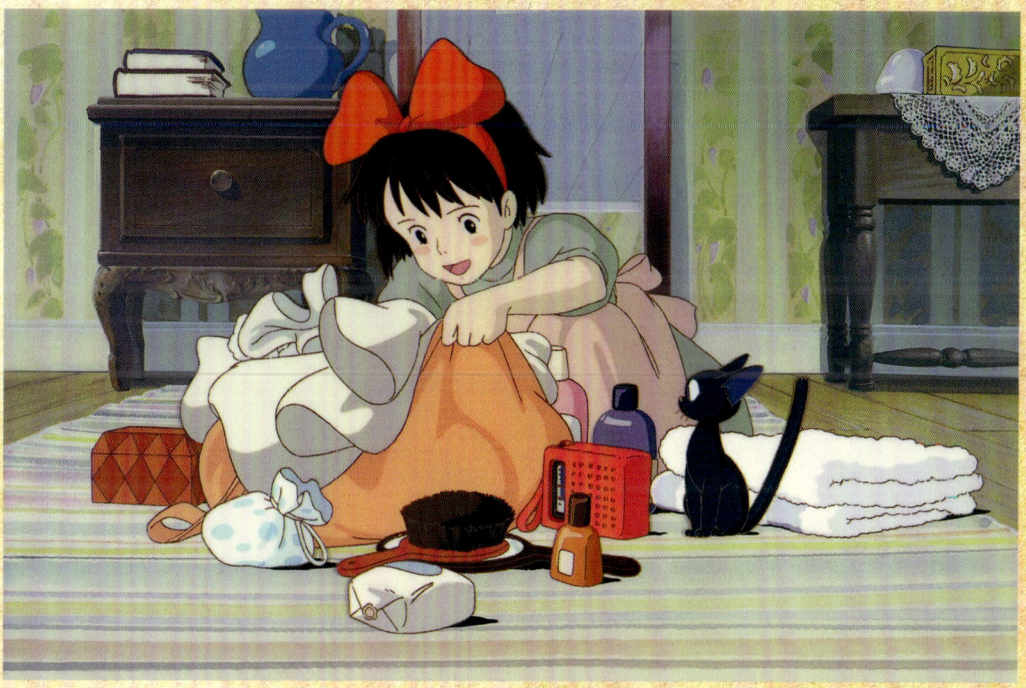

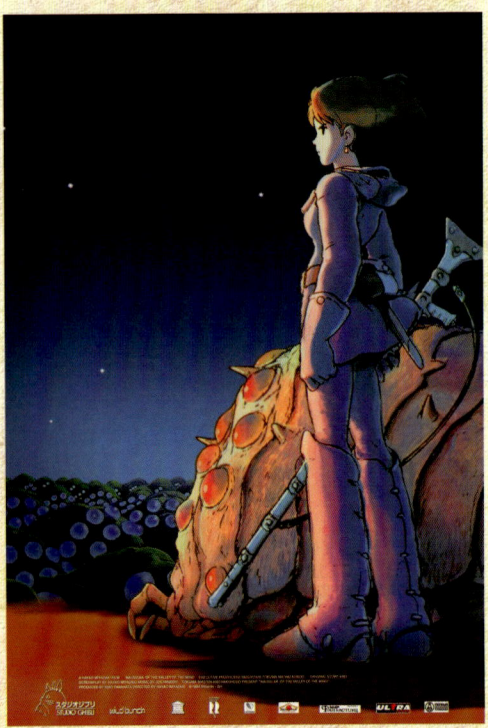

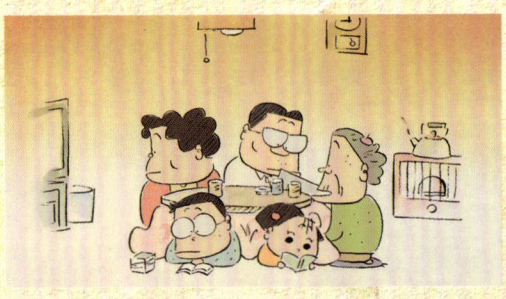

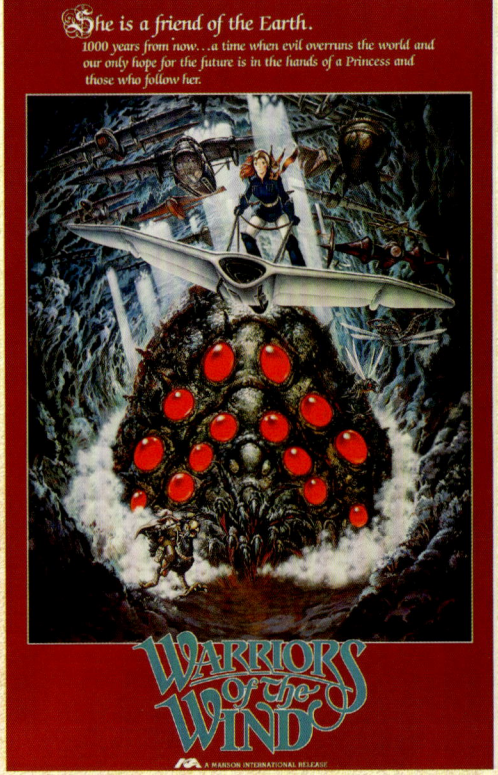

adventures prompted Disney to wait two years before releasing *Princess Mononoke* in theaters, and, not wishing to associate the company logo with the film, Disney entrusted distribution to its subsidiary Miramax.

> *"Disney had never before been involved in producing a foreign film."*

The result was a relative success, with no comparison to the tidal wave in Japan, which put the film at the top of the national box office and displaced *E.T.* from the top spot for all years combined. Nevertheless, Disney invested in Takahata's new film, the atypical *My Neighbors the Yamadas*, which was an adaptation (punctuated by haikus) of a popular manga about the everyday life of a middle-class Japanese family, and in *Spirited Away*, a baroque masterpiece directed by Miyazaki. Disney had never before been involved in producing a foreign film. Gradually, Ghibli productions began to be released regularly in other countries, first in theaters and then on video at a relatively steady pace.

However, with a disorganized chronology of releases (older works intermingled with new ones), it was difficult for the uninitiated audience not to be confused. For example, some viewers lamented the loss of graphic quality between *Spirited Away* and *Castle in the Sky*, which were released internationally a year apart and yet were made fifteen years apart. A classification system on the edge of the DVDs helped restore the true chronology. Since then, most Ghibli works have also been released in lavish HD versions. And now that the agreement with Disney has been terminated, they have been rereleased on VOD and Blu-ray.

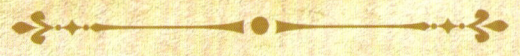

MY NEIGHBORS THE YAMADAS

1999 - ISAO TAKAHATA

After the signing of distribution agreements between Disney and Tokuma (of which Ghibli is a subsidiary), Hayao Miyazaki directed his darkest and most violent film in 1997, *Princess Mononoke*. The following year, Isao Takahata confirmed that the studio had maintained its artistic integrity with *My Neighbors the Yamadas*, a feature film that is as funny as it is disconcerting.

⤜ By Philippe Bunel

Composed of vignettes ranging from the burlesque to the dreamlike, *My Neighbors the Yamadas* explores the Japanese family through Takahata's poetic lens. Despite its sizable budget, the film was a commercial failure, a result of distribution problems and stiff competition from the steamroller films *Star Wars: Episode I—The Phantom Menace* and *Pokémon the Movie 2000*. It also fell short of the Ghibli standards perceived by Miyazaki's adoring public.

A SMALL PROJECT FOR A BIG STUDIO?

My Neighbors the Yamadas is an adaptation of Hisaichi Ishii's manga of the same name, which follows a traditional modern family in a variety of humorous situations. Producer Toshio Suzuki, a fan of these satirical stories, had long wanted to turn them into a film, and he convinced Takahata to direct. The project was not an easy one to produce, however,

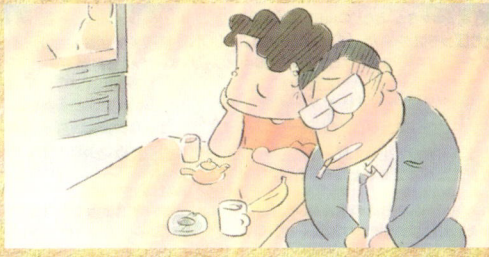

as both the financiers and the artistic team were skeptical about adapting a comic strip consisting of four-frame sketches with simplistic drawings. The project's scope didn't seem commensurate with the studio's recent success with *Princess Mononoke*, but thanks to the genius of Takahata and Suzuki, the budget was ultimately substantial, and the artistic team had to tackle a new technical challenge.

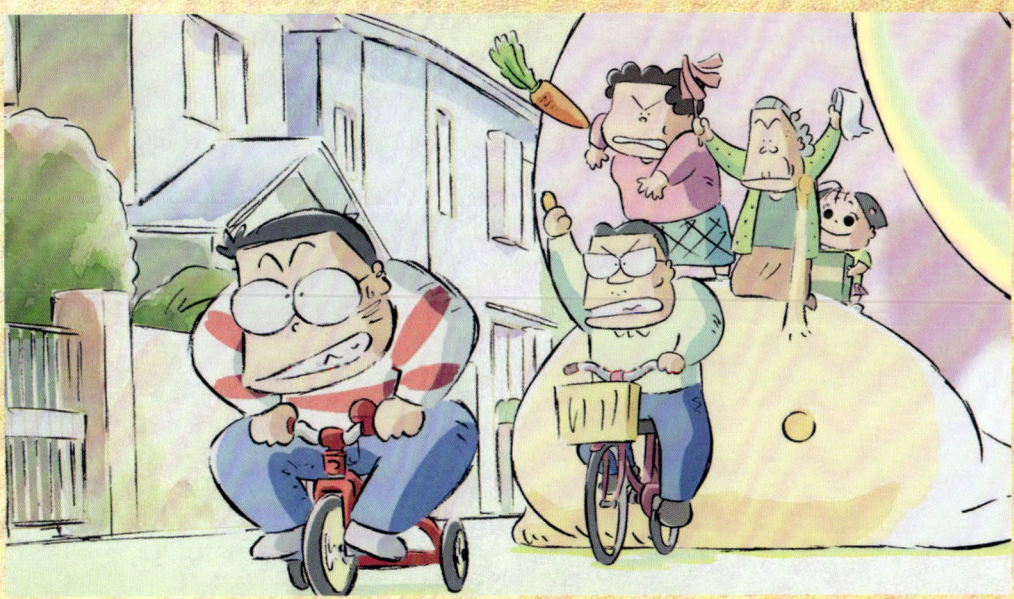

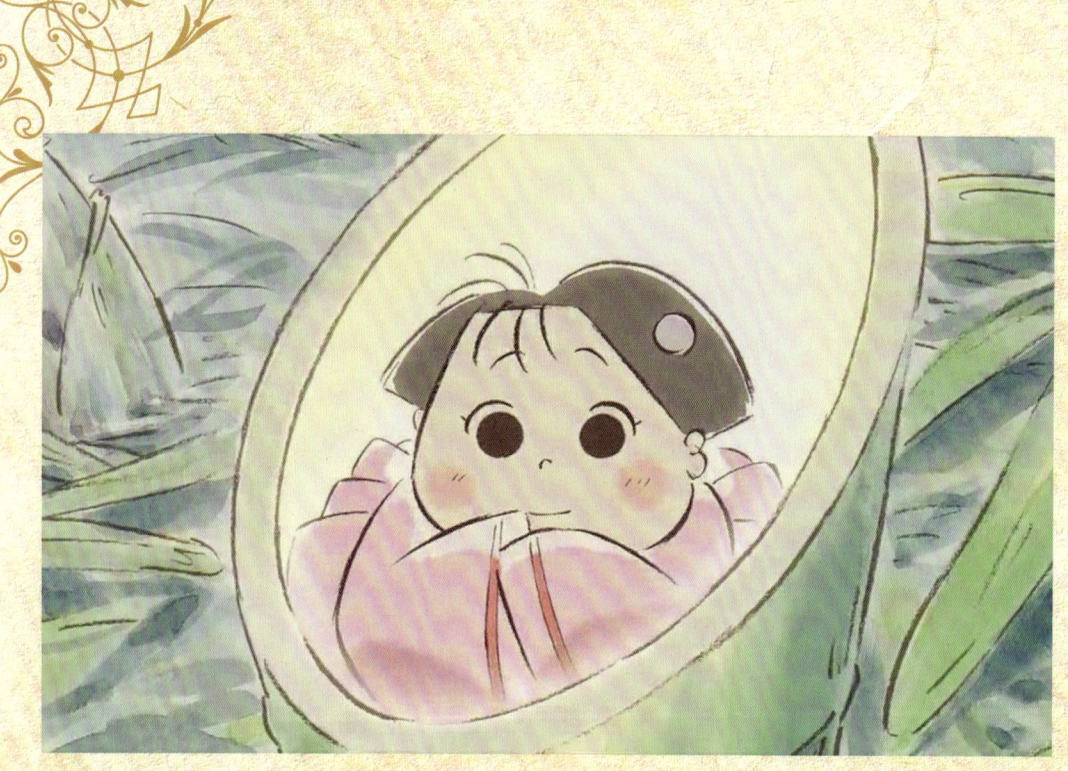

THE COMPLEXITY OF MINIMALISM

Takahata and Miyazaki have always been perfectionists, developing animation techniques such as the layout system, which was optimized during the production of the *Heidi* series. But Takahata's work is very different from that of his colleague in that it has a more social dimension, rooted in reality. This is why *My Neighbors the Yamadas* was a natural step in the filmography of Takahata, who always adapted his direction to his subject matter. In keeping with the author's spirit, Takahata decided to bring the family to life with watercolor-like graphics. To achieve this, he abandoned celluloid and colored the film by computer; this was a new approach for the studio, which invested heavily in computer graphics equipment. But the pencil drawings were similar to the manga, with lines that were almost never closed, which meant that the entire image had to be redrawn with transparent lines to delineate the colorization. As for the decor, the director's compositional work was complex: He didn't cover the entire frame, maintaining a partially blurred style to direct the viewer's attention.

My Neighbors the Yamadas is definitely a film that needs to be rediscovered, along with the melancholy *Only Yesterday*.

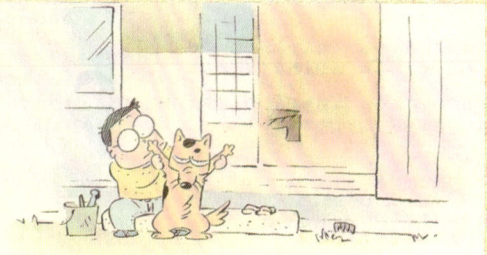

"Takahata's work has a social dimension, rooted in reality."

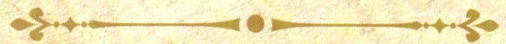

MIYAZAKI'S ACCESSION

❯–◆–❮

Miyazaki at the Forefront

Spirited Away

The Cat Returns

Howl's Moving Castle

MIYAZAKI AT THE FOREFRONT

By Gersende Bollut

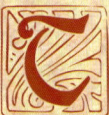The idea for *Spirited Away*, which follows the adventures of a little girl who is forced to work in order to survive in a world that is forbidden to humans, had already sprouted in Miyazaki's mind before the production of *Princess Mononoke*. Miyazaki submitted two adaptations of children's books, including one that he called *Rin the Chimney Painter*, but both were rejected. He then proposed a new project inspired by these works, which was approved. Production began in late 1999 and was completed in June 2001. *Spirited Away* is a film of superlatives. After its release in Japan in July 2001, it paid for itself in just one week, topping the Japanese box office for five months in a row and overtaking *Titanic* to become the biggest box office success of all time (until the 2020 release of *Demon Slayer: Mugen Train*), with over 23 million viewers. It won the Golden Bear in Berlin and the Academy Award for Best Animated Feature Film, cementing Miyazaki's worldwide reputation as well as definitive recognition for Studio Ghibli, which was buoyed by a renewed cash flow.

The quest of the resourceful, hard-working girl at the center of the movie, lost in an *Alice in Wonderland*–style tunnel, was also a hit in France: The media seized on the phenomenon with a massive poster campaign and unanimous critical acclaim, and the film drew 1.5 million curious filmgoers and animation enthusiasts to theaters. There's no doubt that a certain disorientation is guaranteed in the magical world of the film: The heroine wanders through a land where spirits and gods bask in *onsen* (Japanese public baths) staffed by a teeming society of little hands at the ready. The film is imbued with a multitude of motifs specific to Japanese culture that one doesn't need to fully grasp to be captivated by their charm, and is populated by ghosts and witches who are variously surprising, frightening, and endearing.

The more low-key release of *My Neighbors the Yamadas* two years earlier (July 1999 in Japan) marked the end of celluloid in favor of computer technology, which was to become the dominant medium from then on. Takahata was less in tune with producers' expectations and decided to step

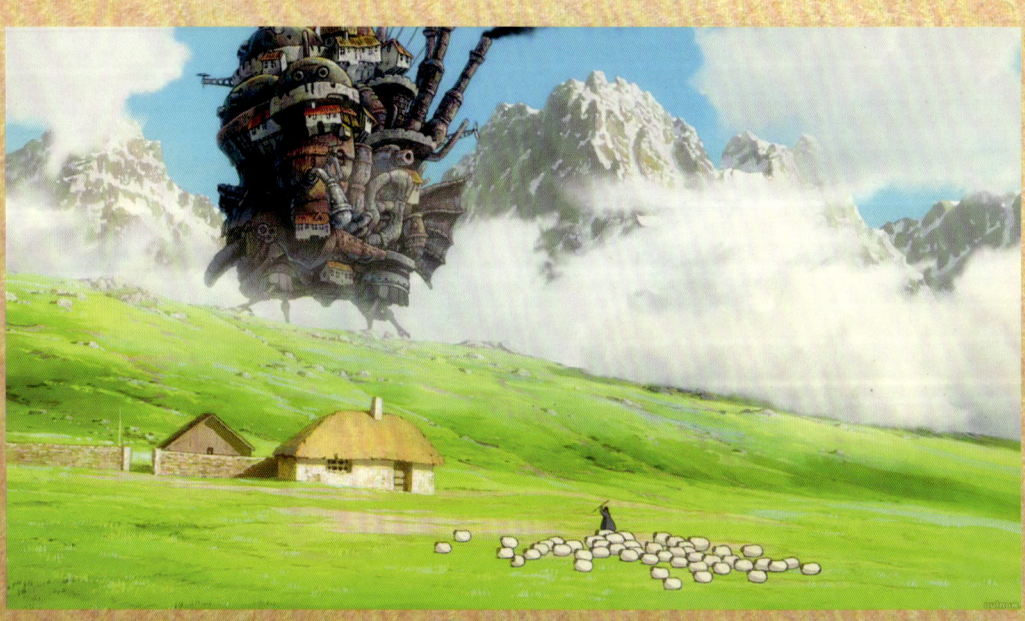

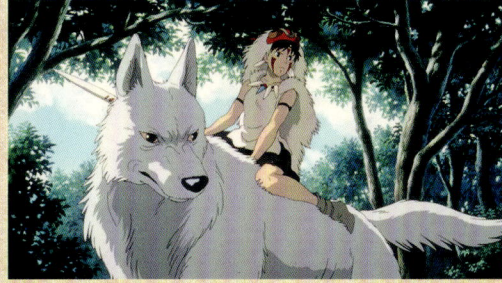

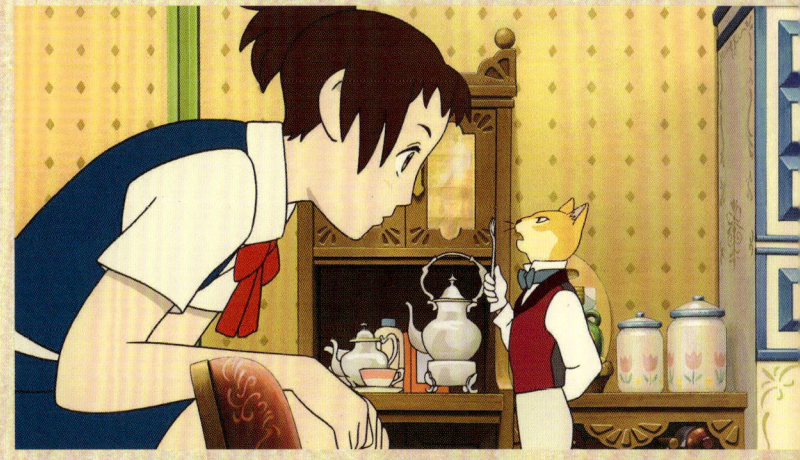

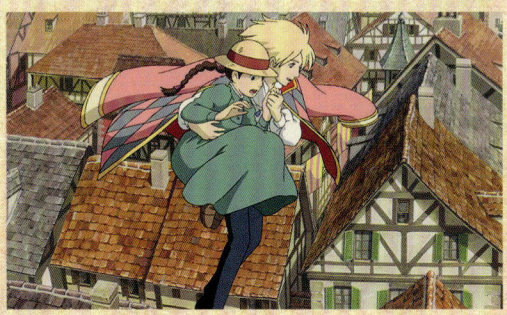

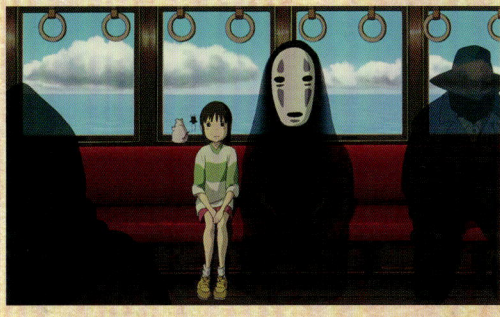

> *"Making a successful film involves a lot of luck; it's almost a miracle."*
> —Mamoru Hosoda

back from the profession in favor of even more personal projects, such as the compilation sketch film *Winter Days*.

As for Miyazaki, he focused on the short films presented exclusively at the Ghibli Museum (there are, to date, thirteen of them), leaving the field open to a new generation of auteurs, like Hiroyuki Morita, who delivered the minor feature *The Cat Returns* in the summer of 2002, and, above all, Mamoru Hosoda, who was tapped to direct *Howl's Moving Castle*, based on a novel by Diana Wynne Jones. But production fell behind schedule, and the young creator left the project after the decision-makers expressed unhappiness with his concept.

Miyazaki took over the abandoned film and relaunched production in February 2003, after a six-month general shutdown. This opulent work, largely influenced by Western motifs, was an unqualified triumph when it was released in late 2004. A few years later, Hosoda was back in the spotlight with the excellent *Summer Wars*, *Wolf Children*, *The Boy and the Beast*, and *Belle*. Asked about his preliminary work on *Howl's Moving Castle*, the filmmaker said in a 2012 interview that he had

been contacted by Ghibli, making no secret of his happiness "at such an offer [after he had] failed the studio's entrance exam." He added, "But my joy doesn't mean that everything went well; it ended in failure. That experience made me realize that making a successful film involves a lot of luck; it's almost a miracle." Asked whether the final film differed from his initial project, he dismissed the question. "Quite frankly, I haven't seen the film directed by Miyazaki, so I don't know, but I'm pretty sure it had nothing to do with my project. I was only thirty-three at the time, and he was over sixty, so obviously, the age difference would make the approach fundamentally different."

SPIRITED AWAY

2001 - HAYAO MIYAZAKI

When Hayao Miyazaki announced his intention to retire, his latest film, *Princess Mononoke* (1997), was a landmark success with over 13 million admissions, giving Miyazaki unprecedented status. The following year, director Yoshifumi Kondô (*Whisper of the Heart*), who had been expected to take over from the master, died suddenly. *Spirited Away* would go into production in 1999 and was already expected to be the master's last film.

By Romain Dasnoy

To this day, *Princess Mononoke* remains the most lavish—almost disproportionately so—historical fresco in the world of animation. The product of three years' hard work and many production delays, the film that could have ruined the studio (as producer Toshio Suzuki liked to say) nevertheless remains one of the most important milestones for Japanese animation in the world. The economic reality that Ghibli faced, combined with Kondô's death, naturally led to Hayao Miyazaki's return to action to lead the production of *Spirited Away*. The film was initially less ambitious than *Princess Mononoke*, but it benefited from excellent promotion and a new media policy that revealed very little of its content at the time of its creation. Released in Japanese theaters four years after the acclaimed *Princess Mononoke*, Hayao Miyazaki's eighth film was a dazzling success, attracting almost 23 million viewers—an all-time record in Japan that would not be broken until 2020. *Spirited Away* garnered several awards around the world, including the Golden Bear at the Berlin Film Festival in 2002, the Academy Award for Best Animated Feature in 2003, and the prestigious Annie Award for Outstanding Achievement for Music in a Feature Production in 2002. And it succeeded in doing the impossible: dethroning *Princess Mononoke*, pure and simple. Was this the result of globalization, or did the movie genuinely appeal to a wide range of audiences? Beyond its undeniable commercial success, this feature was also an artistic achievement, a high point in great film animation. Aesthetically, the director's style represented a continuation of *Princess Mononoke*, very different from what audiences had been used to seeing since *Sherlock Hound*. But Miyazaki's increasingly complex approach also set *Spirited Away* apart from the rest, with its notable depth of field and more lighthearted scenes alternating with epic moments and more intellectual sequences.

> *"The most lavish historical fresco in the world of animation"*

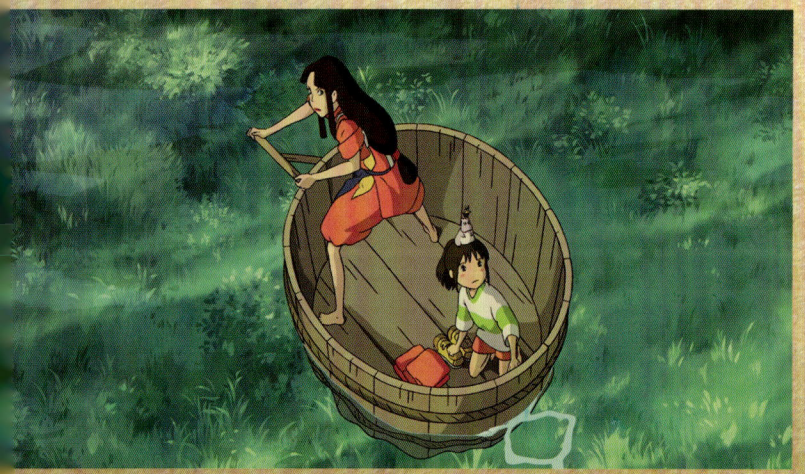

Spirited Away is, above all, a distillation of Hayao Miyazaki's great themes, masterfully executed with a sense of perspective that had been clear since *Princess Mononoke*. Almost as long as the previous film, this new feature added a more human dimension, on a little girl's level, to subjects that went far beyond the first degree of understanding. The passage from childhood to adulthood, a central theme the director treated often, is symbolized here by the transfiguration of a period of life into a highly fantastical place. It is accessible only through a tunnel whose appearance—or the way it is perceived—changes from the beginning to the end of the film. Chihiro, a little girl who is

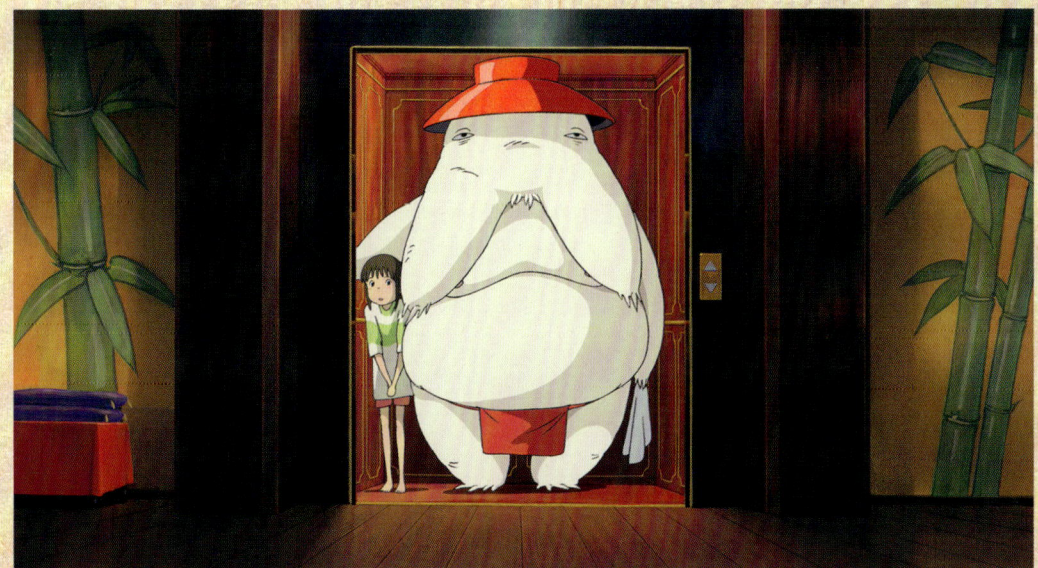

obviously short-tempered and extremely dependent on her parents, goes through that mysterious tunnel. Miyazaki's obvious love of metamorphosis (for example, Chihiro's parents are transformed into pigs, the faceless man's appearance and behavior change, the *onsen* has a "purifying" function for the gods) is complemented by his other great cinematic motifs, giving this film a "definitive" aspect in such narrative elements as the final flight scene with Chihiro and Haku, the role of women, the duality of body and spirit (are the two sisters, Yubaba and Zeniba, a single person?), and omnipresent natural elements.

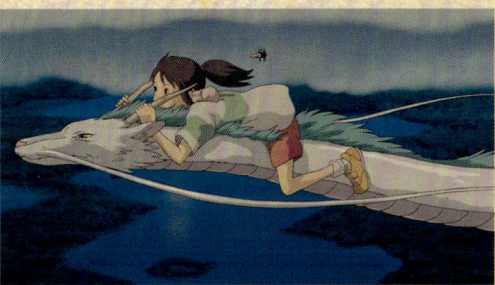

Throughout her adventure, the irreverent Chihiro never loses her ability to provoke situations of all kinds, reminding us that this is a very family-oriented film, renewing narrative links with the Felliniesque *Kiki* and *Porco Rosso*. The film is extremely varied, with masterful writing that moves from one emotion to the next, avoiding the pitfalls of the perhaps overambitious *Princess Mononoke*. Joe Hisaishi's music also reflects this relationship between emotion and narrative. While *Princess Mononoke* featured a thirty-three-track soundtrack, requiring an album of symphonic arrangements to highlight its major themes, Chihiro's story maxed out at twenty-one tracks, already perfectly aesthetic and requiring no symphonic album at all. This vision of harmonizing thematic motifs (for Miyazaki) and musical motifs (for Hisaishi) made the film one of the greatest collaborations seen in an animated movie, with *Ponyo* certainly matching its excellence a few years later. These great moments in cinema include Haku and Chihiro's chase at the beginning of the film (an orchestration repeated in the soundtrack of the French film *Tom Thumb*, also

composed by Joe Hisaishi), the boiler room scene with its purely French aesthetic (in the style of composer Francis Poulenc), the train scene and its sense of infinite sadness (very close to Isao Takahata's work on *Grave of the Fireflies*), and the finale, with its fabulous orchestral layering, directly inspired by the film scores of American composer James Horner.

In short, thanks to the extraordinary inspiration and talent of its creators, *Spirited Away* remains one of the clearest and most beautiful lessons in cinema that has ever come out of Japan.

THE CAT RETURNS

2002 - HIROYUKI MORITA

One year after the triumphant release of Hayao Miyazaki's ninth feature,[1] the studio unveiled its third production that was not directed by one of the company's founders: *The Cat Returns*. It wasn't nearly as ambitious as Miyazaki's or Takahata's films, and was consequently less popular with the public, but Hiroyuki Morita's work is still a success, full of lightness and some beautiful scenes.

➤ By Romain Dasnoy

Still with an eye on well-deserved retirement, Hayao Miyazaki and Isao Takahata, the studio's iconic, hard-to-replace figures, launched production of *The Cat Returns*, bolstered by the success of *Princess Mononoke* and *Spirited Away*. The newly intensified financial and public support allowed them to resume the effort to find replacements in the new generation of directors, an endeavor that had been abandoned with *Kiki's Delivery Service* (which Miyazaki eventually directed) and cut short by the death of Yoshifumi

Kondô (*Whisper of the Heart*) after many hopes had been pinned on him. This new, much less ambitious feature was family entertainment in the purest form, but not without interest. Rather

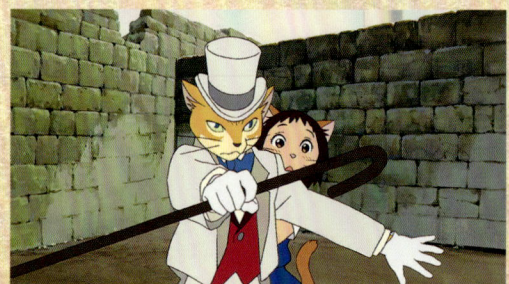

[1.] At the time, it was considered the last of his career.

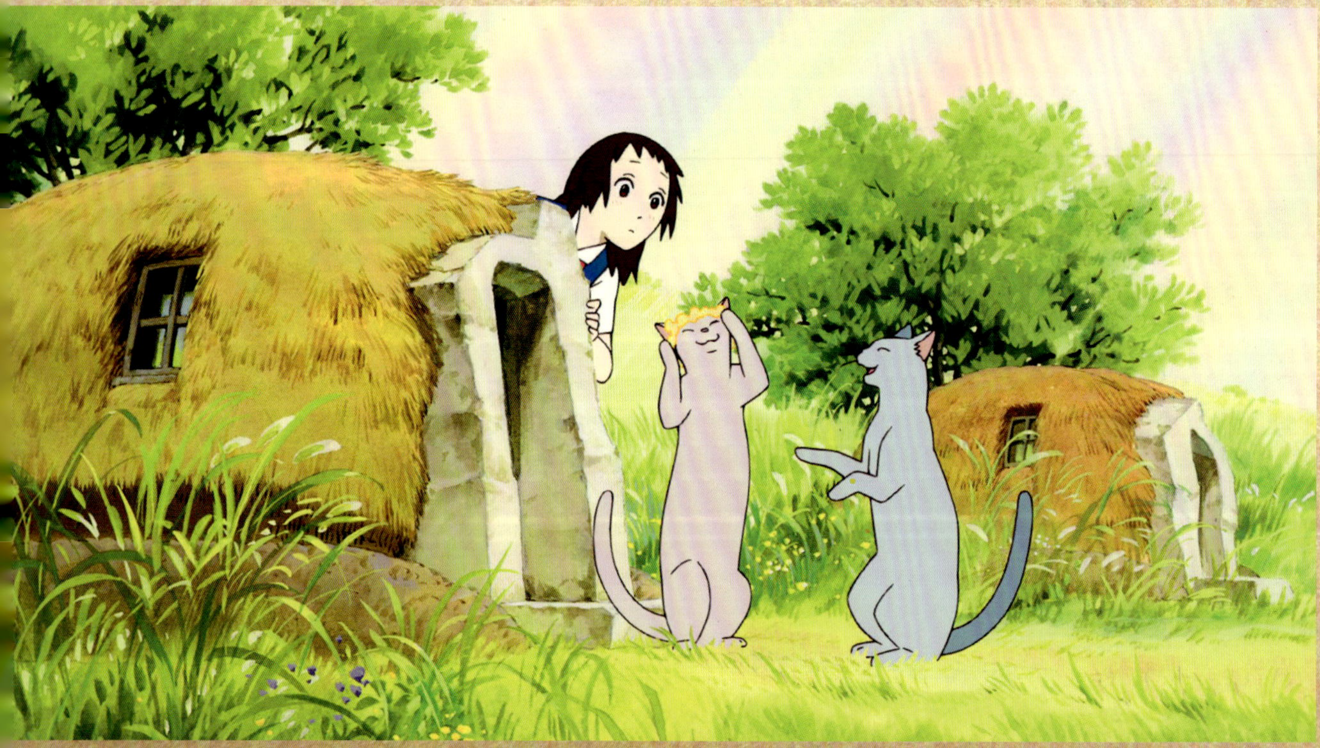

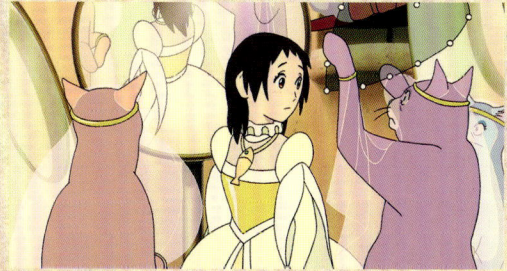

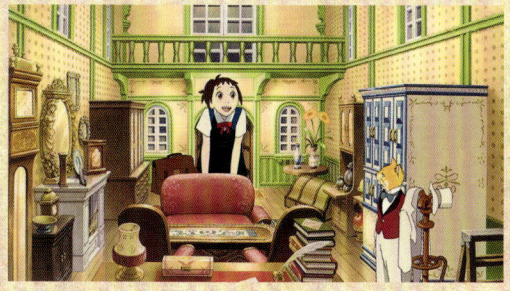

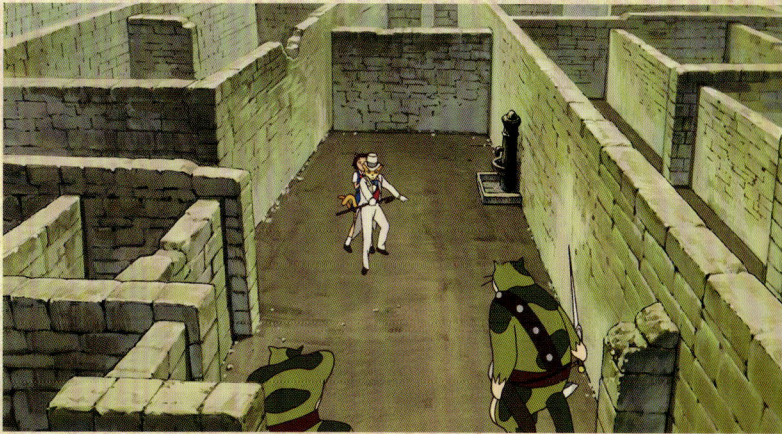

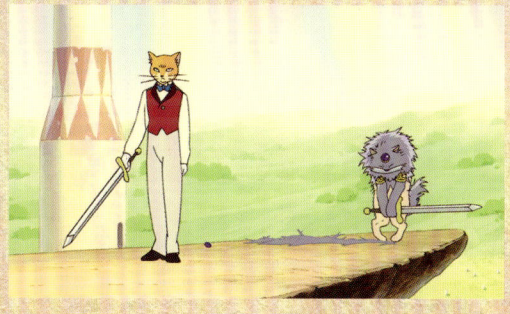

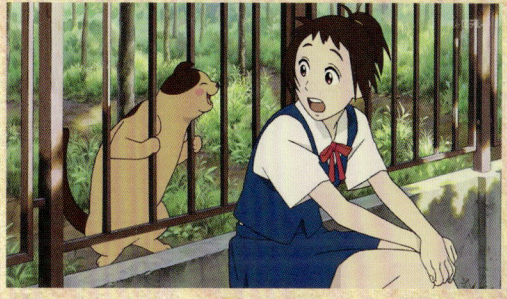

Hayao Miyazaki was drawn to this world and asked her to draft a new story for a short film, which was later turned into a feature film and released in theaters. Although the final product is far from Ghibli's usual standards of quality and depth of field, *The Cat Returns* is still a very respectable production that provides light family entertainment, and not so far removed from *Totoro* or *Ponyo*, minus the excellent writing and artistic ambition.

short (less than an hour and a half) and accompanied by a series of short films from Studio Ghibli, *The Cat Returns* enjoyed minor success in Japanese theaters in the summer of 2002.

The story revolves around a teenage girl, Haru, who rescues a cat one day after leaving her high school and discovers that she can talk to and understand felines. The cat is none other than

"A very respectable production that provides light family entertainment"

Lune, the prince of the cat kingdom. Guided by Baron Humbert von Gikkingen and accompanied by portly Muta (both characters from *Whisper of the Heart*), she sets off for this magical place, where she may be forced to take Lune as her husband, and where strange events will unfold. The tale is reminiscent of *Alice in Wonderland*, with its many metaphors for entering an unknown, fantastical world. In truth, the story is taken from a manga by Aoi Hiiragi, who also authored *Whisper of the Heart*.

HOWL'S MOVING CASTLE

2004 - HAYAO MIYAZAKI

After the resounding success of *Spirited Away* (with over 23 million viewers in Japan), Hayao Miyazaki directed *Howl's Moving Castle* in 2004, concluding a dark and ambiguous parenthesis in his filmography that began with *Princess Mononoke*. Thanks to a bigger budget, the master once again established his dominance at the Japanese box office.

By Philippe Bunel

In 2001, Studio Ghibli announced that it was working on an adaptation of Diana Wynne Jones's fantasy novel *Howl's Moving Castle*. The book describes how young Sophie is transformed into an old lady by a witch, then crosses paths with a strange magician's mobile castle. The director was to be Mamoru Hosoda, a Miyazaki admirer who had worked on the first two *Digimon* films. However, the collaboration between the director and the studio failed, and Miyazaki took over the direction of the film and decided to start again from scratch, much to the dismay of the artistic team. After months of work on the storyboard, production was relaunched at the end of 2003.

Initially scheduled for summer 2004, the film was finally released in November. Although it was not promoted nearly as much as *Spirited Away* (Miyazaki wanted viewers to have the full surprise in theaters), the film was a huge success in its first weeks on the big screen.

A PERSONAL ADAPTATION

It's easy to imagine what a terrible blow Hosoda's departure from production was; the studio was actively seeking a successor to Miyazaki and Takahata, who were both close to retirement. And *Howl's Moving Castle* had all the makings of a legacy film, like Akira Kurosawa's *Madadayo*.

Although Miyazaki's reputation was already well established, he took up a major challenge with this film: that of looking in the mirror and returning to his key themes (grief, family, feminism, and ecology), which he transcended by perfecting his storytelling and graphics. Above all, he projected

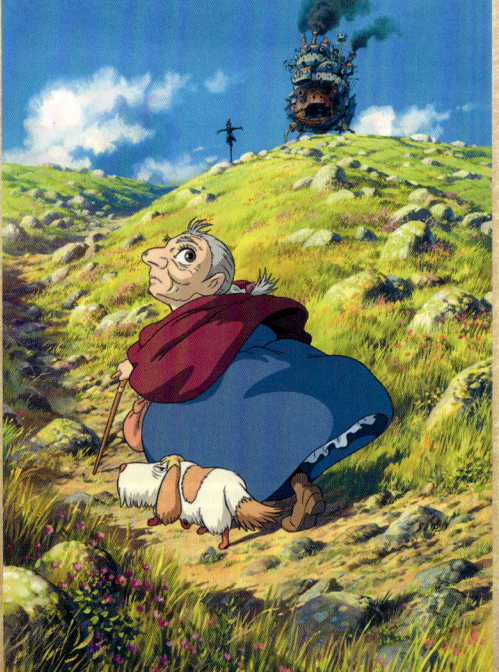

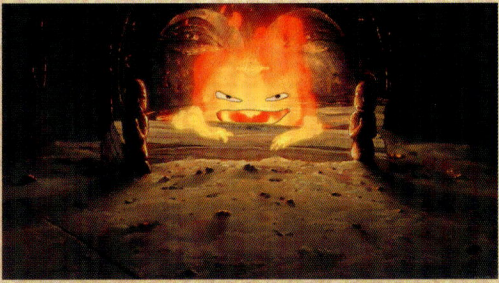

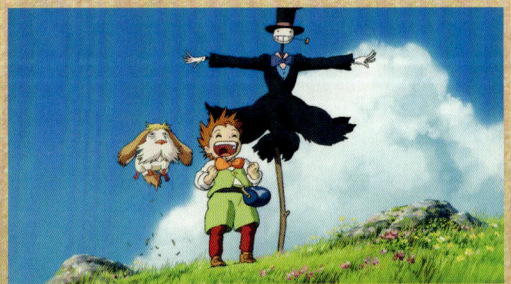

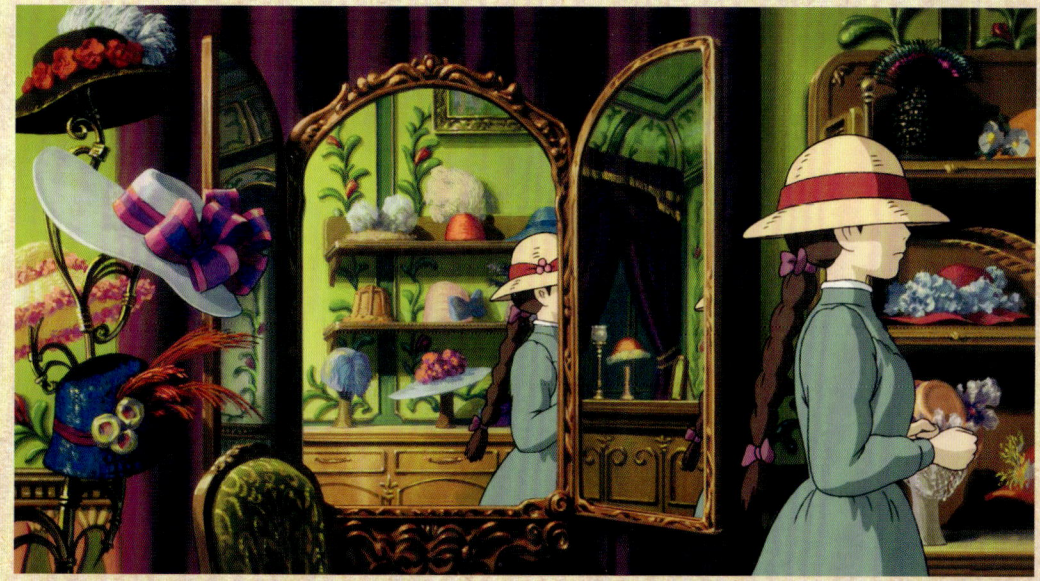

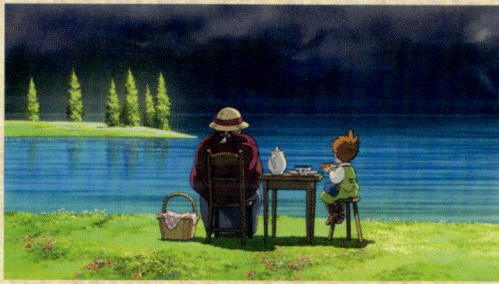

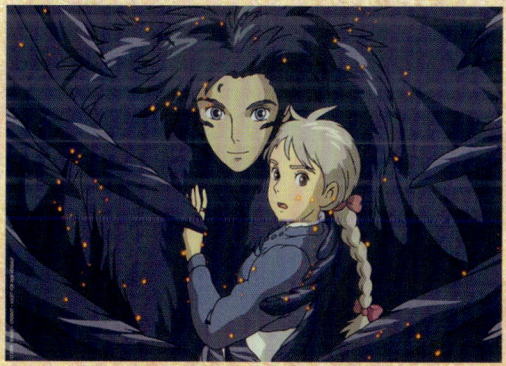

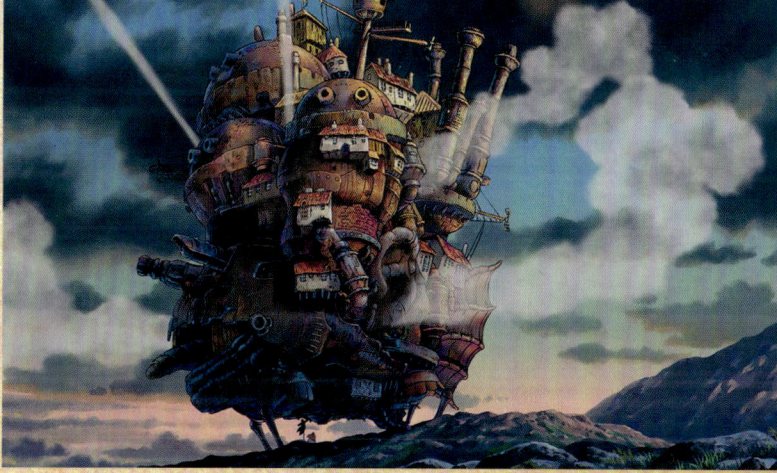

THE ANIMATED CASTLE

Calling the animation first-rate would be an understatement, as the fluidity of movement and the extraordinary crowd shots ensure visual ecstasy at every turn. But the most striking feature of the film is the implausible castle. This steampunk monster wandering through the Alsatian countryside was animated using Softimage 3D software, making it possible to create such distinctive movements with superimposed 2D images. It marked a perfect evolution of the "harmony" technique already used for *Nausicaä*'s Ohmu.

"The fluidity of movement ensures retinal ecstasy at every turn."

himself into the old woman with the heart of a child; she had to overcome back pain and exhaustion to be able to face obstacles and regain her youth. This complex work is the culmination of his style and marks a turning point. This shift was reflected in his next film, *Ponyo*, an ode to the purity of childhood.

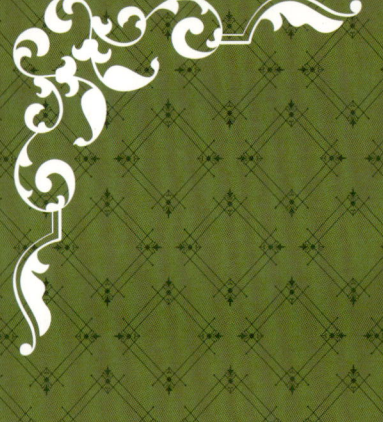

REVIVAL

>-·-<

The Next Generation
Tales from Earthsea
Ponyo
The Secret World of Arrietty
From Up on Poppy Hill

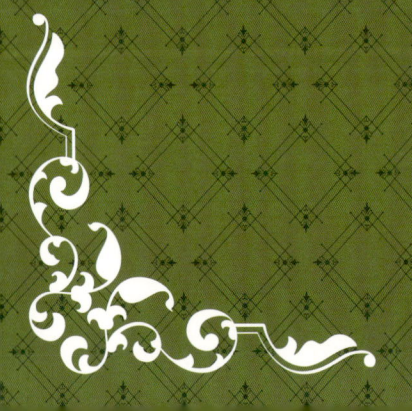
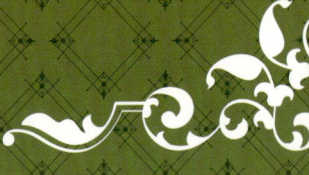

THE NEXT GENERATION

By Gersende Bollut

In 2005, as Ghibli broke away from the Tokuma group and gained its independence, legendary producer Toshio Suzuki announced that the next production would be entrusted to the manager of the Ghibli Museum, who had no directorial training. His name was Gorô Miyazaki. His father: the great Hayao. It was an impressive pedigree, but the patriarch didn't hide his disapproval, to the point that the two men didn't speak to each other throughout the film's production. Completed in eight and a half months, half the time it took for *Spirited Away*, *Tales from Earthsea* was released in the summer of 2006 and proved a great success, despite the bewilderment of critics at the dubious work's lack of originality. Nevertheless, it's hard not to admire this first film, which was inspired by novelist Ursula K. Le Guin's cycle about a prince in search of his identity, the desire of a son crushed by the guiding hand of his father. That same year, new grandfather Hayao Miyazaki focused on *Ponyo*, a project aimed primarily at young audiences that came to him while he was gazing at a storm-tossed ocean. Turning his back on the baroque excesses of *Howl's Moving Castle*, Miyazaki returned to the roots of his work, delivering a simple—some might say simplistic—tale.

The subject of a total news blackout until its release in summer 2008, this contemporary retelling

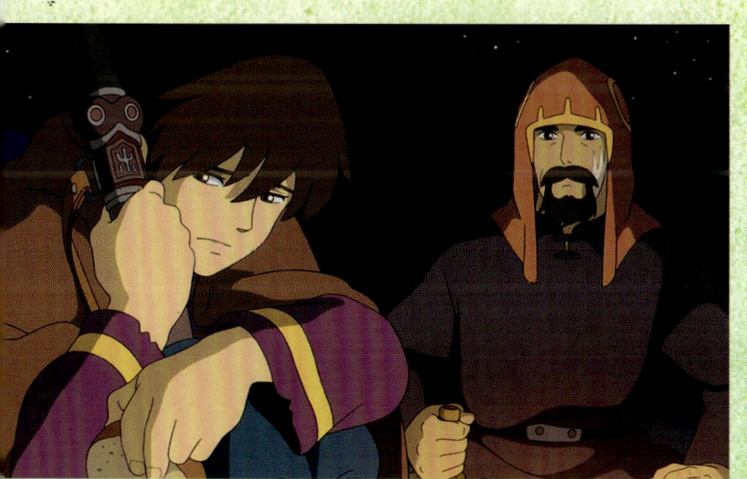

of "The Little Mermaid" was a box office triumph in Japan, ending its run in the same waters (no pun intended) as *Princess Mononoke*. That same year, Kôji Hoshino, the former president of Walt Disney Japan and executive producer of *Spirited Away*, took over as studio president from Toshio Suzuki, who refocused on his work as a producer and member of the Ghibli board of directors.

Suzuki then entrusted the direction of two new feature films to young directors Hiromasa Yonebayashi and, once again, Gorô Miyazaki. Yonebayashi, who had been with the studio for twelve years (including a role as an inbetweener on *Mononoke*), set about adapting English author Mary Norton's children's novel *The Borrowers*. *The Secret World of Arrietty* is punctuated by moments of great beauty, such as the painstaking depiction of a pilfering operation by the tiny characters. Released in Japanese cinemas in the summer of 2010, the film is tender and playful, exploring the budding friendship between a Lilliputian teenager and a full-size human being with infinite finesse. The film's production and message are clearly less ambitious than those of *Spirited Away* or *Mononoke*, and it is therefore not in the same league as its illustrious predecessors.

This time, however, one thing was clear: Studio Ghibli was actively preparing the next generation. This was reflected in Miyazaki's compliment to Yonebayashi, whom he described as "the first director born and bred at Studio Ghibli." All he had to do was turn the trial run into reality. In December 2010, Suzuki firmly denied the rumor of *Porco Rosso 2* that was circulating on the internet and announced a five-year plan for three films set in the Shôwa era (1926–1989): after *Arrietty*, a second project by a young director, and a third that promised Hayao Miyazaki's return to the director's chair. The director who followed in Yonebayashi's footsteps was Gorô Miyazaki, who released a second film in the summer of 2011 that was better received than *Tales from Earthsea*. He reconciled with his father, to the point that the latter took charge of the screenplay (although a few tensions arose during the yearlong production). With *From Up on Poppy*

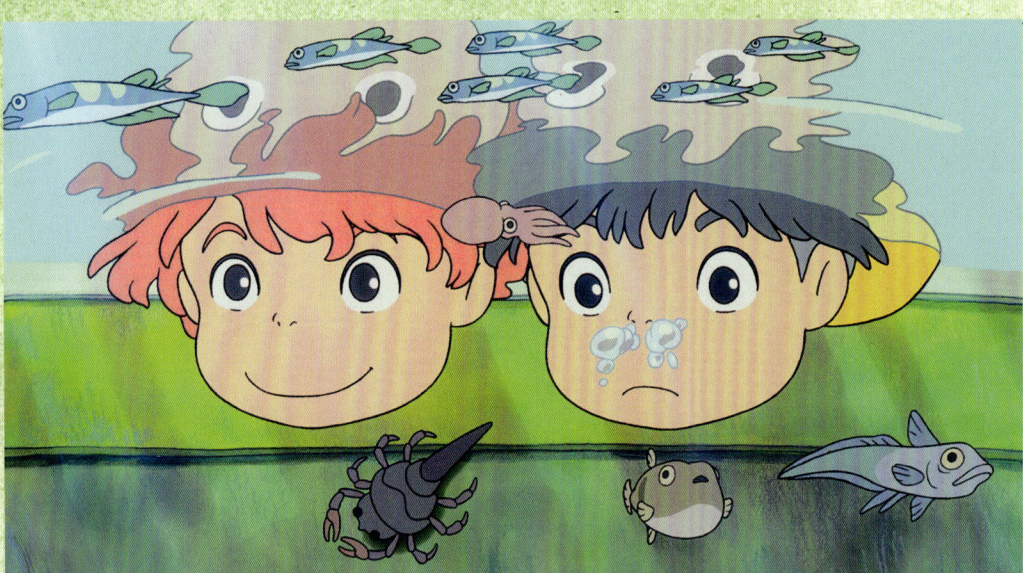

Hill, Gorô created a loose adaptation of a random *shôjo* from the 1980s, which both men had spotted when it was first published.

> "The film shifts between tenderness and humor, and it is tinged with a beautiful melancholy."

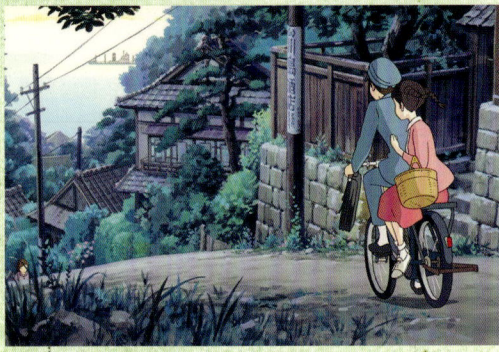

With the time period of the story changed (to the 1960s rather than 1980s) to depict a Japan in the midst of an economic boom and about to host its first Olympic Games, the film shifts between tenderness and humor, and it is tinged with a beautiful melancholy that invites viewers to give in to its charm. But with only four months to go before its theatrical release and the team exhausted from working until midnight every day, the unthinkable happened. On March 11, 2011, an earthquake measuring 9.0 on the Richter scale struck the northeast coast of the island of Honshu, triggering a devastating tsunami and a nuclear accident at the Fukushima power plant. Japan's economy was devastated (losses were estimated at $210 billion), and the effects of the earthquake had repercussions for the film's production, even jeopardizing its release. Once the shock wore off, Hayao Miyazaki encouraged the team to get back to work and brave the planned power cuts by completing the film during the night. Ghibli discreetly kept the promotional campaign for *From Up on Poppy Hill* to a minimum,

releasing it in theaters in mid-July. Nevertheless, critics were enthusiastic, as were Japanese audiences, who made it the most-seen animated film of 2011.

TALES FROM EARTHSEA

2006 - GORÔ MIYAZAKI

The period after *Howl's Moving Castle* was crucial for Studio Ghibli. While Hayao Miyazaki was still officially on his way out, he was reluctant to take a step back. This unwillingness to let go of the studio led producer Toshio Suzuki to put the master's son, Gorô Miyazaki, in the spotlight, assigning him a long-shelved project to direct.

✤ By Romain Dasnoy

In 2005, the sudden arrival of Gorô Miyazaki at the head of this project left many people skeptical, starting with Studio Ghibli's inner circle and collaborators. At that time the director of the Ghibli Museum, Hayao Miyazaki's son had obviously been immersed in animation since childhood. *The Earthsea Cycle*, a fantasy saga by American author Ursula K. Le Guin, was a true inspiration for the creator of *Nausicaä*, who had long wanted to adapt it for the cinema. In the mid-2000s, after the success of *The Cat Returns* (which surpassed *Porco Rosso*'s box office sales), Toshio Suzuki was still looking for a successor to the studio's two founders. He turned to Gorô Miyazaki, who had trained as a landscape architect and had already secretly begun working on the *Earthsea* adaptation project, drawing sketches and a storyboard. Although his father was unhappy with the decision (they didn't speak to each other during the making of the film), production nevertheless went ahead, with Miyazaki's son showing a real passion for the subject and a certain talent for

directing and scriptwriting. *Tales of Earthsea* was a success at the Japanese box office (with 4 million admissions), and despite fierce criticism from the press, it cemented Toshio Suzuki's determination to accelerate the development of films with new directors.

> "The Earthsea Cycle, an American fantasy saga, was a true inspiration for Miyazaki."

The story takes us to the kingdom of Enlad, whose young prince, Arren, sets out on a crusade against the forces of evil, aided by the wizard Sparrowhawk and a girl he meets by chance. Far removed from the *mise en abyme* of Hayao's films, *Earthsea* doesn't shine in terms of originality and subtlety, and it displays a form of Manichaeism that stands in almost stark contrast to the subtlety of the dualism that had been so cleverly developed in Ghibli's previous films. Yet there is no doubt about it: This is a Miyazaki, which only makes the son's true contribution to the awkward situation created by Toshio Suzuki all the more unclear. Yet *Tales from Earthsea* is far from bad, especially for a first film, and should by no means be dismissed. It even offers hope for the future. Is this Miyazaki a name to watch?

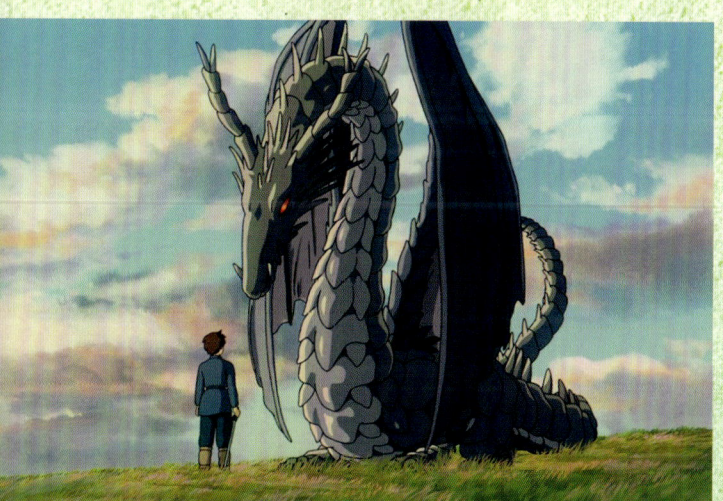

© 2006 Nibariki - GNDHDDT

PONYO

2008 – HAYAO MIYAZAKI

A loose, naive reinterpretation of the Hans Christian Andersen tale "The Little Mermaid," *Ponyo* is both a freshly sweet, touching work and a magnificent tribute to traditional animation.

➤ By Bruno de la Cruz

In early 2006, Hayao Miyazaki began sketching the first images of *Ponyo*, two years after the release of *Howl's Moving Castle*. As was often the case, the director didn't hesitate to draw on his surroundings to fuel his imagination and bring his new creation to life. In this case, Ponyo, a goldfish who wants to become a little girl, was partly inspired by a trip to the seaside, and partly by a novel by Natsume Sôseki (1867–1916), *The Gate*, about a character named Sôsuke living at the foot of a cliff.

> *"A dream where everything becomes possible through drawing"*

There is something indefinably strange about this work. Although far from the class of *Princess Mononoke* or the grandeur of *Spirited Away*, *Ponyo* and its marine world boast a design as charming as it is fascinating. From the opening scene in the ocean to the mischievous antics of this odd water child, the film can be enjoyed like a dream where everything becomes possible through drawing, a clear desire on the part of the team to create a production for the very young, with a less rigid structure.

SEND THE DREAM

Ponyo marked a return to Studio Ghibli's first loves, particularly in terms of aesthetics. *Ponyo*'s clean, simple graphics contrast with Miyazaki's almost exaggerated attention to detail. On location in Setouchi in western Japan, the director remained faithful to his production system: mastering the *e-konte* (storyboards) and laying the foundations of the artistic direction with color sketches, which established the broad outlines of the film's spirit. With the movement of the sea as a huge challenge and his story in mind, Miyazaki was able to more fully launch his project after several delays and hesitations.

Primarily animated by hand, *Ponyo* is a lavishly dreamlike river that required the efforts of more than four hundred artists over a period of almost twenty-five months. Miyazaki himself retouched many of the key poses, and he surrounded himself with loyal collaborators. In addition to Makiko Futaki (the exceptional animator of the tsunami sequence, who died in 2016) and Michiyo Yasuda (the colorist), the contributions of the art director (and incidentally the scenery designer) Noboru Yoshida cannot be underestimated. We also find his name on one of the Ghibli Museum's short films whose background is very close to *Ponyo*'s: *Monmon the Water Spider*. Miyazaki has said, "As you grow up, you must learn to betray your promises. In this film, I wanted to show a child keeping his." And don't worry; the film delivers on its promises as well.

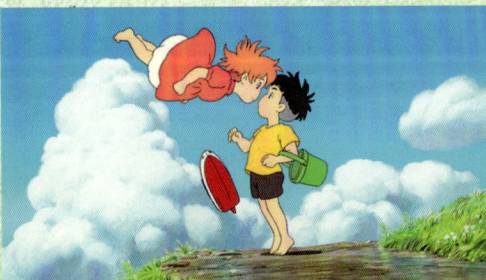

THE SECRET WORLD OF ARRIETTY

2010 - HIROMASA YONEBAYASHI

Arrietty is often overlooked in Studio Ghibli's filmography, but it's an enjoyable, deeply soothing work that perfectly illustrates the adage that good things come in small packages. This was the directorial debut of Hiromasa Yonebayashi, who began his career as an inbetweener on *Princess Mononoke*.

By Gersende Bollut

Adapted from the novel *The Borrowers* by British author Mary Norton, *The Secret World of Arrietty* might be a minor Ghibli film, but its charming world (reminiscent of the more realistic series *The Littles*) reveals a tender film that invites viewers to see the world on an infinitely small scale. At its center is a tiny family who have found refuge in the heart of a peaceful, comfortable, doll-size home set up to their liking, nestled under the floorboards of a wealthy holiday home on the outskirts of Tokyo, where a human-size teenager is being treated for a heart condition. The inactive young man is sensitive to the slightest event that occurs in the house and becomes attached to the Lilliputian girl he happens to spot during one of her nighttime excursions. The family has a habit of discreetly borrowing what they need to survive from those who live in the house. Treated with infinite delicacy and modesty, this budding friendship between a tiny girl and a human escapes all sentimentality. The plot is full of red herrings, taking unexpected and delightful side trips through sumptuous scenery.

The viewer watches the film at the level of the "borrowers" and becomes enthralled by the day-to-day life of this small family unit (a reasonable father, a worried mother, a reckless teenager) as they try to live secretly, avoiding humans, who pose a threat to their stability. The film's clever use of everyday objects means that for Arrietty's family,

> *"The simple but not simplistic story makes Arrietty extremely appealing."*

a clothespin becomes a hair clip, and staples stuck into a beam become stair treads. Punctuated by a number of lovely moments (a visit to a cozy dollhouse, a depiction of a typical borrowing operation), *Arrietty*'s simple but not simplistic story makes the film extremely appealing, despite a few pitfalls (like the lack of depth in the ailing youth's self-effacing temperament) and the fact that it can't compete with classics such as *Spirited Away*, whose production was far more ambitious. The director's themes are similar to those of his peers, with a handful of thieves joining forces against the humans who are a threat to them to ensure their survival, just like nature in *Princess Mononoke* or the tanuki in *Pom Poko*.

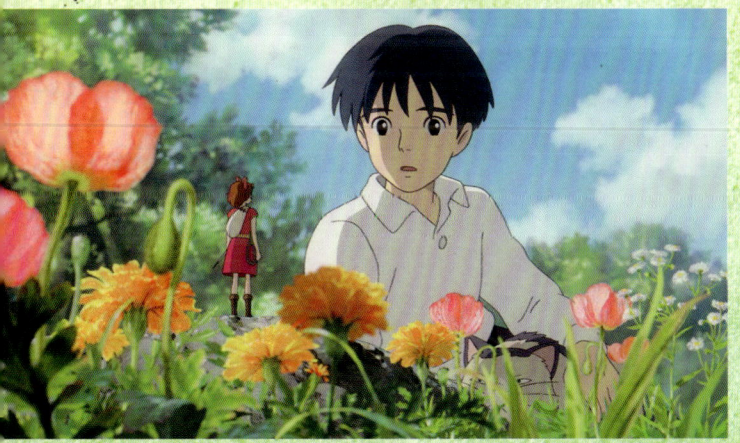

FROM UP ON POPPY HILL

2011 - GORÔ MIYAZAKI

It's not easy being the heir to a luminary like Hayao Miyazaki. Inevitably expected to fall on his face and drawing comparisons with his father, Gorô Miyazaki had his work cut out for him in terms of establishing his own style. After the critical failure of *Tales from Earthsea*, the young director stuck with it, returning with an adaptation of the manga *From Up on Poppy Hill*.

❧ By Pa Ming Chiu

Yokohama, 1963. Ever since her father was lost at sea, young Umi has been silently praying for his return, hoisting signal flags in front of her house on the coast every morning. This moving message of hope inspires her classmate Shun, who turns it into a poem for the school newspaper. The two teenagers grow closer and share their daily lives. In particular, Umi and Shun are committed to saving the former student residence, an old building known as the Latin Quarter. As time passes and they fight side by side, friendship gradually gives way to love, but a terrible family secret threatens their budding romance.

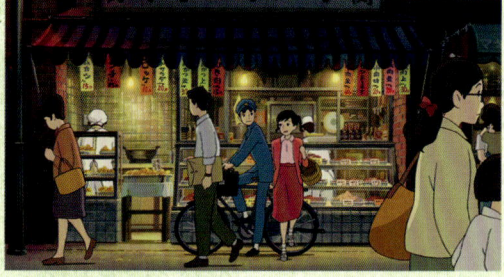

A META FILM?

After falling out with each other during the production of *Tales from Earthsea* (to the extent that Hayao Miyazaki even walked out of the film's premiere, rejecting it), father and son were finally working together. The father was co-writer, and the son was directing again, but this time under the watchful eye of his illustrious father. Was Hayao's presence the reason why *From Up on Poppy Hill* has held up so much better? Or did Gorô learn from his beginner's mistakes and improve considerably? Perhaps a little of both. Only time will tell.

The fact remains that his father's shadow lingered over the project, not only with the more rigorous staging and more masterful storytelling, but also with the underlying themes. The decision to adapt this story was perhaps not insignificant.

Foreshadowing the nostalgic theme of *The Wind Rises*, it's about heritage and building for the future while respecting, understanding, and protecting the foundations of the past. It's only a short step from there to drawing a parallel with Hayao Miyazaki's own studio and his passing the torch to his son.

Gorô's contribution should not be underestimated, however, as he still refused to follow too closely in his father's footsteps, especially in terms of pacing, which is much slower and more contemplative than in his father's films. While this didn't work with the cryptic, almost opaque world of *Earthsea*, it's perfect for this authentic, intimate portrayal of a bygone Japan.

Gorô excelled at framing small silences and fleeting emotions, and even lingered on them, much to our delight. The result is a touching film with plenty of personality whose tone almost reminds us of Takahata. We've seen worse in terms of a late teenage crisis.

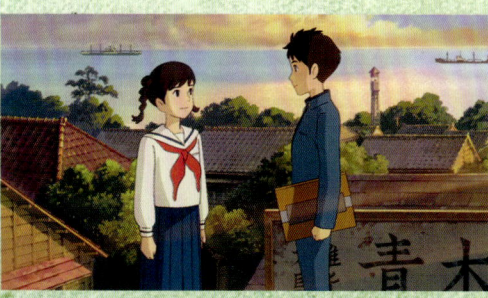

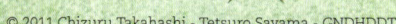

BACK TO THEIR ROOTS

❦

One More Time
The Wind Rises
The Tale of the Princess Kaguya

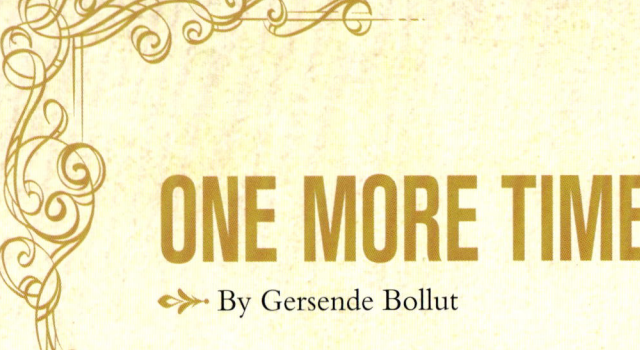

ONE MORE TIME

By Gersende Bollut

No offense is intended to these young filmmakers by acknowledging that, however enjoyable works such as *Arrietty* or *From Up on Poppy Hill* may be, none of them have the makings of Hayao Miyazaki's masterpieces. In his spare time, the *Nausicaä* auteur returned to manga in 2008 with *The Wind Rises*, which was published between 2009 and 2010 in the specialized magazine *Model Graphix*. Behind this title, a tribute to a poem by Paul Valéry, lies the documented biography of Jirô Horikoshi, creator of the Zero aircraft during World War II.

When Suzuki suggested a big-screen adaptation, Miyazaki was extremely reluctant. In his opinion, animated films should be aimed primarily at children, not made for adults. After careful consideration (the filmmaker's wife tried to influence the decision), Miyazaki agreed in early 2011 to tackle the challenge of directing the story of a man who, prevented from becoming a pilot because of his nearsightedness, made his dream come true by becoming an aeronautical engineer. It took the master's "last" achievement—before he did it again with *The Boy and the Heron* (p. 83)—to discover his most intimate, partly autobiographical work. Like the hero, Miyazaki is shortsighted and had neglected his wife to throw himself headlong into his work; like the heroine, the filmmaker's mother contracted tuberculosis. The film is at once dark, realistic, and poignant, a far cry from happy-go-lucky *Ponyo*, and occupies a special place in Miyazaki's filmography. There are no forays into the fantastic, except for a few dreamy digressions; there are unprecedented historical references to the Kantô earthquake and the Great Depression (the government response to which provoked considerable controversy in Japan), and above all, there is a disenchanted vision of human nature that stands in stark contrast to the hope expressed elsewhere over the course of his career.

This eleventh feature met with public triumph upon its theatrical release in the summer of 2013, and it was quickly followed by a sensational announcement: Miyazaki declared that he was retiring for good, at least from filmmaking. This time, it was official. But it only lasted a little while.

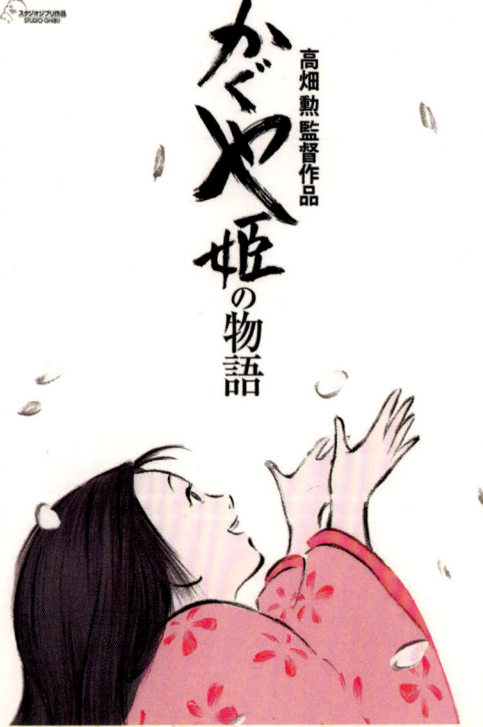

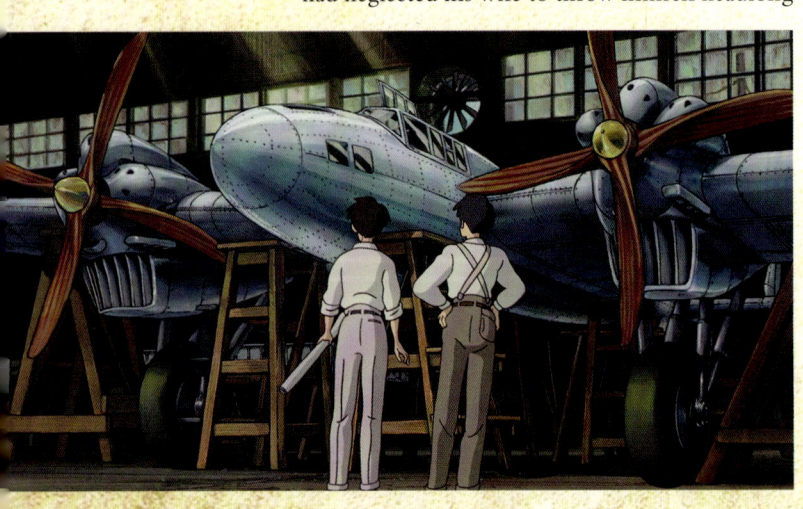

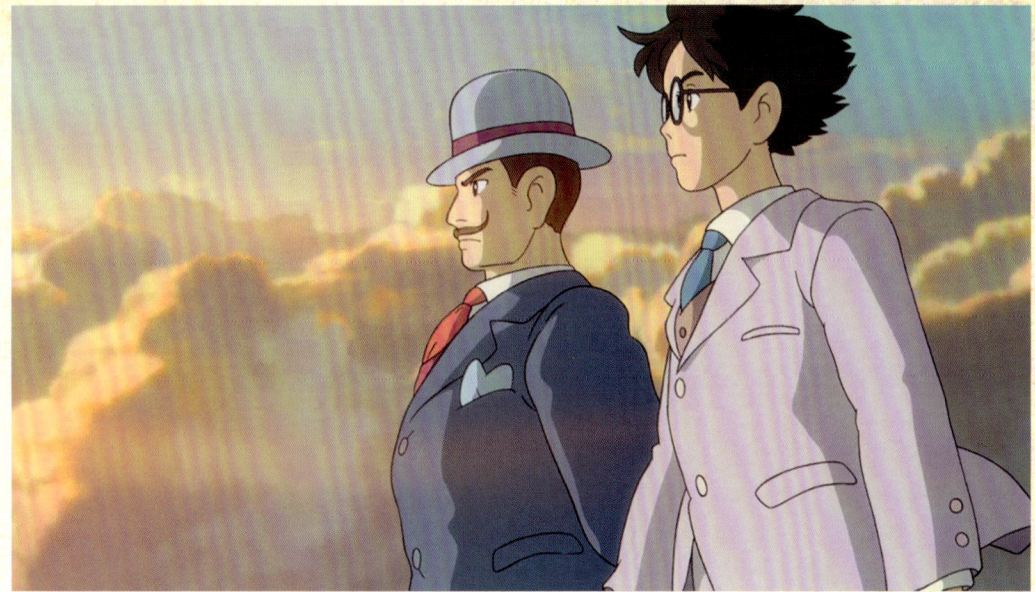

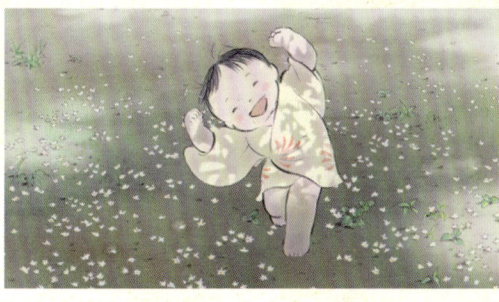

After directing a short film, *Boro the Caterpillar*, the master went on to make another feature-length film.

As for Isao Takahata, he had been absent from the screen for almost fifteen years (*My Neighbors the Yamadas* was released in theaters in 1999), and Suzuki urged him to take on a new project in 2005. After much procrastination, the director decided on a project he had been considering for many years: an adaptation of "The Tale of the Bamboo Cutter,"

"A dark, realistic, and poignant film, a far cry from happy-go-lucky Ponyo"

a tenth-century folk story in which a fast-growing, fiercely free woman refuses to submit to the protocol befitting her rank as a sovereign. As a young Toei employee, Takahata had entered a screenwriting competition to bring the tale to the screen, but the project was ultimately abandoned.

In the early 2010s, the project was back in the spotlight, with a grand, formal ambition that promised to make it a milestone in the history of animated cinema. Studio Ghibli intended to repeat its 1988 feat of releasing *My Neighbor Totoro* and *Grave of the Fireflies* at the same time: *The Wind Rises* and *The Tale of the Princess Kaguya* were scheduled for joint release in 2013. But in February, *Princess Kaguya*'s lagging production pushed the film back to November. *Kaguya* was even longer than *Mononoke*, at almost two hours and twenty minutes, and proved to be the promised masterpiece. Between the brilliant script and the dazzling direction, whose meticulousness and delicacy turned every shot into a work of art (the use of charcoal and watercolor was utterly enchanting), Miyazaki's eternal companion created an instant classic of animated cinema. Although critically acclaimed and presented at Cannes and Annecy, the film wasn't quite as successful commercially.

The Wind Rises
© 2013 Nibariki – GNDHDDTK
The Tale of the Princess Kaguya
© 2014 Hatake Jimusho GNDHDDTK

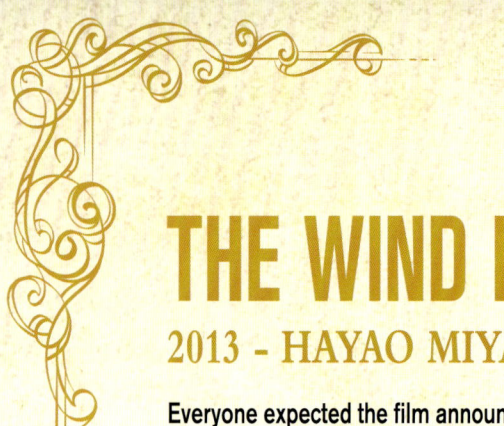

THE WIND RISES

2013 - HAYAO MIYAZAKI

Everyone expected the film announced as Miyazaki's last to be a dreamlike, enchanting journey. In this contrarian historical melodrama, the master takes us on a tour of his favorite themes, but most of all reveals a facet of his personality that was previously hidden from the public, like an artist who drops his mask upon leaving the stage.

✦ By Matthieu Pinon

In interwar Japan, little Jirô Horikoshi will never be able to fulfill his dream of becoming a pilot because of his poor eyesight. So he turns to engineering and aircraft design, work that's in increasing demand as World War II approaches. Despite the scale of the tragic events shaking his country (earthquake, economic crisis, escalating war), the young man has just one thing on his mind: creating the best airplanes. The only person who can compete with his artistic obsession is Nahoko, whom he meets on a train. The encounter opens with a line by Paul Valéry: "The wind rises; we must try to live."

THE WIND RISES . . .

Every Miyazaki film is dedicated to flight, to the wind, to that ethereal element that cannot be seen or conveyed directly, except through its consequences. What a challenge! While it was at the heart of the conflict in *Nausicaä of the Valley of the Wind,* here it becomes the driving force behind the love story, a character in its own right. How would Jirô and Nahoko have found each other without gusts of wind carrying away a hat or a parasol? The scene of the paper airplane sent to the balcony, which shows a restraint that is rare in Miyazaki's work, is probably his greatest victory over the challenge.

The fluid camera movement that follows the slight bending of the airplane is a counterpoint to the film's other key scene, the Kantô earthquake of 1923, whose violence is expressed in still shots with ultra-tight editing. After this fit of rage, the wind's threat becomes more lurking and omnipresent as international tensions build.

> *"Every Miyazaki film is dedicated to flight, to the wind, to that ethereal element that cannot be seen or conveyed directly."*

WE MUST TRY TO LIVE

Suffering from tuberculosis, Nahoko leaves the mountain sanatorium where she is exposed to snowy air (a strikingly poetic scene) to go back to her love, even if it means risking death. The film is melodramatic to the core and warns viewers right from the start, with a dreamlike shot of a colorful aircraft destroyed by filthy, jagged mechanical parts. Reality harshly takes over from dreams. This time, Miyazaki draws us into a world that actually existed, with dreams serving only to illustrate the characters' psyches.

The departure is made all the clearer by the fact that, for the first time, Miyazaki takes a long time to develop his story and focuses on heroes who are (now) adults. Constant through the years, Jirô's devotion to his quest for the perfect plane (he even takes inspiration from the curve of mackerel bones during a meal) takes precedence over his life

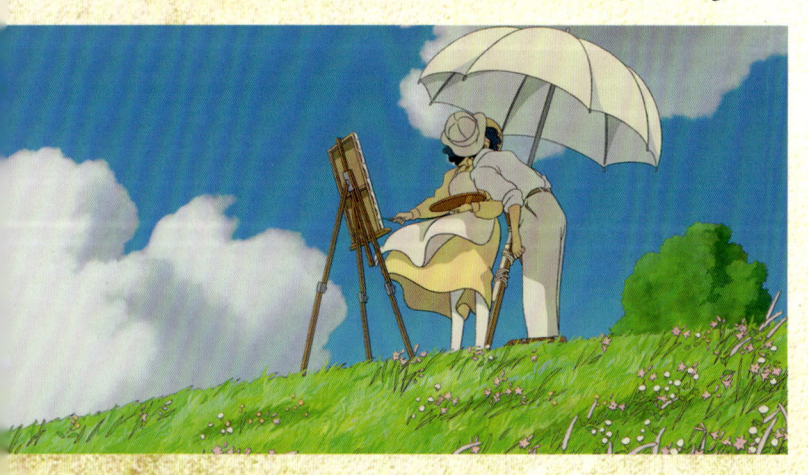

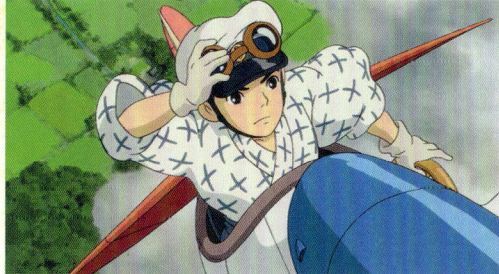

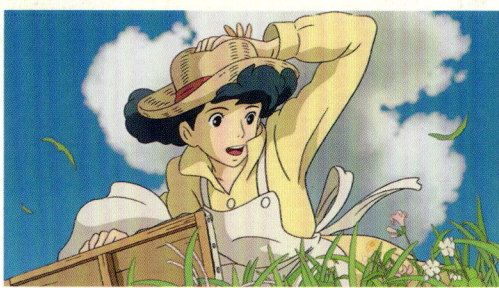

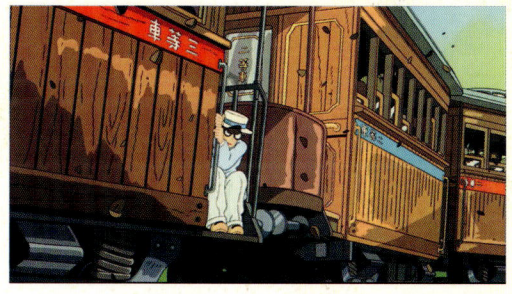

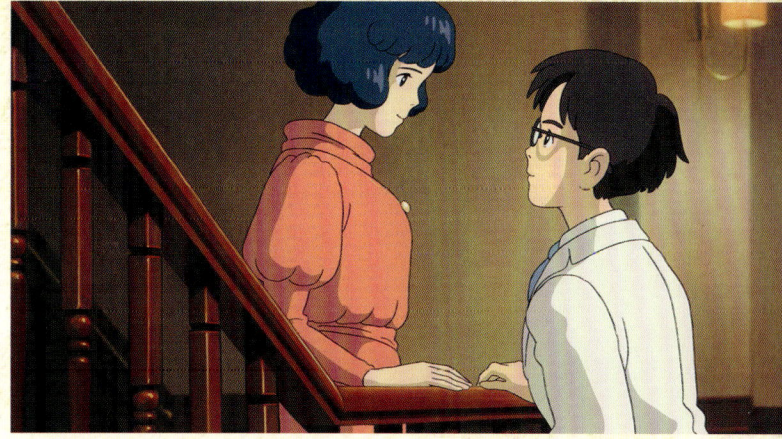

(in a poignant scene, he draws with one hand and holds Nahoko's with the other) and reputation (his planes will be used by kamikazes). In this respect, choosing Hideaki Anno to voice Jirô was perfectly fitting. Sometimes regarded as king of otaku and an animator adored by Miyazaki, the *Evangelion* director lent his disillusioned, unsentimental voice to a hero for whom everything seems to be slipping away. Everything except his one passion and his one love, the only two things that keep him going.

IN SHORT, IT'S DIFFERENT

The project's origins lie in a short manga of a few dozen pages that Miyazaki created for a model-making magazine. Blending a love story inspired by Tatsuo Hori's autobiographical novella *The Wind Has Risen* with Jirô Horikoshi's biography, the story fell into the hands of producer Toshio Suzuki.

In a documentary, Suzuki confessed that he was angry over *Ponyo*, which brought nothing new to Miyazaki's body of work. Suzuki urged him to step out of his comfort zone and refrain from using any fantastic elements in a film that draws on history and fictionalized biography. Thinking that this would

be his last feature film, the director, who was then in his seventies, took up the challenge.

The Wind Rises gave him a chance to reflect on his career. The film features vintage airplanes like *Porco Rosso*, the tuberculosis found in *My Neighbor Totoro*, the steampunk atmosphere of *Howl's Moving Castle*, and a song by Yumi Arai (who had two tracks in *Kiki's Delivery Service*). Without a doubt, this is a Miyazaki film like none that had been seen before.

It is impossible not to see the character Jirô's sacrifices as an echo of the director's life and his decades of devotion to his art; in both cases, it's all about following one's dreams to the end, despite the obstacles. This echo tragically resonated right in the middle of production, when an earthquake struck the country in March 2011. The impressive earthquake scene was the focus of the entire Studio Ghibli team, whether they were expressing themselves with their brushes or behind the microphone.

Miyazaki decided to experiment with sound effects for airplane and car engines and other elements, using sounds that studio members produced by mouth. Suzuki wanted innovation, and he wasn't disappointed. But that wasn't the case with the Japanese public. *The Wind Rises* failed to match *Ponyo*'s box office success, and lagged far behind *Spirited Away*, *Princess Mononoke*, and *Howl's Moving Castle*. Although more difficult to access than most of his filmography, *The Wind Rises* remains the best film for understanding Hayao Miyazaki.

THE TALE OF THE PRINCESS KAGUYA

2013 - ISAO TAKAHATA

Isao Takahata's final film, *The Tale of the Princess Kaguya*, is a synthesis of the director's leitmotifs in both form and content. The film stands out for its technique, with design that sharply contrasts with that of other Ghibli productions.

By Matthieu Pinon

While Miyazaki is a filmmaker of lyricism and excess, Ghibli's other half favored a more humanistic, intimate approach to deeply Japanese themes. Family relationships against a backdrop of war (*Grave of the Fireflies*, page 27), folk legends (*Pom Poko*, page 43), and neighborhood bonds (*My Neighbors the Yamadas*, page 49) are all aspects of everyday Japanese life enhanced by a discreet but clear technical standard, a far cry from his colleague's epic shots.

With *The Tale of the Princess Kaguya*, Takahata combined his favorite themes. Taken from the oldest written tale in Japan, the film follows the early years of Kaguya, who is discovered by a bamboo-cutting peasant in the hollow of one of his plants. Once grown up, she strives above all else to remain independent, not hesitating to spurn her suitors by entrusting them with impossible missions, and eventually returning to her true family on the moon.

Like *My Neighbors the Yamadas*, *The Tale of the Princess Kaguya* hides a treasure trove of inventive and creative animation beneath its seeming simplicity. Every movement is deeply considered, with certain passages destined to become benchmarks for any aspiring animator, who needs to own the DVD to

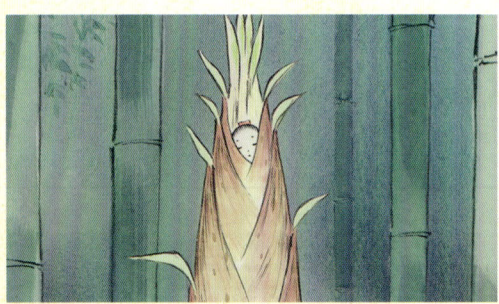

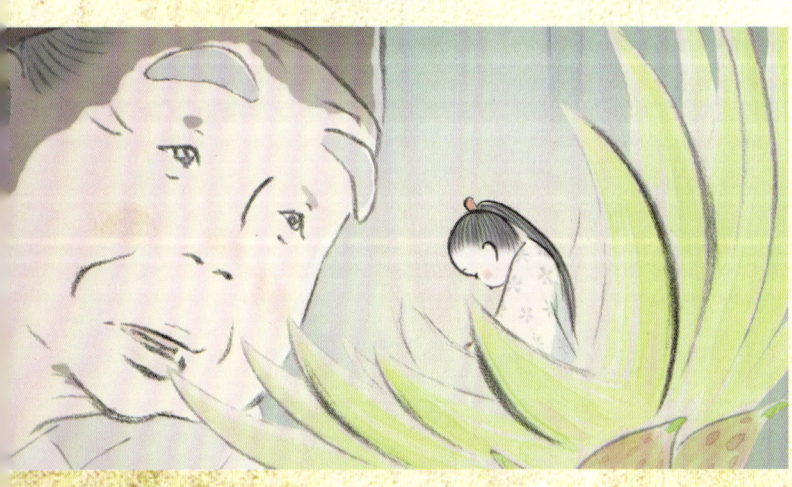

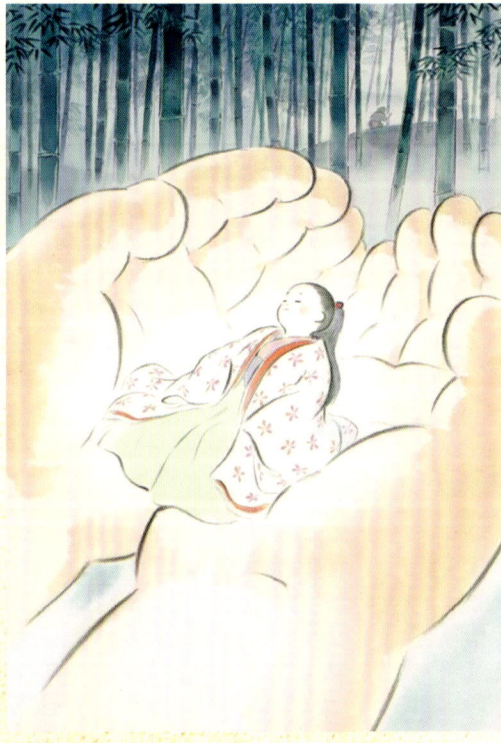

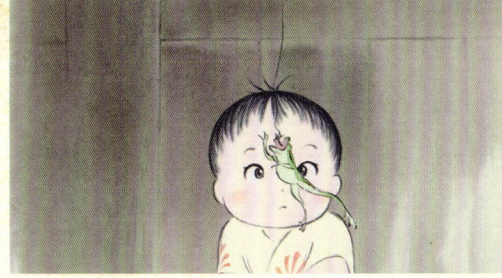

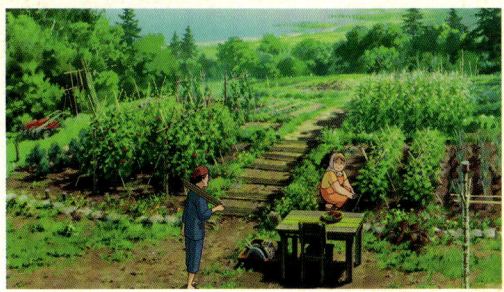

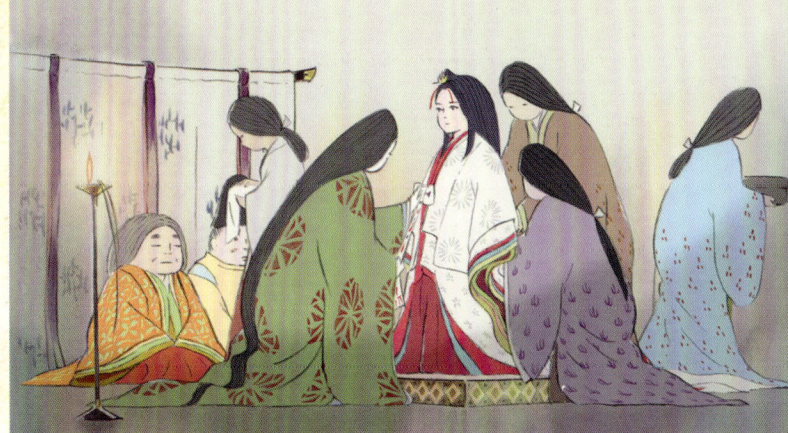

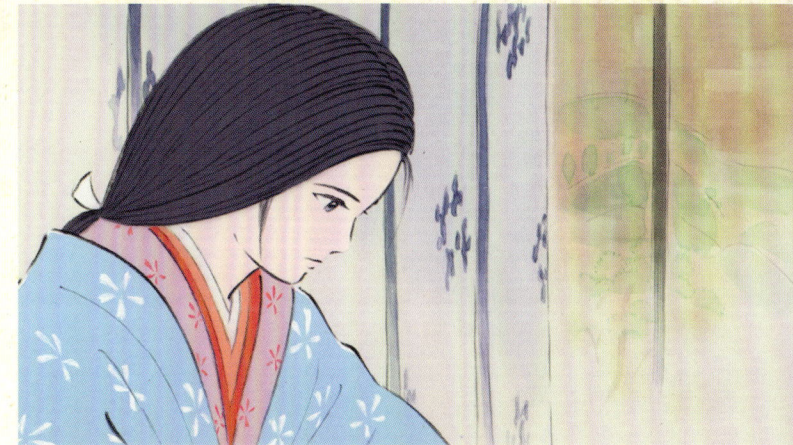

study all its subtleties. Among the many fine scenes of a quality that only Ghibli can produce, we must single out a long shot in which the heroine, running madly, sheds her kimonos one by one (a metaphorical abandonment of her human condition), as well as the final sequence in which she and her heavenly family are finally reunited.

One can only applaud the challenges met by Takahata and his team, unless one's name is Toshio Suzuki. Foreseeing the end of an era as Miyazaki and Takahata reached a venerable age, the producer wanted the directors to go out with a bang. Twenty-five years after the simultaneous release of *Totoro* and *Grave of the Fireflies*, Suzuki wanted to coordinate the release dates of *The Wind Rises* and *Princess Kaguya*. Unfortunately, *Princess Kaguya*'s production schedule went out the window, forcing him to postpone its theatrical release by six months, and nipping a carefully thought-out marketing plan in the bud. Miyazaki discussed the decision in the documentary *The Kingdom of Dreams and Madness*, not mincing his words about his friend and colleague's inability to manage time. What remains is a memorable film, a masterpiece for Takahata, Ghibli, and the world of animation, which will undoubtedly inspire a whole new generation of animators in Japan and beyond.

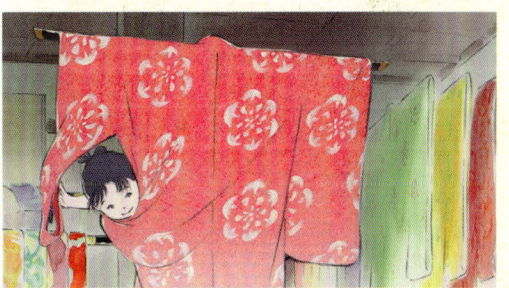

"A masterpiece in the world of animation, which will inspire a whole generation of animators"

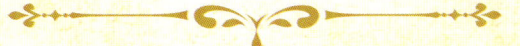

A NEVER-ENDING STORY?

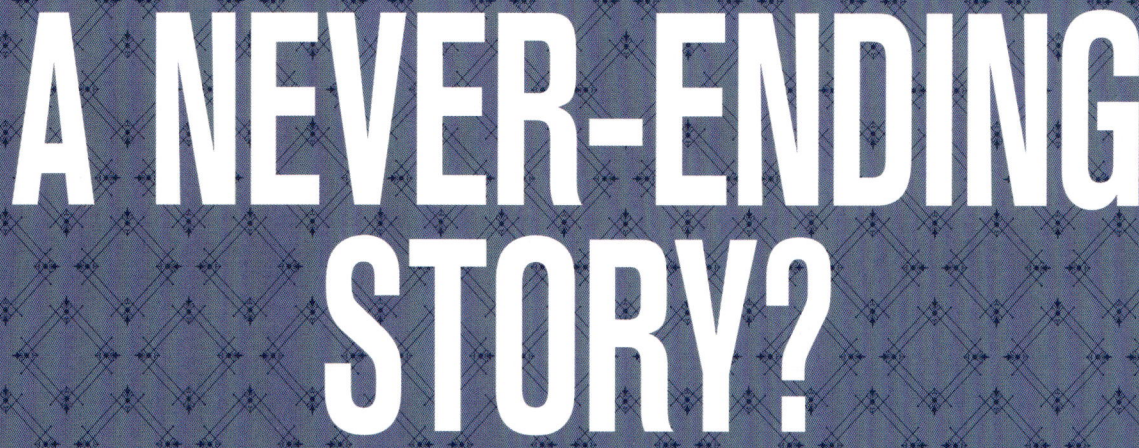

The End of an Era
Ronja, the Robber's Daughter
When Marnie Was There
The Red Turtle
Earwig and the Witch
The Boy and the Heron

THE END OF AN ERA

By Gersende Bollut

hree years after *Arrietty*, Hiromasa Yonebayashi directed his second feature, *When Marnie Was There*, which marked the end of thirty years of sparkling creativity at Ghibli and the official divestment of the studio's pillars. Initiated during the production of *The Wind Rises*, this project arose from the filmmaker's desire to overcome the frustrations of making his first film. Miyazaki himself persuaded him to submit a new project to Suzuki, who was quickly won over by the idea of adapting the novel *When Marnie Was There*, a children's book written in the late 1960s by British author Joan G. Robinson. Miyazaki appreciated it so much that he included it in the list of fifty books he strongly recommended. Thanks to a comfortable production deadline of a year and a half, Yonebayashi delivered his final version in the summer of 2014. The film featured a highly poetic script but suffered from

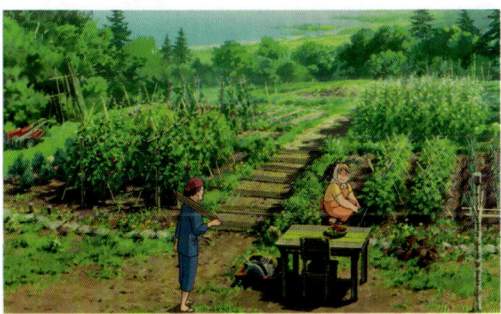

a slow and sometimes poorly controlled pace and struggled to attract audiences; its box office receipts in Japan were three times lower than those of his first film in its first ten days of release.

A few months earlier, Suzuki had stated in a radio broadcast, "Above all else, Ghibli is a company that produces a film and then releases it in theaters. If it's successful, we make another one. Every

> "When Marnie Was There
> *marked the end of thirty years*
> *of sparkling creativity.*"

time, a film's success determines the company's future direction. *Marnie*'s results will be important for the future. Public support and earnings will determine whether or not we go ahead with a new film. If the results are good, we may make another film immediately. If they aren't, we may wait a while." What happened next is well known: On August 3, 2014, just five months after Suzuki's departure was announced, the studio finalized a major restructuring and the suspension of all feature film production until further notice. It also refocused its operations on rights management and the Ghibli Museum. Would it be able to bounce back in the future?

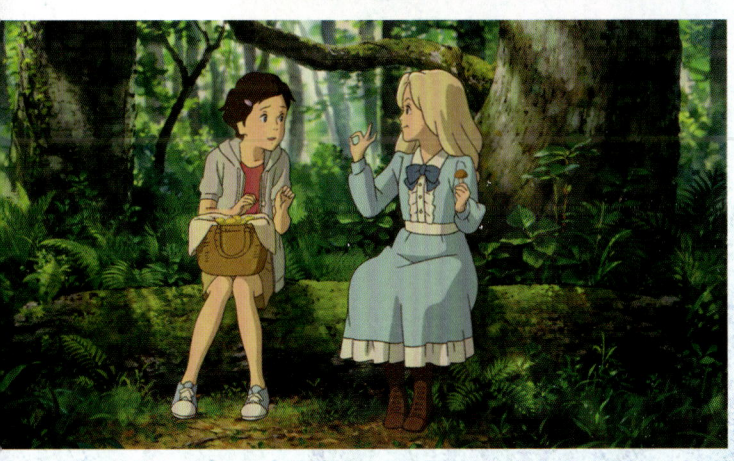

When Marnie Was There
© 2014 GNDHDDTK

RONJA, THE ROBBER'S DAUGHTER

2014 - GORÔ MIYAZAKI

A collaboration between Polygon Pictures and Ghibli (from afar) for the Japanese channel NHK, *Ronja, the Robber's Daughter* was a project headed by Gorô Miyazaki, stretching over twenty-six episodes of twenty-six minutes each. Broadcast in Japan in the fall of 2014, this adaptation of the novel of the same name by Swedish author Astrid Lindgren marked Ghibli's first attempt at the TV series format.

➤ By Emma Mahoudeau-Deleva

 ntil this point, Ghibli had almost never diversified into television, remaining true to the reason for its creation: the desire to take its time and offer high-quality feature films entirely under the studio's control. It wasn't until Gorô Miyazaki showed a strong belief in this project that the studio behind such animated wonders as *My Neighbor Totoro* and *Spirited Away* launched its 3D CGI TV series with Polygon Pictures. While the visual quality is decent and the watercolor backgrounds live up to their promise, *Ronja* remains a far cry from the initial TV experiments of masters Miyazaki and Takahata during their early years at Toei (*Wolf Boy Ken*, *Sally the Witch*, the lively *Heidi* series, and *Future Boy Conan*). The years had passed, and *Ronja, the Robber's Daughter* was made for children, with a tale centered on learning about nature, the rules of life, and so on.

A SLOW RHYTHM THROUGH THE SEASONS

While the younger Miyazaki may not have reached the same level as his father, he still managed to get away from the ninety-minute format and develop a story spanning more than eleven hours that follows the childhood and coming-of-age of the mischievous and slightly rebellious Ronja. Unfortunately, the main characters lack charisma; those who have

it are caricatures, like the girl's father, who rolls on the ground whenever he's upset! Ronja is the daughter of Mattis, a vicious highwayman who lives in a castle in the woods and spends his time robbing the middle class to feed his wife—a strong woman with big red braids—and his gang of six losers. His life revolves around plundering and hatred, as does that of Borka, another criminal who is equally

"A tale centered on learning about nature and the rules of life"

dim-witted and has a son, Birk, who was born on the same day as Ronja.

Everyone adores and pampers the little girl, and when she turns ten, she is finally allowed to see the world and go for walks in the forest. Her life unfolds according to the seasons and her discovery of her environment, without her experiencing any real drama or trauma. Even when Ronja falls asleep in the forest and is annoyed by gray dwarfs (nasty creatures that attack when they smell human fear), she manages to escape thanks to her thieving but very protective father. *Ronja, the Robber's Daughter* is an average series, produced with a more modest budget than the studio's masterpieces, but it lives up to its promise with young children.

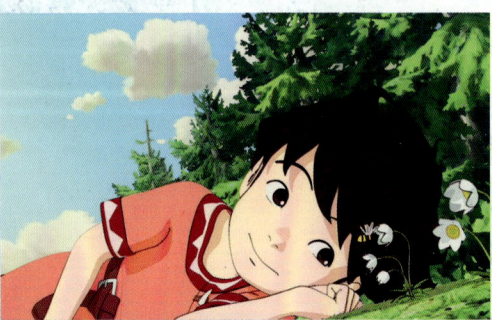

WHEN MARNIE WAS THERE

2014 - HIROMASA YONEBAYASHI

Some films don't leave you unscathed; you exit the theater teary-eyed and heavyhearted. *When Marnie Was There* is one of them. Directed by Hiromasa Yonebayashi and nominated for the 88th Academy Awards after its 2015 stateside release, *When Marnie Was There* was proof—if any were needed—that Yonebayashi was a future grand master of Japanese animation. With his personal touch, he gave the studio a new lease of life, surpassing the master's son in talent and finesse.

By Emma Mahoudeau-Deleva

ayao Miyazaki lifted Yonebayashi out of anonymity in 2010, entrusting him with the adaptation of *The Secret World of Arrietty*. Although he was already a leading animator, Hiromasa Yonebayashi himself was reportedly surprised to have been chosen to direct this script by the master, based on the novel by Mary Norton. He was given the opportunity to prove himself, and Yonebayashi made the most of it with a fresh work that won the Japan Academy Film Prize for Animation of the Year in 2011 and enjoyed great international success (particularly in the United States). The director, who joined Studio Ghibli as an inbetweener in 1996 and became an animator in 2001, had made his mark on *Spirited Away* and *Howl's Moving Castle*. Moving up the ranks, two years later he served as an assistant animation director on Gorô Miyazaki's *Tales from Earthsea*. In 2014, *When Marnie Was There* was his second feature film as a director (the screenplay is credited to him, Keiko Niwa, and Masashi Andô), and his last for the mythical studio. Hiromasa Yonebayashi quit after this commercial semi-failure and joined Studio Ponoc, which was founded by Yoshiaki Nishimura, the producer of *The Tale of the Princess Kaguya*.

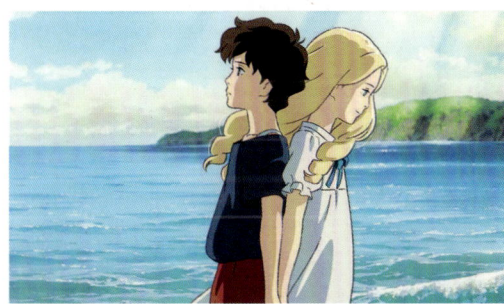

> *"Anna has a passion that allows her to express and channel her violence: drawing."*

ANNA: THE THROES OF PREADOLESCENCE

After the lively and spirited young Arrietty, Hiromasa Yonebayashi turned his focus to Anna, a preteen girl who isn't always nice to her "aunt," who is actually her adoptive mother. Not only is she withdrawn and unpleasant, but she also has no friends, because she has trouble controlling her temper. Her aunt juggles the girl's mood swings with the sadness of having no real support from her husband, who is always away on business, and decides to send Anna to the seaside to treat her asthma and put some distance between herself and the rebellious young upstart. A child whose parents died in mysterious circumstances, Anna is not a simple girl, and she doesn't let others get away with anything. She's not very kind to herself, either, and is

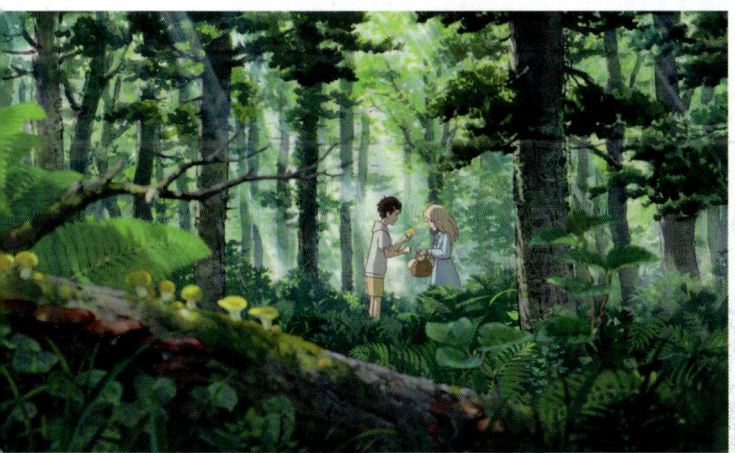

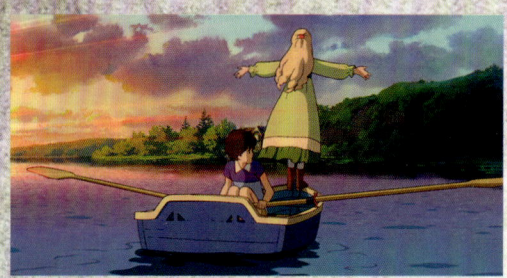

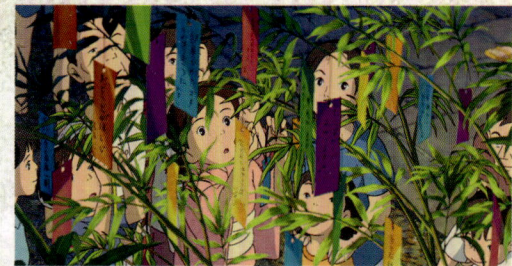

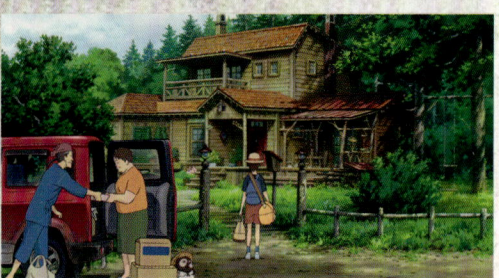

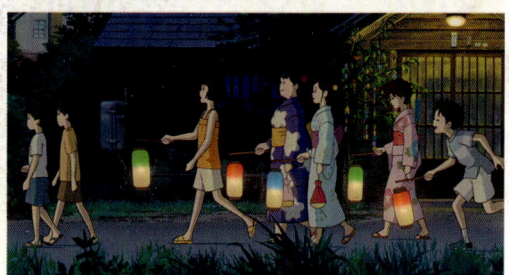

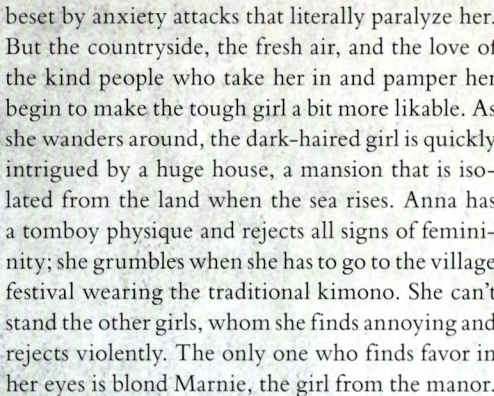

beset by anxiety attacks that literally paralyze her. But the countryside, the fresh air, and the love of the kind people who take her in and pamper her begin to make the tough girl a bit more likable. As she wanders around, the dark-haired girl is quickly intrigued by a huge house, a mansion that is isolated from the land when the sea rises. Anna has a tomboy physique and rejects all signs of femininity; she grumbles when she has to go to the village festival wearing the traditional kimono. She can't stand the other girls, whom she finds annoying and rejects violently. The only one who finds favor in her eyes is blond Marnie, the girl from the manor.

MARNIE: THE LIGHTNESS OF BEING

Anna has a passion that allows her to express and channel her violence: drawing. She sets her sights on the mysterious mansion and, paradoxically, even though she sketches it every day, never perceives its changes. Like in an Edgar Allan Poe tale, the viewer senses that something is wrong, that there's a flaw. Hiromasa Yonebayashi's skill is in taking us by the hand and, like Anna, sliding us into Marnie's life; she is so beautiful, so lively, so radiant. He plays with the physical contrast and opposition between the two young girls: Anna, the brunette with short hair and surprisingly dark blue eyes, with little inclination toward gentleness, and Marnie, the coquette with her long blond hair, her European looks, and her dresses from another time. She's evanescent and stubborn, seeming to have stepped out of another era. These moments of freedom with Anna take her away from her cantankerous governess. She lives as if suspended above the waters that encircle her house, and

remains very mysterious, insisting on secrecy. At a time of budding love, the plot is sometimes ambiguous, with the girls passionately declaring their friendship, vowing to see each other again, and more. They see each other only after dark, and when Anna misses the meeting, the mirage disappears without her realizing it. The arrival of a new family in the manor doesn't dispel her belief, as she is convinced of Marnie's existence.

PUZZLING ORIGINS

As a counterpoint to the serious, dramatic characters that Anna and Marnie ultimately are, the key to the ending is provided by two characters: Sayaka—the comic relief—is the young girl who arrives at the house, finds Marnie's diary, and leads the investigation, while a painter who has memories of the place helps Anna finish the puzzle of Marnie's origins and finally move on with her life.

When Marnie Was There is a unique film in Studio Ghibli's filmography. Adapted from the British novel of the same name by Joan G. Robinson, the feature failed to achieve the anticipated success, despite its undeniable merits. Hiromasa Yonebayashi has since directed *Mary and the Witch's Flower*, produced by Studio Ponoc, a feature that bears the hallmarks of the Ghibli school.

THE RED TURTLE

2016 - MICHAEL DUDOK DE WIT

A Japanese-French-Belgian co-production made by a Dutch animator at Prima Linea in Angoulême, France, with artistic direction by Ghibli, the very existence of the *Red Turtle* project was somewhat perplexing. Infused with these influences, Michael Dudok de Wit's universal film is a masterpiece that has won awards at several festivals.

➤ By Matthieu Pinon

he director will long remember his first feature film. After graduating in 1978, the twenty-five-year-old worked for a few years in the London studio of Richard Purdum[1] before setting off on his own. Dudok de Wit became known for his animated commercials for companies such as United Airlines and AT&T.

The director then made a name for himself at film festivals with his shorts, including *The Monk and the Fish* (1994), which was nominated for an Academy Award in 1995, and *Father and Daughter* (2000), which won the Oscar in 2001. Drawn entirely from tea, *The Aroma of Tea* was his last short film to be shown at a festival, in 2006. After ten years of work, Dudok de Wit made a spectacular return to the screen with his very first feature film, which enjoyed the support of both the general public and critics, via Studio Ghibli.

MR. & MRS. ROBINSON

The sole survivor of a shipwreck, a man is stranded on a desert island. Once he has adjusted to his new life as a hunter-gatherer, he devotes all his energy to returning to civilization. However, each of his

> *"It's hard to say more about this film without ruining the viewing experience with spoilers."*

attempts ends in abject failure: A gigantic red turtle destroys his makeshift raft. Why is it holding him back? How can he fight such an adversary? And is it really an enemy?

It's hard to say more about this film without ruining the viewing experience with spoilers. Combining the themes of his previous works (the obsessive struggle with a marine animal in *The Monk and the Fish*, the journey of a lifetime in *Father and Daughter*), Dudok de Wit's feature works above all through metaphor, and at no point seeks to justify its twists and turns. By following the whole life of its Robinson Crusoe–like protagonist, *The Red Turtle* achieves a universal power, but one that will

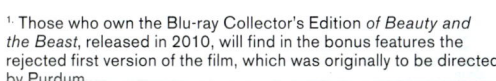

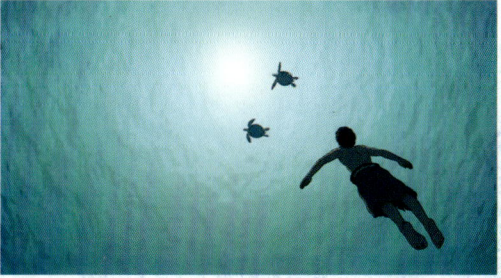

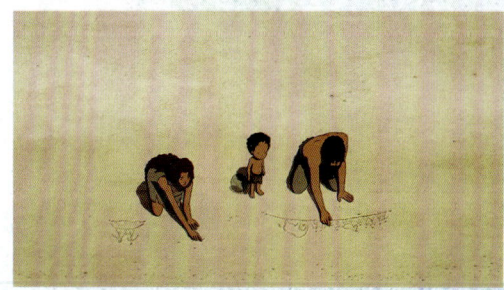

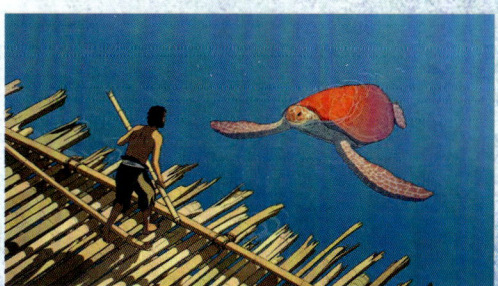

[1]. Those who own the Blu-ray Collector's Edition *of Beauty and the Beast*, released in 2010, will find in the bonus features the rejected first version of the film, which was originally to be directed by Purdum.

be perceived differently by different viewers, depending on their personalities and histories.

This universality is reinforced by the absence of intelligible dialogue for eighty minutes. This constraint, which is shared by all his previous works, is effective for a short film but risky in the longer format. However, it reinforces the atmosphere of the lost island, enhanced by a delicate score by Laurent Perez del Mar (*Wolfy, the Incredible Secret*). With no spoken disruptions, the viewer can focus on the physical evolution of the characters over time—several dozen versions of each of them!

AN ISLAND BETWEEN SKY AND WATER

The island that serves as the story's setting has many facets, from hostile to protective to fertile. These variations are enhanced by subtle lighting effects and intense work on the scenery: After an initial manual phase, the charcoal sketches were scanned before computer colorization. The process is highlighted by Dudok de Wit's sense of framing, contrasting the verticality of a bamboo forest with the horizontality of a beach, all united in the sensual curve of the island's overall topography.

Each shot is fixed, except for a few forced tracking shots, and thus becomes a veritable tableau, whose apparent simplicity conceals considerable thoughtfulness. The slightest movement serves a carefully crafted composition, reminiscent of the masters of *ligne claire* drawing, most notably the Belgian artist Hergé. Ghibli is unquestionably responsible for this sheer aesthetic beauty.

UNIVERSAL LANGUAGE

Won over by the Dutch director's short films, Isao Takahata took the initiative of contacting him to offer Studio Ghibli's artistic support when he wanted to begin production on his first feature film. Dudok de Wit jumped at the chance, much to the delight of the company's directors, who had no one else in mind for their first collaboration with a non-Japanese director. After seeing *Father and Daughter*, Miyazaki had even contemplated the idea of a collaboration.

The director traveled between Angoulême, where the film was made with French (Why Not, Wild Bunch) and Belgian (Belvision) capital, and Tokyo, where he received sound advice from experienced masters. "Suggestions," de Wit said, "but each time repeating that it was my film, and I had to choose for myself. [...] The respect they have for the director's choices, regardless of commercial considerations, is impressive."[2]

When Dudok de Wit offered to change the tidal wave scene after the real-life tsunami of 2011, Studio

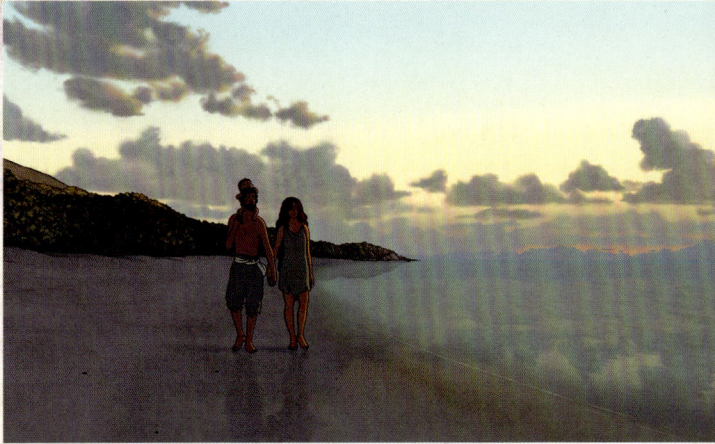

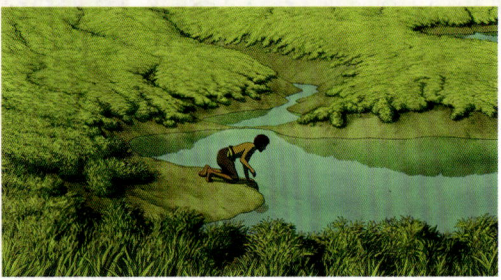

Ghibli objected. Not only does the passage serve the film's plot, but it treats this natural disaster without compromise or pathos.

The film dazzled international critics, winning the Un Certain Regard Special Jury Prize at the Cannes Film Festival and opening the Annecy Festival. But Japanese audiences were not impressed. One week after its release, the film achieved nine times fewer admissions than *A Silent Voice*,[3] which was also released on September 17 ($329,000 versus $2,771,000). This blow is a reminder that even more than Studio Ghibli, it's the Miyazaki name that attracts audiences to theaters.

[2.] www.liberation.fr/cinema/2016/06/28/la-tortue-rouge-jevoulais-une-qualite-de-silence_1462691/
[3.] Film based on the manga of the same name by Yoshitoki Ôima, available from Ki-oon.

EARWIG AND THE WITCH

2020 – GORÔ MIYAZAKI

Studio Ghibli's much-criticized transition to 3D went smoothly with this new production by Gorô Miyazaki. In keeping with the spirit of the studio, *Earwig and the Witch* is a lighthearted film for the whole family. And, at last, the director was standing on his own two feet.

➤ By Stéphanie Chaptal

t would be an understatement to say that professional relations between the Miyazakis had been strained since Gorô made his directorial debut with *Tales from Earthsea*. Whether the son was settling a score with his father on the big screen, or they were collaborating with varying degrees of tension on *From Up on Poppy Hill*, Gorô Miyazaki's work for Studio Ghibli has always divided audiences and critics alike, as they don't see the same magic as in his father's films. After a stint in television with *Ronja, the Robber's Daughter* for Polygon Pictures, Gorô Miyazaki made an eagerly awaited return to the Ghibli fold with another TV movie and, above all, the studio's first 3D CGI feature. It was the studio's first feature film after 2016's *The Red Turtle* (a co-production with Europe). Released during the COVID-19 pandemic, *Earwig and the Witch* didn't get the theatrical attention it had hoped for, except in Japan and at a few festivals abroad. Instead, it was picked up by Netflix, which added it to its catalog on November 18, 2021.

Earwig and the Witch tells the story of Earwig, an orphan abandoned as a baby by a red-haired

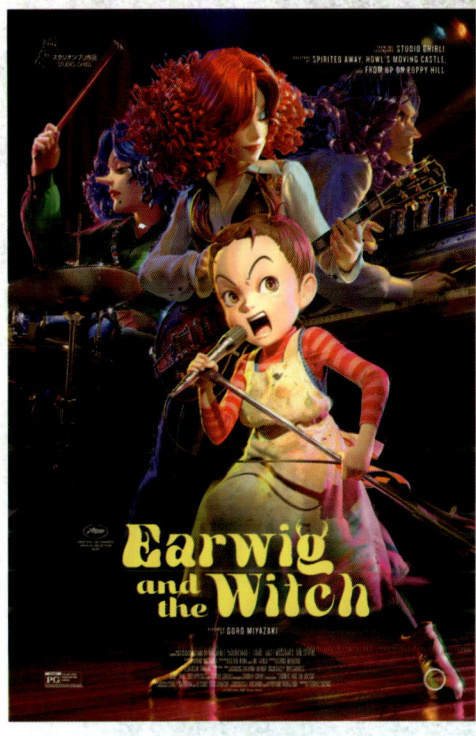

witch. As she enters adolescence, she finds herself in the care of a rather peculiar adoptive family. The blue-haired witch who chooses her is looking for a helping hand to do all the tedious chores, and the pointy-eared man who lives with her wants peace and quiet so as not to trigger all the fires of the underworld. And unlike the people who ran the orphanage, they are unlikely to give in to Earwig's whims, unless she manages to charm them.

Like his father's *Howl's Moving Castle*, *Earwig and the Witch* is an adaptation of a novel by Diana Wynne Jones. Except that *Howl's Moving Castle*, the inspiration for Hayao Miyazaki's film, was aimed at fantasy-loving teenagers and adults while *Earwig and the Witch* was intended for a young audience (ages

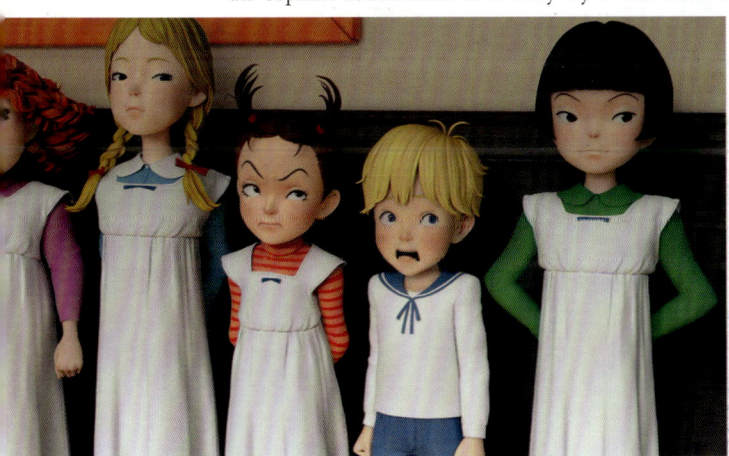

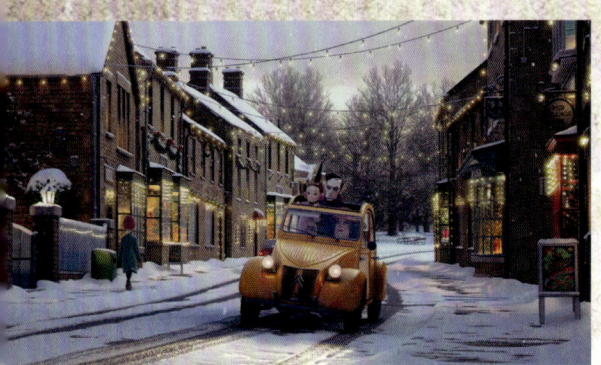

near as unpleasant as feared. Some scenes (on the roof of the orphanage, the concert sequences, the opening chase) are even beautiful. And the characters' facial expressions show the perfect fluidity that is Ghibli's trademark. The plastic aspect has not disappeared, particularly in the witches' hair, but it is justified by the story. In particular, it underlines how the witches use their powers and how magic influences their appearance, making their hair move in unnatural ways.

> *"The characters' facial expressions show the perfect fluidity that is Ghibli's trademark."*

From the very first scenes, this entirely computer-generated 3D film carries the viewer along, immersing them in the heart of the story. On a personal level, the 3D aspect also offered a huge advantage: It enabled Gorô Miyazaki to avoid most of the comparisons that could be made with his illustrious father and to finally establish his own style at Studio Ghibli.

eight to twelve). To turn it into a feature-length animated film that would appeal to a wider audience, the story had to be expanded. This was done by adding more depth to secondary characters, particularly the witch Bella Yaga and Mandrake, and even those that were only mentioned in passing in the book, like Earwig's mother. Moreover, by imagining a common musical past for these three, Gorô Miyazaki and the screenwriters, Keiko Niwa and Emi Gunji, also changed the tone of the story.

Music, especially a very British pop-rock sound, plays a key role. Supported by a lively soundtrack, the plot is fast-paced from the very first scene to the last, which keeps the audience from dwelling on some of the script's weaknesses, such as the mother's fate or the revelations about Earwig's father. The change of pace from Gorô's previous works is evident right from the start, with an impressive car chase opening the film. The featured car, the Citroën 2CV, is Hayao Miyazaki's favorite, and its license plate reads "MYA 13 CW," in a sequence that is reminiscent of the opening scene of the elder Miyazaki's *Lupin III: The Castle of Cagliostro*. In the film, as in the book, the threats hanging over Earwig are merely a pretext for entrusting her to the orphanage, never to be mentioned again. The shared memories of the three primary adults and their special relationship with Earwig soften the girl's pesky side and make her more sympathetic to viewers.

While the film borrows many of Hayao Miyazaki's signature elements, the Gorô touch is obvious. Earwig is a self-centered rascal who drives everyone up the wall. Like the witch and the "demon" who take her in, she has a malicious streak that always pushes her a little too far. Even the cat Thomas can't calm her down. But despite all her shortcomings, the little girl proves endearing, gradually winning the hearts of the characters she meets and the audience. And what about the 3D aspect? While the promotional stills and the first trailer may have raised concerns about the characters' rigid plasticity, the result—apart from a few scenes—is nowhere

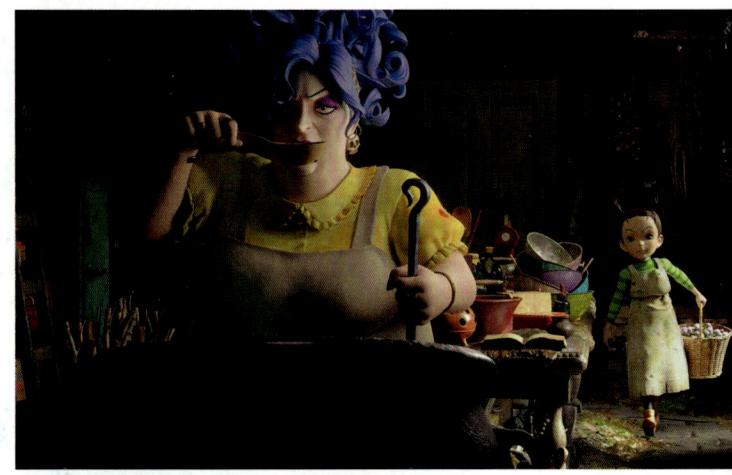

THE BOY AND THE HERON

2023 – HAYAO MIYAZAKI

By Mario Pasqualini (*Dimensione Fumetto*)

astern numerology is highly complex and philosophically linked to both the theory of yin and yang and to geomancy, which interprets the future based on the space that surrounds us (a concept found in feng shui, for example, and no, the layout of the bed and windows inside a house has nothing to do with it). To greatly oversimplify this esoteric, four-thousand-year-old discipline, we can remember that Chinese soothsayers not only divided the ecliptic band into twelve astronomical zones, but also the entire sky into ten segments called "trunks" and the entire earth into twelve segments called "branches," thus covering all 360 degrees. The result is a complex sexagesimal system called *ganzhi*, which is contained in a compass that represents colors, animals, cardinal points, elements, body parts, times of day, and, in general, everything that surrounds us, everything that's part of life.[1] However, the most renowned system within *ganzhi* is that of the twelve animals of the Chinese zodiac, including the rat, buffalo, tiger, and boar (or pig), one for each year. These animals pass through the five elements of metal, water, wood, fire, and earth. Once the twelve animals have passed through the five elements, sixty years have passed, forming a life cycle. According to the same Eastern thought, the twelve stages in five phases over sixty years represent a lifetime.

On July 14, 2023, *Kimi-tachi wa Dô Ikiru ka* (literally *Do You Live?* but titled *The Boy and the Heron* in English), Hayao Miyazaki's twelfth feature film, was released in Japanese cinemas, concluding five phases in sixty years of work.

A whole lifetime.

FIVE DISTINCT PHASES

Miyazaki lived through a large part of the history of Japanese animation, passing through five distinct phases that corresponded to very different works, ideas, and ways of working.

The first phase, 1963–1971, was at Toei Doga, known internationally as Toei Animation. A recent

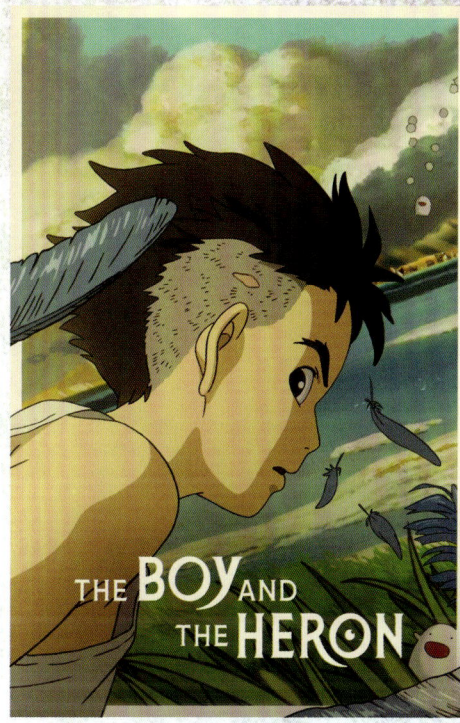

The art book's cover

graduate in economics, a degree he never used (as is often the case with the Japanese, who tend to earn their degrees purely for the prestige, no matter what the subject), Miyazaki joined Toei as an artist, as he had always cultivated his talent for drawing even while studying other subjects. He worked his way up to animator on series adapted from comic books. Under the direction of historic animator Yasuo Ôtsuka, Miyazaki became a *sakuga* animator (equivalent to an animation director in Western cinema) alongside his colleague Yôichi Kotabe on the groundbreaking film *Horus: Prince of the Sun,* directed by Isao Takahata. This was the starting point for these four incomparable artists.

The second phase was at A Production (1971–1973). It lasted only a few years, but it was crucial in the career of filmmaker Yasuo Ôtsuka. A freelance artist, he joined A Production, followed by Kotabe, Miyazaki, and Takahata. It was there that Miyazaki worked on the first series of *Lupin III* and

[1]. Paola Di Felice, *L'universo nel recinto. I fondamenti dell'arte dei giardini e dell'Estetica tradizionale giapponese*, Olschki, Florence 2012.

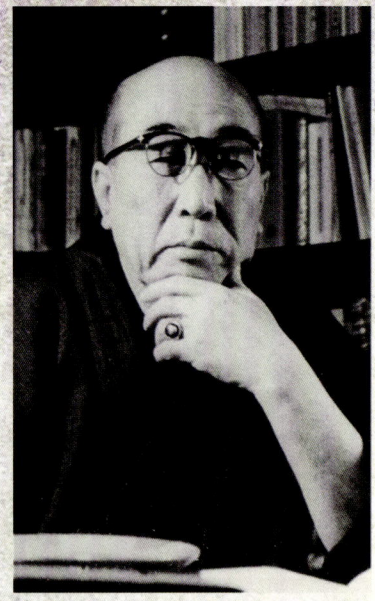
Edogawa Ranpo. R.R.

noons, WMT produced series such as *Heidi*, *3000 Leagues in Search of Mother,* and *Anne of Green Gables*, which were public and critical successes. During the incredibly problematic production of *Anne of Green Gables*,[2] Miyazaki lost it (the Japanese expression would be "overturning the tea table") and left Nippon Animation, only to quickly reverse his decision.

The fourth phase was at TMS (1979–1981). It was a very short but crucial period. Miyazaki and Ôtsuka directed the Italian-Japanese co-production *Sherlock Hound* and returned to work on the Lupin III franchise, both by participating in the second feature in the series, *The Mystery of Mamo*, and, above all, by directing the feature film *The Castle of Cagliostro,* in 1979. The production of this legendary film was itself mythical, as it was completed in just six months. From the initial concept to the final production, with a colossal effort, it was entirely conceived, written, storyboarded, drawn (characters and perhaps even animation), and directed by Miyazaki. Nevertheless, more than forty years after its release, the film remains astonishing for its sheer number of ideas. With his first cinematic work, Miyazaki had already produced a masterpiece in the history of cinema, not only in animation and not only in Japan.

The fifth phase is the Tokuma Shoten and Studio Ghibli era (1981 to the present). After the mixed success of *The Castle of Cagliostro* (it wasn't a great commercial success, at least at first), the monthly

developed his interest in children's literature (which he was less fond of as a child, preferring authors who were ostensibly unsuitable for his age, such as the founder of Japanese detective fiction, Edogawa Ranpo, and progressive philosopher Genzaburô Yoshino, whose landmark novel was *Kimi-tachi wa Dô Ikiru ka* (*How Do You Live?*). The four artists' unsuccessful attempt to adapt *Pippi Longstocking* into animation evolved into two *Panda! Go Panda!* short films, released in 1972 and 1973. While the first is just cute, the second is interesting to watch today, as it contains the beginnings of many ideas and visual touches that Miyazaki would develop over the decades, from Papa Panda rolling off the roof, like in *Lupin III: The Castle of Cagliostro*, to the flooded country featured in *Ponyo*; from his interest in depicting food to the final scene with the train on the water, which is echoed in both *Spirited Away* and the end of the documentary *The Kingdom of Dreams and Madness*, in which Miyazaki makes the moving declaration, "You can, in animation," summing up a precious realm of possibilities in four words.

The third phase was Zuiyô Eizô/Nippon Animation (1973–1979). In 1973, the four animators changed studios again, joining Zuiyô, a production company that had fallen on hard times with bankruptcies and name changes. They produced true masterpieces there, including original series such as *Future Boy Conan* in 1978, directed by Miyazaki himself for NHK, and adaptations of literary works for the major *Sekai Meisaku Gekijou* project, better known in the West as *World Masterpiece Theater*. Originally intended for a thirty-minute slot on Fuji TV on Sunday after-

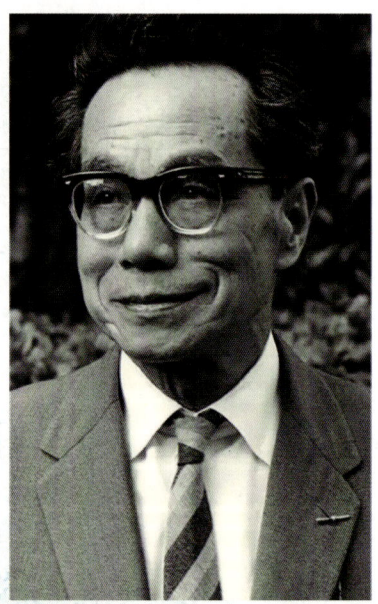
Genzaburô Yoshino. R.R.

2. Matteo Watzky, *Anne of Green Gables* on Animétudes, May 8, 2022 | https://animetudes.com/2022/05/08/anne-ofgreen-gables.

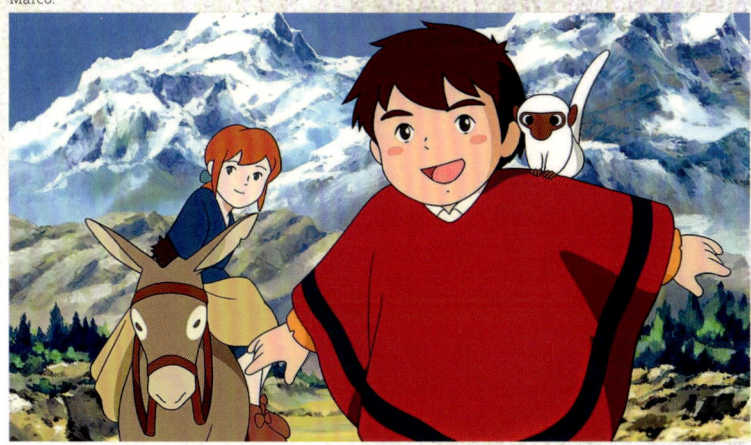
Marco.

animation magazine *Animage*, published by Tokuma Shoten, commissioned Miyazaki to create an episodic comic for them, with editor Toshio Suzuki at his side. The result was *Nausicaä of the Valley of the Wind*, published from 1982 to 1994, and adapted into a feature film in 1984, just as the comic had begun. Unlike the *Lupin III* film, *Nausicaä* was a major hit, and immediately recognized as a turning point in the history of Japanese animation. The film's success convinced Tokuma Shoten to trust Miyazaki and his team, leading to the creation of Studio Ghibli within the publishing house on June 15, 1985. The rest is history.

TWELVE FILMS

How many other filmmakers in the world can boast an artistic career as impressive as that of Hayao Miyazaki, with an output consisting exclusively of historic, significant, extraordinary works, and in particular a filmography ranging from the excellent to the absolute masterpiece? Very few, if any. It's no wonder that choosing a favorite Miyazaki film is an extremely difficult task. It's a tough choice. They're all so different! His filmography is truly remarkable not only for its artistic and box office value, but also for the amazing diversity of themes, styles, and historical-geographical settings. There is a huge difference between one title and another, but at the same time, they consistently maintain a distinct narrative language, content, and form.

SIXTY YEARS

The last film, *Kimi-tachi wa Dō Ikiru ka* (*The Boy and the Heron*), brings the series to a glorious close with what is undoubtedly Hayao Miyazaki's richest, most complex, most personal (or self-referential, if you prefer), most colorful, most abundant, and perhaps even most significant film.

It single-handedly captures all of Miyazaki's themes, languages, visual motifs, moral ideas, cha-

racter types, and distinctive writing styles. Children flying through the sky? Yes. A magical girl? Yes. A determined boy? Yes. An isolated country house? Yes. Kindly and cantankerous old women? Yes. People who speak simply and others who speak in a sophisticated manner? Yes. Incredibly rich, multi-colored, sparkling decor? Yes. Races up steep stairs and over tiny ledges? Yes. Round, four-colored stained-glass windows and large doors with question-mark handles? Yes, yes, and yes again. Heads popping out of tiny windows/holes into the void? Yes. Flowing blood? Yes. Flying objects, perhaps from outer space? Yes. Magic in various forms?

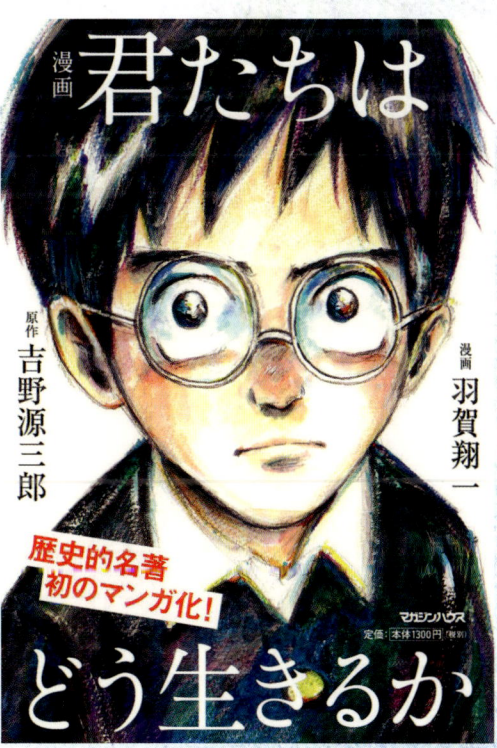
Cover of the manga adaptation.

Marco
© 1976 Nippon Animation

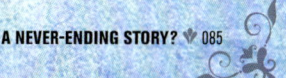

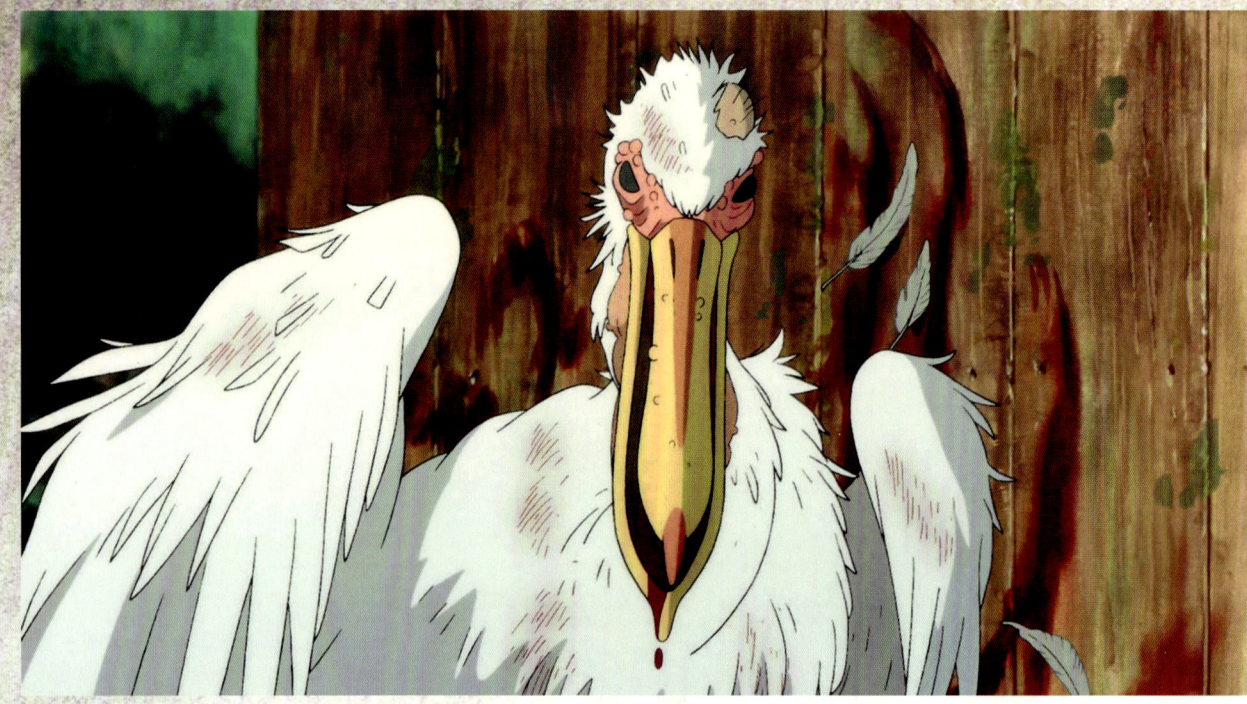

Yes. Miscellaneous creatures? Yes. Planes, means of transport, and engines? Yes. Food, food preparation, Japanese food, Western food, and takeout food? Yes, of course. Tea? Obviously! The film is so visually rich that it's almost excessive, and the viewer has to see it several times to take it all in. Despite this visual abundance, the writing remains front and center, and at times the artist's message seems to be the focus, rather than the narrative itself, particularly in the final section, in a pure *sekai-kei* (world-themed) style. But since this film brings Miyazaki's career to a close, perhaps some of his artistic "excesses" can be forgiven.

The Boy and the Heron offers two hours of complete immersion in the mind of an artist who delivers his spiritual legacy to the world: The world is beautiful, life goes on, and it is up to every one of us to take that first step toward the future.

Yes, it really is a simple, clear, sincere message.

ON THE ROAD TO *KIMI-TACHI WA DÔ IKIRU KA*

The film's production itself also sparked the interest of Japanese animation fans. Unlike all of Studio Ghibli's previous works, *The Boy and the Heron* was not produced under the supervision of a "commission,"[3] a group of sponsors, companies, and various producers who usually invest not only financially, but also decide on the artistic direction the production should take. In this case, the film was financed completely independently by Studio Ghibli and distributed by Toho, thus allowing considerable creative freedom, which is clearly visible in terms of theme and narrative. Gathering the scant information revealed, we knew before the film's release that preproduction had apparently begun in 2017, taking as its starting point the for-

mative novel *Kimi-tachi wa Dô Ikiru ka*, published in Japan in 1937, one of the early readings that Miyazaki has mentioned as having had a major influence on him. The film's title was inspired by the novel, but not its plot, which is entirely original and unrelated to that of the book.

The novel would be difficult to adapt for animation. It tells the story of the daily adventures of a fatherless child who lives with his mother and uncle, with whom he has a deep intellectual bond and who helps him in his "discoveries." For example, watching the crowds from the terrace of the Wako department stores in the Ginza section of Tokyo, he understands that humanity is a single organism made up of individuals, just as matter is made up of individual molecules. Or when looking at a package of powdered milk made in Australia, he realizes that every individual object is the end result of a production process involving many people, many stages of work, and so on. In short, it's a coming-of-age story that invites young people to rise above selfishness and individualism, embrace humanity and compassion, and become part of the complex, *bishu* (beautiful and ugly at the same time) system we call "the world." It's almost a *sekai-kei* text that was written at a time when the expression didn't yet exist. In 2017, producer Toshio Suzuki revealed in an interview[4] that Miyazaki intended his new film as a gift for his grandson before he died. *Ars longa, vita brevis* (art is long, life is short): The filmmaker is going to die but his art remains, and the film was meant to specifically address the process of mourning a departed loved one.

[3] Matteo Watzky, "Hayao Miyazaki's *How Do You Live*?" on *Full Frontal*, July 14, 2023 | https://fullfrontal.moe/how-do-you-live-review.

On January 21, 2019, Vincent Maraval, co-founder of international film distribution company Wild Bunch, visited Studio Ghibli,[5] where he learned that two films were in production, one by Hayao Miyazaki and the other by Gorô Miyazaki. He expressed his excitement on Twitter, writing that "the drawings are a-maz-ing!" On December 18, 2019, France-based Italian jazz musician Giovanni Mirabassi, co-founder of the Jazz Eleven label and a huge anime fan, released a second album of jazz rearrangements of anime tracks, following *Animessi* (2015), which featured music from several films. The new album was entitled *Mitaka Calling* (Mitaka is the city in Tokyo Prefecture where the Ghibli Museum is located), and the cover featured what appeared to be a Studio Ghibli illustration of a child running through a crowd toward a fire. It was later confirmed[6] that it was indeed an illustration from Miyazaki's layout of *The Boy and the Heron*, a gift from the director to his musician friend.

Over time, more fragmented information emerged, revealing that the film's head animator was Takeshi Honda, a long-standing collaborator of Hideaki Anno's at Studio Khara who is highly regarded by Miyazaki, assisted by only about sixty other animators (with only five CGI animators, as can be noted in the film's credits). The composer was the faithful Joe Hisaishi. Suspicious coincidences (congratulatory messages, bouquets of flowers, etc.) suggested that Kenshi Yonezu had written a song for the film, which was later confirmed. There was no promotion prior to the film's release. Producer Toshio Suzuki explained that when he was young, there were no trailers or other such nonsense, yet everyone went to the movies.[7]

He also cited as an example the film *The First Slam Dunk*, which was a great success despite very limited promotion.[8] (Suzuki exaggerated the point; in reality, that film did benefit from promotion,[9] but it was very targeted and very enigmatic so that it would have more impact and be tinged with a symbolic mystery.) It has been pointed out[10] that Studio Ghibli generally spends considerable sums

on promotion, and this could simply have been a way of saving part of the budget for this self-produced film (and keeping a low profile at a time when Suzuki was in the media spotlight for economic scandals[11]). As a result, no other poster was produced apart from the cryptic one we know, with details of a sketch by Miyazaki, and no trailer, flyer, teaser, press kit, or anything else. Suzuki was confident that word of mouth would bring the

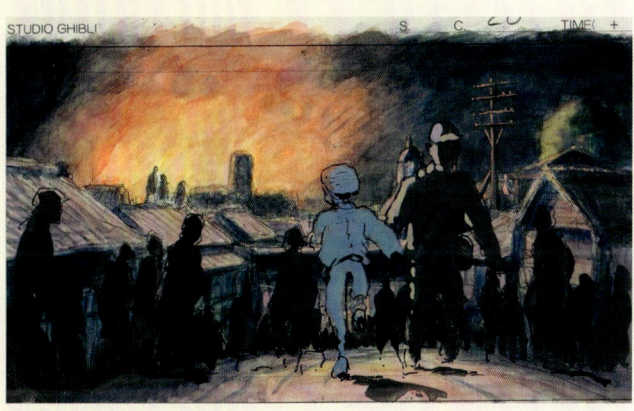

film the success it deserved. In any case, the names of the trailer editors and communication managers are mentioned in the film's credits, so some form of promotion did exist, but only after the film's release. In August 2023, Studio Ghibli gradually began releasing information, images, music, and more.

The film remained relatively unknown until its theatrical release, even among anime fans. On the day of its release, theaters weren't as full as they had been for the master's previous films, which repeatedly broke Japanese box office records and kept Studio Ghibli afloat for years in the face of

4. Report on the status of Hayao Miyazaki's new feature from Studio Ghibli producer Toshio Suzuki: "2019 release is 'not possible' " on *Natalie*, April 29, 2017 | https://natalie.mu/eiga/news/230849.

5. "Le fils de Hayao Miyazaki serait, lui aussi, de retour dans les Studio Ghibli pour un nouveau projet!" on *Hitek*, January 21, 2019 | https://hitek.fr/actualite/goro-miya-zaki-fils-hayao-miyazaki-projet-en-preparation-studios-ghibli_18381.

6. "Hayao Miyazaki disegna la copertina del nuovo album di Giovanni Mirabassi" on *Go Nagai World*, November 12, 2019 | www.gonagaiworld.com/hayao-miyazaki-disegna-la-copertina-del-nuovo-album-di-giovanni-mirabassi.

7. "Ghibli producer explains unusual promotion for mystery Miyazaki film," on *NHK World-Japan*, July 13, 2023 | www3.nhk.or.jp/nhkworld/en/news/backstories/2575.

8. "Studio Ghibli's Producer Decides Not Revealing Any Plots of Hayao Miyazaki's Latest Film Prior to Release Date" on *Cinema Daily US*, December 28, 2022 | https://cinemadailyus.com/news/studio-ghiblis-producer-decides-not-revealing-any-plots-of-hayao-miyazakis-latest-film-prior-to-release-date.

9. Mario Pasqualini, "*The First Slam Dunk* – Takehiko Ino'ue e l'arte della narrazione sul campo da basket" on *Dimensione Fumetto*, March 6, 2023 | www.dimensionefumetto.it/the-first-slam-dunk-takehiko-inoue-e-larte-della-narrazione-sul-campo-da-basket/.

10. Marlen Vazzoler, Latest news on Facebook, June 10, 2023.

11. "Studio Ghibli co-founder accused of spending company funds on Thai girlfriend" on *Thaiger*, March 30, 2023 | https://thethaiger.com/news/national/studio-ghibli-co-founder-accused-of-spending-company-funds-on-thai-girlfriend.

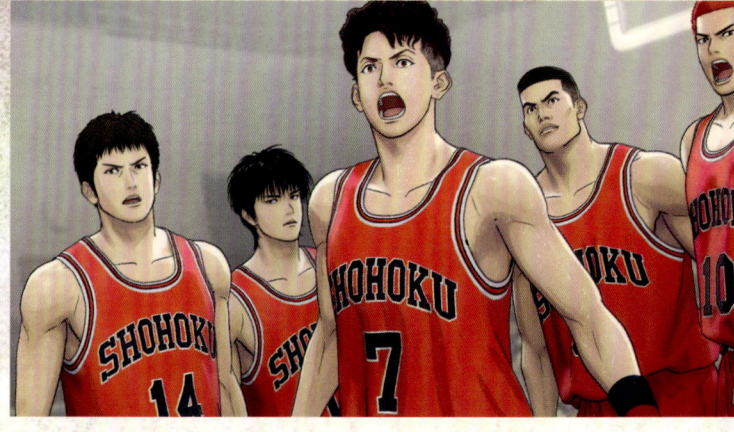

Isao Takahata's spending and the mixed commercial success of other directors.

STORYLINE

Tokyo, "the third year of the war"[12]: An alarm sounds in the middle of the night to warn of a fire in a hospital.[13] Little Mahito Maki[14] rushes to the scene, only to discover that his mother, Hisako, who was being treated there, has perished in the flames.

Not long after, Shoichi, Mahito's father, marries Natsuko, the younger sister of the late Hisako,[15] and is expecting a child with her. Mahito treats her coldly, not accepting her as his new mother. The family moves to the country[16] to live in a large villa belonging to the mother's family, just like so many others migrating from the city because of the war. The villa is near the factory producing parts for military aircraft where Shoichi is the director. A group of elderly people look after the villa, including seven colorful old women, each very different from the next.[17] One of them is strict, irritable Kiriko, who is always looking for tobacco. When Mahito arrives at the villa, he is greeted by a gray heron[18] living in the garden, which Natsuko claims is welcoming him. Exhausted by the long journey and his new life, Mahito falls asleep under the gaze of Natsuko and the heron outside the window, which seems to be calling to him.

REALITY VS. IMAGINATION, OR: TO YOU, MY SINCERE SOUL

Ten years after his already highly personal *The Wind Rises*, which was then his second or third "last film" (it should be remembered that the director has on several occasions announced his departure, not from animation in general, but only from feature film directing because of his advanced age), Miyazaki returned to the big screen with *The Boy and the Heron*, depicting an even more intimate and moving story. Once again, there are numerous more or less autobiographical references that are sometimes conveyed through metaphors, from a sick mother to a father working in aircraft production, from evacuation to the country because of bombing attacks in the city to a passion for reading. Much of the young Hayao shines through in Mahito.

The First Slam Dunk
© I.T.PLANNING, INC. © 2022 THE FIRST SLAM DUNK Film Partners
The Boy and the Heron
© 2023 Studio Ghibli

[12.] No specific date is given in the film. During the first half of the twentieth century, Japan waged an almost continuous war, at least from 1912 to 1949, with various individual conflicts that began in different years and accumulated. As a result, the date of the "third year of the war" is not obvious, as it does not specify which war it refers to. In any case, given the context (clothing, miscellaneous objects, the scene with the veterans' procession, etc.), we can assume it's the 1940s. If we think it's the Second Sino-Japanese War, then it's 1940, while if we think it's the Pacific War, then it's 1943. The year is clarified at the end of the film.
[13.] There is no mention of whether the fire was caused by the war or simply occurred at the time of the war. In the panoramic scenes of the fire, there are no planes or bombs, and the hospital is the only building on fire, so it could be a tragic accident for other reasons.
[14.] The surname is made up of the ideogram 牧 (*maki*), meaning "to raise, graze, look after livestock," while the first name is made up of the ideograms 眞 (*ma*), meaning "truth," and 人 (*hito*), meaning "person," so "honest person." It is therefore an evocative name that can be translated as "honest shepherd."
[15.] In traditional Japanese society, particularly in the upper social classes, it was quite common for widowers/widows to remarry with one of the deceased spouse's close relatives, as the bond between the two families was considered more important than the specific bond between the two people.
[16.] Probably in Shizuoka Prefecture, where most of the displaced were housed during World War II.
[17.] This is probably a reference to the seven dwarfs in the "Snow White" fairy tale—more specifically to Walt Disney's 1937 film *Snow White and the Seven Dwarfs*, because in the Brothers Grimm's original story, the seven dwarfs are all identical, rather than being portrayed as distinct personalities. The tale is also mentioned later in the character of Himi.
[18.] In Japanese, "heron" is 鷺 (*sagi*, pronounced /saghi/), which is a homophone of 詐欺 (*sagi*), meaning "fraud, deceit," and 詐偽 (*sagi*), meaning "lie, imposture." The contrast with the protagonist's name, which means "person (who tells) the truth" or "honest person," is obvious.

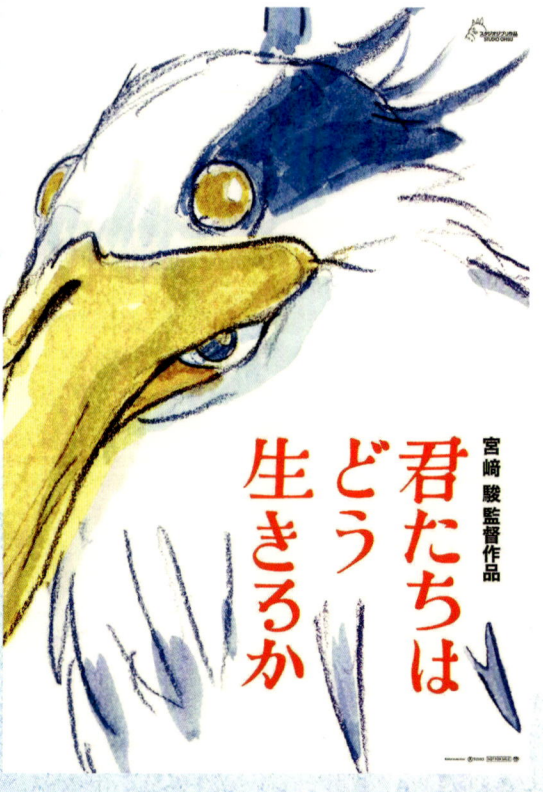

宮崎 駿 監督作品

君たちはどう生きるか

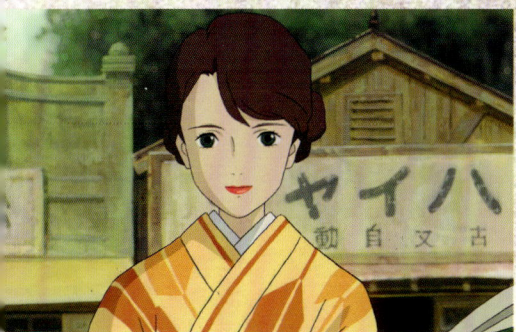

POSSIBLE INTERPRETATIONS OF THE PLOT: THE IMPORTANCE OF HONESTY AND THE CHOICE TO LIVE

The elements of adventure and geographical space in the film are supported and made more obvious by a series of stark oppositions.

The first aspect is the clear division of the story into two parts, marked by a precise liminal passage where the characters "shift" into a dreamlike dimension where their actions influence reality. As the viewer watches a dream scene with real-world repercussions at the beginning of the film, they can't help wondering whether the characters are dreaming or if everything is real. Toward the end, however, the issue is explained by the theory of parallel worlds (a classic element of science fiction, fantasy, and horror) but becomes irrelevant, as it gradually becomes clear that Miyazaki's priority is not narrative clarity, but communicating a message identical to that of the Yoshino novel from which it takes its title: the importance of young people choosing to be part of the world. The word *sekai* (world) is repeated many times as the film nears its finale, pointing very clearly to a familiar trope in which the protagonist's interiority corresponds to the outside world and vice versa.

As a result, the protagonist's personal calm and the rest of the world influence each other. The internal and external coincide, yin and yang together. Although Miyazaki had already touched on this theme in *Ponyo*, where the world seems to react to Ponyo's changing moods, it reaches its peak here through cryptic dialogue and more explicit imagery (the most frequently used being that of building blocks). The film uses many opposites in addition to the internal and the external, such as town and country, inhabited villa and abandoned tower, humans and birds, youth and old age, day and night, birth and death, war and peace, and many other specular concepts that Miyazaki employs not to create division, but to create union. This is precisely at the heart of the aforementioned theory of yin and yang, whereby harmony can be achieved only through the union of opposites. Individual elements, taken on their own, are sterile, but when brought together, they take on value. Nothing is beautiful in itself, but it is beautiful when contrasted with something ugly, which has value and a reason to exist because it is intrinsically linked to the others. This is what Yoshino teaches in his 1937 novel.

This concept is supported by the abundant use of visual and narrative symbols and allegories, to the extent that after first viewing the film, audiences emphasized its complexity.[19]

Interpreting a film is just as important as interpreting dreams, as the events and images represent psychoanalytic phenomena. For example, the painter Takashi Murakami has compared the film to the mysterious cryptic monolith in the manga *Nausicaä of the Valley of the Wind*,[20] trying to decipher

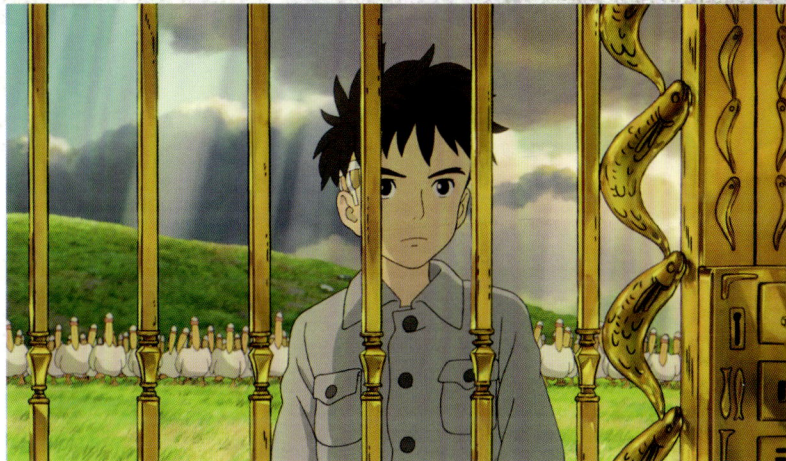

certain iconographic aspects. These range from the tomb inspired by Arnold Böcklin's 1883 painting *Island of the Dead* (which Sigmund Freud loved) to more subtle allusions, such as the Western colonization of Asia represented by the Indies Company fleet to the hypothesis[21] that the flight of the parakeets might represent the student riots of the 1970s, and that Uncle/Takahata/Einstein might be a "creative" artist, and as such, use the stone blocks found in art academies for observational drawing. This doesn't mean that the film can be appreciated solely for its pure narrative or representational values. It remains exciting, entertaining, colorful, masterfully animated, and generally crafted to the best of Studio Ghibli's ability. The film is exceptional and

19. 宮崎駿『君たちはどう生きるか』はなぜ難しいのか?: 実はシンプルなあらすじを解説 on Ongakuteki, ongakuronteki, July 20, 2023.
20. Takashi Murakami, tweet from July 22, 2023 | http://twitter.com/takashipom/status/1682755314976952324.
21. Takashi Murakami, tweet from July 23, 2023 | https://twitter.com/takashipom/status/1682860453419171840.

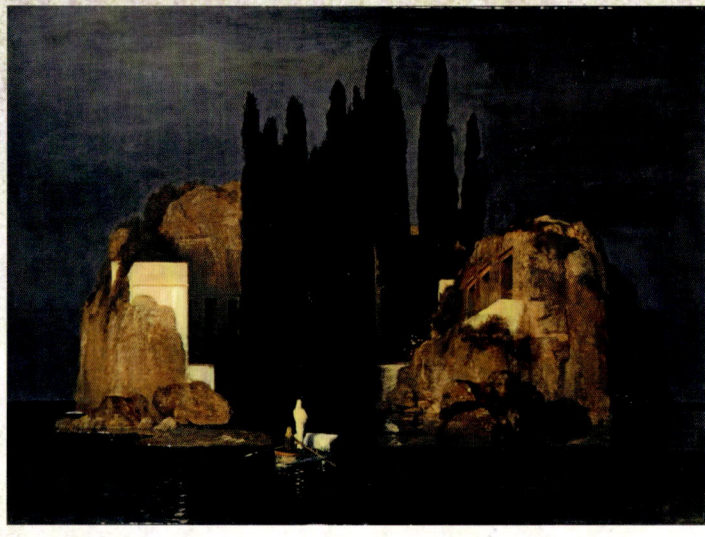

very rich, even in its "superficial" aspects. At the same time, the film constantly invites the viewer to explore its "deep" part and to hypothesize about its meaning. Here are a few ideas:

• (Hypothesis suggested by the author's wife.) Natsuko is happily pregnant but, faced with Mahito's grouchiness, she realizes the complexity of bringing up a child and decides to reconsider her decision to have a baby and perhaps abort it, or at least think about it. However, patriarchal society, symbolized by the all-male parakeets, doesn't accept this decision. They don't eat her because the child is important (more important than she is), but they have locked her in a room where she is tormented by the problems represented by the streamers that hover around her incessantly (problems perceived as being nothing more than strips of paper). There's only one way out of this prison, and that's through the affection of loved ones. The moment Mahito calls her "Mom," Natsuko realizes that she wants the child, and makes the choice to get up and leave the room. The streamers (i.e., the problems) envelop and trap her, and the only solution is to stand together, to cooperate, and to escape from the mental prison into the outside world, which can exist and be beautiful.

• (Hypothesis suggested by writer Natsuki Ikezawa in the September 2023 issue of *Switch*[22] magazine.) Mahito represents Hayao Miyazaki himself. He reads a lot. From the city (the family), Miyazaki moves to the countryside (leaves the family and enters the world of animation). Natsuko and the seven old women could be colleagues in the early days of his career. Inside the world of animation, he finds this remote, magical tower that is unlike any other place (it represents Studio Ghibli), although there are others (which are all anima-

tion studios). Inside the tower, we find the busy Heron Man (Toshio Suzuki) and the wise uncle (Isao Takahata) who keeps the world going with his genius. Mahito finds himself an outsider in this world and can't replace the uncle (Miyazaki feels himself to be an animator, not a director), so all he can do, now that the uncle is gone (Takahata having passed away), is make the tower collapse (with the end of his career, Studio Ghibli ceases to exist as it has until now and either dies or becomes something else, which can be just as beautiful).

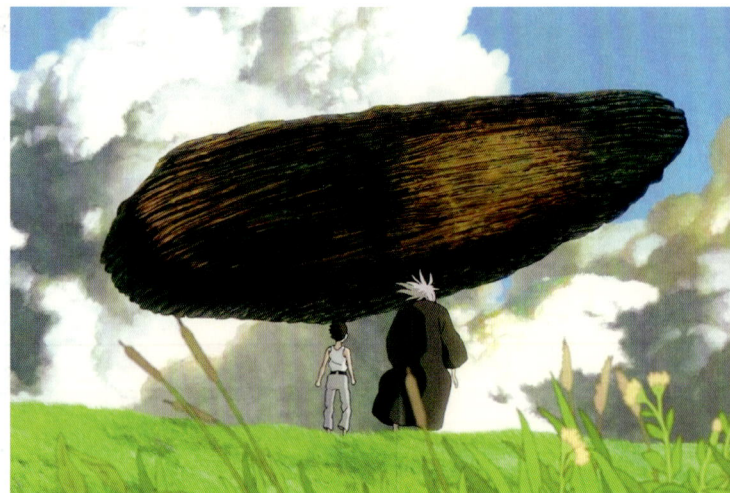

And these are just two possible interpretations. A thousand others could be found, given the film's many symbols: the toads surrounding Mahito, the pelicans, the instruction to not look back at the

Island of the Dead
Kunstmuseum Collection, Basel, Suisse.
The Boy and the Heron
© 2023 Studio Ghibli

22. Natsuki Ikezawa (ed.), "Studio Ghibli's Daring Journey" (in Japanese) in *Switch*, September 2023.
23. 大小暦 | 日本の暦 (The Japanese Calendar) on *National Diet Library* | www.ndl.go.jp/koyomi/chapter2/s1.htm.

tomb like in the myth of Orpheus and Eurydice, the objects in Kiriko's house, the numbers on the doors, the embroidery on the curtain in Natsuko's room, the thirteen blocks stacked every three days to represent the passage of time (in the ancient Japanese lunisolar calendar, there were twelve months, to which a thirteenth, called *uruzuki*, was added every three years to regularize the length of the year[23]). Everything speaks to the viewer. The film's great richness lies in the fact that it is fun to watch as a fantasy adventure, but also opens the door to many complex interpretations.

values in human relationships are: honesty with oneself and with others to begin a happy life, which is certainly possible and can be beautiful.

The Japanese concept of *bessekai* is vaguely like that of the "alternate dimension" or "parallel world" in science fiction. It should definitely not be confused with the concept of 別世界 *isekai*, which has recently become popular thanks to the many works that use it. An *isekai* is a world totally different from the *konsekai*, like that of a fantasy video game, while a *bessekai* is another version of the *konsekai*, an alternative vision of the world we know,

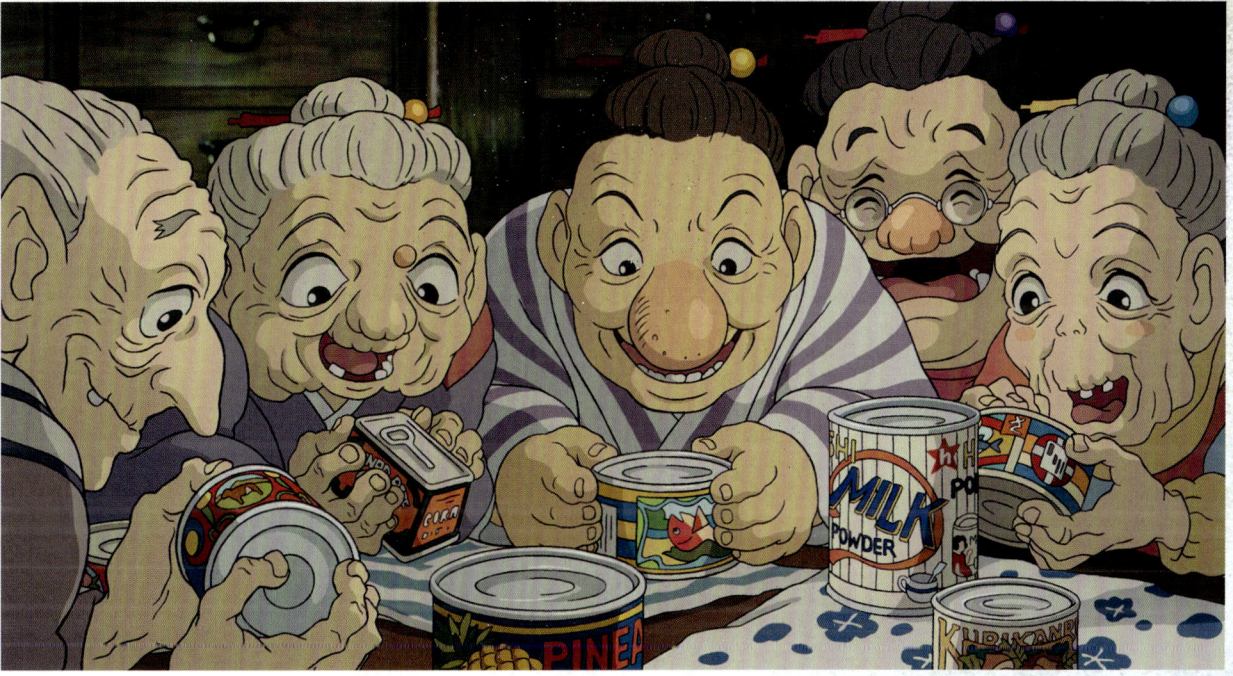

FROM THE SPOON TO THE CITY[24]: GEOGRAPHICAL SPACE IN THE STORY AND THE DECISION TO TRAVEL

In light of Miyazaki's earlier works, a third, highly abstract interpretation may be suggested:

• (The author's hypothesis.) One place exists and the other doesn't: The villa represents reality while the tower symbolizes dreams, or illness, or some alteration of the basic psycho-physical state. Or, as suggested by the setting of 1943–1945, the city is the 今世界 *konsekai* ("this world," the real) and the countryside is the 別世界 *bessekai* ("another world," the imaginary). The latter is an "other" place where people take temporary refuge from the stresses of everyday life and embrace a period of contemplative pause and self-reflection, ultimately understanding what the fundamental

apparently more or less similar in form but characterized by a different philosophy or worldview.

In this sense, Mahito's entry into the tower, just like Lupin's entry into Cagliostro, Nausicaä's into the forest, Pazu and Sheeta's into Laputa, Satsuki and Mei's into the camphor tree, Kiki's into the city, Porco's into the workshop, Ashitaka's into the foundry, Chihiro's into the *kami* baths, Sophie's into the moving castle, Ponyo's into Sôsuke's house, and Jirô's into the factory, symbolizes entry into a *bessekai*, meaning an "other" place where you can

24. Slogan by architect Ernesto Nathan Rogers, taken up by Max Bill in 1952. "From the spoon to the city" means that a common method can be applied to the design of both small objects and cities, that small things act on the large; the small scale affects the grand scale.

experience a philosophy that is different from the one you're used to, and from which you can emerge forever changed.

This is precisely the process that takes place in the *kekkai* (equivalent to the Greek term *temenos*, "sacred ground") of Shinto shrines, or in the *chashitsu* (tearooms) where the *chakai* (mistakenly called the "tea ceremony"[25]) takes place, leading to self-alienation. You are no longer yourself; you are another person, another thing.

Simply put, Mahito's journey takes place mainly in his mind, and ultimately leads him to make a choice about his life, as is the case in all Hayao Miyazaki films. From Lupin choosing honesty and leaving Clarisse's house, to Sen choosing honesty by leaving the baths to take the train to Zeniba's house (Miyazaki himself pointed out that the film could have ended there[26]), to Mahito choosing honesty by

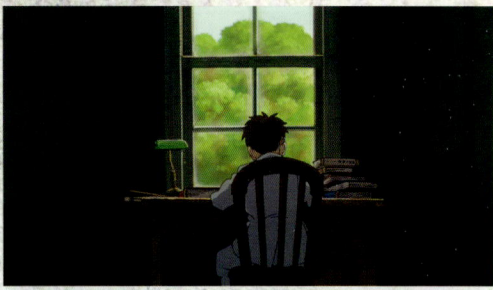

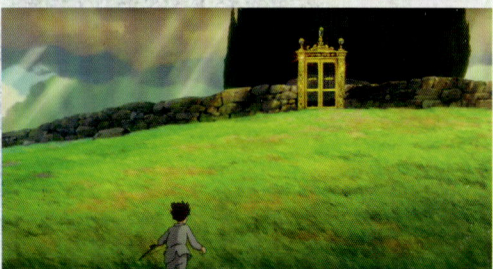

leaving the World Below (place of comfort) to face the World Above (real life), with all its advantages and disadvantages. Thus, the ultimate meaning of the film, its moral (to use a fairy-tale term), was already clearly written in its original title: *How Do You Live?* Will you always choose the easiest, most comfortable solution, or will you be honest with yourself and with others, even if it means experiencing some discomfort?

Right up to the end, Miyazaki reveals himself to be a dialectical intellectual, using his customary language of space to communicate his intense creativity. In all his films, the narrative phase is preceded by the spatial design phase,[27] as it is the characters' movement that generates the animation and consequently the narrative. *The Boy and the Heron* is no exception.

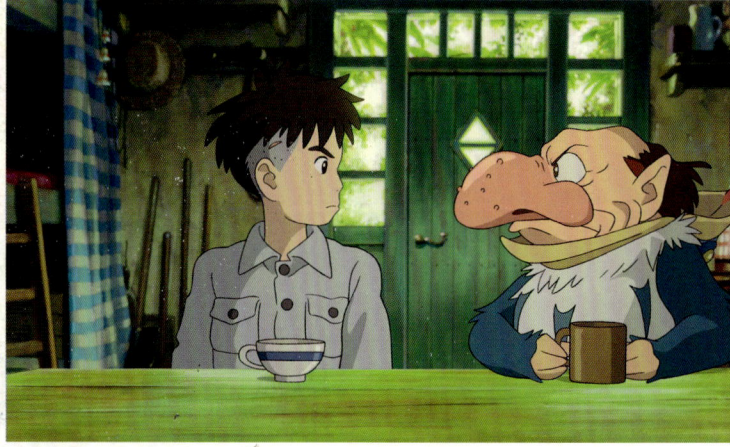

The film itself opens with a striking example of movement as narrative: a frenetic scene in which Character A runs across town to Character B, only to discover that B has died. This running scene is a deliberate choice of staging, as it would have been possible to use a thousand other approaches to communicate the same information to the viewer.

Character A could have already been there with B and witnessed the death scene, or A could have received a phone call or been talking to someone, or A could have been looking at a photo of B while crying, or the police could have gone to A's house to notify him, or something else. The director dismissed these alternatives because they would have been static, and nothing is ever static in a Miyazaki film. So he envisioned a scene in motion where A runs to B through a space to learn the information. "You can, in animation."

And, of course, if everyone is on the move, then the space must be thought through; this has been Miyazaki's standard practice since *The Castle of Cagliostro*, although his methods have changed. Discussing the setting of the 1979 film, Miyazaki declared,[28] "For a while, I used Hitchcock's method, but then I told myself I'd never do it again. I was young back then. I used it for *Lupin III: The Castle of Cagliostro*. Concentrating on the last scene, preparing the story, and meticulously assembling the

[25]. Okakura Kakuzo, *Le Livre du thé*, Garzanti, Milan, 2015.
[26]. Hayao Miyazaki and Takeshi Yoro, *Mushime to Anime*, Tokuma Shoten, Tokyo 2002 | www.interactiongreen.com/hayao-miyazaki-quote.
[27]. Mario Pasqualini, "Genesis – Hideaki Anno ovvero l'erede di Hayao Miyazaki" on *Dimensione Fumetto*, December 22, 2020 | www.dimensionefumetto.it/lerede-di-hayao-miyazaki/.
[28]. 『ルパン三世 カリオストロの城』豆知識まとめ (" 'Lupin III: The Castle of Cagliostro' Trivia Summary") on the fan site *Studio Ghibli Hikoshiki*, January 16, 2015 | https://ghibli.jpn.org/report/cagliostoro.

individual scenes, I first placed the castle here and the lake there, prepared the action scene, and made sure that each location was always shown at least twice, that is, the same location shown this way and that way, changing the camera's point of view. By doing this, I established my rules for building scenes. It was a kind of mental game, very interesting, well, as interesting as it could be, but I decided not to pursue it. I had the feeling that if I continued with that method, my work would suffer. That's why I only used it for *The Castle of Cagliostro*."

Miyazaki was referring to the fact that Alfred Hitchcock created his settings by first developing the space. Famous examples include the Bates Motel and the mother's house in *Psycho*, the real-life San Francisco locations where the characters evolve in *Vertigo*, and the extreme case of *Rope*, which was shot in unity of space and time, where the synchronized movement of camera and actors in entirely interior spaces was fundamental (paradoxically, the trailer was shot outside). Although Miyazaki had firmly sworn off using Hitchcock's method, he returned to it in the most complex way possible in *The Boy and the Heron*.

In every Miyazaki film, the characters' movement through space defines how the plot progresses. This is particularly true and apparent in *The Castle of Cagliostro* and *The Boy and the Heron*, which closely follow Hitchcock's methodology described above, giving extreme importance to spaces (far more than to many characters), showing them from different angles, filling them with details that carry metaphorical meaning, and using them as focal points for external plot and internal character development.

As previously mentioned, the film's great narrative complexity, in terms of both plot and character development, is largely based on contrasts, many of which are spatial: city/country, traditional house/*yashiki*, villa/garden, house/school, inhabited

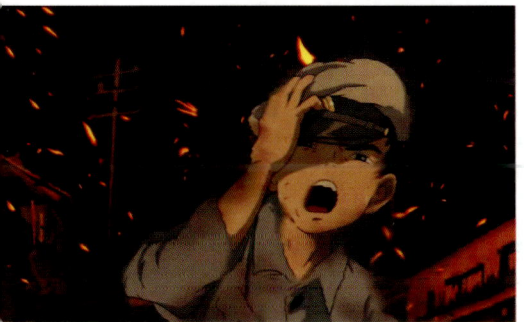

house/abandoned tower, and so on. All these horizontal contrasts in the World Above are matched by vertical contrasts in the World Below: above/below, grave on the hill/boat on the sea, sea/Kiriko's house, entrance at the bottom of the stairs/entrance at the top of the stairs to go to the uncle's house, garden below/cottage above, and so forth.

Speaking of opposites, it's interesting to note how Miyazaki's very first and very last films are perfectly specular (mirror images) in many respects, suggesting that this was a deliberate—or perhaps unconscious—choice on the part of the director, as if to come full circle:

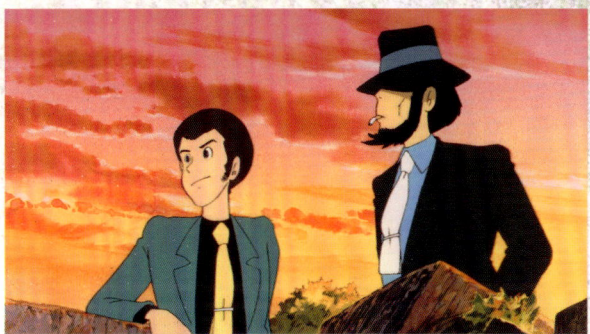

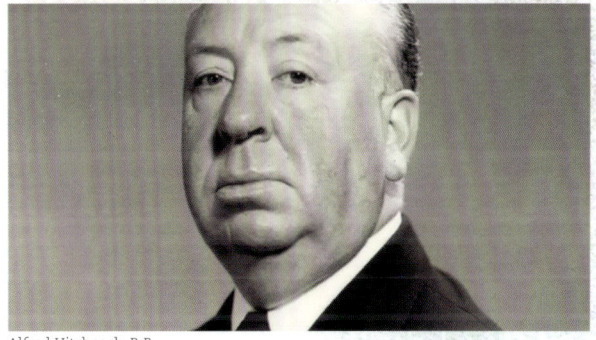

Alfred Hitchcock. R.R.

- A totally different reinterpretation of a childhood book (*The Haunted Tower* by Edogawa Ranpo)/A totally different reinterpretation of a childhood book (*How Do You Live?* by Genzaburô Yoshino)
- Six months of frantic work/Six years of slow work
- Unmarried virgin/Woman who is already married and pregnant
- Working-class urban area and mysterious separate area reserved for a select few (the castle)/ Working-class urban area and mysterious separate area reserved for a select few (the villa)
- Two worlds separated horizontally (rest of the world and the Grand Duchy of Cagliostro)/

Two worlds separated vertically (World Above and World Below)
- Offensive male servants/Defensive female servants
- Saving a girl who loves you and whom you'll never see again/Saving a girl who doesn't love you and whom you will see again
- Plot centered on a mysterious tower that collapses in the end/Plot centered on a mysterious tower that collapses in the end
- Finding a hidden building/Destroying a hidden building.

And the list could go on and on. *The Castle of Cagliostro* and *The Boy and the Heron* truly represent the two pillars of Miyazaki's career. Confirmation of the above comes from the 2015 edition of Edogawa Ranpo's novel *The Haunted Tower*, published in Japan by Iwanami Shoten and introduced by a short comic by Hayao Miyazaki entitled ぼくの幽霊塔 *Boku no yurei-to* (*My Haunted Tower*), in which the porcine-featured creator recalls how much he loved the novel in his youth.

The comic says:

Sixty years ago, there was a small rental bookshop in town where I discovered Edogawa Ranpo's *The Haunted Tower*. I still remember the covers wrapped in wax paper. I had forgotten that I had rented this book for 20 yen for three days and two nights.

[Onomatopoeia: Bo-bom-bo-bom! How exciting! Very scary and beautiful!]

When I liked a book, I read it again and again.

[Off-screen voice: "Hurry up and go to sleep!"]

And so on. Amazingly, in the comic where the wax paper covers are mentioned, the back cover of *How Do You Live?* appears next to *The Haunted Tower*. It seems that Miyazaki's destiny had preordained these two books to be literally the alpha and omega of his life and artistic career.

In any case, the similarities between *The Boy and the Heron* and Miyazaki's previous films are not limited to *The Castle of Cagliostro*. As already noted, it's easy for the director's fans to recognize direct references to all his previous films in many scenes, including the settings. For example, the ruined outer parts of the Parakeet King's tower resemble Cagliostro's burned-out villa, the parakeets' tower with its lofty spaces is reminiscent of the stacked houses in Pazu's village, and Himi's house is

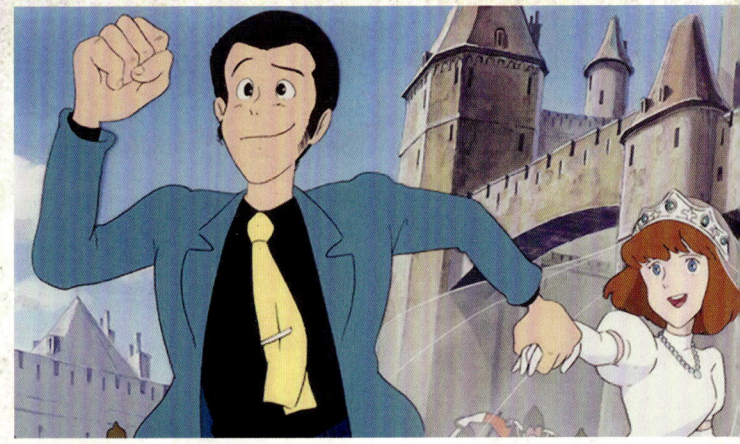

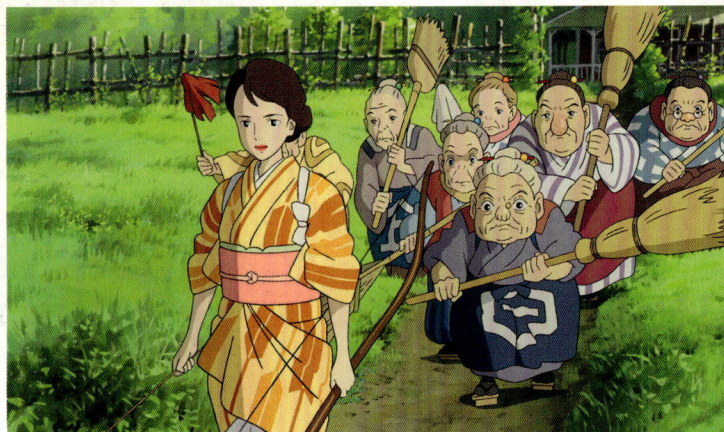

virtually identical to Hauru's childhood home, but with even more flowers.

All in all, even the setting confirms that Miyazaki could have retired with a simpler film, but instead chose to make what is probably the most complex film of his entire career.

FROM BOOK TO FILM: THE CONNECTION TO YOSHINO AND WALT DISNEY

As we have seen, we had little information about the film before its release, other than that it borrowed the title, themes, and poster font from Yoshino's novel *How Do You Live?*, but not the plot, which was to be of a fantastic nature. In fact, the film's storyline has nothing to do with that of the book, yet there are many connections.

The most abundant references are small, varied allusions scattered throughout the film, but present nonetheless. Some are cryptic (for example, in the novel, the protagonist's father dies, but in the movie, it's his mother), while others are explicit (such as the jar of powdered milk brought to the villa). There are lots of little details that someone who has read the novel can enjoy finding.

But as much fun as it is to spot these micro-references, it's absolutely impossible to ignore the most important macro-reference: The book itself appears in the film. Mahito finds and reads it toward the end of the first part, that of the World Above. The work moves him to tears, and it is precisely the reading of the book that prompts the boy to change his attitude toward Natsuko; she is first treated coldly, then recognized as worthy of being treated with the same affection as he is. As the poet sings, "I am human and I need to be loved, just like everybody else does." Yoshino's book is a kind of atypical coming-of-age novel, which in no way leads the protagonist to realize that he is special or better than others, to see any individualistic value in himself, or to achieve any specific dreams, but instead celebrates the unity of all humanity as the ultimate richness of humankind: to feel a part of something greater that touches us all, to never feel superior, but to see in everyone a singular value that is no less important than our own, above and beyond any social, economic, geographical, ethnic, or other differences. This is a unique text, especially considering the cultural context in which it was published, namely the highly ideological and militarized Japan of 1937.[30]

In one of the pages written to the main character, Co-per-kun, a middle-school student, by his uncle, the man says, "If you think about it, every day, you're nothing but a 'consumer' of things, from the indispensable to the superfluous, and you don't produce anything tangible. Yet, even if you don't realize it, every day you produce something else in large quantities. What is it? [...] As human beings, we absolutely must think about the answer to this question."

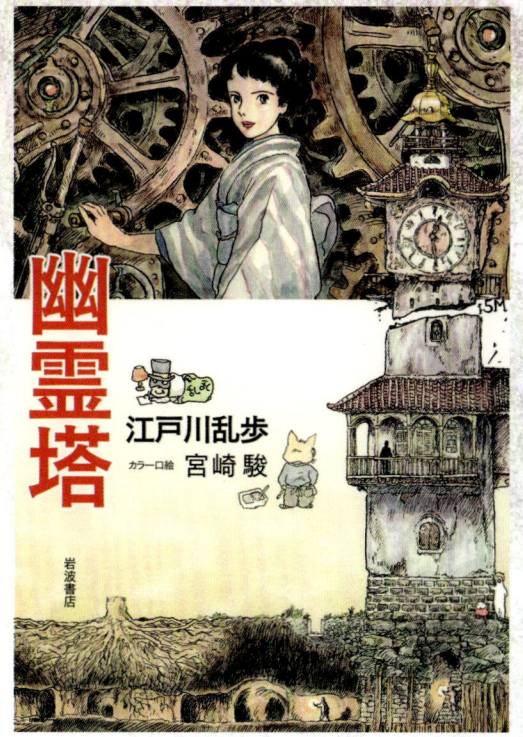

The answer is surely not money, power, or consumer goods, but love. In another passage, written to his nephew and his friends who want to become powerful like Napoleon Bonaparte to get back at the bullies who are harassing them, the uncle writes in praise of the military man's impressive social and political rise, and paradoxically concludes with, "For all his vital energy, what did Napoleon really achieve?"

The answer is that, compared to humankind's long journey on Earth, nothing at all. Twenty years of fleeting fortune and power, ending in a miserable death on a miserable island. *Sic transit gloria mundi*.[31] What was the point of killing all those wretches in all those battles? Nothing. Let's try, as we all head toward the same conclusion (death), to behave with kindness and love for our fellow humans, for a fuller, richer, happier experience of life. And that is why Mahito chooses to love Natsuko, even though she is not his real mother.

In this sense, the film's title is particularly important, as it is not a summary of the plot, but rather a direct question that Miyazaki is asking viewers; in fact, one that he has always asked viewers: "How do you live?"

---

30. Kenneth G. Henshall, *Storia del Giappone*, Mondadori, Milan, 2017.
31. Thus passes the glory of the world.

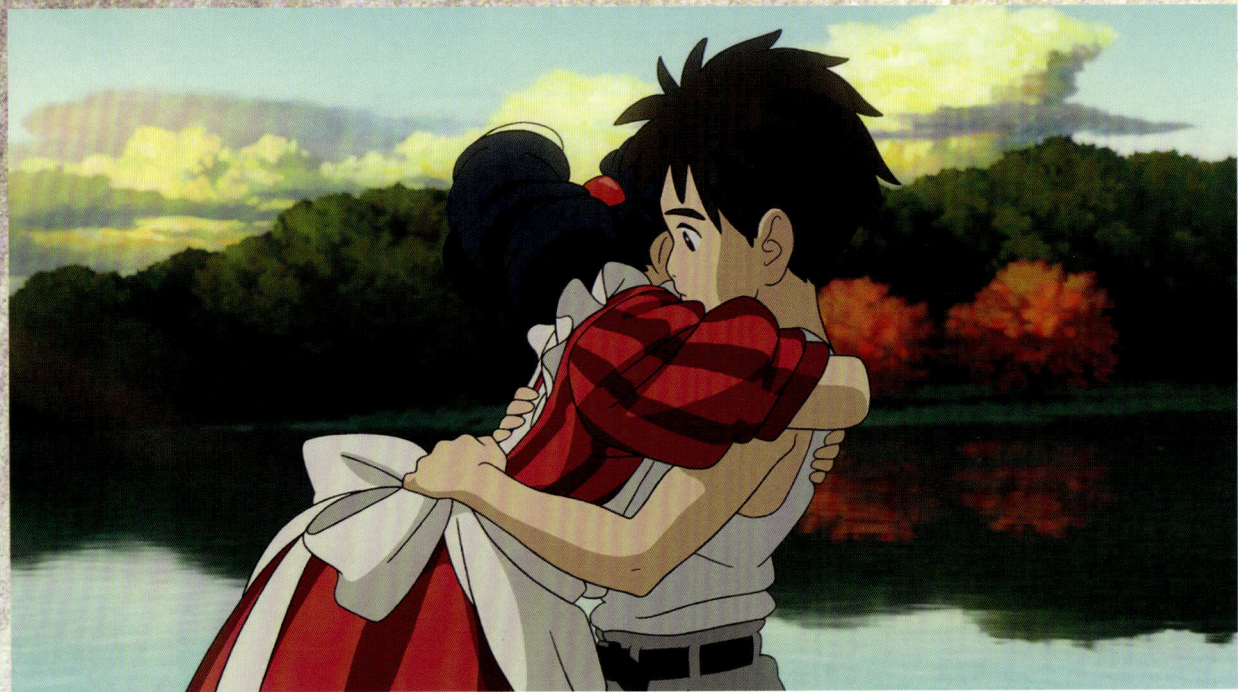

In the North American version, the title *The Boy and the Heron* was preferred, and it was subsequently adopted in other Western languages. Perhaps this is a reference to Paul Grimault's iconic film *The King and the Mockingbird*, which both Miyazaki and Takahata adored.[32] It's not a bad title, but it loses the feeling of direct address, or even of the direct relationship between director and audience, giving the impression that the film is about a boy and a heron. This is reductive; it's a story about choosing how to live. The plot is a pretext, a gigantic Hitchcockian MacGuffin,[33] and the scene in which Mahito confesses that he lied is the one that really sustains the whole film. Paradoxically, *The Boy and the Lie* would have been a better title (especially as "lie" is *sagi* in Japanese, a homophone of "heron," so it would have been perfect).

As for Walt Disney, it is easy to spot several references in the film to the visual world of Disney's animated features. Miyazaki and Disney have shown a totally complementary attitude in the way they relate to and understand cinema in general and animation in particular.[34] Although the Japanese filmmaker has been critical of the Disney studio's output from the 1980s onward,[35] he has never expressed a negative view of the American film-maker and the works produced during his lifetime, stressing that Disney was a producer and he himself was an animator, like the Nine Old Men,[36] for whom he has enormous respect.[37] There are actually small but significant similarities between the pre-1966 Disney classics and Studio Ghibli's films, particularly in terms of specific technical solutions.

In *The Boy and the Heron*, there are references to at least two elements of Disney's imaginary world: Snow White and Alice. In both cases, the references are more to the original texts (the Grimm brothers' fairy tale and Lewis Carroll's novels) than to the American films, but some details, such as the characterization of the seven old women as the seven dwarfs (where Kiriko would be Grumpy) and the descent into the World Below/Wonderland with its very Disney-like parakeets could be somewhat veiled references.

In conclusion, *The Boy and the Heron* offers such a wealth of ideas, readings, interpretations, stratifications, and literary, cinematographic, architectural, artistic, and cultural leads in general, that it surprises the viewer and establishes itself as the most complex film in Miyazaki's entire filmography. An extraordinary finale to an extraordinary career.

32. 高畑勲監督が語る映画「王と鳥」 先見的で、きわめて今日的 on the official Studio Ghibli website | www.ghibli-museum.jp/outotori/takahata/.

33. A method popularized by Alfred Hitchcock that involves using a concept, object, place, etc., as a motivator to advance the plot, without having any intrinsic meaning or value.

34. Mario Pasqualini, "Disney e Miyazaki attraverso lo specchio – La natura" on *Dimensione Fumetto*, June 30, 2016 | www.dimensionefumetto.it/dem01/.

35. Post from May 29, 2020, on *DVDizzy Forum* | www.dvdizzy.com/forum/viewtopic.php?t=33551.

36. Studio mainstays from the 1920s to 1980s.

37. "悪人を倒せば世界が平和になるという映画は作らない 宮崎" on *ITmedia Business*, November 27, 2008 | www.itmedia.co.jp/makoto/articles/0811/27/news004_3.html.

MUSIC AND MASTERS

As in (almost) all Miyazaki films, the soundtrack here includes instrumental pieces composed by Joe Hisaishi and existing songs or songs written for the occasion, notably Kenshi Yonezu's song "Chikyuugi," which is used for the end credits. The two musicians had previously collaborated in the same roles for Ayumu Watanabe's 2019 film *Children of the Sea*.

Hisaishi's contribution emphasizes the film's division into two parts. In the first, realistic section, the accompaniment is extremely sparse in instrumentation, dominated by numerous solo piano pieces, and almost clumsy at times, with melodies often reduced to two notes, or even a single note in the case of the heron character's introductory leitmotif. In the film's second, more dreamlike section, the themes soften, and the musical arrangement is enriched by ethereal orchestral textures, in keeping with the style to which audiences have become accustomed.

The end result differs considerably from the composer's previous works for Miyazaki. If you listened to it independently of the film's images, it could

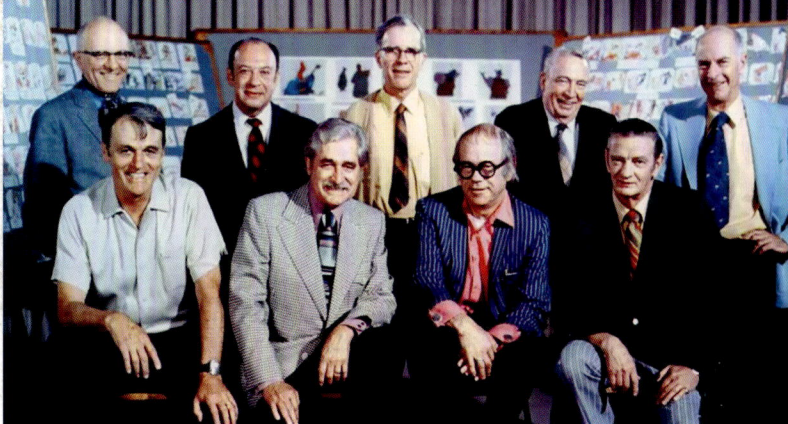

almost seem like a concert for piano and orchestra, so predominant is the solo instrument, and it would be hard to imagine this music as a movie soundtrack. Yet, as always, Hisaishi's music fits perfectly with Miyazaki's images: an unconventional soundtrack for an unconventional film.

Although Yonezu's work differs from his previous creations, it is still brilliant. The singer, formerly an innovative composer for the voice synthesizer Vocaloid under the pseudonym Hachi, has talked about being personally chosen by Miyazaki himself after he heard him on the radio singing "Paprika," a 2018 children's song he wrote, performed by the multicultural group Foorin for NHK's *Minna no Uta* program. It was used as a leitmotif to celebrate the arrival of 2020 and the Tokyo Olympics. "Paprika" was—and still is—a resounding success, and virtually every child in Japan, from kindergarten to high school, knows the words and choreography by heart.

After the tremendous success of "Paprika," Yonezu instantly rose from young pop hopeful to Japan's number one new star. Since 2018, Yonezu has written around seventeen songs for TV series, films, video games, and specials, including "Umi no Yurei" for the film *Children of the Sea*, "M87" for the film *Shin Ultraman*, and "KICK BACK" for the anime series *Chainsaw Man*.

The Nine Old Men.
From left to right, top row: Milt Kahl, Marc Davis, Frank Thomas, Eric Larson, and Ollie Johnston.
From left to right, bottom row: Woolie Reitherman, Les Clark, Ward Kimball, and John Lounsbery.

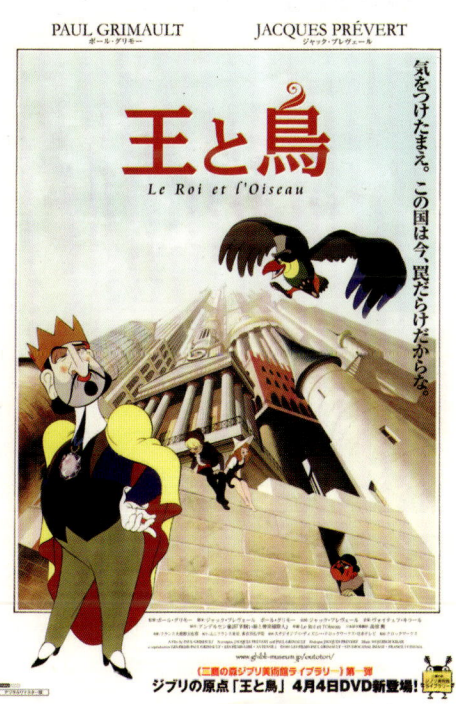

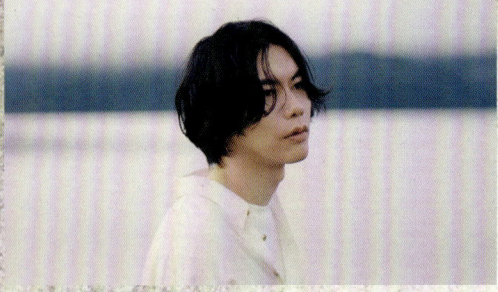

Kenshi Yonezu. D.R.

"Chikyuugi" was written in 2019, before many of the songs mentioned, and today it "sounds nostalgic" to its own creator.[38] Directly inspired by the film, the singer said he wrote the lyrics after reading the five volumes of storyboards (!!!) provided by Miyazaki. The title itself means "globe," once again emphasizing the *sekai-kei*. It features an unusually sparse arrangement for Yonezu (the instrumentation includes only voice and piano accompanied by bagpipes, percussion, and backup vocals) and incorporates ambient sounds, such as the creaking of the piano seat.

Musically, it's another barcarole, a form often used by the musician, with a refrain reminiscent of a nursery rhyme: It takes some time to get it into your head, but once it's there, it stays there.

The physical version of the single includes a small 160-page booklet and a Miyazaki illustration for the film on the cover, a considerable bonus.

The book features many photos by Tomohiko Ishii that show the song's creative process: Yonezu contacted by Miyazaki and Suzuki, Yonezu reading the storyboards (the cover of the first volume, containing shots 1 to 220, bears the layout board depicting the fire that was also on Giovanni Mirabassi's album *Mitaka Calling*), Yonezu composing with his guitar while reading the storyboards, Yonezu presenting the song lyrics to Miyazaki and Suzuki, Miyazaki and Suzuki pleased and touched, and the film's end-of-production party with Joe Hisaishi, Miyazaki, Suzuki, and Yonezu sharing a barrel of sake. A cross-interview between Suzuki and Yonezu and the song lyrics complete the book.

In short, the soundtrack is rather different from those of Miyazaki's other works but is nonetheless highly polished and perfectly in tune with the film.

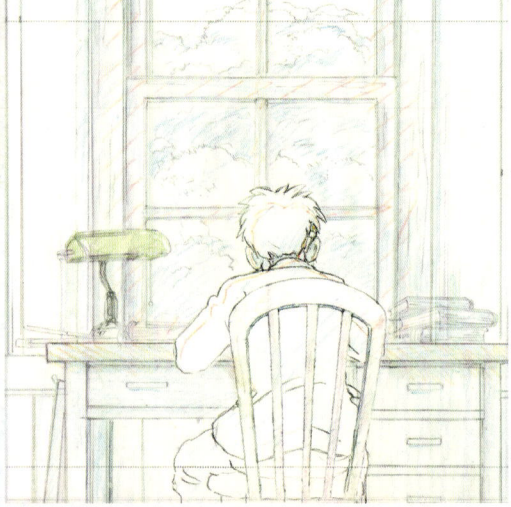

"Chikyuugi" (Known internationally as "Spinning Globe").

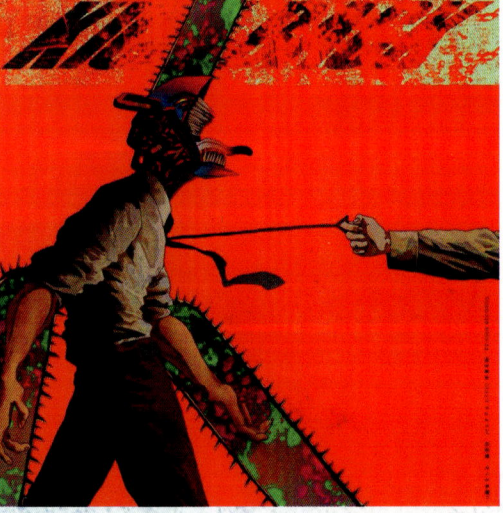

"KICK BACK."

38. Kenshi Yonezu, tweet from July 14, 2023 | https://twitter.com/hachi_08/status/1679685709232484352.

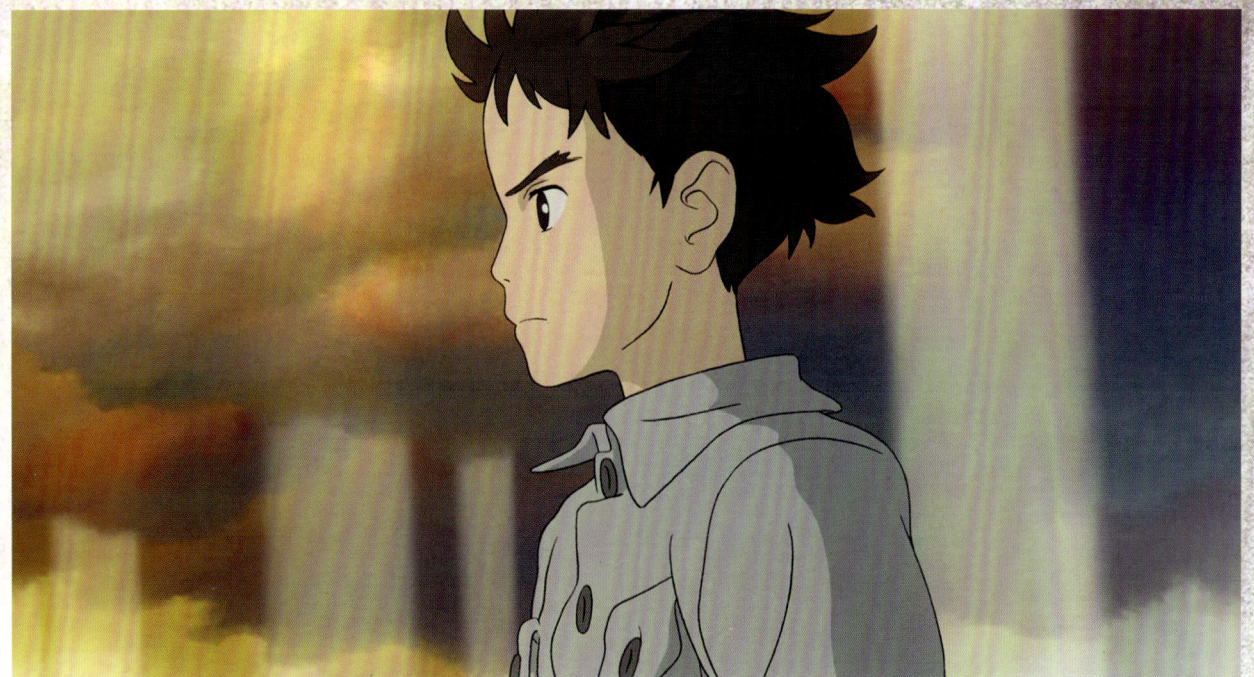

A NEW LIFE

Sixty years, twelve films, five phases, countless contrasts, and a single message: Life is worth living, and to do that, you must choose to live it. Is this a mundane message? Absolutely not. Every day, every person faces countless problems that can make the world and life seem more difficult than they really are.

At eighty-two years of age, sixty of which have been spent at the work table, Miyazaki has given us what some speculated might be his final film, a declaration of love for life, and therefore also for nature, for peace, for individual and collective rights, for equality, for all the principles he has believed in and constantly fought for without ever backing down, to the point of sometimes being controversial or dubbed an idealistic old man, which he has never been and never will be, whatever his age.

The Boy and the Heron brings Hayao Miyazaki's artistic cycle to a close, and for that reason alone, it deserves to be celebrated, and the man recognized as a director who could have retired with an "easy" film, but chose to make such a rich, thoughtful, well-structured one. He took the risk of making what could become his most complex, studied, even representative film, but also his most controversial. Yet this is also a sign of vitality and marked innovation throughout his career, and even beyond. If Chinese numerology is any indication, he could now be embarking on a new cycle of life and art. Who knows?

In the film's final shot, Mahito closes a door behind him and moves on, continuing with his life. The credits do not include the word *End*: This is the first and only Miyazaki film that has no ending, looking eternally toward the future.

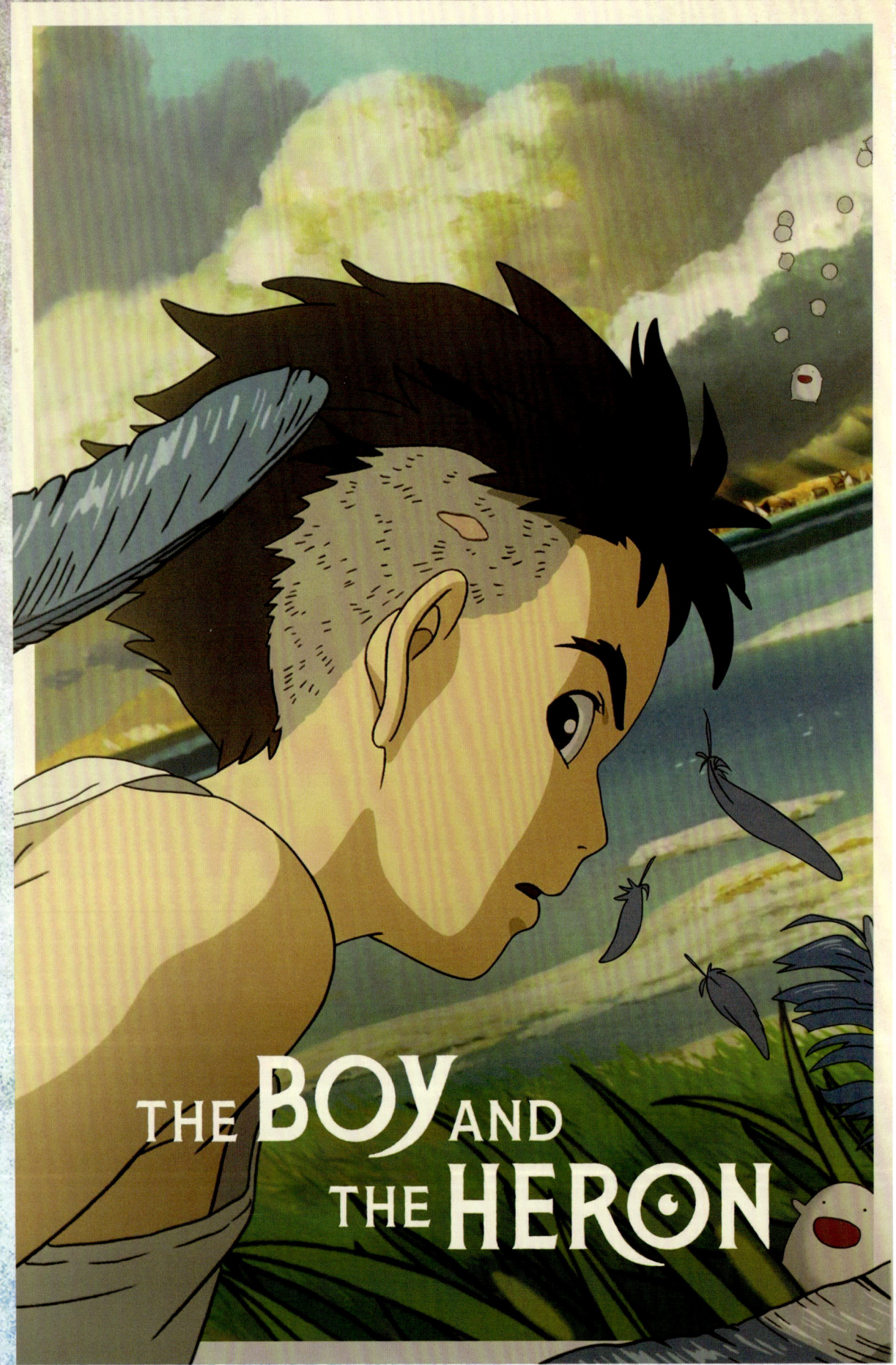

THE GHIBLI SUCCESSORS

In the face of exponential production growth, most studios are gradually being reduced to the role of service providers, losing their uniqueness. Built on strong artistic and structural convictions, Studio Ghibli has maintained its policy of producing little but (very) well. Toshio Suzuki, Hayao Miyazaki, and Gorô Miyazaki remain the only forces capable of carrying the studio forward since the death of Isao Takahata. But for how long?

By Bruno de la Cruz

The question of the succession of the Ghibli style raises a number of relatively broad issues, not least of which is the very definition, the dogma, of the Ghibli school. Is this style ultimately reflected in Hayao Miyazaki's films, Isao Takahata's films, the themes addressed, or the studio's technical approach? It's a huge question. In Japan, the longevity of an artistic trend is not the prerogative of a single structure, relying more than ever on intertextuality and influence between works and artists. Just as Gainax (*Neon Genesis Evangelion*, *Gurren Lagann*) was collapsing, Trigger (*Kill la Kill*) was born, perpetuating the school of limited, stylized, referential, uninhibited animation in the wake of animator and director Hiroyuki Imaishi. For Ghibli, which has been copied more than once, the question arose almost belatedly with the 2015 launch of Studio Ponoc.

STUDIO PONOC: THE GOOD STUDENT

While there remains a gap in terms of quality, the relationship between Studio Ghibli and Studio Ponoc is obvious, given that the latter was co-founded by producer Yoshiaki Nishimura (*The Tale of the Princess Kaguya*, 2013) and director Hiromasa Yonebayashi (born in 1973), one of Ghibli's rising talents. After working as a solid animator and co-directing the *My Neighbor Totoro* spinoff *Mei and the Kittenbus* (2002), he became lead director of *The Secret World of Arrietty* (2010) and the excellent *When Marnie Was There* (2014). But success was not to be. With *Mary and the Witch's Flower* (2017), Studio Ponoc's first film, Yonebayashi unabashedly invoked his training studio ("to make an animated film with techniques acquired at Ghibli," he said at the time of the film's release), garnering praise from Miyazaki himself. In the wake of the superb omnibus *Modest Heroes*[1] (2018) and its 2023 film, *The Imaginary* (directed by

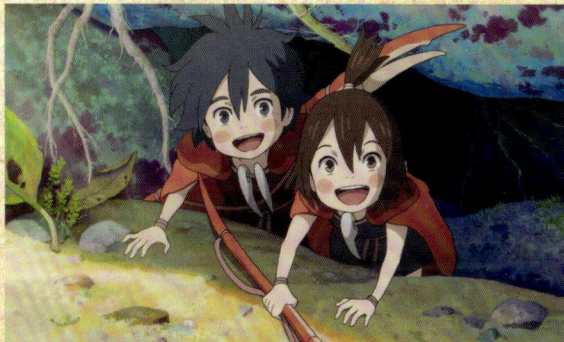
Modest Heroes

Yoshiyuki Momose, another Ghibli contributor), Studio Ponoc combines reality and fantasy with technical skill[2] and a universal message that bring it somewhat closer to Studio Ghibli in the great wave of good-natured, accessible Japanese animated films that have flooded the market over the last ten years.

MISSED OPPORTUNITIES

Masaaki Yuasa (born in 1965, *Lu over the Wall*), Keiichi Hara (born in 1959, *Colorful*), and Makoto Shinkai (born in 1973, *Your Name*) have often been heralded as the new Miyazakis by distributors looking for a bankable benchmark, but they in no way represent an extension of Ghibli cinema.

[1.] It features three short films linked by the care with which they were produced: *Invisible*, the jewel in the trio's crown, was directed by the brilliant animator Akihiko Yamashita (*Spirited Away*, *The Wind Rises*). It tells the story of a man made invisible by society. *Kanini & Kanino*, written and directed by Hiromasa Yonebayashi, tells the story of a family of crab children. Finally, Yoshiyuki Momose directed *Life Ain't Gonna Lose*, a human drama that raises awareness of the danger of food allergies. Incidentally, the producer also wanted Isao Takahata to direct a short film.

[2.] Studio Ponoc is close to the studio Dehogallery, which is responsible for producing backgrounds. Founded by Yoshiaki Nishimura, Nobuo Kawakami, and Hideaki Anno in 2015, Dehogallery is made up of artists who worked with Ghibli and is advised by veteran art directors Kazuo Oga and Yôji Takeshige.

Yuasa is attached to convoluted storytelling and visual experiments, Hara would like to return to live action after *The Wonderland* (2019), and Shinkai (with the exception of 2011's *Children Who Chase Lost Voices*) offers tales that are too contemporary and urban. Ironically, it was Makoto Shinkai's poaching of the regular Studio Ghibli talent Masashi Andô (born in 1969) for the character design of *Your Name* that won over the general public. Andô also co-directed the adaptation of *The Deer King* (2021), a fantasy novel by Nahoko Uehashi, whose graphic design inevitably evokes *Princess Mononoke*. In reality, apart from Yonebayashi and possibly Hiroyuki Okiura (born in 1966 and director of 2011's *A Letter to Momo*), the Ghibli succession had two names: Yoshifumi Kondô (1950–1998) and Mamoru Hosoda (born in 1967). Kondô died of a ruptured aneurysm at the age of forty-seven while in the middle of production on *Princess Mononoke* (see this book's article "A Time of Recognition"), while Hosoda, who had always dreamed of Ghibli, had to jump ship during the (stormy) production of *Howl's Moving Castle* (2004). However, the former employee of Toei Animation (a studio for all audiences) has an interesting profile: His films are spectacular and have succeeded in combining science fiction and fantasy to create initiatory journeys that appeal to everyone. He has been creating steadily for the past ten years with his Studio Chizu.

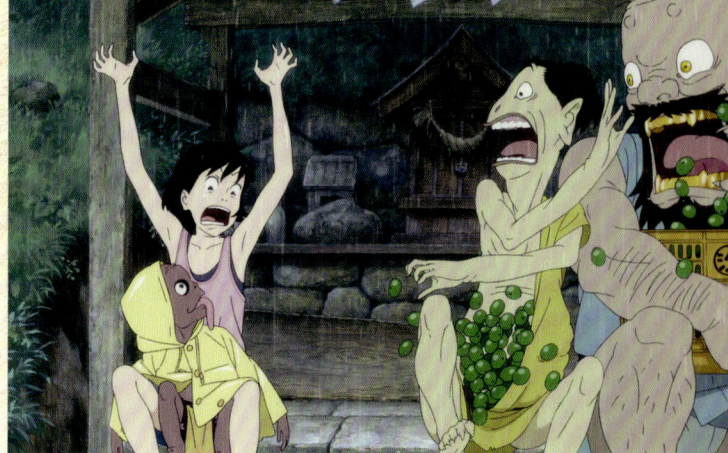
A Letter to Momo

will hold, especially as his decision-making power remains predominant.[3] Not to mention that, in the wake of the retirement of the great producer Masao Maruyama (co-founder of Madhouse and founder of MAPPA studios), the question of Toshio Suzuki's successor arises. It's not easy to find a man who is capable of managing strong tempers, identifying talent, providing human and financial resources, and standing up to sponsors and the press.

HIDEAKI ANNO: THE DREAM

The name may come as a surprise, but Hideaki Anno (born in 1960) is ideally suited to lending his talent to Studio Ghibli. For a start, Miyazaki and Anno have a strong friendship and deep respect for each other, with Anno having often worked as an animator for Miyazaki (since *Nausicaä of the Valley of the Wind*, 1984), as well as delivering the voice performance for the lead role in *The Wind Rises* (2013) and having had two of his films produced by Ghibli (*Love & Pop* and *Shiki-Jitsu*). Second, Anno knows how to do it all (write, animate, design, direct) and is familiar with the pressures of a studio (he founded Khara in 2006 to rebuild his iconic *Neon Genesis Evangelion*) and a high-budget production. This would be a wonderful way to come full circle.

More than simply a part of Miyazaki's legacy, Gorô's evolution fills the gaps left by Isao Takahata and Yoshifumi Kondô, and Ghibli's future lies in its approach as a demanding studio. Predictions aside, only Hayao Miyazaki knows what the future

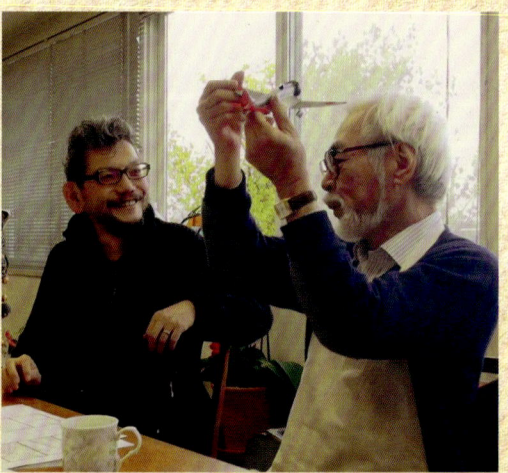
Hideaki Anno and Hayao Miyazaki.

3. In the documentary *Never-Ending Man: Hayao Miyazaki* (2016), he states that he has given up on looking for a successor.

THE MUSICAL REALM

❖

Joe Hisaishi
Ghibli Composers: Cécile Corbel,
Michio Mamiya, Yûji Nomi
Ghibli and Music

JOE HISAISHI

Joe Hisaishi's work is indelibly connected to director Hayao Miyazaki and Studio Ghibli, and it has made him the most famous and popular Japanese composer in the world. But beyond his orchestral and sometimes conventional style, which has been developed largely in Miyazaki's films, lies a much more complex artistic personality, somewhere between music for pictures, musical experimentation, and pure classicism.

By Romain Dasnoy

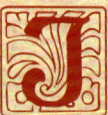oe Hisaishi's career may have exploded in the mid-1980s with the unforgettable and trailblazing *Nausicaä of the Valley of the Wind*, but it took root a few years earlier, emerging in a surprisingly wide variety of genres and sometimes extreme approaches.

Introduced to music at an early age, Mamoru Fujisawa (Hisaishi's real name) began his career in the 1970s when, as a young man, he produced his first events on the Japanese underground scene. These evolved around the idea of a certain cultural revival for Japan, which then inevitably involved music and breaking with traditional conventions, with an eye to the West. The 1970s in Japan were a time of industrialization and globalization and synonymous with rebuilding identity, particularly after the student revolts in Tokyo in 1968.

At the movies, auteurs such as Hiroshi Teshigahara (*Woman in the Dunes*) and Yoshishige Yoshida (*Eros*

+ Massacre) completely redefined the notion of narrative, bringing it ever closer to that of the West. Later, the emergence of electronic groups, such as Ryûichi Sakamoto's Yellow Magic Orchestra with its epic, hallucinatory covers of Martin Denny and the Beatles, turned the music industry on its head.

> *"A surprisingly varied career, in terms of genres explored and his approaches"*

It was in this pursuit of transfigured aesthetics that Joe Hisaishi began his career, moving between electronic and acoustic music. His first two studio albums were collaborations with the Mkwaju Ensemble (*Mkwaju*, 1981) and the Wonder City Orchestra (*Information*, 1982), with Hisaishi conducting and composing. His third studio album arrived three years later, signed "Joe" and entitled *a-Bet-City*. Composed around the time of his first work for animation, such as *Amazing Sarutobi* and *Genesis Climber Mospeada*, Joe Hisaishi's first personal works are surprising in more ways than one: Far removed from the lofty orchestral flights heard in his later music for animated films, his early compositions are more reminiscent of musicians such as Steve Reich or, at the other extreme, of electro-pop with uninspired lyrics. This approach, with its often minimalist and heavily electronic elements, is one of the most interesting facets of the Japanese composer, who was clearly torn between his true musical identity and the need to produce commercial pieces in line with the times.

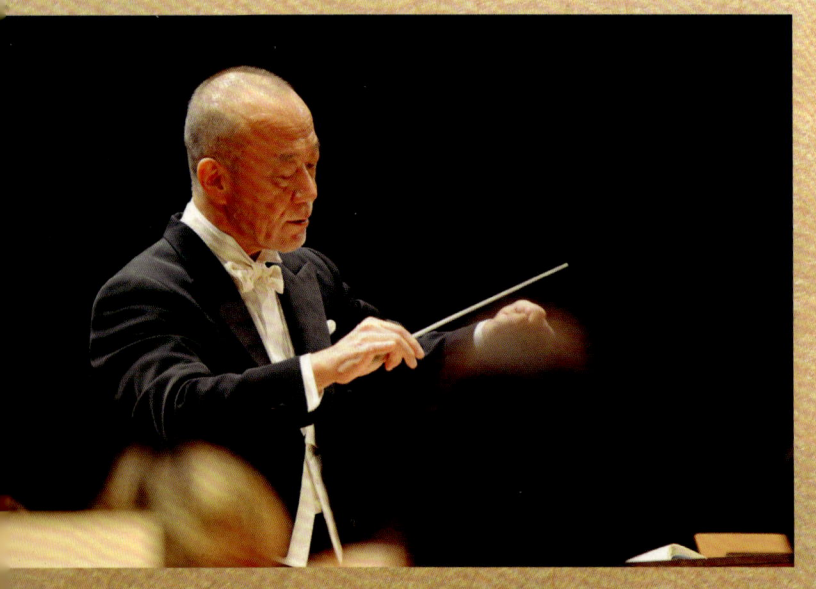

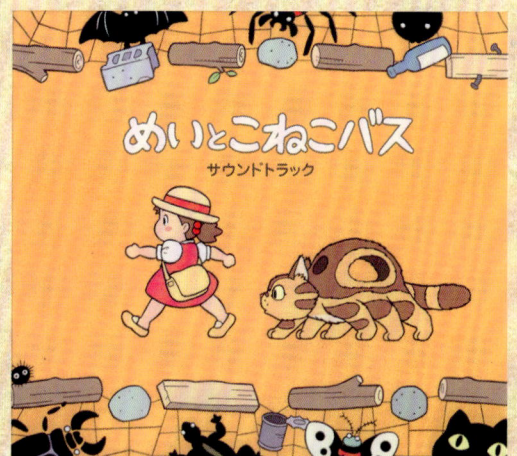

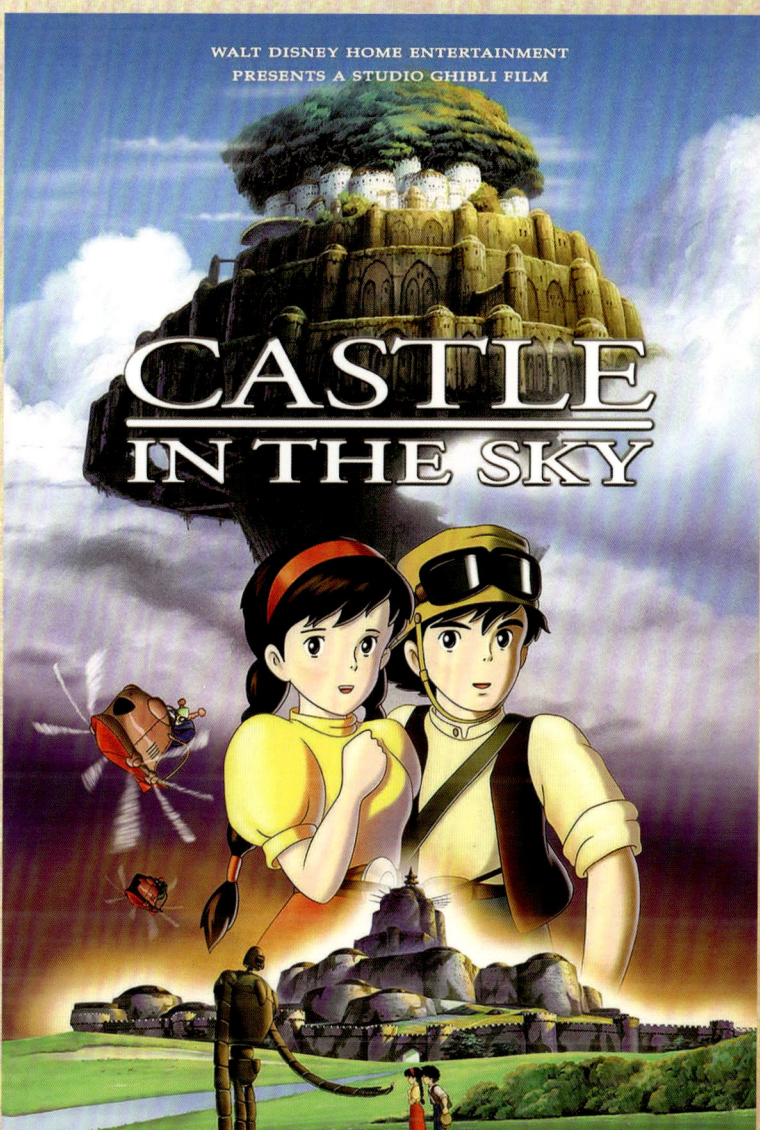

TAKEOFF

"I arrived in a large room, where there was nothing but a table, a chair, and a gentleman sitting there, looking a little lost," Joe Hisaishi recalls of his first meeting with Hayao Miyazaki[1]. "He began to explain the story, the characters [...], even getting up on his chair to show me what was going to happen! I was really fascinated, watching him and thinking what an unusual guy he was."

In 1984, while working for the Victor Entertainment and Tokuma Japan labels, Joe Hisaishi was approached by the producers of Hayao Miyazaki's second film, *Nausicaä of the Valley of the Wind*. This meeting gave rise to a forty-year collaboration that would have a lasting impact on the entire film industry. The *Nausicaä* score would be one of the most flamboyant of their careers. Divided between electronic and orchestral music, *Nausicaä*'s soundtrack subtly blends classical influences with the more electric sounds of the time, for a finished product with a wide range of colors and emotions. This collaboration, on similar artistic terms, continued in 1986 with *Castle in the Sky* and with *My Neighbor Totoro* two years later. Due to health problems, Joe Hisaishi continued to work extensively with computers on *Totoro*, calling on the orchestra for support only very sparingly.

During these years, Hisaishi was increasingly in demand, with anime themes, commercials, and documentaries, as well as many arrangements and original compositions for increasingly significant titles, such as the animated films *Robot Carnival* in 1987 and *Venus Wars* in 1989, the live-action film *Maison Ikkoku – Apartment Fantasy* in 1986, and NHK's famous series of CGI documentaries on the human body from 1989 to 1997.

At the same time, his solo career took him to increasingly surprising territory, as evidenced by the 1989 album *Pretender*. Somewhere between jazz, pop, and New Age and featuring covers of old songs and sounds from previous films (notably the audio samples from a Pygmy tribe used in *My Neighbor Totoro*), the album is a marvelous reminder of a time when the composer was still searching for the right tone.

After several top-quality documentaries, the dawn of the 1990s enabled Joe Hisaishi to not only manage his productions better, but also to gain further recognition with an encounter that changed his way of thinking about music.

[1] Interview by Olivier Fallaix and Ilan Nguyên, *AnimeLand* Special Issue No. 3 (2000).

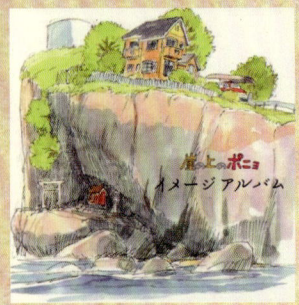
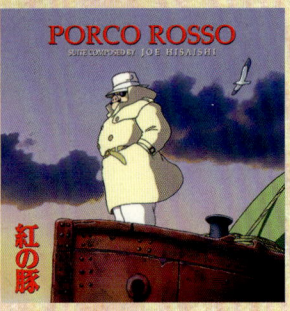
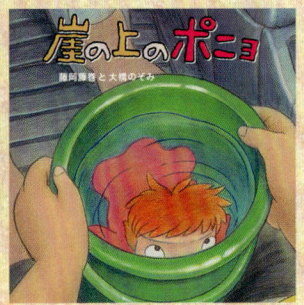
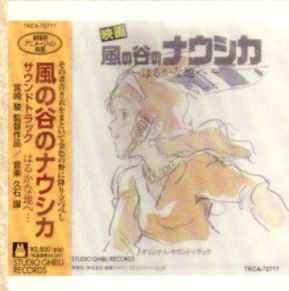

THE MYTHICAL COLLABORATION

"When I'm making a film, I always have the verb 'hone' in mind, and I keep pestering the composer to write music in that spirit. Joe not only indulges this whim, but also composes music that brings out the images in my film. Each of his scores crystallizes my film, giving it its own flavor."
—Takeshi Kitano, about Joe Hisaishi[2]

An exceptional figure on the Japanese audiovisual scene, Takeshi Kitano began directing in 1989 after Kinji Fukasaku stepped down as the director of *Violent Cop*; the movie's reception was negative. His third feature, 1991's *A Scene at the Sea*, was shot, edited, and ready for release but had a real aesthetic problem: It wasn't an action film, the heroes were hearing impaired and mute, and there wasn't a note of music. The film's production team called in Joe Hisaishi.

He himself didn't really understand how he could fit into Takeshi Kitano's very special world.

Watching the film was a huge revelation. Kitano's work was minimalist in style, playing with the frame and off-screen elements, and featured a love story sprinkled with touches of dry humor and a lot of poetry; it perfectly embraced facets that had been difficult for composer Joe Hisaishi to express. The soundtrack, with its variations on Erik Satie, remains one of the most incredible achievements in Japanese cinema, a synergy made all the more astonishing by the fact that it was created after the film was considered complete.

STARDOM

With the rise of globalization, Hayao Miyazaki and Takeshi Kitano crossed continents to present their films at the biggest film festivals in existence. Meanwhile, Joe Hisaishi was increasingly in demand. Formerly very eclectic, he was refocusing on orchestral music with a European touch, clearly identifying his inspirations (Italian with Nino Rota in the late 1980s and early 1990s, like in *Kiki* and *Porco Rosso*; Viennese in the 2000s with a waltz style, as in *Howl's Moving Castle*, *Welcome to Dongmakgol*, and his score for Buster Keaton's *The*

[2.] Comments in the album booklet for *Works I* by Joe Hisaishi (1997).

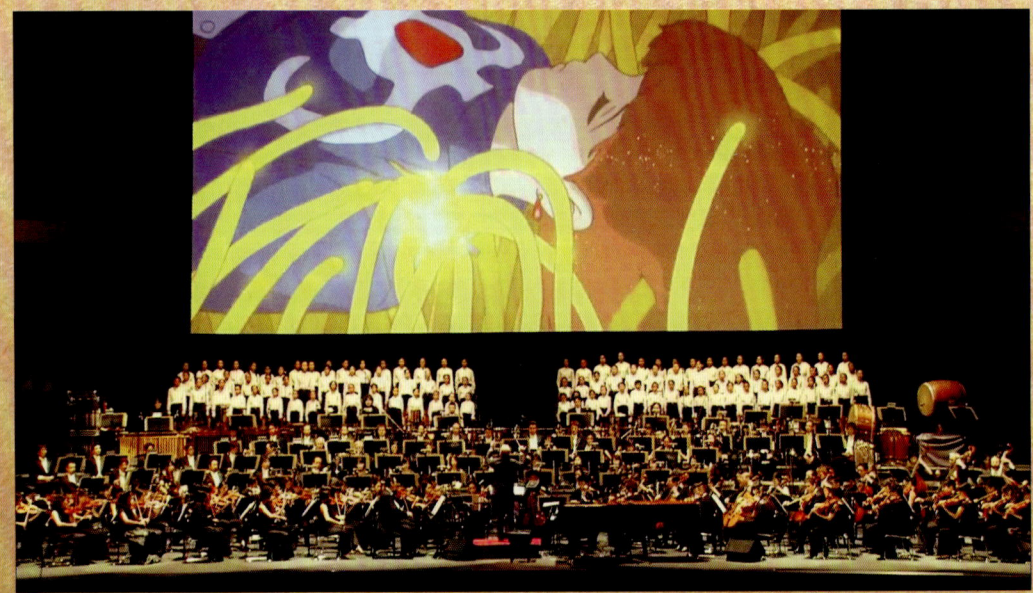

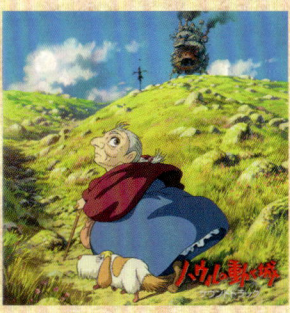 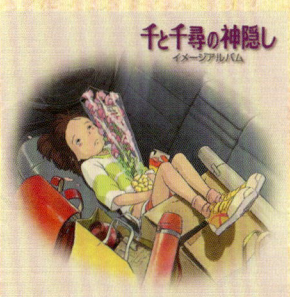 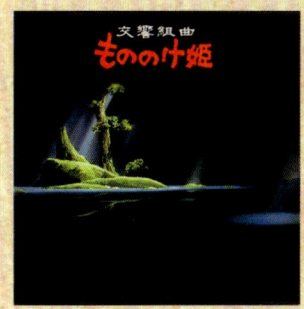 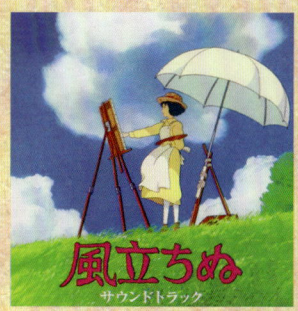

General). Between dazzling concerts featuring his great film scores and more personal albums (*Shoot the Violist* from 2000, *Asian X.T.C.* from 2006, and *Minima_Rhythm* from 2009 are gems of minimalist music), Joe Hisaishi continued to develop his taste for orchestration and the ever-dominant role of the piano. As artistic director of the World Dream Orchestra, he has produced albums that are

> *"Hisaishi produces albums that are veritable declarations of love for Western music."*

veritable declarations of love for Western music, covering George Gershwin, Jerry Goldsmith, John Williams, Lalo Schifrin, and Michel Legrand. The effects of globalization began to make themselves known in the 2000s, when he was called upon for the French film *Tom Thumb*, with a score that was very close to—and often better than—that of *Spirited Away* (both films were released in 2001). He was invited to the Cannes Film Festival in 2004 to rework the music of a Keaton classic. He is also involved in Hong Kong cinema, gives master classes at leading schools, and travels the world to receive awards and give performances; it may well be that Joe Hisaishi, well beyond his collaboration with Hayao Miyazaki, has become one of the most significant composers in the history of Japanese music.

JOE HISAISHI'S WORK FOR STUDIO GHIBLI

★ Hayao Miyazaki film

2023 *The Boy and the Heron*★
2018 *Boro the Caterpillar*★ – short film
2013 *The Tale of the Princess Kaguya*
2013 *The Wind Rises*★
2010 *Ni no Kuni* – video game
2008 *Ponyo*★
2004 *Howl's Moving Castle*★
2003 *Okaasan no Shashin* (*Mother's Photo*) – original album with a track by Hisaishi
2002 *Mei and the Kittenbus*★ – short film
2001 *Spirited Away*★
1997 *Princess Mononoke*★
1992 *Porco Rosso*★
1989 *Kiki's Delivery Service*★
1988 *My Neighbor Totoro*★
1986 *Castle in the Sky*★
1984 *Nausicaä of the Valley of the Wind*★

GHIBLI COMPOSERS: CÉCILE CORBEL, MICHIO MAMIYA, YÛJI NOMI

Music is a crucial element in visual arts (cinema, video games, animation, etc.) and has a special resonance in Studio Ghibli films. The studio's output wouldn't be what it is without Joe Hisaishi. But he's not the only one to have made an impression on viewers: Cécile Corbel, Michio Mamiya, and Yûji Nomi have also made their mark.

By Romain Dasnoy

CÉCILE CORBEL

In 2010, Cécile Corbel, a Celtic singer and harpist from Brittany, France, was chosen to compose the score for Hiromasa Yone-bayashi's *The Secret World of Arrietty.*
Corbel is an exception in the French music world. Since her debut in the mid-2000s, she has accompanied herself on a Celtic harp, a smaller instrument than the classical harp (requiring extra effort on the part of the instrumentalist, who has to operate levers to alter the desired note and obtain semitones). Corbel's repertoire is, of course, Celtic, but she also draws on more continental influences and sings in a number of languages, including Gaelic, English, and Hebrew. For *Arrietty*, Corbel delivered a soundtrack of rare purity and lightness, which was most welcome on this "minor" Studio Ghibli film.

MICHIO MAMIYA

A great name in Japanese music, Michio Mamiya was most closely associated with Isao Takahata on three films, only one of which was for Studio Ghibli. But he's still someone to remember!
At the age of ninety-five, Mamiya was still one of the leading figures of contemporary "classical" music in Japan. His work includes pieces for orchestra, choir, solo instruments such as the piano, and theater. In 1968, he wrote the soundtrack for Isao Takahata's *Horus: Prince of the Sun.* They collaborated again in 1982 for *Gauche the Cellist* and in 1988 on the unforgettable Ghibli production *Grave of the Fireflies.* A persistent rumor claimed that Joe Hisaishi was scheduled for this film but was already busy with a Miyazaki project. Nevertheless, Michio Mamiya remained an exceptional composer with a very refined style. Some of his music is available in Europe on labels like Naxos, although most of his work has never left Japan, either on an album or in concert. Michio Mamiya died on December 11, 2024.

YÛJI NOMI

Little known to the public, and especially to movie fans, Yûji Nomi is a composer who earned his stripes in the 1980s on some excellent productions, particularly with the great Ryûichi Sakamoto.

Nomi keeps a relatively low profile, even in Japan, but he remains a composer of surprising credentials, collaborating with Ryûichi Sakamoto on films such as Bernardo Bertolucci's *The Last Emperor*, series like *Phoenix* (2004, adapted from a manga by Osamu Tezuka), and his two credits at Ghibli. The 1995 film *Whisper of the Heart* and its 2002 sequel, *The Cat Returns*, are clearly not the studio's most popular titles and didn't heighten the composer's profile. But, notably, *Whisper of the Heart* was the first Ghibli film directed by someone other than the two founders, Yoshifumi Kondô. Musically speaking, the experiment was a success, with Yûji Nomi doing extremely well with these two works.

GHIBLI AND MUSIC

Rarely has a studio been as musically identifiable as Ghibli. The recipe is simple on paper: strong emotions, sufficient time to develop ideas, and a masterful genius for melody. Some other studios or composers can boast of making their mark on the industry in this way, but Ghibli remains unique in its relationship with music, distinguishing itself with a powerful authenticity.

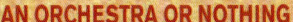 By Romain Dasnoy

J nherited from the late 1960s with the arrival of jazz, where Japan remains an exceptional scene (the legendary composer of *Lupin the Third*, Yûji Ôno, formed a trio with the incredible American drummer Lenny White in the 1970s), electronic music began to make inroads into Japanese animation, mainly for budgetary reasons. But the aesthetic was there and could not be dissociated from this era of creative innovation. Joe Hisaishi, a young composer with a keen interest in new technologies, wrote the music for *Nausicaä of the Valley of the Wind,* combining classical (using Brahms and Handel) and more electronic sounds. These elements would later be featured in 1980s films such as *Castle in the Sky* and *Robot Carnival*. This use of the great names of the classical and baroque repertoire, however, opened a breach that had already been tapped into by Isao Takahata, who a few years earlier had collaborated with Michio Mamiya on the superb, entirely acoustic score for *Gauche the Cellist*, in which the cello is king. *Grave of the Fireflies* adopted the same formula, moving closer than ever to so-called traditional cinema. However, it wasn't until the late 1980s, with *Kiki's Delivery Service*, that Miyazaki and Hisaishi really got into the *Cinema Paradiso* spirit and devoted more time, and even budget, to the essential element of music.

AN ORCHESTRA OR NOTHING

Some of Isao Takahata's films are like musical potpourri: *Only Yesterday, Pom Poko,* and *My Neighbors the Yamadas,* which also feature some unforgettable pieces (the *Yamadas* three-beat "theme" is absolutely wonderful), are social chronicles of varying degrees of realism, rooted in a certain everyday reality that imposes a pluralistic form on the music, which is sometimes directly integrated into the narrative. As

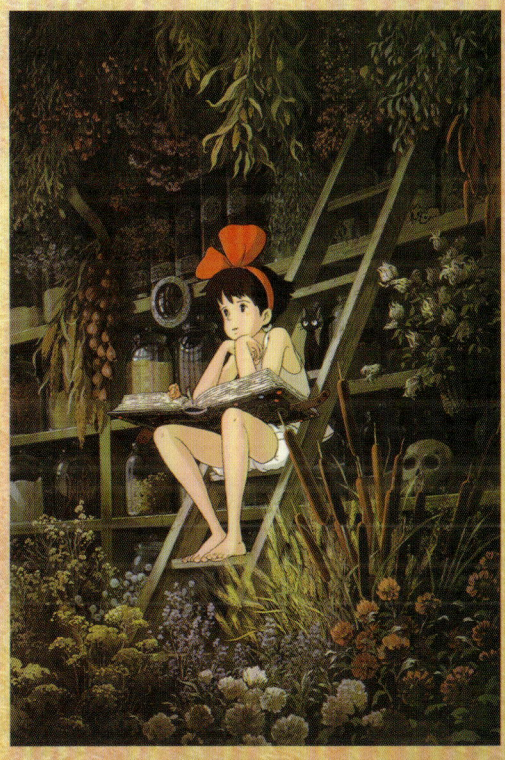

for Hayao Miyazaki, he developed works with very Western overtones, such as *Kiki's Delivery Service* and *Porco Rosso*. This period enabled Joe Hisaishi to paraphrase the European cinema he loved so much, and to write fully orchestral scores with a harmonic development that was distinctly classical in approach. After *My Neighbor Totoro*, which still bore the strong influence of computer-assisted music but was packed with illustrative ideas that were very close to American burlesque cinema where Mei pursues the small Totoros is an ode to Warner Bros. animation), *Kiki* surprises with its classical approach and contrasting themes in a film that is far more artistically ambitious.

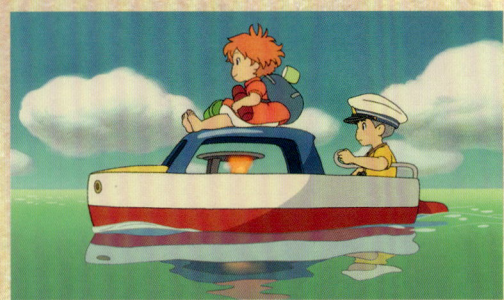

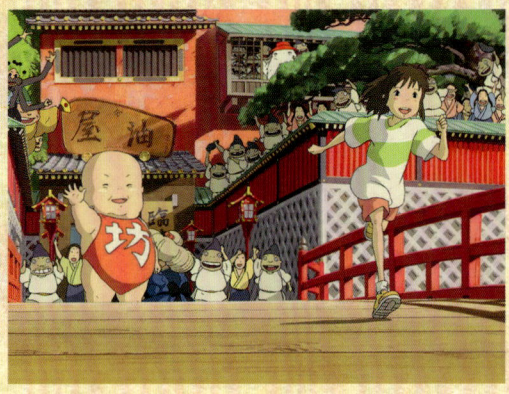

We also note an interesting and unusual use of string instruments (and an ever-increasing fascination with flight, portrayed here with the help of a highly polished orchestration), as well as more typical instruments related to the Italian atmosphere of the film (like mandolin and prepared piano). This knowledge would be developed in Joe Hisaishi's solo work, where he gradually abandoned his desire to make pop albums to develop his passion for the orchestra, and in the inimitable *Porco Rosso*, with its musical devilry full of counterpoint and dissonance, starting with its theme—which is almost reminiscent of a certain John Williams—and its tonal changes worthy of Nino Rota in Fellini's *Amarcord*.

ONGOING AMBITIONS

In the studio's drive to go further and be stronger, *Whisper of the Heart* was like a UFO: a new director, a rather lightweight story that was far removed from

> "It wasn't until Kiki that Miyazaki and Hisaishi dedicated more time to the essential element of music."

Miyazaki's fantasies, and a score that showed a certain aesthetic regression with its virtual instruments and piano with awful reverberations. In 1997, the master got things back on track with Japan's most ambitious animated film, which even received rave reviews from Akira Kurosawa. Heavily influenced by American works such as James Horner's score for *Braveheart*, the *Princess Mononoke* soundtrack, by Joe Hisaishi, doesn't surpass that movie's symphonic vision, but it does reach a pinnacle for music used with images, employing an extraordinary variety of instruments. Miyazaki's next four films upheld the same extremely rigorous quality standards, and composer Hisaishi reinvented his technique, orchestration, and classical references (Wagner in the wave scene in *Ponyo*, Poulenc in

the boiler scene in *Spirited Away*) or more contemporary ones (Horner and his harmonization in *Spirited Away*, John Williams and his orchestration in *Howl's Moving Castle*).

Ghibli offers its viewers two musical trends. On the one hand, there are films that are independent of one another, both aesthetically and narratively, with a wide variety of musical approaches (as in the films of Isao Takahata); on the other, there are the eagerly awaited films of Hayao Miyazaki, whose thematic and literary developments are precisely identified, and who has been working with the same composer for forty years. The latter offers a coherent synergy of aesthetic logic, which has truly changed the way we perceive music in pictures. According to Miyazaki,[1] Hisaishi's music is magnificent, embellishing the images and making them even better. We couldn't agree more!

[1] Comments in the album booklet for *Works I* by Joe Hisaishi (1997).

WHEN GHIBLI TELLS A STORY

>-◄·►-◄

Is There a Ghibli Style?

IS THERE A GHIBLI STYLE?

People often say that there is a Ghibli animation style based on fluid sequences, as opposed to the limited animation from other Japanese studios, but it's undoubtedly more difficult to group the narrative filmmaking of directors as different as Hayao Miyazaki and Isao Takahata—not to mention the studio's other artists—under a single banner. Nevertheless, we're going to attempt to describe the common ground between these stories.

> By Bounthavy Suvilay

While many studios offer feature films adapted from popular *shônen* manga like *Dragon Ball*, *Pokémon*, and other tales of adventure and combat, Ghibli specializes in portraying the evolution of feelings, whether they're emotions linked to love or the discovery of the world. This recurring theme is undoubtedly related to the influence of Isao Takahata, for whom the realistic representation of human behavior was always a central consideration.

SHÔJO AND THE EVOLUTION OF FEELINGS

Most Ghibli films are adaptations of *shôjo*, literature for girls, or sentimental stories. But unlike most other such productions, the studio doesn't use exaggeration or systematic humor to illustrate characters' behavior. Instead, the goal is to make characters believable through the authentic portrayal of various emotions.

For example, the TV movie *Ocean Waves* (1993) was adapted from a story by best-selling novelist Saeko Himuro. It takes a realistic look at the world of Japanese teenagers, following the everyday life of a high school student who spends her time working hard at school to achieve the best possible results so she can apply to Tokyo's prestigious universities. It's not a farcical caricature like the romantic comedy *Maison Ikkoku*, but rather a subtle portrayal of the complexities of love.

Similarly, in *Whisper of the Heart* (adapted from Aoi Hiiragi's *shôjo*), Yoshifumi Kondô cleverly portrays the love affair between the mischievous Shizuku Tsukishima and the mysterious Seiji Amasawa.

They get to know each other after a difficult start, and their mutual admiration drives them to

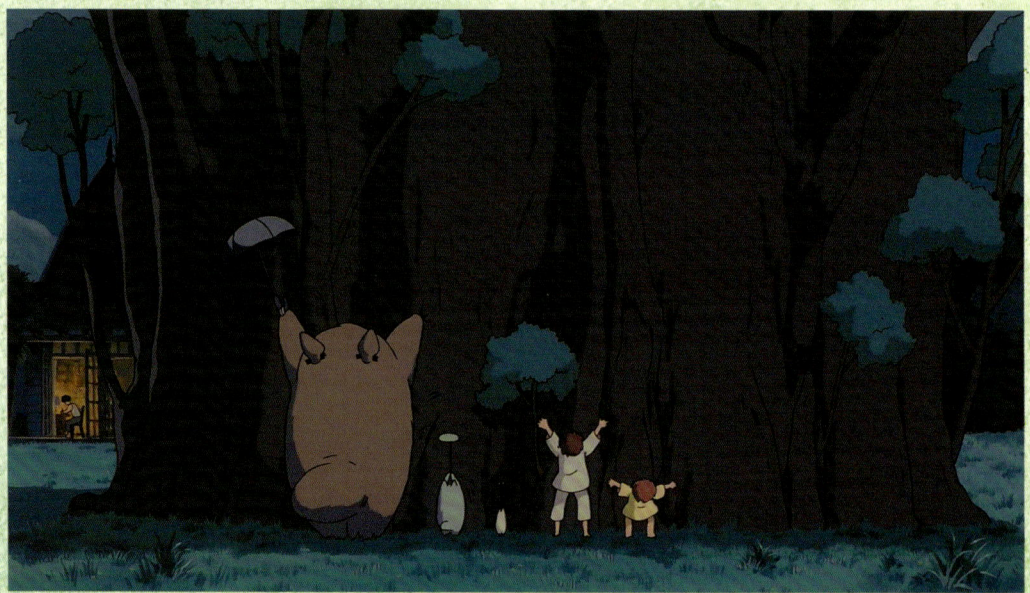

excel in their respective fields. More recently, the couple formed by Umi and Shun in *From Up on Poppy Hill* is made realistic by the sincerity of its dialogue, in which the girl expresses herself honestly and directly. Once again, this is an adaptation of a *shôjo*, with screenwriter Tetsurô Sayama working from the manga created by Chizuru Takahashi.

Perhaps the most striking example of this realism in romantic feelings is Isao Takahata's *Only Yesterday*. Returning to the scenes of her childhood, Taeko Okajima recalls moments spent with her family and rediscovers her history from a different angle. Parallel to her story with Toshio in the present, she recalls the behavior of two boys when she was at school, and better understands how to react to her feelings.

In addition to the beginnings of love, Ghibli stories tend to show the passage to adulthood, or at least to greater independence. These are coming-of-age stories, often centering on a female character. In

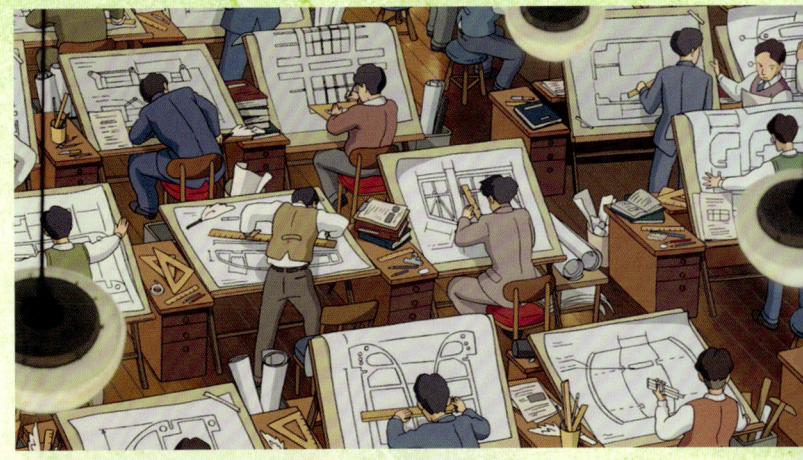

> "Graphics can be extremely stylized without detracting from the realism of the characters."

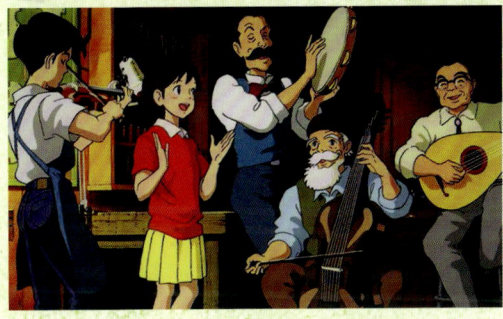

Only Yesterday, young Taeko discovers new activities that take her away from her parents and samples the previously untasted fruit that binds the family together in a shared curiosity and rejection. In *Ponyo*, *Spirited Away*, and *Kiki's Delivery Service*, girls learn to fend for themselves without their parents. In *Kiki*, Miyazaki departed slightly from the original work by Eiko Kadono. Instead of dwelling on the young witch's magical powers and keeping a light tone, the director added more dramatic elements: the loss of her powers and an airship needing rescue at the end of the film. Unlike Takahata, who seemed to strive for a certain restraint in his representations, Miyazaki appears to prefer artifice designed to thrill the audience. While most Ghibli directors aim for a coherent, credible portrayal of their characters' feelings to give them depth, Miyazaki prefers to depict characters in action, and is less interested in describing emotions, as exemplified by his adaptation of Diana Wynne Jones's *Howl's Moving Castle*. He abandons the romantic intrigues of the original work in favor of more visually spectacular representations of metamorphoses and other feats.

This desire for truth in the portrayal of characters can be found in even the most seemingly fanciful films. In *My Neighbors the Yamadas*, Takahata chose a character design that was faithful to the original manga and far removed from photorealism. But

this didn't prevent him from accurately depicting the everyday life of a traditional Japanese family, where the grandparents live with the next generations. Ghibli proves that graphics can be extremely stylized without detracting from the realism of the characters.

IDEALIZED PAST

The realistic depiction of feelings goes hand in hand with almost documentary-like precision in the description of everyday life. In *Only Yesterday*, scenes set in 1966 abound with typical details that plunge Japanese viewers into a nostalgic remembrance of the past. CRT televisions (using cathode ray tubes), old TV programs, and period music all combine to immerse the audience in a bygone Japan. These everyday details can also fascinate Western viewers, who discover ways of life that are both familiar and exotic. Who hasn't been drawn to the Japanese meals in Ghibli films? But above all, Takahata's aim was to portray Japan's transition from a postwar economy to a modern consumer society, when farming is no longer "natural." In many Ghibli films, the artists seem intent on celebrating a past where nature was still respected and mentalities were different, with less focus on mass consumerism. This idealization of the past reinforces the underlying critique of the modern world. Two of Miyazaki's adaptations move the action

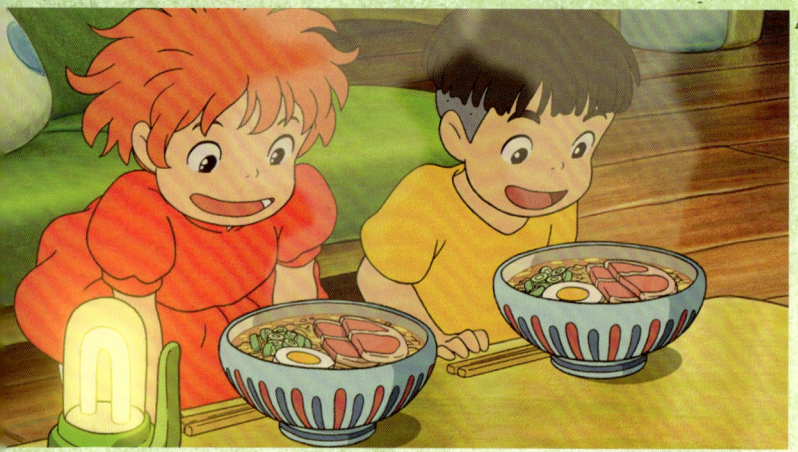

cated the fields and forests surrounding the cities. In *Porco Rosso* and *The Wind Rises*, the director is able to project himself back to his favorite period, when airplanes were still considered technological masterpieces (even though they were formidable weapons of war). Both airplane pilots and creators were heroes, whereas these days, flying is like taking a cab. In the documentary *The Kingdom of Dreams and Madness*, we can see Miyazaki explai-

> *"The artists seem intent on celebrating a past where nature was still respected."*

back in time. In *Howl's Moving Castle*, he erased all hints of the twentieth century, whereas the novel did include some. The European-inspired settings refer to much earlier times. Similarly, by shifting the plot of *Poppy Hill* from the present day to 1963, the elder Miyazaki and his son gave themselves the means to reconstruct the daily life of the period, corresponding to Hayao's first working years as a young man. Here again, the soundtrack provides a nostalgic backdrop, and Japanese audiences can recognize hits from the era. Notable buildings are presented in ways that enhance the sense of reality. This preservation of the past is undoubtedly a far more positive vision than that found in other films. Even in a film as fanciful as *My Neighbor Totoro*, Miyazaki paints a painstakingly realistic picture of a bygone era. Mei and Satsuki discover the Japanese countryside of the 1950s, a time when intensive urbanization had not yet eradi-

ning to his team of animators how people greeted each other in those days, with what he sees as less abrupt manners than today.

Are these films to be seen as the ramblings of aging artists who know they are closer to death than to their youthful past? It's possible. After all, Miyazaki is in his eighties, and Takahata died in 2018, at the age of eighty-two. They met in the 1960s, a time when they were able to dream of a different way of making feature films, and subsequently founded Ghibli. It's probably no coincidence that their films are set in the past or in a fantasy world, as if they were trying to avoid portraying a reality that they found disappointing or troubling.

In *Pom Poko*, Takahata explicitly pays homage to the past with a parade of tanuki transformed into folk characters. Shigeru Mizuki, a specialist in *yokai* (spirits and supernatural phenomena

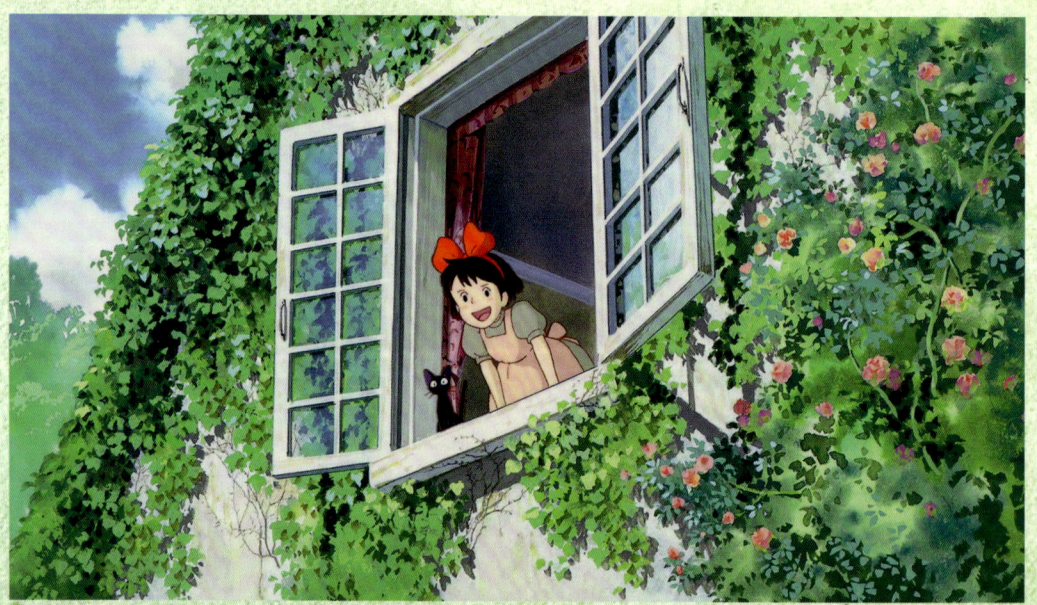

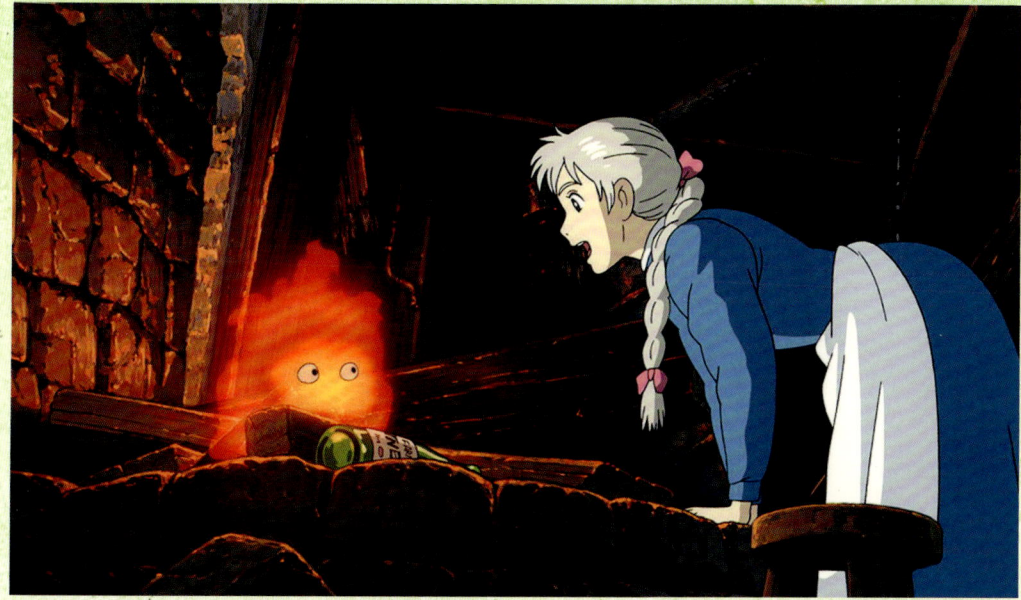

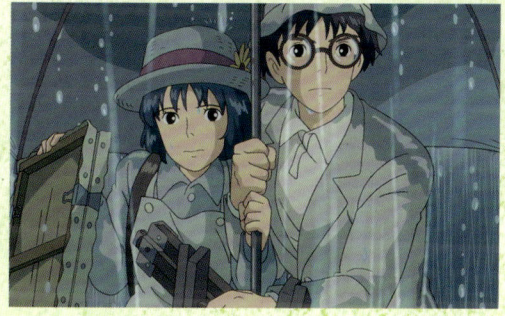

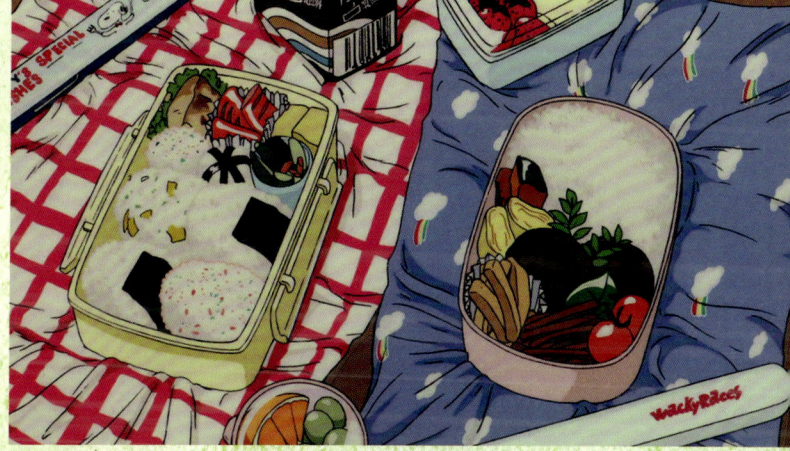

in folktales), was involved in the creation of this "spectral" march, which ends dramatically with the death of one of the sages and commercial exploitation by humans. The wonderful yet bitter sequence no doubt sums up the filmmakers' mixed feelings about modern Japan.

Of course, idealizing the past doesn't mean celebrating war. On the contrary, for Miyazaki and Takahata, animation is a means of denouncing the folly of warring humans. *Grave of the Fireflies*, adapted from Akiyuki Nosaka's short story, allowed Takahata to open with a scathing line: "September 21, 1945; that was the night I died." This initial sequence and the film's conclusion are original creations by the director, which enabled him to heighten the emotional impact of the long suffering of the two orphans in a modern Japan that treats them with indifference and relegates them to misery.

In *The Wind Rises*, Miyazaki created his own version of the historical figure who invented the planes flown by kamikazes during World War II. In his view, Jirô Horikoshi was first and foremost an airplane enthusiast, not a nationalist responsible for thousands of deaths. He wanted to separate technical beauty from human tragedy.

EUROPEAN POSTCARD
Delving into characters' psyches and into the past is often accompanied by a hint of the exotic for Japanese audiences. One could almost say that all Ghibli films follow the formula of Takahata's brilliantly executed *Heidi* series, which is an adaptation of a story for girls set in nineteenth-century Europe. In 1973, Takahata took part of the production team to Switzerland and Germany to scout out the region and gain a better

understanding of Western lifestyles, and to avoid making mistakes in the representation of the girl's daily life in the mountains and the city. The result is a joyful series aimed at a family audience, in which we learn through Heidi's eyes how she lives self-sufficiently in the mountains with her grandfather, feasting on pieces of bread and cheese before rolling in the grass of the Alpine pastures. Her time in the city is sadder but provides an opportunity to depict the daily life of the petty middle class, with its stranglehold of rules. Thanks to the success of the series, Nippon Animation adapted a children's literature classic every year. Takahata went on to produce other series in the collection.

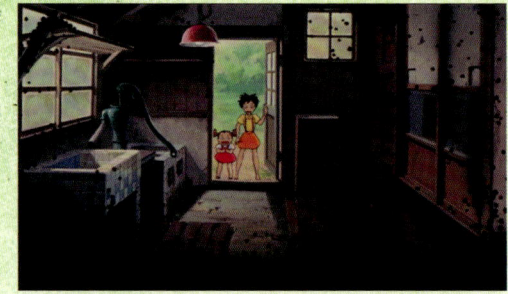

As for Miyazaki, he had worked with his mentor to prepare an adaptation of *Pippi Longstocking* and took the opportunity to make his first trip to the West. He traveled to Sweden to meet the author, who vetoed the project. But the trip wasn't altogether in vain, as the Scandinavian landscapes were later featured in *Kiki's Delivery Service*. To create that film, Miyazaki returned to Sweden with his team to take a maximum number of photos of Stockholm and Visby.

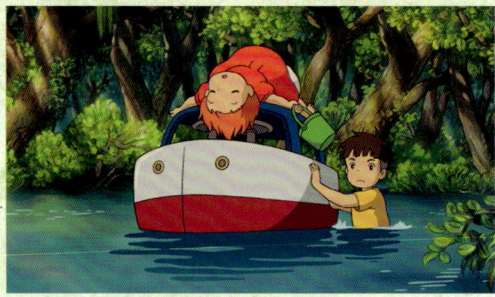

The result is a colorful city that seems to combine all the old-fashioned charms of various European cities in one place. Unlike Takahata, who sought to give a realistic image of daily life in the Alps in the nineteenth century, Miyazaki combined European

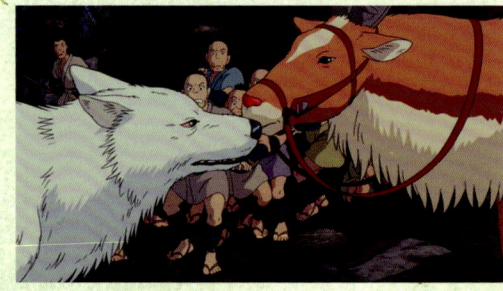

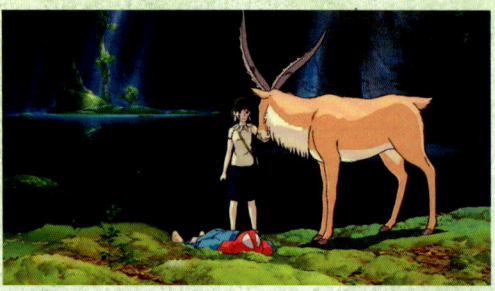

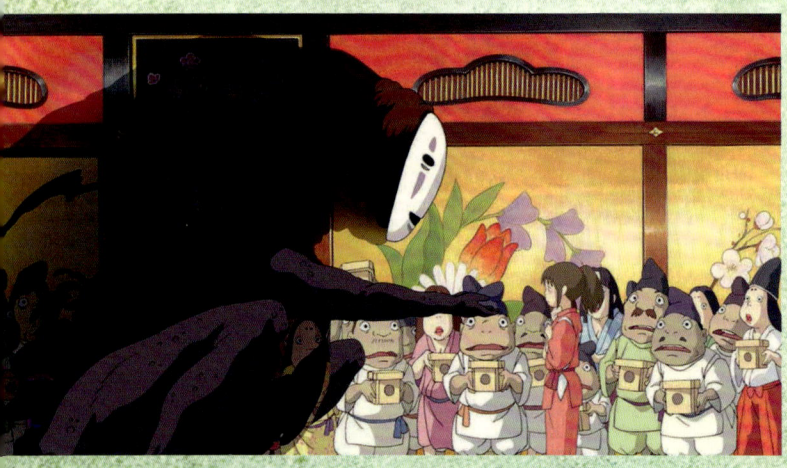

"To create a dreamlike, exotic West for Japanese audiences"

postcards to create a unique, utopian atmosphere. For Western audiences, this is a kind of reverse exoticism. Usually, we find foreign countries, and Japan in particular, exotic. Ghibli is primarily aimed at a Japanese audience, and what's exotic for them is Europe, with its old cities and historic architecture. This desire to create a dreamlike, "exotic" West for Japanese audiences was already present in Miyazaki's previous works: *The Castle of Cagliostro* offered a fanciful variation on Italian mountain towns, while *Castle in the Sky* reinterpreted English mining towns during the Industrial Revolution. For Western audiences, it's a novel change of scenery, inviting them to rediscover familiar elements that have been foreignized by cinematic interpretation. The same slightly familiar yet unreal atmosphere

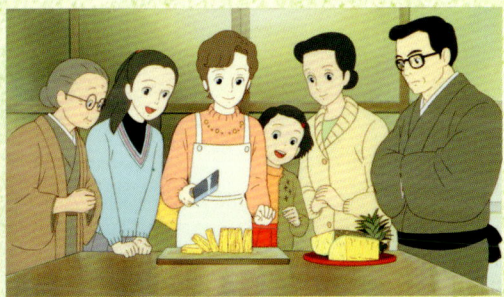

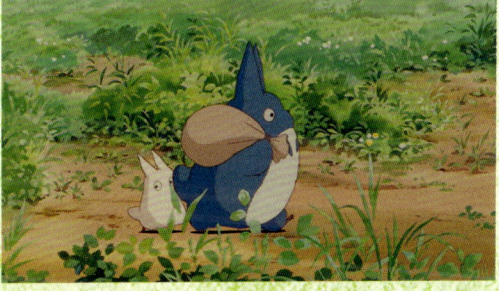

can be found in 1920s Italy in *Porco Rosso* and the transformed French town of Colmar in *Howl's Moving Castle*.

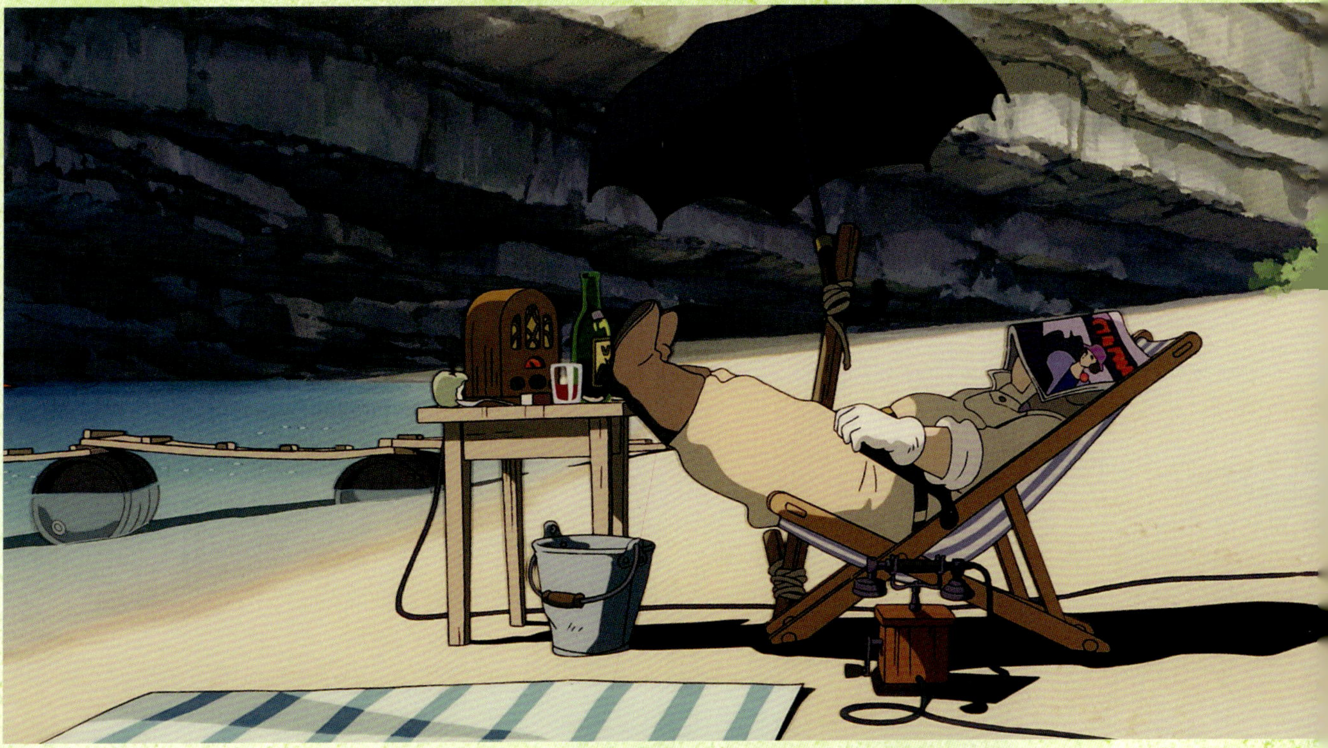

To a lesser extent, this reverse exoticism can be found in other Ghibli films, such as *The Cat Returns*, where Baron wears a suit and top hat and lives in a Western house. In *Tales from Earthsea*, the team mixes references to paintings of European cities and architecture to create an imaginary world inspired by Ursula K. Le Guin.

A STREAM OF TRANSFORMATIONS

The transformation of European cities through the imagination and sensibilities of Japanese artists preceded the explosion of metamorphoses in Ghibli productions. By taking up and adapting Japanese folklore of shape-shifting beings, Miyazaki invented the creatures in *My Neighbor Totoro* and, above all,

those in *Spirited Away*. Multiple deities rub shoulders in the bathhouse, where the young heroine encounters both the Radish Spirit and Okusaresama, a putrid being that is none other than a river polluted by human waste. Just as Miyazaki cleans the stream near his home every Sunday, Chihiro washes the god to restore him to his original form. As for No-Face, he's a faceless black shape that seems to embody modern consumerism.

The multiple visual metamorphoses in this film are a response to the transformations of traditional Japanese animals in *Pom Poko*. While Takahata focused on tanuki, cats, and foxes, which were forced to mutate to defend their territory and survive, Miyazaki created his own fantastic bestiary. In Takahata's work, the summoning of ancient Japanese beliefs is the sign of a rupture between the balance of the past, when man lived with nature, and the modern world, which rejects the nonurban environment. We find the same idea in a less humorous form in the epic tale of *Princess Mononoke*, with the forest deities imagined by Miyazaki. Between the boar god transformed into a monster and devastating the village at the beginning of the film and the deer god that is decapitated at the end, there is definitely no place left for these beings linked to nature in the human world. As with *Nausicaä*, the director invented a new, oversized bestiary for the postapocalyptic world of the science fiction story; in *Mononoke*, Miyazaki embodies natural forces in beings of monumental proportions. And in both stories, these giants are decimated by humans.

Subsequently, sequences of metamorphoses became increasingly frequent in both directors' works, as if they were seeking to escape the all-too-disappointing reality of their contemporaries. Transformations are at the heart of the story in *Howl's Moving Castle*, where the protagonists fall victim to a variety of spells: A young heroine becomes old, a magician transforms into a winged creature, and a fire demon and scarecrow inhabit the film's world, inspired by a story by an English novelist. Besides transformations, the film offers a change of scenery, thanks to its geographical, temporal, and cultural distance.

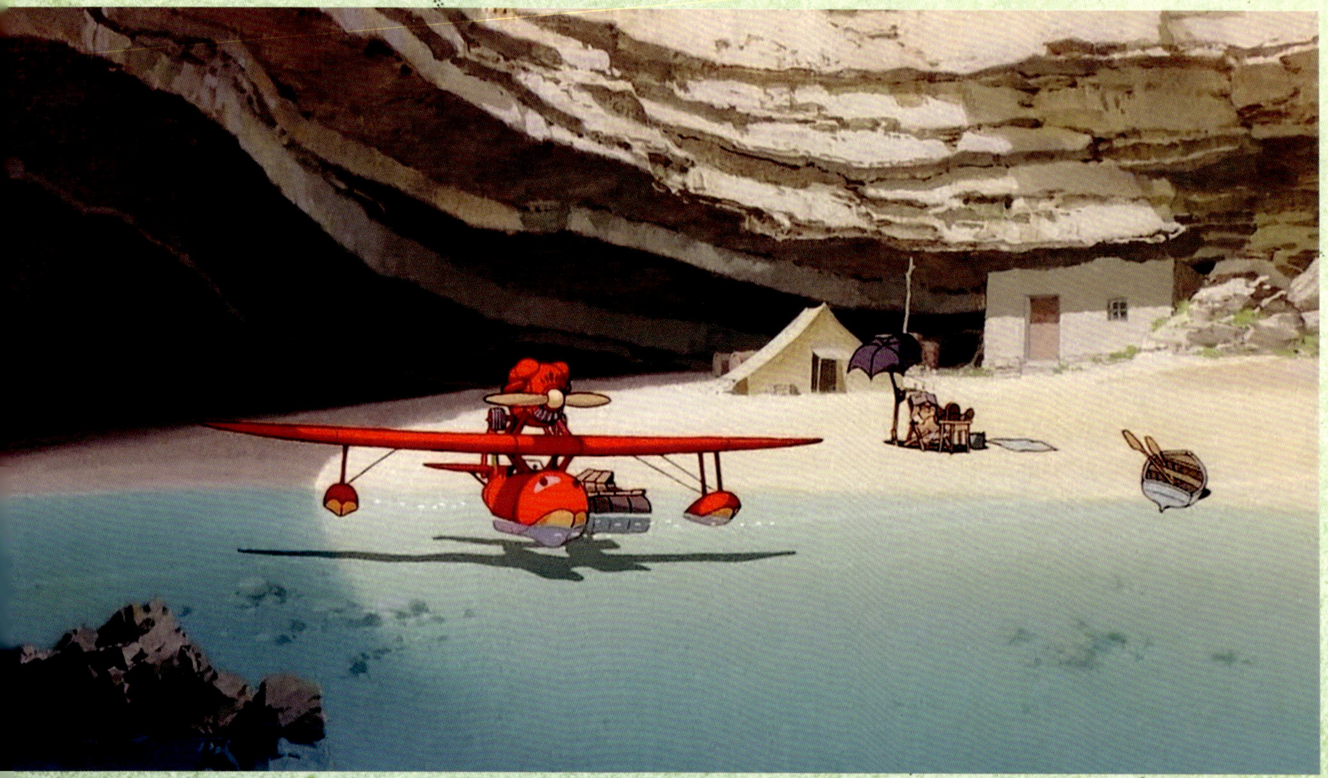

In *Ponyo*, everything seems to be a pretext for metamorphosis. The daughter of a magician and a deity, the small heroine transforms several times before taking human form and following her friend. The tsunami is a dramatic element, but above all, it becomes the pretext for upheaval in the territories designed by humans: Water obliterates

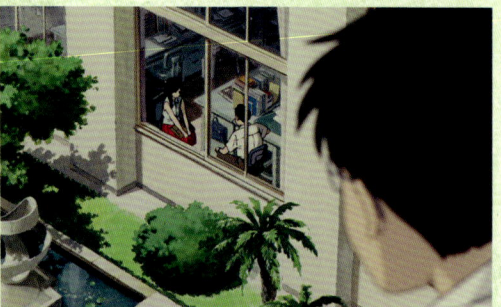 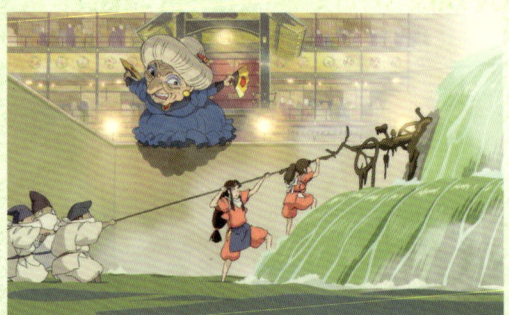

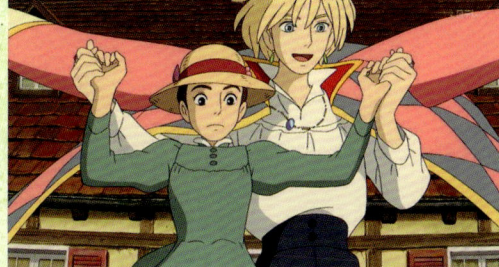

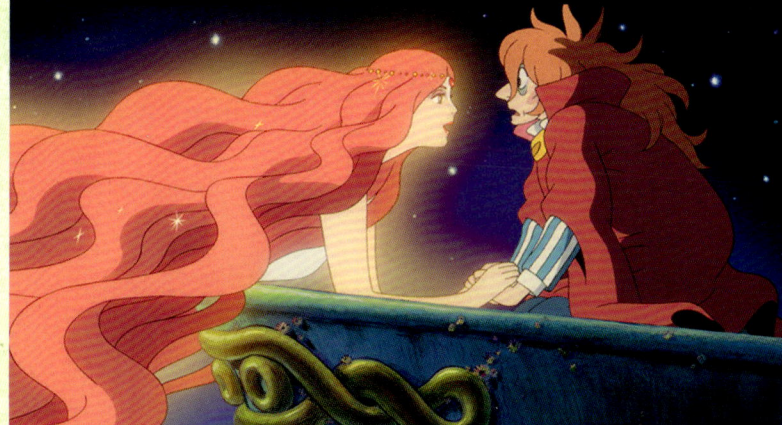

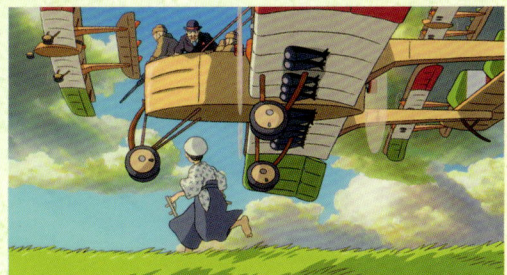

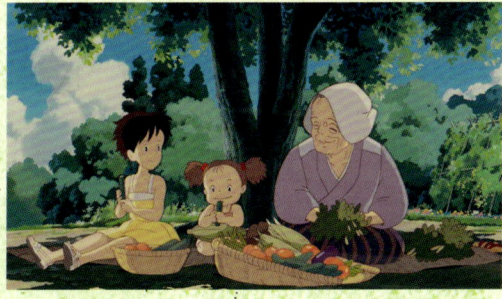

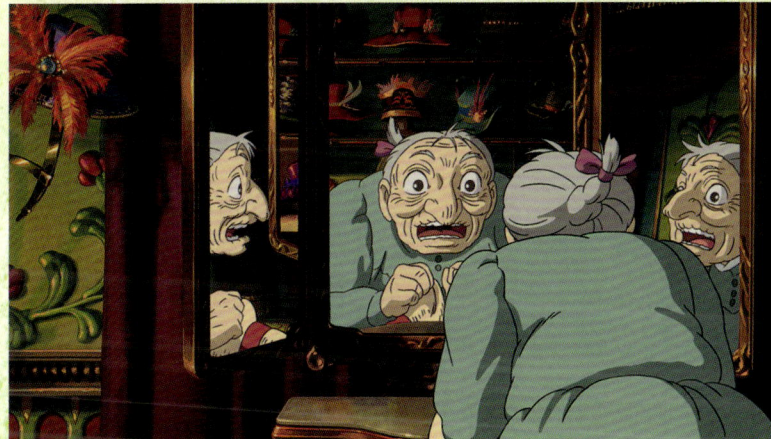

roads, boats replace cars, and retirees become agile again.

Likewise, Takahata's last two films focus on graphic transformations: a standard Japanese family in a giant sleigh, a confrontation with bikers that changes the way characters are treated, and a princess born in a bamboo plant who grows rapidly before returning to her family.

Although Miyazaki and Takahata's initial aim was to produce films for an adult audience with an accurate depiction of feelings, this credo gave way to an increasingly fanciful treatment of their stories, as the two directors allowed themselves to be transported by graphic experiments and metamorphoses that distanced them from strict realism.

Ocean Waves
© 1993 SAEKO HIMURO – GN
Whisper of the Heart
© 1995 Aoi Hiiragi/Shueisha – Nibariki – GNH
Only Yesterday
© 1991 Hotaru Okamoto – Yuto Tone – GNH
Howl's Moving Castle
© 2004 Nibariki – GNDDDT
My Neighbor Totoro
© 1988 Nibariki – G
The Wind Rises
© 2013 Nibariki – GNDHDDTK
Kiki's Delivery Service
© 1989 Eiko Kadono – Nibariki
Porco Rosso
©1992 Nibariki – GNN
Ponyo
© 2008 Nibariki – GNDHDDT
Princess Mononoke
© 1997 Nibariki – GND
Spirited Away
© 2001 Nibariki – TGNDDTM

REIMAGINING FEMALE CHARACTERS

→·←

The Ghibli Woman

THE GHIBLI WOMAN

While Studio Ghibli has always stood out for its consistently high graphic quality, both in its designs and its animation, it has above all raised public awareness through strong themes, like the environment and the innocence of childhood. In addition to these hallmarks, its normalization of female roles has brought a new facet to heroism to the screen.

By Philippe Bunel

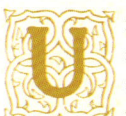ntil the 1970s, female characters in animation were regularly relegated to a supporting role, or even just used as a foil to build up the hero's masculinity. A few exceptions heralded the empowerment of women: Jeanne (*Belladonna of Sadness*) and the title character of *Cleopatra* were the protagonists of erotic films in which men tried to subdue them at every turn. As for Lady Oscar in the TV series *The Rose of Versailles*, she had to conceal her femininity to meet her father's and society's expectations. While these adaptations draw upon foreign mythology, they reflect ancestral Japanese machismo. Directors played on this not-so-ordinary level of sexism to develop intense female characters. *Shôjo* manga were becoming increasingly popular, and even *mangaka* Gô Nagai and Leiji Matsumoto created female icons such as the eccentric Honey Kisaragi (*Cutie Honey*) and the buxom sisters Maetel and

Emeraldas in *Galaxy Express 999*. Meanwhile, live-action exploitation films were disconcerting in their concept of the vengeful woman (like *Female Prisoner #701: Scorpion* and *Lady Snowblood*). Gradually, people got used to seeing temperamental, rebellious women in fiction, whether from imaginary worlds or inspired by real life. Takahata and Miyazaki contributed to this feminist trend in radically different ways.

"They have their own turmoil, making it easy to identify with them, while also adding great richness to the story."

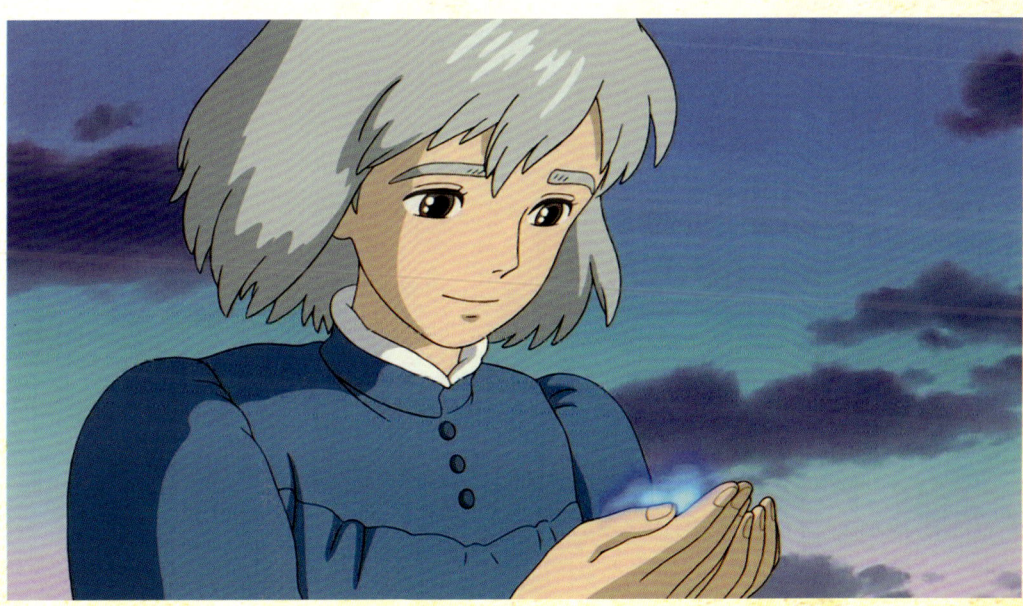

FEMINISM FOR MEN

In the 1980s, heroines made their marks in a multitude of works. But even though Masamune Shirow created major female roles in the mangasphere (*Appleseed*, *Dominion*, *Ghost in the Shell*), he always externalized the sexual impulses of his protagonists, echoing the cinema of the 1970s. There was a certain perversity in the creation of his heroines (later confirmed by his work as an erotic illustrator), which responded to a male fantasy. Works such as the TV series *Dirty Pair* and *Cat's Eye* were part of this trend, in which independent young women couldn't resist showing off their curves in flattering outfits, much to the delight of creator and fans alike.

At that time, *shôjo* wasn't as diversified as it is today, and the niche audience was very large (supported by the rise of OAVs, or original animated videos, the equivalent of today's direct-to-video) and mostly male, which explains how fan service came about. And while the emphasis on women could have been an opportunity to win over female viewers who didn't identify with action stories, it quickly becomes apparent that the attractive fictional women were ultimately hypervirile (sometimes aided by cybernetics), fulfilling well-known hero standards for such qualities as fearlessness, strength, beauty, and humor. Things had changed: Viewers were still following adventure and science fiction series, but they were now falling in love with the main characters! Women were no longer submissive, but they were idolized to the extreme.

This ambiguity is what sets Takahata and Miyazaki's work apart. Their films break out of these compartments to appeal to a wide audience. There are many secondary interpretations, and their heroines are free of sexual attractions. In fact, the worlds they portray have completely assimilated women as pillars of society, starting with the first film from what would become Studio Ghibli: *Nausicaä of the Valley of the Wind* (1984).

THE NAUSICAÄ MODEL

In 1981, Takahata directed the wonderful *Chie the Brat*, a logical sequel to *Heidi*, in which he returned to the eternal struggle of a young girl seeking self-esteem in a world bogged down by archaic values.

With *Nausicaä of the Valley of the Wind*, Miyazaki placed his young heroine in this continuum, but via a fantasy world not subject to misogynistic norms, at least not as far as this princess is concerned. She's totally freed from the conventions that should be respected by a person of her rank. Nausicaä is fearless, like the hero of *Future Boy Conan*, but above all, she achieves peace of mind and a sense of responsibility. Her status as a woman is never called into question on the grounds that she might be frail or delicate. In this way, the boundaries between genders are shattered in a surprisingly natural way. *Nausicaä* represents the purity of youth in search of fulfillment, with no cleavage, no marriage, and no prejudice. This vision serves as the basis for Ghibli heroines, who don't need to impose themselves on society to exist.

> *"While Ghibli's temperamental women fascinate with their combativeness, men are not excluded."*

PHYSICAL NEUTRALITY

With their familiar faces of similar design and outfits that might well be worn by someone who's very conservative, Ghibli's female characters display no sensuality, making them easy to identify with. And while these young women are still romantic, romantic relationships are not their goal, unlike in Disney princess films, where romance is clearly the aim.

The focus on charismatic women is also the cornerstone of that American movie company, but its approach is profoundly different from that of the Japanese studio. It's true that the charming princesses gradually gain charisma and independence over time, showing just how far women can break free from the conventions of the classic fairy tale. They are blessed with features that set them apart from one another, but these usually correspond to beauty stereotypes that distort the notion of purity, influencing the gaze of both the other characters and the viewer. Beauty thus becomes an unconscious criterion, just like dress, an elegant attitude, or graceful movements, with bodily overexpressivity becoming an integral part of the personality. In contrast to

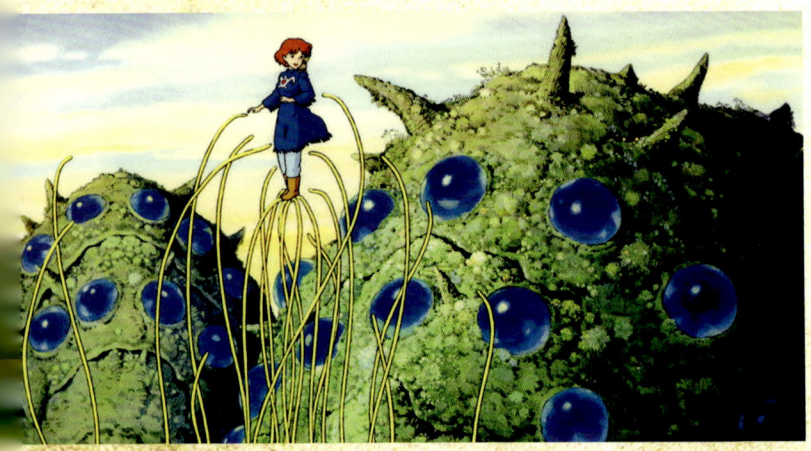

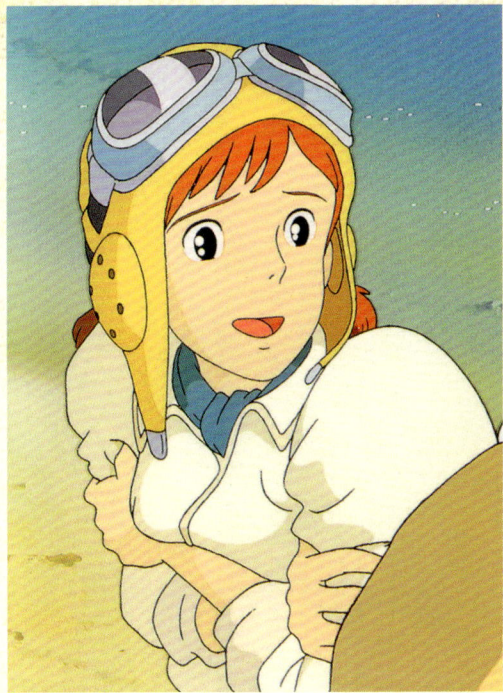

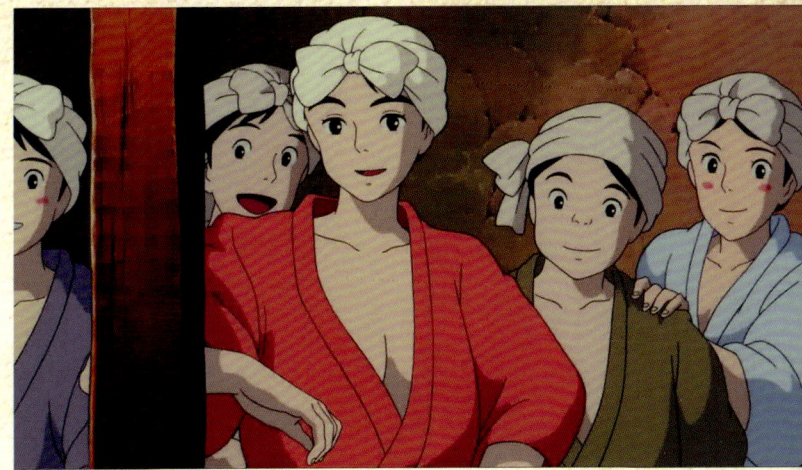

Ghibli, and despite the fact that the quest for innocence is one of Disney's fundamental values, the heroines are subjected to excessive feminization, supported by marketing that is as powerful as it is distressing, and which encourages superficiality. And, unfortunately, making characters into stars further divides the girl/boy realms. While Mulan and Belle occasionally stand out from the crowd, it's little Lilo (*Lilo & Stitch*) who comes closest to the works of the Japanese studio. This is partly because, at that time, Disney still found it difficult to accurately portray children (a fundamental truth that has since been forgotten; poor Princess Sofia), and partly because she's a typical young girl with real worries and an extraordinary destiny. It's a character concept in a more self-effacing genre, the essence of which Ghibli has always maintained.

But where Disney joins most Japanese productions is in its adaptability to trends, thus offering characters that correspond to the expectations of the moment. Ghibli is exactly the opposite. The studio has never given in to this opportunistic game, although it is generally essential to the success of a movie and a company. Thus, the recurring anime clichés (outgoing girl, taciturn girl, or shy girl with glasses, for example) never make it into the productions, which instead favor unexpected characters such as the young/old Sophie (*Howl's Moving Castle*), wild and unapproachable San (*Princess Mononoke*), tomboyish Fio (*Porco Rosso*), and even ordinary-looking Chihiro (*Spirited Away*).

FLEEING SEXUALITY?

However surprising Ghibli's vision of women may be, could it perhaps be seen as a form of fear of a more invasive femininity, at the risk of losing realism? Although very real, physical attraction is always sidestepped with the absence of gender differentiation, or even blamed when it comes to the temptation or drive of more stereotypical characters. Gina, the magnificent singer in *Porco Rosso*, hints at her attraction to the pig-headed aviator; and her other seducers, who use their virility as a sign of charm, appear laughable to the audience. This process of ridiculing the domineering male is repeated in Takahata's *My Neighbors the Yamadas*, where he revisits the role of the housewife, and in the preconceived destiny that convention imposes on Princess Kaguya. Takahata depicts not only gilded cages, but also jailers (the husband, the suitors, the father) who are themselves blinded by the innate nature of an absurd national machismo.

In fact, Ghibli conveys utopian values, allowing female audiences to project themselves into these adventures while pausing the anti-prejudice alarm bells. There is restfulness, even relief, that is rarely found elsewhere.

STRONG SPIRIT

But if you take away women's physical assets and this conflict, conscious or otherwise, with patriarchal society, what's left that is so compelling? It turns out that character really does come to the forefront. The characters' personalities are varied and profound. These young women all have their own turmoil, which varies in severity depending on the film, making it easy for us to identify with them, while at the same time adding a richness to the story. Who hasn't felt nostalgic about their childhood? Who hasn't been sad about moving away? Who hasn't worried about their mother's

health when she was hospitalized? Who hasn't been shattered by the loss of a loved one? Who hasn't had to work hard to earn a living? And, in a more extreme situation, who has experienced war and starvation while trying to survive with their older brother? The characters carry these obstacles with them, forging their individuality. In this way, the images in each film become more immersive, just as the decisions made during the narratives become more meaningful.

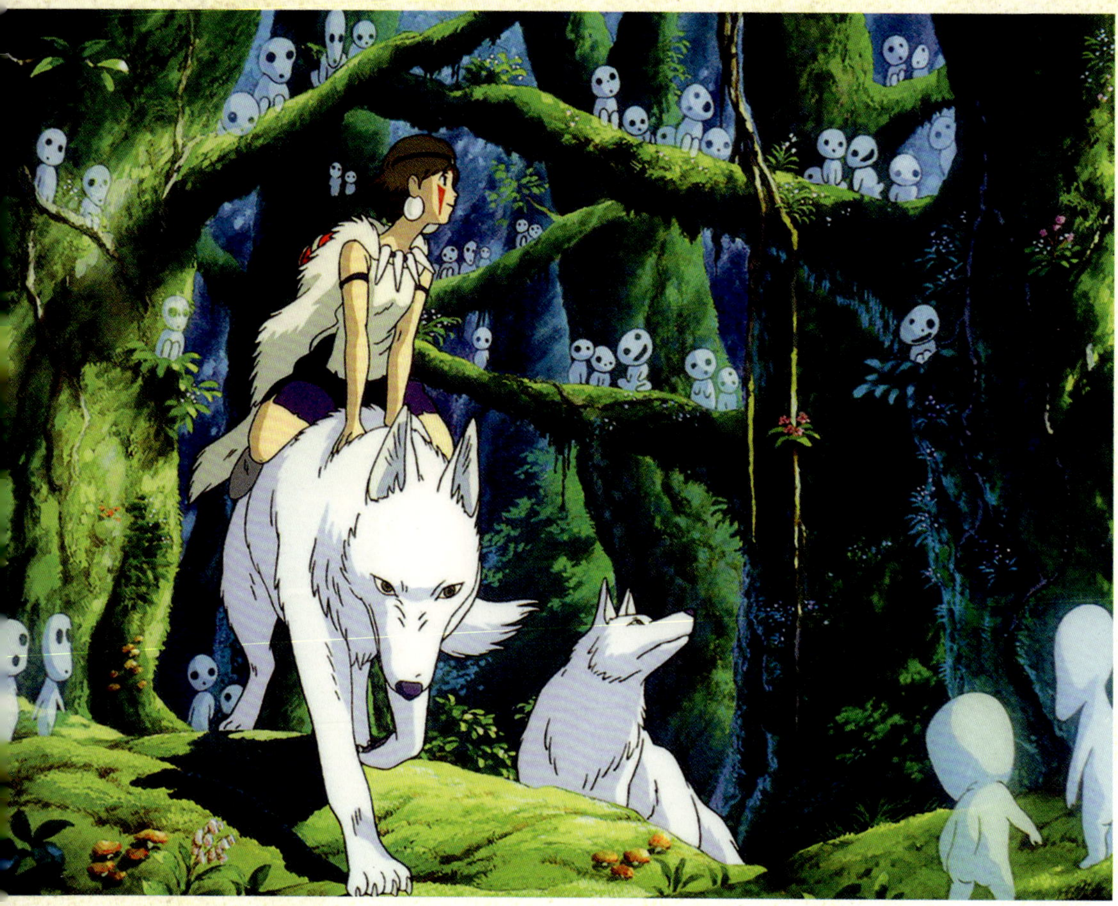

In the end, Ghibli depicts dark stories with tortured characters, which explains their sensitive personalities. But the strength of conviction of these young girls and women proves to be quite innovative, and sometimes daring, as exemplified by the many matriarchal structures present in the films. This provides further proof of the filmmakers' complete confidence in women's self-sufficiency, whether in their homes (*Ponyo*, *From Up on Poppy Hill*), their businesses (*Porco Rosso*, *Spirited Away*), a micro-society (*Princess Mononoke*), or even a city (*Howl's Moving Castle*).

MALE DUOS

Of course, while Ghibli's temperamental women fascinate with their combativeness, men are not excluded. There are feelings of love and friendship, but the male character's masculinity never impinges on the balance of the relationship. And because each character has their own goal, the heroine's doesn't overshadow that of her partner. As a result, we see complementary duos such as San and Ashitaka, Sophie and Hauru, and even Ponyo and Sôsuke.

THE EXTENDED UNIVERSE

❧ • ☙

The Ghibli Museum
The Ghibli Exhibition
Donguri Stores
Video Games
Ghibli in Advertising
The Theme Park
Ghibli Collaborations

THE GHIBLI MUSEUM

Unlike the gaudy theme parks dedicated to Disney productions, the Ghibli Museum—from its conception in 1997 by Hayao Miyazaki to its opening in 2001 under the direction of his son Gorô—offers visitors an enchanting, soothing experience in communion with nature. This is a guided tour of a magical place nestled in a quiet, upscale Tokyo suburb.

⤖ By Gersende Bollut

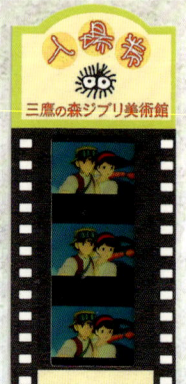

GHIBLI MUSEUM, MITAKA

In the vast majority of cases, visiting a museum requires no reservation, except for school groups. The Ghibli Museum, however, has been an exception to this rule, with huge numbers of visitors since its opening on October 1, 2001. Before you can hope to enter the lair dedicated to the works of Miyazaki, Takahata, and company that was directed for many years by Gorô Miyazaki (before he was spurred on by a desire to direct movies, including *Tales from Earthsea* in 2006, *From Up on Poppy Hill* in 2011, the series *Ronja, the Robber's Daughter* in 2014, and *Earwig and the Witch* in 2020), it's a good idea to book your ticket in advance—at least three months before the date you plan to visit—with the Keikaku travel agency (https://keikaku-japan.com/) or through Lawson Entertainment (https://l-tike.com/st1/ghibli-en/sitetop). Despite being warned by friends and family, the author of these lines had the unfortunate experience of being turned down when he tried to make a reservation a month before

the trip and was forced to use his "connections" at Ghibli to obtain the precious ticket. Even if you proclaim your unconditional love for the studio's films to the museum's front desk, you won't be granted any such favors, so make sure you reserve your ticket well in advance, or you'll be turned away at the entrance.

> *"The museum reveals its wooden architecture, all flowing lines and curves."*

If you're already in the area, you can also buy your ticket in one of the Lawson stores, but the process requires a perfect command of Japanese. As proof of its ongoing success, at the end of May 2015, for the first time in its history, the museum introduced a lottery for the distribution of tickets for the summer period, with a view to curbing the shortage caused

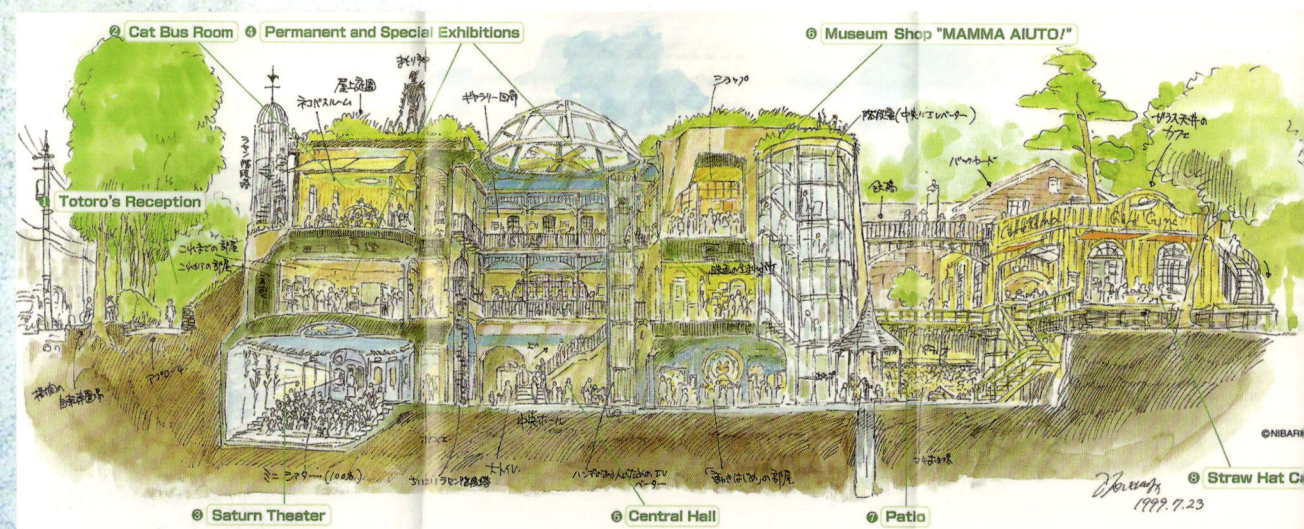

② Cat Bus Room   ④ Permanent and Special Exhibitions   ⑤ Museum Shop "MAMMA AIUTO!"

① Totoro's Reception

③ Saturn Theater   ⑥ Central Hall   ⑦ Patio   ⑧ Straw Hat C[afé]

1999.7.23

©NIBARI

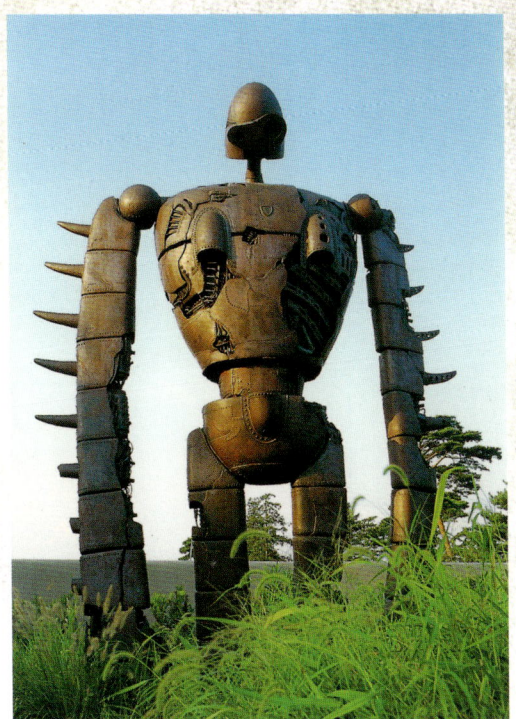

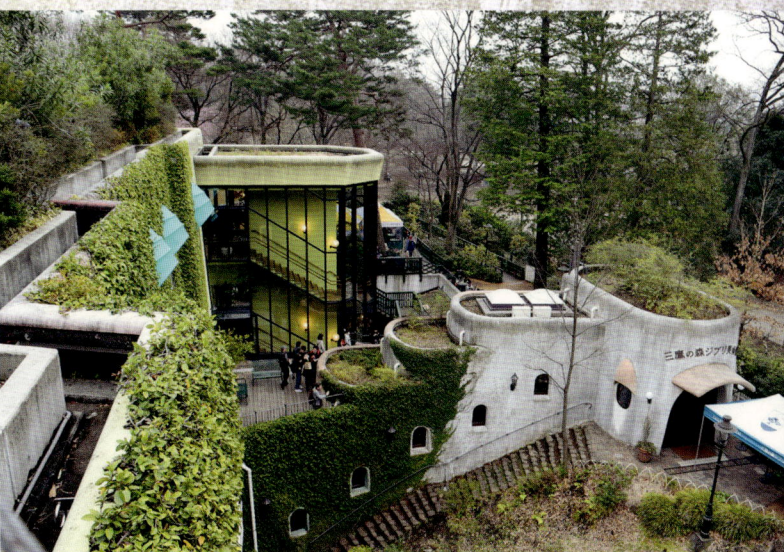

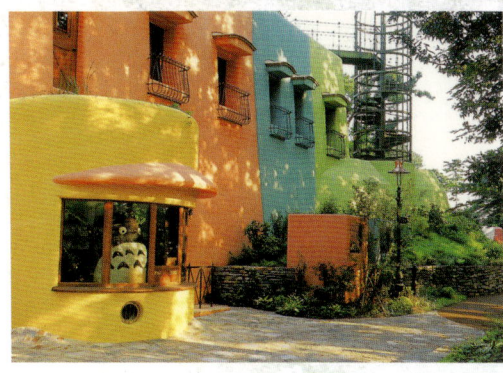

by speculators who buy up a stock of tickets so they can sell them at a premium on auction sites. Now that you've got your ticket, let's get down to business. Follow the guide!

ENCHANTMENT

After taking the Chuo or Sobu subway line from Tokyo to the Mitaka station on the outskirts of the city (a twenty-minute trip), the lucky traveler takes a few steps to a sign topped by a smiling Totoro that points the way to the eagerly anticipated museum. The sign leads to a bus stop from which a shuttle makes regular round trips to the building at an affordable price, although you can walk to the museum while enjoying the pleasant Tokyo countryside in about fifteen minutes.

A magical place is then revealed: Greeted by a life-size Totoro placidly seated behind a counter (just a few yards away from the real counter with flesh-and-blood employees), visitors enter the environmentally friendly venue. Built in the heart of the majestic Inokashira Park, the building features wooden architecture whose flowing lines and curves fit seamlessly into the natural surroundings. There's bicycle parking nearby, and signage that blends in with the scenery; for a second, you almost don't notice the main building, as it marries harmoniously with the vegetation in a respectful tribute to Mother Nature.

The validated ticket, which entitles the holder to a map of the museum and a piece of film that will prove useful during the visit, gives access to the central hall, from which visitors can enter three exhibition rooms: two permanent ones and a temporary one dedicated to a specific production or theme (see box on page 135). Some of the display cases are playful, revealing an adorable articulated puppet of Mei chasing a Totoro in a loop, several very short films playing in a loop in what looks like a projection booth, and a gorgeous zoetrope of *My Neighbor Totoro*. Other displays are educational, featuring a multitude of sketches, sets, storyboards, and celluloid films which, because of the local culture, are barely protected, as no one here would dream of the possibility of anyone trying to walk off with them. It's a matter of trust. The documents on display fascinate the youngest visitors (who are amazed to see their heroes come to life) and make the general public more aware of the process of creating an animated film, and the exhibition rounds out fans' knowledge with the meticulous reconstruction of an animator's studio. Visitors can discover many of Miyazaki's annotated documents, as well as his main sources of inspiration. Whether it's literary classics, reference works (many of them French), or the model of a seaplane for *Porco Rosso*, the wealth of information piled haphazardly captures the creative energy, with vivid details that avoid any sense of a rigid, dusty repository.

EASY ON THE EYES

Nearby, an attractive eighty-seat movie theater lets you watch one of the short films made exclusively for the museum! This is one of the special features of the Ghibli Museum: Upon presentation of a piece of film received at the entrance (which, fortunately, can be kept afterward), and depending on the time of year, visitors have access to the Saturn Theater, which shows the same production repeatedly throughout the day. Make sure you don't blink, though, because due to the large number of visitors, you'll be able to see the short film only once. So there's no need to rush off at the end of the screening to enjoy it a second time in the magnificent room, with its *Porco Rosso*–themed ceiling and tram-shaped projection booth, where you can admire the projectionist's work.

To date, thirteen short films have been produced: *The Whale Hunt* in 2001; *Koro's Big Day Out, Mei and the Kittenbus, Imaginary Flying Machines, The Ornithopter Story: Fly, Hiyodori Tengu!*, and *The Invention of Imaginary Machines of Destruction* in 2002; *House Hunting, Monmon the Water Spider,* and *The Day I Bought a Star* in 2006; *A Sumo Wrestler's Tail* and *Mr. Dough and the Egg Princess* in 2010; *Treasure Hunting* in 2011; and lastly, *Boro the Caterpillar* in 2018. Nine of them were directed by Hayao Miyazaki and, frustratingly, not available to see again, unless you return to the museum regularly or hope for a very hypothetical video release (currently ruled out, as it would deprive the museum of one of its main draws). During our spring visit, we were treated to *A Sumo Wrestler's Tail*, a hilarious adaptation of a traditional tale in which an old peasant couple who live in a mountain house come to the aid of mice who secretly participate in sumo tournaments every night, fattening up their skinny little tenants to give them strength. The film's meticulous direction, endearing characters, and irresistible ending make it a real gem.

AND THE WALLET!

The rest of the visit is spread over several floors. On the second story, children can climb the gigantic plush Catbus with contagious pleasure (even if we've all kept a childlike spirit, access is strictly limited to young visitors); the museum roof, reached by a spiral staircase, is where you'll find an impressive reproduction of the iconic robot from *Castle in the Sky* (and it's the only place in the museum where photographs are allowed); and the cafeteria is guaranteed to be 100 percent organic (the house specialty is a fruit sandwich).

There's plenty of room to stroll around, admiring the interior architecture and the attention to detail in the decor, as exemplified by the magnificent stained-glass windows featuring the studio's key characters. Collectors will be especially keen to visit the museum's two exclusive boutiques. The first, Tri Hawks, is primarily aimed at connoisseurs, with its multitude of specialized books on Ghibli. Manga and essays are mostly in Japanese, but art books, some of which are very rare (each short film

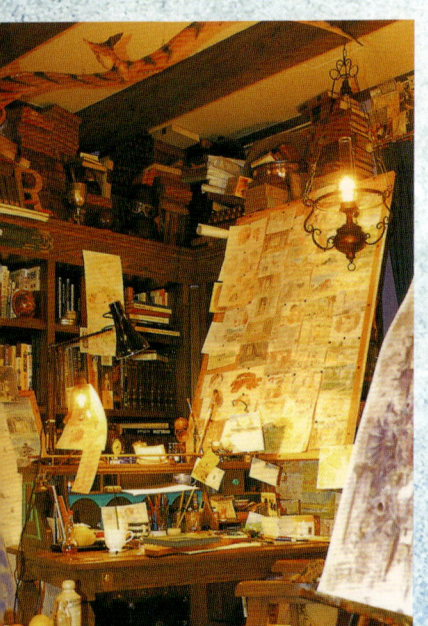 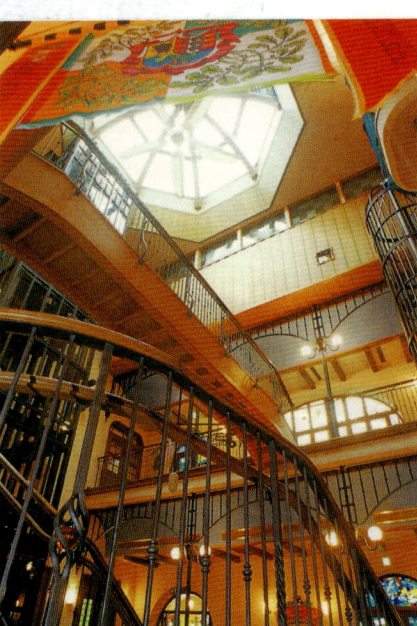 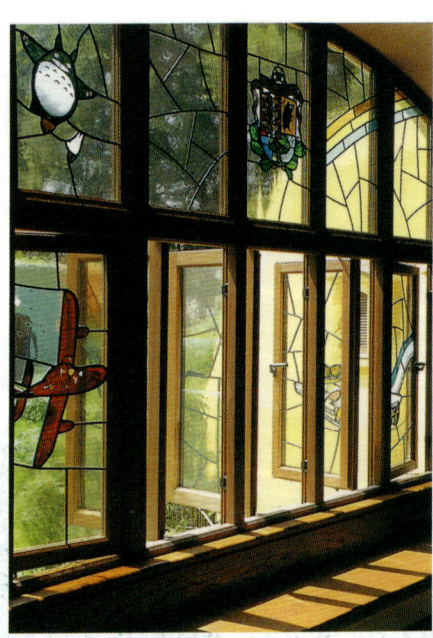

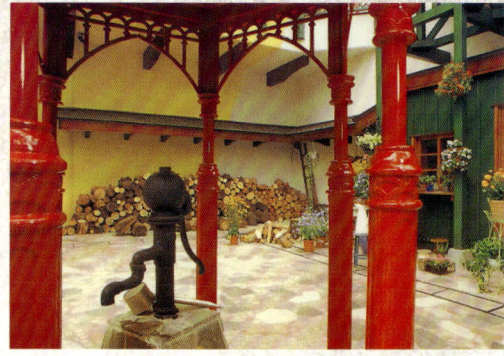

produced for the museum has its own richly illustrated booklet), are a joy for fans.

The second shop, Mamma Aiuto, is more for the general public, and it's a bit of a madhouse when you have to elbow your way through the crowds. There, you can find a wealth of merchandising products, both more (statues, jewelry) and less (cookies, pins) collector's items, not to mention OSTs (original soundtracks), DVDs, and Blu-rays of the studio's works. However, given the prohibitive prices of some items, the better-stocked Donguri stores[1] dotted around the country might be preferable. There are no fewer than forty shops selling a whole range of figurines, bags, tableware, garden accessories, and household linen, at the risk of endangering your bank account (we can't recommend the one in Tokyo Station enough). In all, you should allow at least two hours for a tour of the Ghibli Museum, a unique place that perpetuates the atmosphere of the definitively enchanting works.

TEMPORARY EXHIBITIONS

Every year, starting in May, a temporary exhibition takes up residence at the museum. After those devoted to *Castle in the Sky* and *Spirited Away*, and the tributes to the great Russian director Yuri Norstein and the Pixar and Aardman studios, the fifteenth exhibition was entitled *Welcome to The Haunted Tower: Perfect Popular Culture*. Largely supervised by Hayao Miyazaki, this exhibition shed light on Edogawa Ranpo's novel *Yureito* (*The Haunted Tower*, for which there is also a manga adaptation published by Glénat), which was an acknowledged influence—among others— on *The Castle of Cagliostro*. While we were there, we were able to enjoy the previous exhibition, *The Nutcracker and the Mouse King*, featuring figurines, dioramas, creative workshops for youngsters, and illustrations from various world editions of Ernst Theodor Amadeus Hoffmann's renowned German fairy tale, which made a strong impression on Miyazaki when he immersed himself in it during the 2013 holiday season, just after he retired. Other more recent exhibitions have included *Painting the Colors of Our Films* (2018), *"Sketch, Flash, Spark!"* ~ *From the Ghibli Forest Sketchbook* (2019), *Earwig and the Witch* (2021), *Future Boy Conan* (2023), and *The Boy and the Heron Part 3: Background Art* (2024). All further reasons, as if any were needed, to return to the Ghibli Museum once a year and explore its rooms.

[1.] The Benelic group's chain of stores dedicated exclusively to Ghibli merchandise, divided between Donguri Republic and Donguri Garden stores. More details at https://benelic.com and www.kanpai-japan.com/travel-guide/donguri-official-ghibli-shops.

Photo credit: Gersende Bollut

© Ghibli Museum

THE GHIBLI EXHIBITION

From July 7 to September 11, 2016, the Roppongi Hills observation deck was swarmed by thousands of Japanese fans, who were prepared to stand in line for hours just for a few dreamy moments. It was a sixty-seven-day celebration of Studio Ghibli's thirtieth anniversary, with an eagerly awaited retrospective exhibition.

By Matthieu Pinon

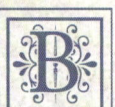

By night, Roppongi is famous for its chic restaurants, trendy bars, and exciting nightclubs. By day, it's the business district, where multinational headquarters rub shoulders with embassies and luxury boutiques. It's Tokyo's international crossroads, mixing tourists, partying students, high-ranking businessmen, and local families. The 787-foot-tall Mori Tower rises above it, with a panoramic observation deck on the top floor that offers a breathtaking view of the capital. It provides an exceptional backdrop for the Mori Art Museum's temporary exhibitions and was ideal for the retrospective of a studio adored by the Japanese and visitors from other countries alike.

THE SLOW CLIMB

The exhibition's announcement didn't go unnoticed! Although it predated the studio's creation, *Nausicaä of the Valley of the Wind* was featured on the exhibition poster, a subtle tribute to the film on whose postapocalyptic ashes Ghibli was built. But the real surprise came two weeks before the opening. Studio head Toshio Suzuki found the idea of a proposed 2,300-yen ticket (about $15) unacceptable, and finally won his case: Admission was set at 1,800 yen (around $12), the price of a movie ticket in Japan. The diplomacy of the apology message, published on the official Ghibli website, was contradicted by a caricature of an out-of-control Suzuki, drawn by Miyazaki.

> *"Many visitors had come for the Miyazaki aura rather than for Ghibli."*

By contrast, visitors lined up in complete silence for up to four hours on a spiral staircase with an unobstructed view and guaranteed warmth through the glass roof in the early September heat wave. Don't worry, they think of everything in Japan: An employee was on hand to offer bottles of water for 100 yen (less than a dollar), which were appreciated by young and old alike. The intergenerational crowd was largely made up of children, even though the eyes of many adults shone with the same gleam of anticipation.

At last, the way in! The ultrafast elevator to the fifty-fourth floor! Despite the breathtaking views,

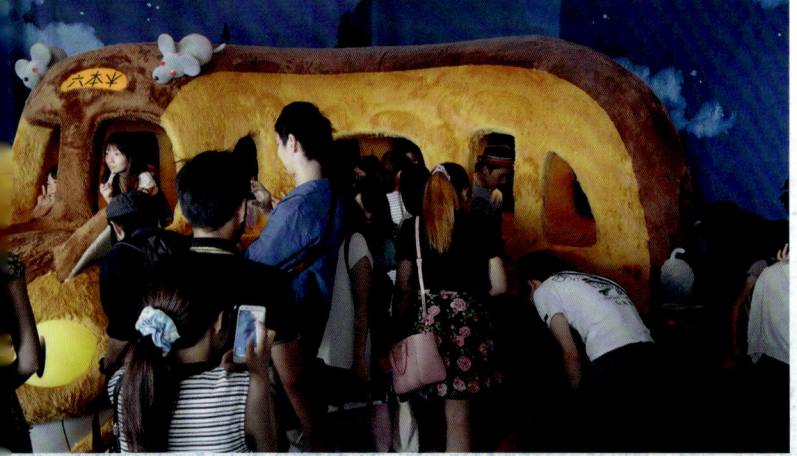

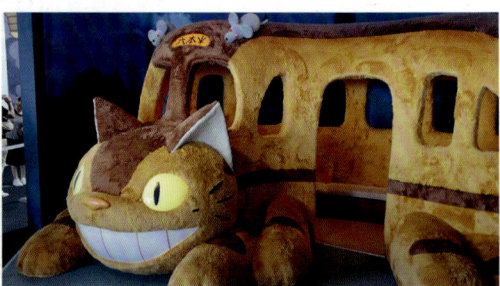

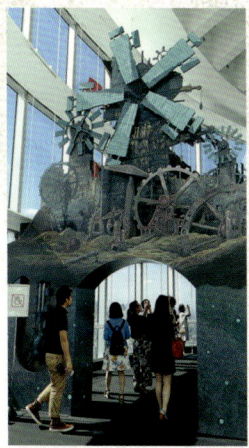
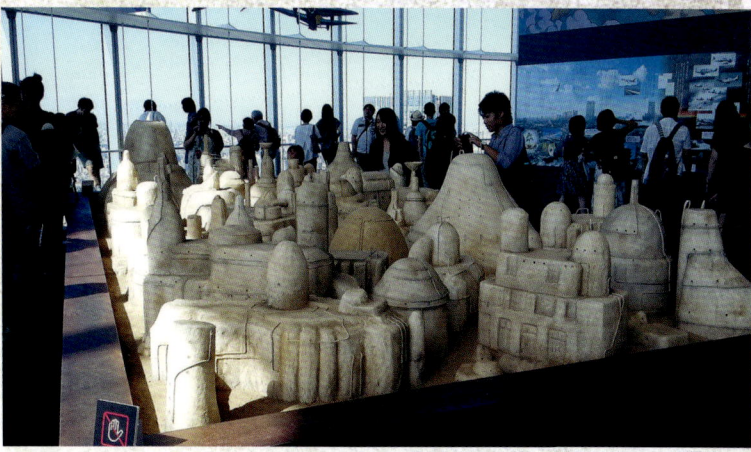

there were many sighs of disappointment at the "No Photos" sign at the entrance to the exhibition dedicated to The Red Turtle, the studio's latest production. Paradoxically, the focus on this film did little to boost awareness of Michael Dudok de Wit's feature, which had not yet been released in Japan. Despite the large number of exclusive *Red Turtle* working documents on display, visitors rushed through that part of the exhibition space to get back to the classics as quickly as possible.

TO THE TOP

In any case, the guards left us no choice but to move on! Visitors had to be kept moving to let in those who were waiting, and we were kindly asked not to linger in front of the giant Totoro who welcomed us into the first room, which featured all the Japanese posters from Ghibli productions, or the next room, whose wallpaper featured all the advertisements published in the press over the past thirty years. The re-creation of Suzuki's office might *seem* like a funny detail, but it demonstrated the efforts made by every section of the studio, including marketing.

These efforts have paid off, as can be seen in the treasure room: Life-size statues, ultralimited quantities of goodies, various gifts, and foreign posters all provided concrete proof of the studio's success over three decades. Many of the items came from the Ghibli Museum, and the event will probably remain the only opportunity to admire the Golden Bear and Oscar proudly displayed in their cases.

In turn, visitors' patience paid off. Anyone who has visited the Ghibli Museum has experienced the frustration of being deprived of the Catbus, which is only for children. Here, anyone could get into the giant stuffed animal, in an avalanche of selfies limited to less than two minutes on the attendant's stopwatch.

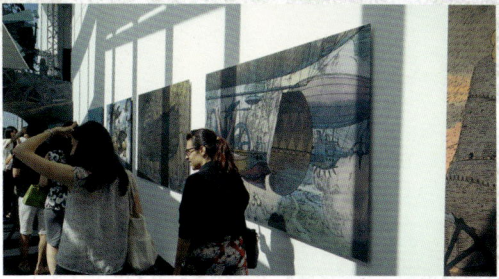

With smartphones and digital cameras so commonplace, the final gigantic room in the exhibition, an ode to the flying machines that have appeared in the movies, was the place to be. The aircraft reproductions, set against a blue summer sky, gave the impression of reliving the flights from *Porco Rosso* or *Castle in the Sky*: A giant model straight out of *Castle* rose and fell above a diorama landscape that looked like something out of *Nausicaä*.

RETROSPECTIVE OR JUBILEE?

Ultimately, the most instructive thing about the event was its audience. Drawn into this compact, ever-moving crowd, we realized that visitors of all ages and genders had come primarily for the Miyazaki aura rather than for Ghibli, neglecting the works of other directors (Takahata films, Yoshifumi Kondô's *Whisper of the Heart*, Hiroyuki Morita's *The Cat Returns*, etc.) even though they were equally represented. This resolutely mainstream retrospective proved, if proof were needed, just how much Totoro has remained the darling of the Japanese public, with plush toys of the character filling the store at the expense of more recent productions. Sadly, this rush for nostalgic stuffed toys confirms that, for the Japanese, Ghibli is now mostly a thing of the past.

Photo credits: Matthieu Pinon

DONGURI STORES

Between the shamelessly imported counterfeits that have been available for too long around the world and limited opportunities to buy the real thing outside Japan, fans of tie-in merchandise are left with nothing but tears in their eyes. Unless they want to buy a one-way ticket to Tokyo.

By Gersende Bollut

or any true Studio Ghibli fan, a trip to the other side of the globe is like a pilgrimage. Apart from the must-see museum on the outskirts of Tokyo, to which we devote an article on page 132, or, for the more adventurous, a detour to the island of Yakushima, which inspired the lush forest in *Princess Mononoke*, the most fun activity—but also the most painful for the wallet—is to visit one of the thirty-seven Donguri stores spread across the country (the name literally means "acorn," an item immortalized in *My Neighbor Totoro*). Far better stocked than the Ghibli Museum's Mamma Aiuto boutique, which also charges exorbitant prices, these outlets are brimming with Ghibli merchandise that is impossible to find elsewhere—unless you pay a premium price in carefully selected boutiques or on auction sites. Supervised by the Benelic group and officially approved by the studio, the chain of boutiques is a veritable Ali Baba's cave for merchandising enthusiasts. In addition to the traditional plush toys and figurines, you can find a variety of accessories ranging from useful to frivolous, including picture frames, sophisticated stationery, bedding, tableware, and bags featuring the characters from the films that have forged the studio's reputation (in terms of popularity, Totoro; *Jiji*, the cat in *Kiki's Delivery Service*; and Ponyo come out on top), DVDs and Blu-rays of the aforementioned works (with a few new releases thrown in), as well as a selection of products for babies that will make even people without offspring fall in love. There are scores of quality items to tempt you to decorate your home and your daily life or treat your loved ones to 100 percent official products.

> *"Simply discovering one of these stores is enough to fill you with wonder."*

MIGHTY OAKS FROM LITTLE ACORNS GROW

Discovering one of these stores, whether in a tourist district or a subway station, is enough to fill you with wonder. A Totoro on a wooden sign usually dominates the entrance to attract the attention of the enlightened traveler, who is only too happy to make a shopping stop. But beware: Not all Donguri offer the same items. While the flagship products figure prominently everywhere, some are specific to a particular outlet, as the author of these lines found with several characters from the *Spirited Away* mini set, which were available in limited quantities in only a handful of Donguri shops. In a friendly musical atmosphere featuring Joe Hisaishi's compositions, enthusiasts are sure to enjoy wandering through spacious, bright, often lavishly decorated stores displaying the most unusual items, from a

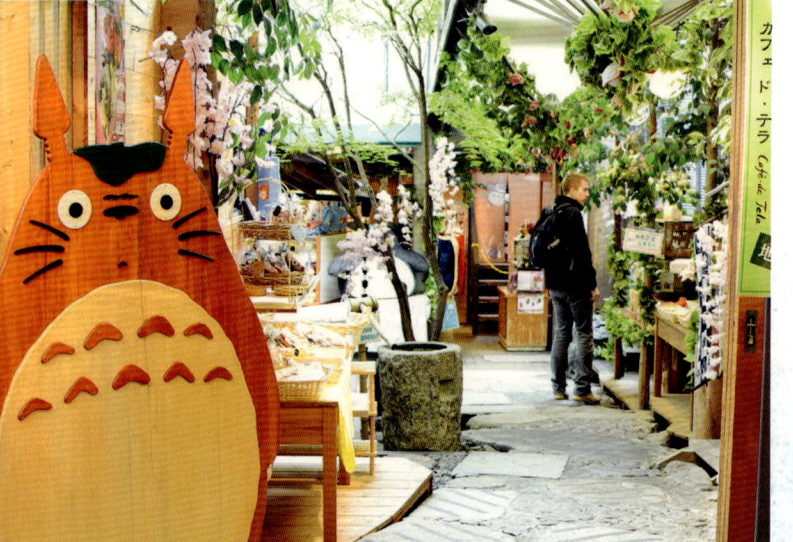

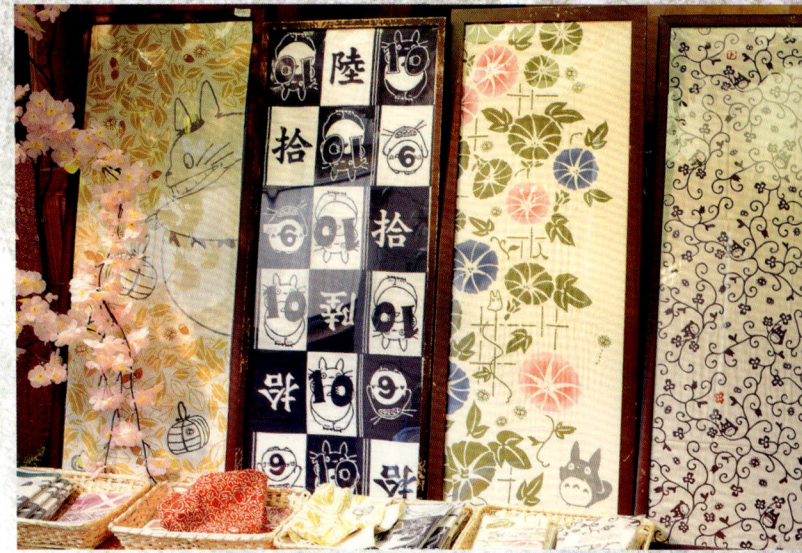

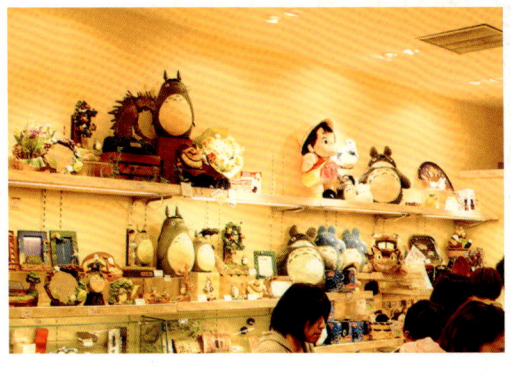

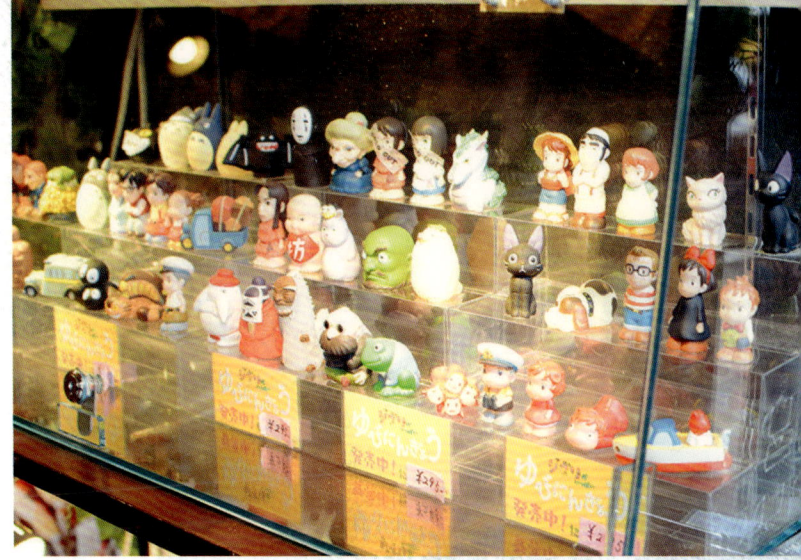

flowerpot shaped like the robot's head in *Castle in the Sky* (with a humidity tester adorned with the fierce Teto from *Nausicaä of the Valley of the Wind*) to a sumptuous translucent bust of the Deer God from *Princess Mononoke*, after he was decapitated by the sinister Lady Eboshi. Whether located underground (Tokyo Station), in a busy district (Kyoto), or away from the tourist hotspots (Mount Koya), each Donguri has its own unique identity, and the temptation to enter every single one of them is irresistible, even if you've already had the pleasure of visiting one during your travels in Japan. In addition, some stores offer a separate counter where customers can drop off collected acorns, which are then transferred to Okawa to help reforest this village of around four hundred souls on the island of Shikoku. This ecological cause, which is extremely important to Hayao Miyazaki, is reminiscent of the momentum generated in the late 1980s by Frédéric Back with his wonderful short film *The Man Who Planted Trees*, adapted from a short story by Jean Giono.

Photo credits: Gersende Bollut

VIDEO GAMES

Because there's a strong connection between Japanese animation and video games, Studio Ghibli has logically invited itself into the creative process for certain games. But here again, true to its reputation, the studio has opted for quality over quantity. Here's a quick overview.

✏ By Bruno de la Cruz

his is now true in both directions, but Japanese animation was originally a showcase for video game production. With the possibility of integrating video sequences on disc, Japanese video games benefited from high-quality animated opening sequences, and the same was true of adaptations for other consoles. These introductions, which were often short and previously featured in commercials, benefited from top-notch workmanship to seduce the audience, even though they were sometimes more attractive than the game's main content.

Studio Ghibli has had relatively few forays into the world of video games. Nevertheless, it's fair to say that when it does get involved, it doesn't do things halfway. The studio's first major game project was *Jade Cocoon: Story of the Tamamayu*. In this role-playing game (RPG) developed by the Genki studio and released on PlayStation in December 1998, the player embarked on a quest in a fantasy world to fight, collect, and merge various creatures. The turn-based role-playing game's mechanics were a little cumbersome, but the atmosphere was dreamlike enough to appeal to fans of the genre. The world imagined by Hayao Miyazaki, a sort of cross between *Princess Mononoke* and *Nausicäa of the*

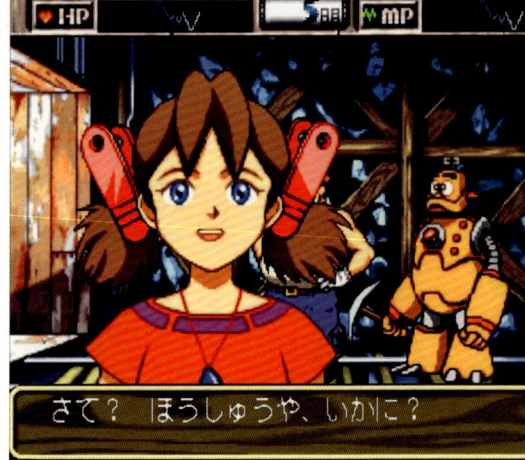

Wonder Project J2.

Valley of the Wind, was based on the master's usual themes. To present it properly, Ghibli produced a beautiful two-and-a-half-minute introduction, a spectacular sequence that sets the scene without really revealing the game's mechanics, and which would be accompanied by cut scenes from the game.

Animator Katsuya Kondô was heavily involved in this project. The artist not only designed the characters but also did much of the art direction, which is presented in a special art book. The book also includes storyboard pages and a manga section, allowing players to learn more about the characters and extend the game experience. Speaking of extensions, *Jade Cocoon* was given a second opus in 2001, on PlayStation 2. This game was set two hundred years after the events of the first *Jade Cocoon*, and once again relied on Kondô's art direction. Unfortunately, the animated scenes are replaced by relatively poor sequences produced by the game engine.

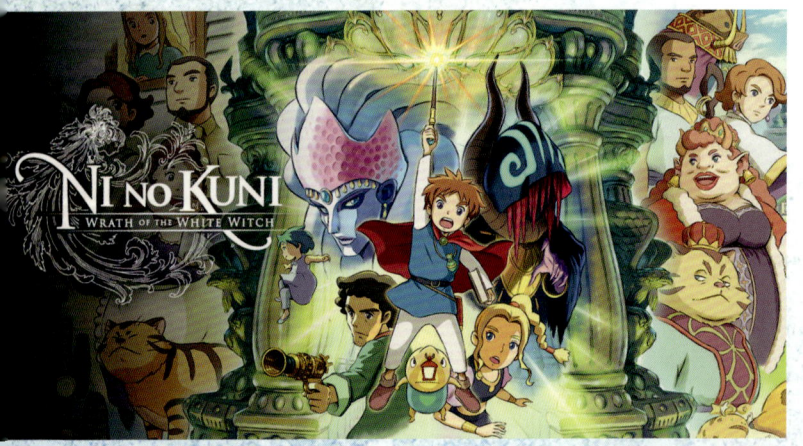

MONSTERS EVERYWHERE

Studio Ghibli didn't give up on RPGs based on "collecting and fighting little monsters." In 2002, it took part in the PS2 game *Magic Pengel: The Quest for Color.* In this rather pleasant product where players could generate creatures, studios Ghibli and Gainax produced the final sequence. This fresh, watercolor ending directed by Osamu Tanabe was a real treat, supported by the designs of veteran artists Yoshiharu Sato (*My Neighbor Totoro*) and Masashi Andô (character designer for *Your Name*).

Another, lesser-known game also benefited from a Ghibli look. In *LostMagic*, a modest RPG-RTS (real-time strategy game) released on Nintendo DS in 2006, the player took on the role of a young blond mage. The game's character design by Yoshiharu Sato was quite appealing. Similarly, the point-and-click saga *Wonder Project J2* (which had an interface never seen before in Europe) also involved Ghibli talent. For the 1996 Nintendo 64 opus, Akihiko Yamashita (future regular animator at Studio Ghibli and Studio Ponoc) created a character design whose heroine, with two enormous clips in her hair, inevitably brings Arrietty to mind.

LEVELING UP WITH LEVEL-5

In 2011, Ghibli marked its most famous video game collaboration with the *Ni no Kuni* saga, a small RPG marvel developed by the excellent Level-5 studio (which also created the *Professor Layton* series). Once again, this was a turn-based RPG set in a world of fantasy and small creatures, in which a young hero battled the forces of evil. While the first entry in the saga was released in 2010 on Nintendo DS, it was the PS3 version (*Ni no Kuni: Wrath of the White Witch*) that hit it big in the West. With its enchanting, benevolent, colorful, accessible universe, the adventure had everything it took to appeal to several generations of gamers. Above all, *Ni no Kuni* benefited from the studio's talent and exacting standards on every level, including characters, settings, artistic direction, Joe Hisaishi's music, and animated sequences. With a style that was streamlined but never simplistic, the game perfectly captured the Ghibli spirit, and the studio didn't compromise on its artistic ambition. In fact, with a big name like Yoshiyuki Momose directing the cut scenes, this was a truly interactive and immersive film. Even though the characters lost some of their vitality in the game, the roundness and warmth of the "Ghibliesque" art remained. It was a real tour de force that won over the studio's fans as an extension of its enchanting, epic world.

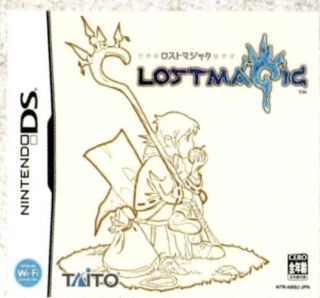

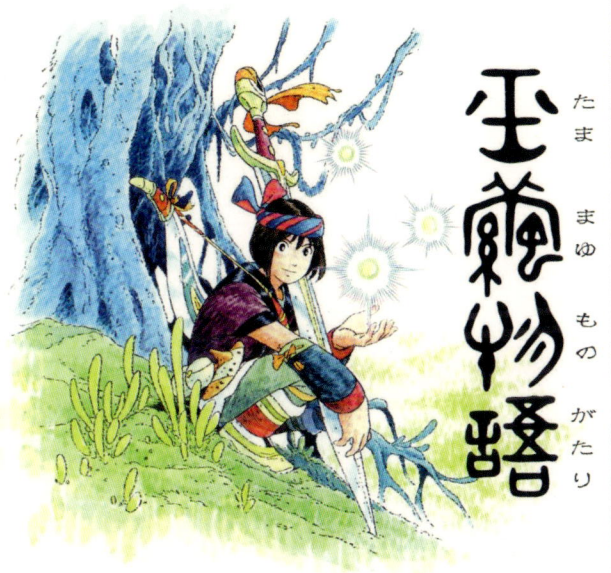

Magic Pengel: The Quest for Color.

It was only logical that the franchise should be brought to the big screen, but contrary to expectations, the studio OLM (*Pokémon*) handled the production.

GHIBLI IN ADVERTISING
QUALITY IS SERVED

From cotton swabs to socks and scissor holders, the Japanese are often very inventive when it comes to displaying their worlds on consumer products. While the marketing department of Toei Animation (*Dragon Ball*) remains a benchmark in the field, it often comes up with relatively conventional ads. Other players in the market, such as Studio Ponoc and Studio Ghibli, are seen as more adept at creating genuine short films, even when they're used for advertising.

➤ By Bruno de la Cruz

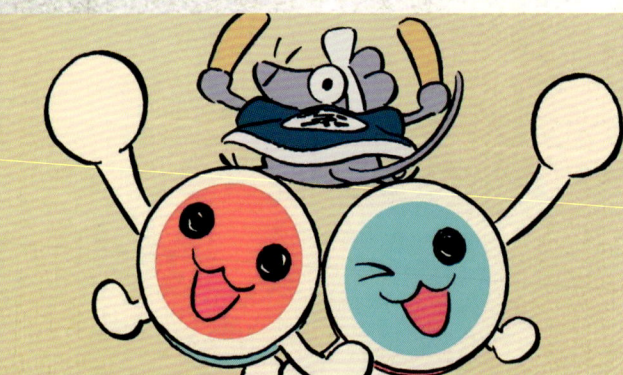

Taiko no Tatsujin.

O-UCHI DE TABEYÔ (2003–2004)

Six fifteen-second films were produced for the House Foods brand of ready-made meals. Hayao Miyazaki and Yoshiyuki Momose were at the helm of these commercials, which skillfully blend traditional animation and CGI, alternating between winter and summer scenes. As is often the case with Studio Ghibli, the graphic rendering of the meals is outstanding, and these ads, set to Joe Hisaishi's musical compositions, are among the company's most technically successful.

YOMIURI SHIMBUN (2005)

In a more penciled style, somewhere between *The Tale of the Princess Kaguya* and *My Neighbors the Yamadas*, these fifteen- and thirty-second films are dedicated to the historic daily newspaper *Yomiuri Shimbun*, founded in 1874. They show Japanese people during the Edo period, newspaper in hand. It's delicate, lively work by veteran animator Osamu Tanabe, who also had a hand in *The Tale of the Princess Kaguya* and *My Neighbors the Yamadas*.

TAIKO NO TATSUJIN (2015)

Publisher Bandai Namco approached Studio Ghibli to celebrate the fifteenth anniversary of its video game *Taiko no Tatsujin*, a hugely successful rhythm and drum simulation game for Nintendo Switch. Thanks to the cute, rounded work of animator Katsuya Kondô, Studio Ghibli presents a mouse bouncing on the drum. The *kawaii* and traditional style is a perfect match for the product's artistic approach. Note that DLC (downloadable content) made it possible to play songs from *My Neighbor Totoro*, *Kiki's Delivery Service*, and *Ponyo*.

MARUBENI (2016)

One of the studio's most interesting works brings together three advertisements from 2016 dedicated to the animation of *emakimono* (painted narrative scrolls, which some consider to be the ancestor of manga) for green energy supplier Marubeni. A panoramic shot allows us to follow anthropomorphic characters animated with delightful action enhanced by wonderful brushstrokes. It's a remarkable bit of work by Katsuya Kondô, the studio's usual reliable animator.

You can find some of the ads (self-promotional or commissioned works) on the Blu-ray *Ghibli Full Special Short Shorts 1992–2016.*

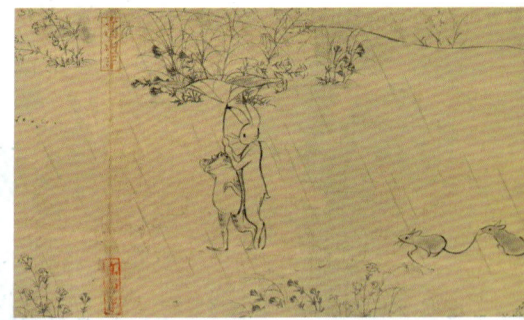

Ad for Marubeni.

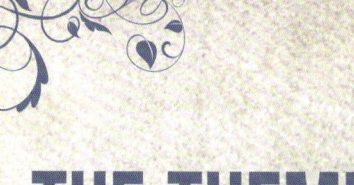

THE THEME PARK

At the time of writing, the successor to Isao Takahata and Hayao Miyazaki is still unclear, but the Ghibli brand continues to expand. Its latest incarnation is the launch of a theme park based on the studio's films.

◆▶ By Stéphanie Chaptal

s if the museum weren't enough, Studio Ghibli has opened a theme park based on its films. Ghibli Park, run in partnership with *Chunichi Shimbun*, opened on November 1, 2022, at the Earth Expo Memorial Park in Aichi Prefecture near Nagoya, the site of the 2005 World Expo. It features five distinct zones, three of which have been accessible since the opening, one that opened at the end of 2023, and one that opened a few months later. The first to open were the 80,000-square-foot Hill of Youth, combining the worlds of *Whisper of the Heart* and *From Up on Poppy Hill* with late-nineteenth-century science fiction elements like those found in *Castle in the Sky*; the 45,000-square-foot Ghibli's Grand Warehouse (the commercial area with stores, restaurants, a children's playground, and a theater); and finally, Dondoko Forest, a large, wooded area of around 215,000 square feet surrounding the existing replica of Satsuki and Mei's house in *My Neighbor Totoro*, which has been there since 2005. These areas were subsequently joined by Mononoke

Village, featuring life-size replicas of buildings from the film *Princess Mononoke*, such as the Tatara Forges, and a small play area, accessible to all free of charge, based on the world of *The Cat Returns*. The 290,000-square-foot Valley of Witches, dedicated entirely to the films *Howl's Moving Castle* and *Kiki's Delivery Service*, offers a mini amusement park and life-size replicas of buildings from both feature films, including the famous castle. The elevator tower near Ai-Chikyuhaku Kinen Koen station, inspired by *Castle in the Sky*, is also accessible free of charge and leads to the park itself, then to the Hill of Youth.

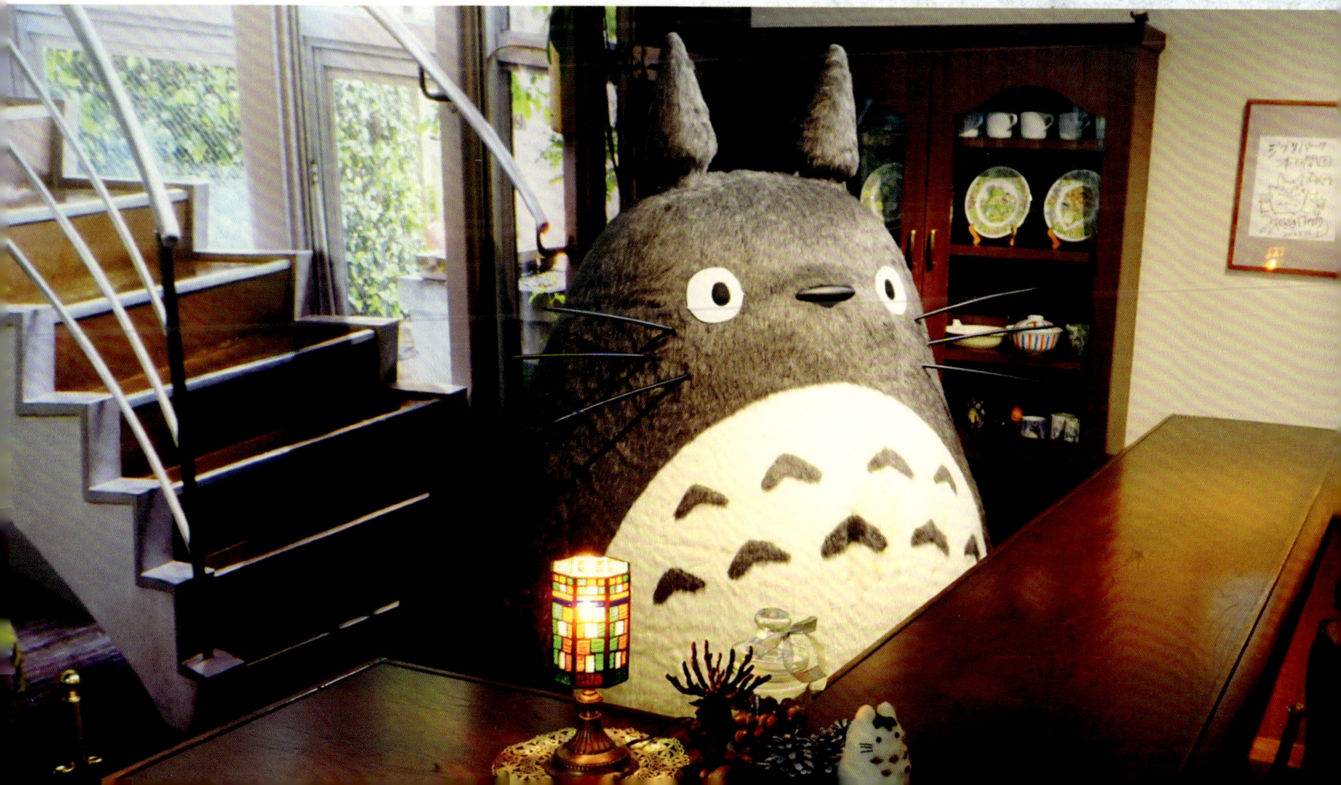

Ghibli Park was designed first and foremost as a theme park, but it is not intended to be an amusement park with a multitude of roller coasters and other spectacular rides, like those found in Disney parks or the recent Nintendo World extension to Universal Studios in Osaka. In a July 2020 interview on the occasion of the exhibition dedicated to the upcoming launch of Ghibli Park, Gorô Miyazaki, who trained as a landscape architect and was the designer and first director of the Ghibli Museum before becoming the park's director, explained, "I've always thought that theme parks with large mechanical attractions as most people imagine them don't suit Ghibli." Instead, the emphasis here is on immersion in the world of the films, with a replica of the garden and aircraft from *Castle in the Sky*, a giant steampunk elevator leading to the boarding house from *Poppy Hill*, the shops from *Spirited Away* in the shopping area, and a 170-seat movie theater showing Ghibli shorts, which had previously been shown exclusively at the museum.

Unlike the Ghibli Museum, the park doesn't take you behind the scenes of Studio Ghibli and animation in general to learn how the various works were made, but simply immerses you in the worlds portrayed in the films and lets you share the experiences of the characters. So much so, in fact, that the Valley of Witches was the last section of the park to open to the public because it was inspired by the studio's most European-set films, and the designers wanted to use typically European materials such as oak, chestnut, and ash wood to re-create the bakery where Kiki works and Sophie's millinery shop in *Howl's Moving Castle*. As these species are rarely used in Japan, they had to have them cut and wait until the wood was dry enough to be used as building material. To compensate, it was decided to add another element—The House of Witches—which is a reconstruction of the house of Bella Yaga, the blue-haired witch who takes in Earwig in *Earwig and the Witch*.

In the spring of 2024, five electric Catbuses from Toyota went into circulation to take visitors from one part of the park to another. According to Keiji Yamamoto, one of the carmaker's project managers, "The challenge was to give the impression of a living creature capable of moving at any moment. We gave it a round shape and a matte paint finish. We used soft, plush upholstery for the seats." Just like the interior of Mei and Satsuki's favorite means of transportation in the film. And these are accessible even to adults, unlike the Catbuses in the park's play areas and at the Ghibli Museum, which are reserved for those under twelve.

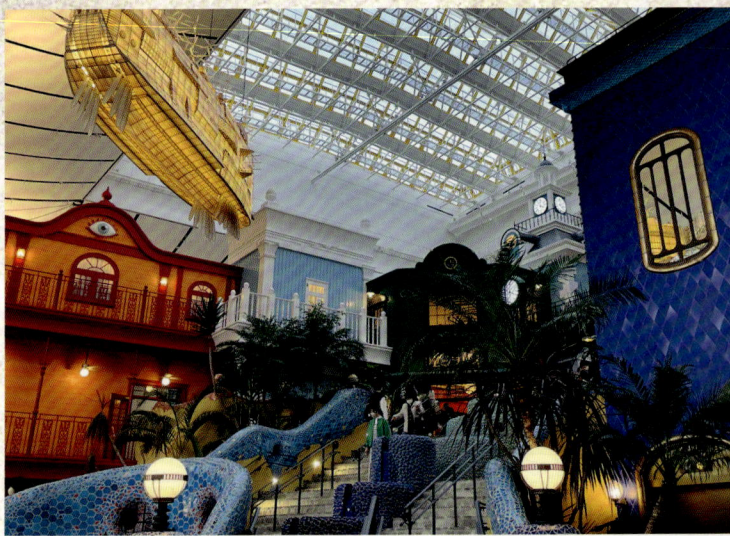

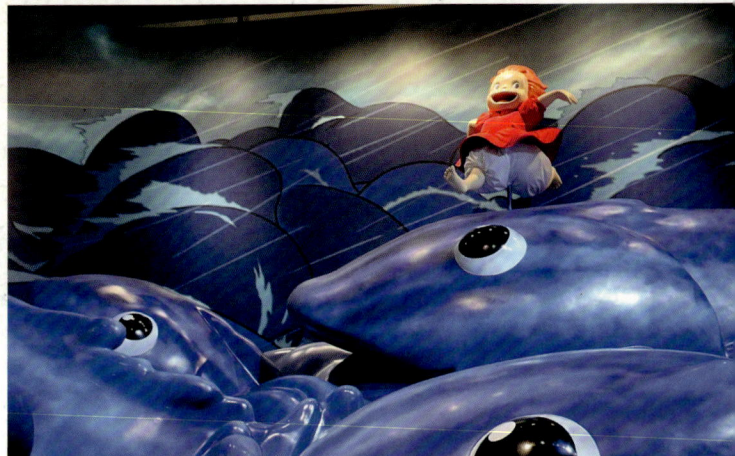

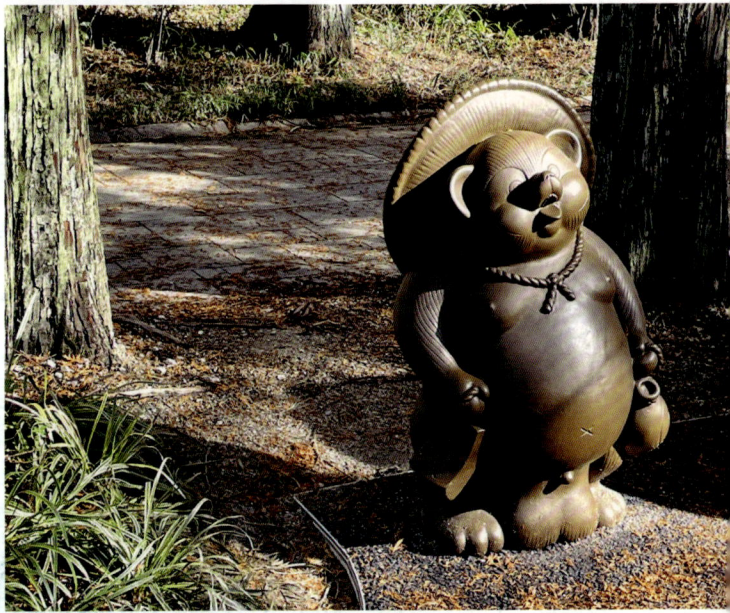

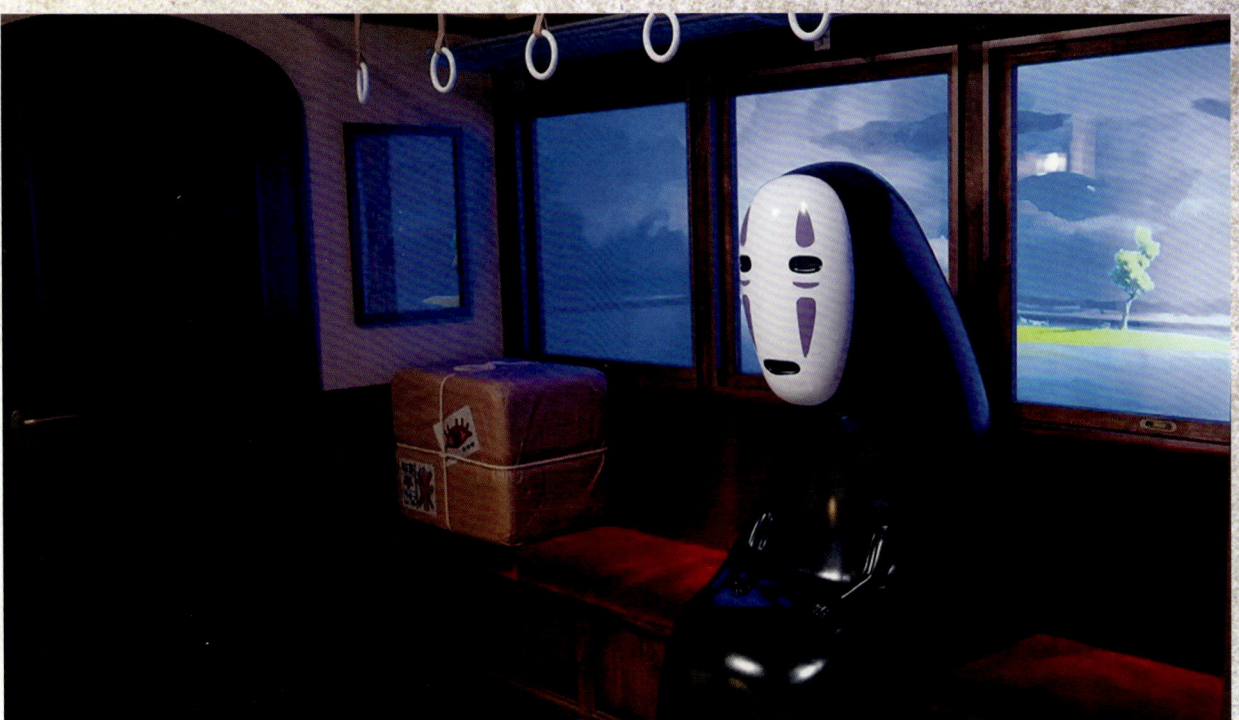

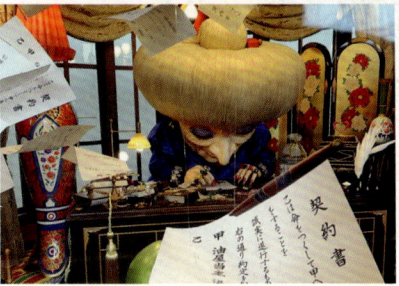
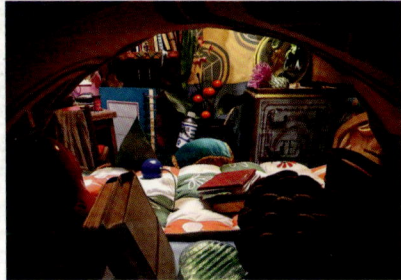
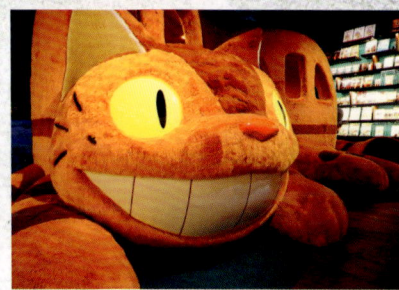

HOW TO GET THERE

The park is a four-and-a-half-hour drive from central Tokyo. Getting there by train requires patience: First, go to Nagoya (about one hour and forty minutes by train from Tokyo, at the fastest), then take the Higashiyama subway line (journey time: twenty-eight minutes) and a second small train called Linimo, which takes about fifteen minutes to reach the park entrance. If you prefer the bus, there is also a shuttle bus from Nagoya bus station to the park's station. Like for the Ghibli Museum, you need to book your tickets well in advance. For a visit scheduled for April 2024, for example, tickets went on sale on the official website, www.ghibli-park.jp/en, on February 10, 2024, beginning at 2 p.m. local time.

A distinction is made between domestic visitors (in other words, Japanese people and permanent residents) and international tourists. Once again, following the Ghibli Museum's example, the park's visitor capacity is deliberately controlled and set quite low, at a maximum of five thousand people per day. This is to ensure optimum visitor comfort. Here's a fun detail: Cosplay is permitted and even encouraged, so you may come across Totoro, Haru, No-Face from *Spirited Away*, or San during your visit, without knowing whether they're park employees or visitors just like you!

And how much does the visit cost? It's free for children under four, and varies between 3,500 and 7,800 yen for adults, depending on the day of the week and the scope of the visit. Children between four and twelve pay half price, as do disabled visitors and their caretakers. It's also possible to purchase a ticket for specific areas of the park, starting at 1,000 yen per zone.

GHIBLI COLLABORATIONS

Dragon Ball, Neon Genesis Evangelion, Berserk, Lupin the Third, and *Ghost in the Shell 2: Innocence* are some of the projects that Studio Ghibli has been involved with to varying degrees. Although it's seen as a unique studio with a firm policy, it's not a reclusive village with impenetrable borders. In fact, it's quite the opposite.

By Bruno de la Cruz

In the Japanese animation industry, it's often said that Japan is a single animation studio. This expression reminds us that a series or film is very rarely produced by a single studio. Given the workload and the pace broadcasters set, the studio primarily responsible for animation delegates some parts here and there to others, usually at a low cost. These elements can be extremely varied, and may involve a few seconds of animation, complete episodes, photography management, set creation (often the domain of specialized studios), cleaning up pencil drawings for a few shots, or editing. In general, the lead studio handles key scenes and episodes in-house, while delegating the less essential parts to other companies. It's also important to understand that when this subcontracting is ordered by very large studios like Toei Animation (which is often involved in large-scale adaptations like *Dragon Ball* and *Digimon*), orders are placed with less talented studios (which is why some episodes are so technically

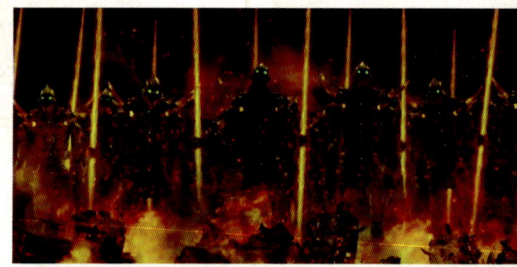

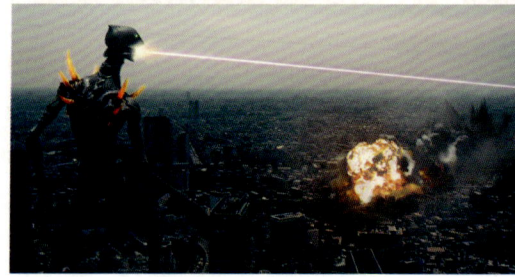

Kyoshinhei Tôkyô ni Arawaru. Giant God Warrior Appears in Tokyo.

weak). Beyond the theoretical, this methodology often depends on the relationships that producers or directors have with their colleagues, and it's not uncommon for negotiations (one could almost say "gentlemen's agreements") to take place between artists: A studio or director will agree to help another only if the other party reciprocates.

This means that while Studio Ghibli has lent a hand with several series, it has also called on other studios (Production I.G, for example) to participate in the production of its films. Nevertheless, Ghibli shoulders the lion's share of the work (it has all the departments needed to produce a film), and this is what sets it apart from the others.

GHIBLI X HIDEAKI ANNO

As mentioned in the "Ghibli Successors" section, Hayao Miyazaki and Hideaki Anno share a relationship marked by respect and admiration. So when it came time to make the ambitious *Neon*

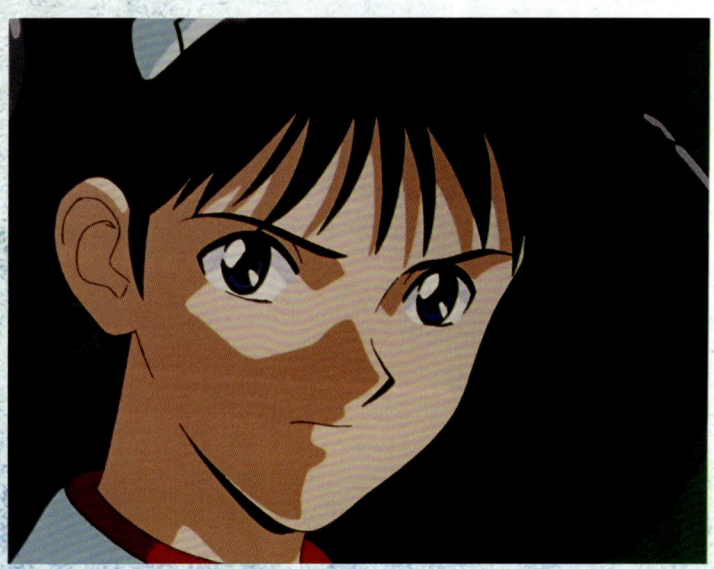

Shinji in Neon Genesis Evangelion.

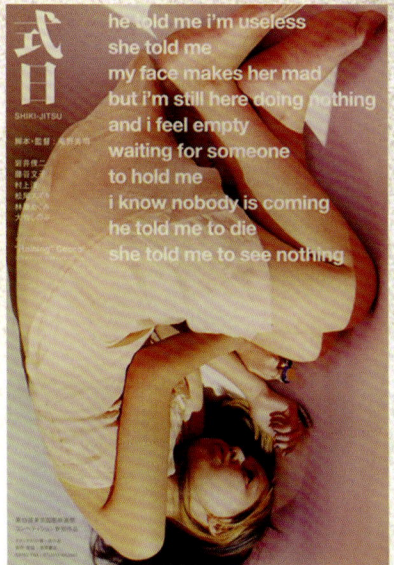

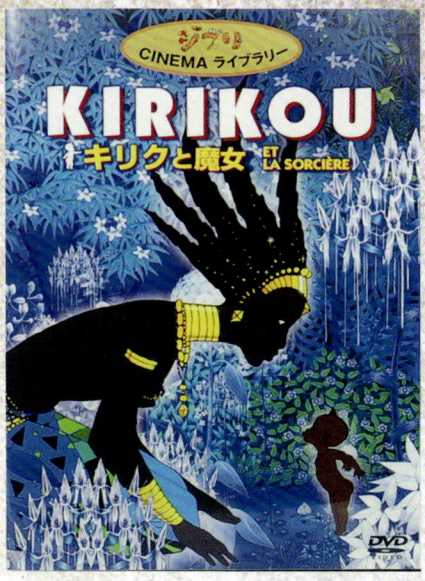

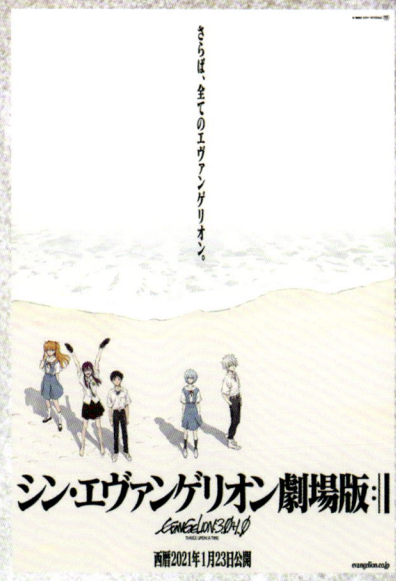

Poster for the film *Shiki-Jitsu*.

Poster for the film *Evangelion: 3.0+1.0 Thrice Upon a Time*.

Genesis Evangelion series (1995), whose production was far from straightforward, Anno and the Gainax studio called on Ghibli to produce much of Episode 11. If you're familiar with Studio Ghibli's films, the faces of Shinji Ikari (the main character) and the other characters will look very familiar. It's important to note that the animation director and the episode's supervisor both assumed (or accepted) that the Ghibli style would be clearly apparent in the final rendering. It's not uncommon for animation directors to rigorously adapt the animators' drawings to the model sheet (the graphic document used as a reference by the animators). Let's just say that Ghibli, as a major studio, takes advantage of its reputation and connections to set itself apart from the rest. As an aside, Anno, who wanted to ask Ghibli for several episodes, sold his request to Miyazaki by explaining that there would be no *mecha* (mechanical elements, such as robots or ships), but only scenes from everyday life.

Ghibli's involvement with *Evangelion* lasted until 2021: While it was delivering *Evangelion: 3.0+1.0 Thrice Upon a Time*, the masterly metaphysical conclusion to its *mecha* tetralogy, Ghibli helped Anno again by lending him equipment.[1] That's what collaboration is all about!

WE'RE GOING LIVE!

The relationship between the studio and Hideaki Anno continued throughout the 2000s with several projects. First came *Shiki-Jitsu* (also known as *Ritual*, 2000), a live-action film produced by Studio Kajino, a subsidiary of Ghibli founded by Yoshiyuki Momose and Toshio Suzuki. The film is an adaptation of the autobiographical novella *Tohimu* by Ayako Fujitani, daughter of actor Steven Seagal. In this experimental, metafictional medium, Hideaki Anno explored depression and paternal relationships through the encounter between a filmmaker and a young woman. But the umbilical cord between Anno and Miyazaki goes even further, with *Giant God Warrior Appears in Tokyo* (2012). In that case, the film was directed by Hideaki Anno's friend Shinji Higuchi, the king of *tokusatsu* (special effects) and unlikely camera angles, using models and CGI to stage a giant creature attacking Tokyo. *Kaiju* (giant monsters), blue skies, and destruction were on the agenda, in line with Anno's filmmaking style. A similar formula was already served up in 2002 with *The Invention of Imaginary Machines of Destruction*. This short, created for the Ghibli Museum exhibition *Laputa, Castle in the Sky, and Imaginary Science Fiction Machines*, showed the destructive power of weapons of war, using traditional animation and scale models. Ghibli has also produced other live-action projects, such as the 2001 feature *Satorare* (*Transparent: Tribute to a Sad Genius* directed by Katsuyuki Motohiro), as well as distributing foreign films such as *Tales of the Night* and *Kirikou and the Sorceress*. Ghibli's range of activities and collaborations is extremely diverse.

[1] Fun fact: Another of Studio Ghibli's traditional animation tables migrated to Mamoru Hosoda's Studio Chizu.

TRIBUTE
ILLUSTRATIONS

➤ • ⬅

Gaëlle Autin
Oussama Bouacheria
Elsa Brants
Pa Ming Chiu
Nicolas David
Bruno de la Cruz
Amandine Girard
Aimé Jalon
Kanthesis
Guillaume Lapeyre
Ulysse Malassagne
Nicolas Mitric
Audrey Molinatti
Camille Moulin-Dupré
Emmanuel Nhieu
Radja Sauperamaniane
Tony Valente

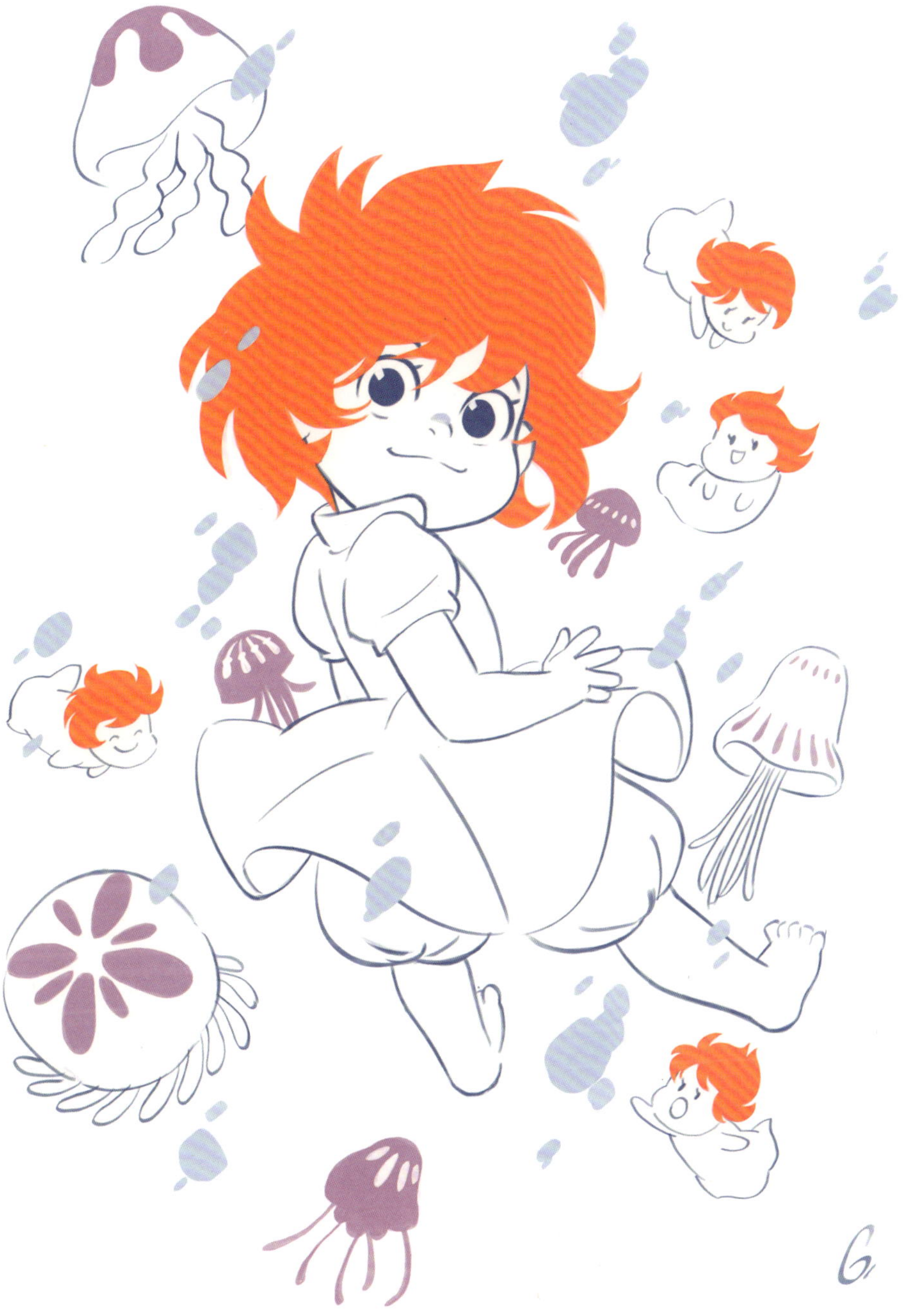

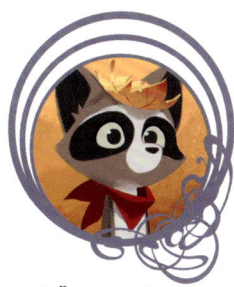

GAËLLE AUTIN (GALOU)

Character designer in animation

Favorite Ghibli film:
Kiki's Delivery Service

Why did you choose this drawing?
I drew this picture because I love everything that is cute.

Titles:
• *Martin Mystery*
• *Rekkit Rabbit*
• *LoliRock*

http://gaelleautin.com
http://facebook.com/Galoupop

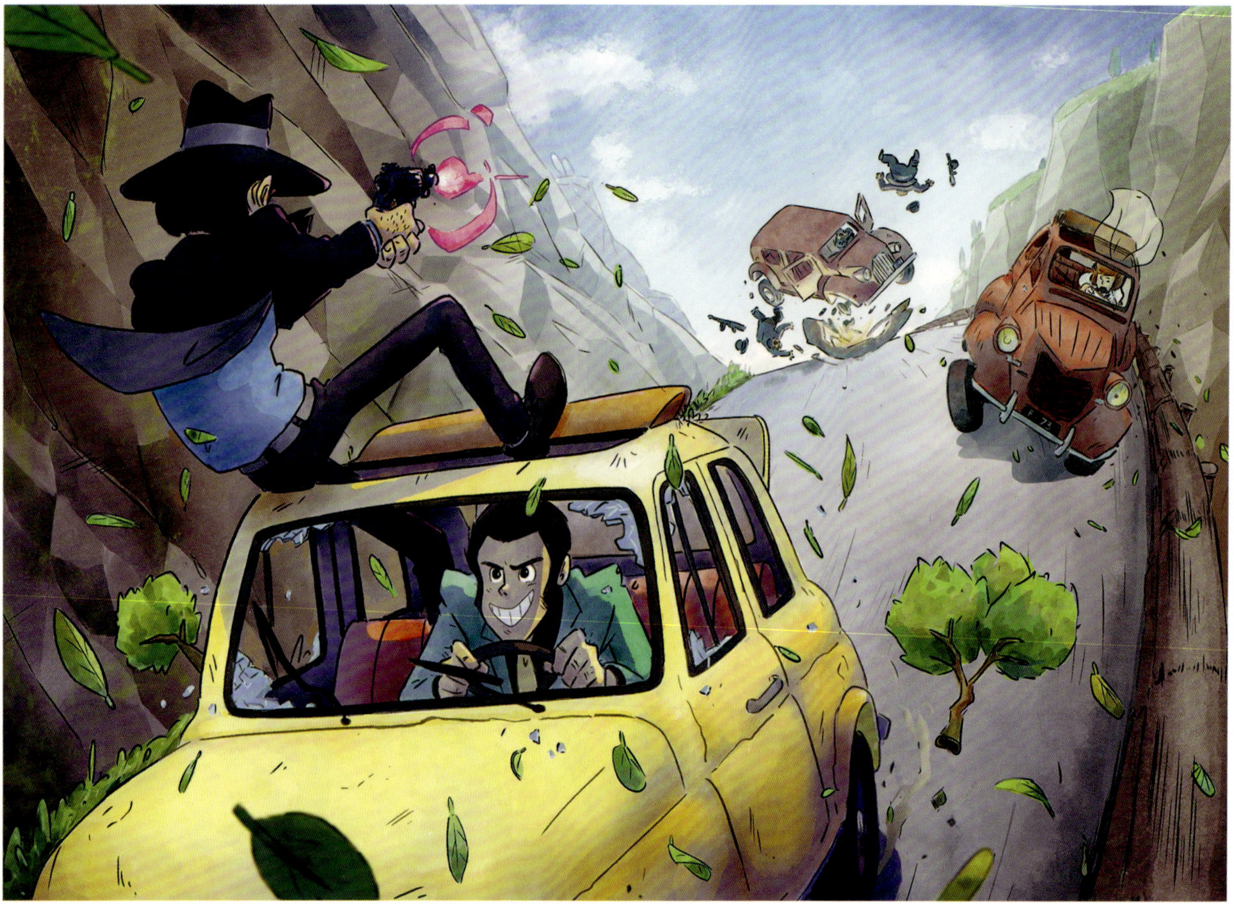

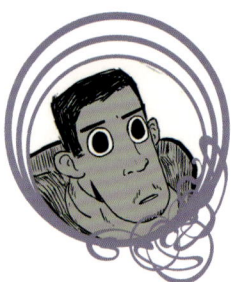

**OUSSAMA
BOUACHERIA**

Director, story artist

Favorite Ghibli film:
*Lupin III: The Castle
of Cagliostro*

**Why did you choose
this drawing?**
It's one of my favorite
animated films, pure
and simple. I must
have seen it a million
times. I love Miyazaki's
work from the late
1970s and early
1980s, especially
Future Boy Conan and
Sherlock Hound.

Titles:
• *Kairos*

• *Mune: Guardian of the Moon*

• League of Legends World Trailer
2016

https://twitter.com/PetitCachottier

www.instagram.com/oussama_
bouacheria_/

www.studiolacachette.com/

https://oussamabouacheria.tumblr.com/

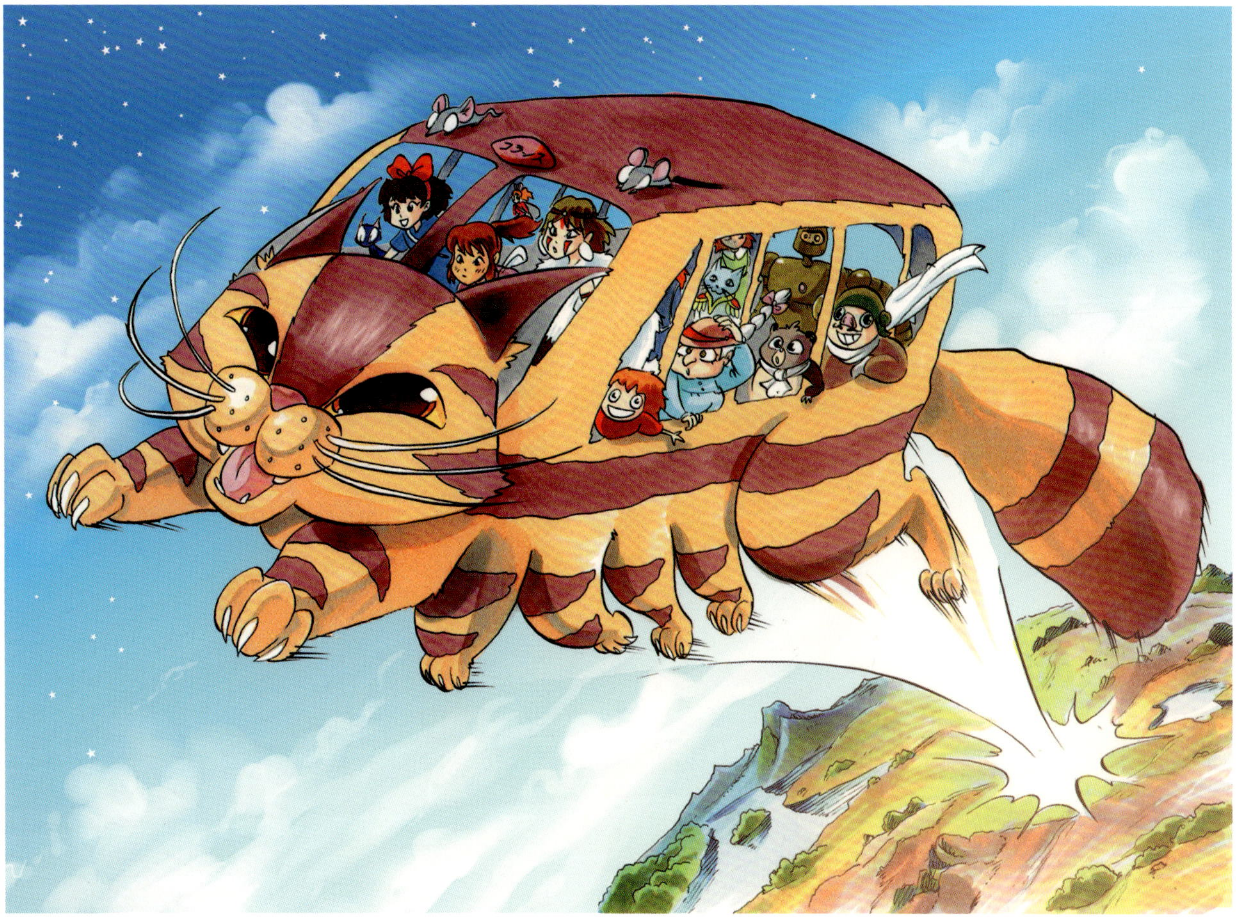

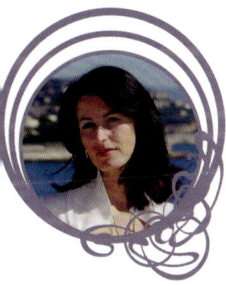

ELSA BRANTS

Manga author

Favorite Ghibli film:
My Neighbor Totoro
(The scene where the trees grow has always made me cry with joy.)

Why did you choose this drawing?
I dream of having my own Catbus! When I visited the Ghibli Museum, I was an adult, and therefore far too tall to be allowed inside the reproduction Catbus. It was so frustrating!!!

Title:
Save Me, Pythia
(Kana)

www.facebook.com/elsa.brants

https://twitter.com/elsabrants

www.instagram.com/elsabrants/

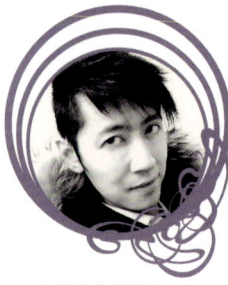

PA MING CHIU

Journalist, screenwriter, author

Favorite Ghibli films:
My Neighbor Totoro and *Princess Mononoke*

Why did you choose this drawing?
Princess Mononoke is one of my three Ghibli favorites (along with *Totoro* and *Castle in the Sky*), and I think San is a magnificent heroine, wild and strong, yet sensitive and flawed.

Titles:
• *Alice & Valentine* (Jungle)
• *A.M.E.S.* (IOS)

www.facebook.com/paming.chiu

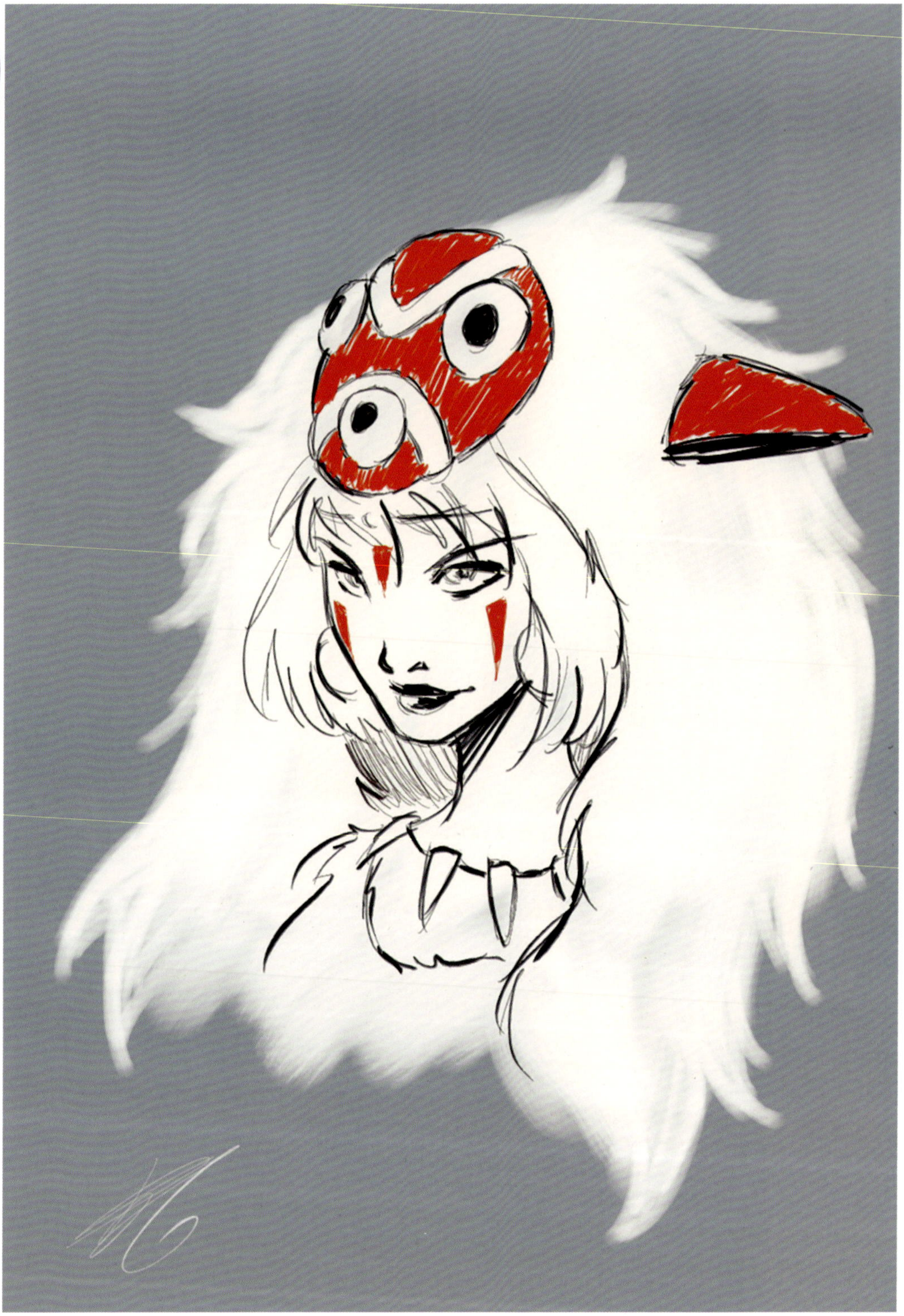

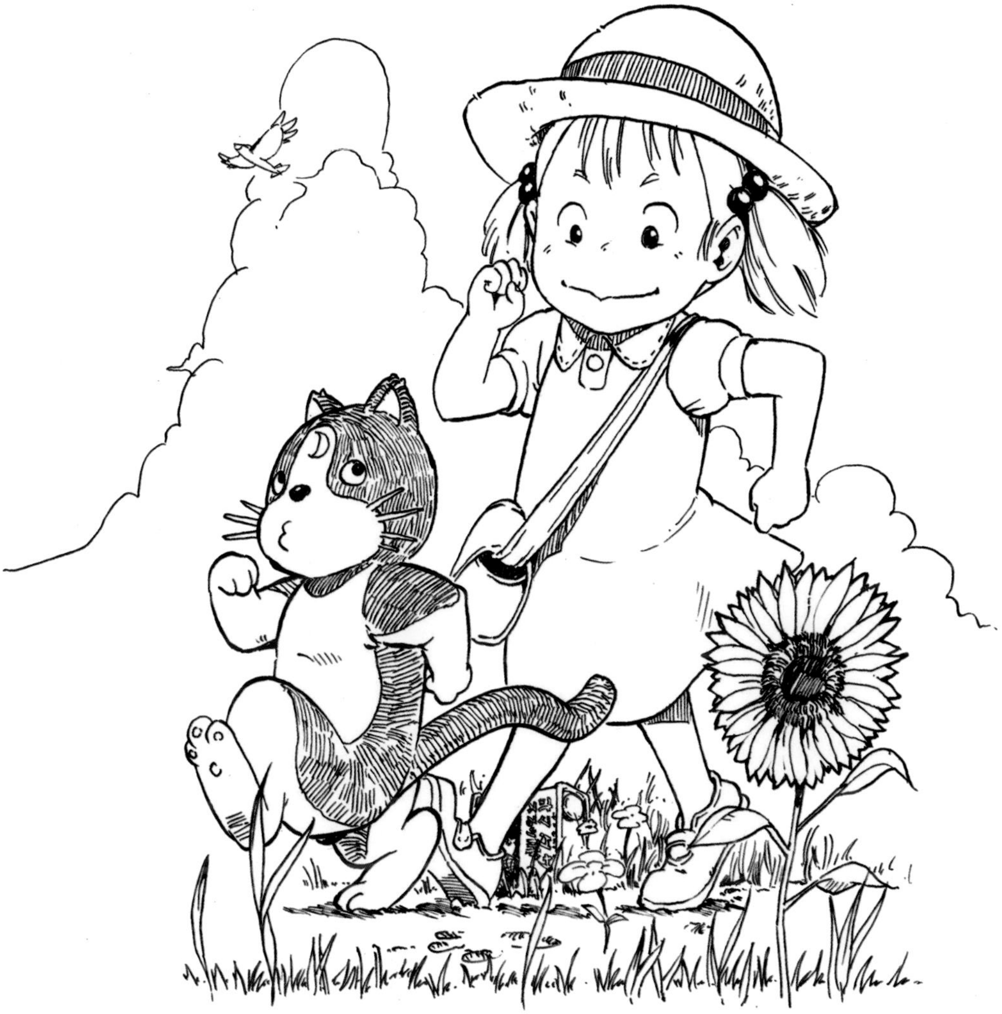

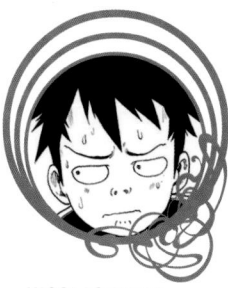

NICOLAS DAVID

Manga author

Favorite Ghibli film:
My Neighbor Totoro

Why did you choose this drawing?
I tried to bring out the nostalgia of *Totoro* and many Ghibli films such as *Chie the Brat*, but I realized afterward how off-base I was, as that one was made before Studio Ghibli was founded.

Title:
Meckaz (Olydri Éditions)

www.facebook.com/
nicolasdavidmeckaz

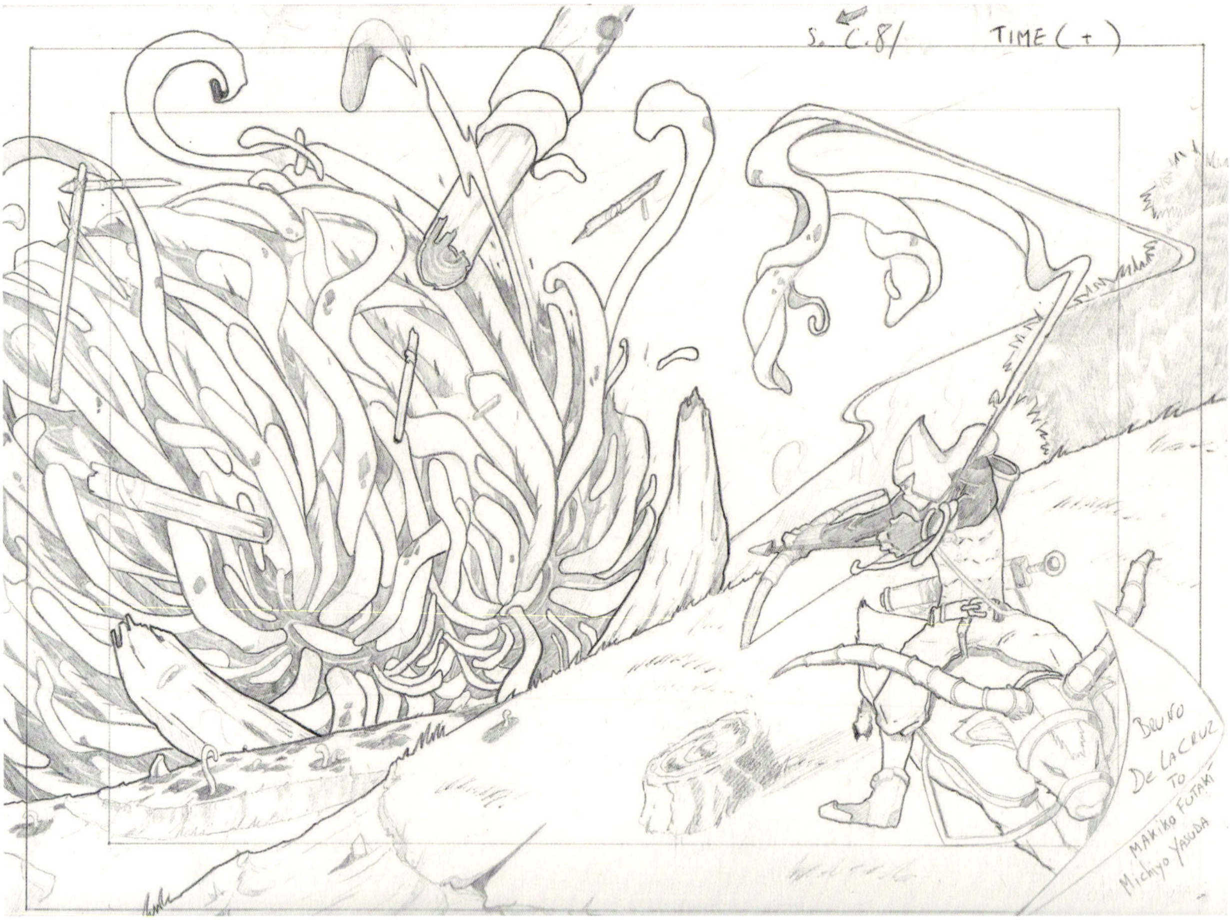

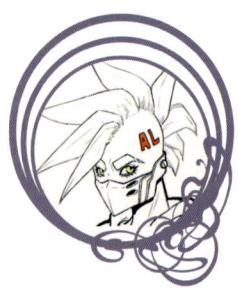

BRUNO DE LA CRUZ

Journalist

Favorite Ghibli film:
Ponyo

Why did you choose this drawing?
Ghibli is almost an artisanal production. So I chose one of my favorite scenes, where Ashitaka is being chased by a demon boar, and did the whole thing in pencil, in layout style. It's also a (modest) tribute to two of the studio's historic artists.

Titles:
• *AnimeLand*
• *AnimeLand X-tra*

www.instagram.com/ono_dlc

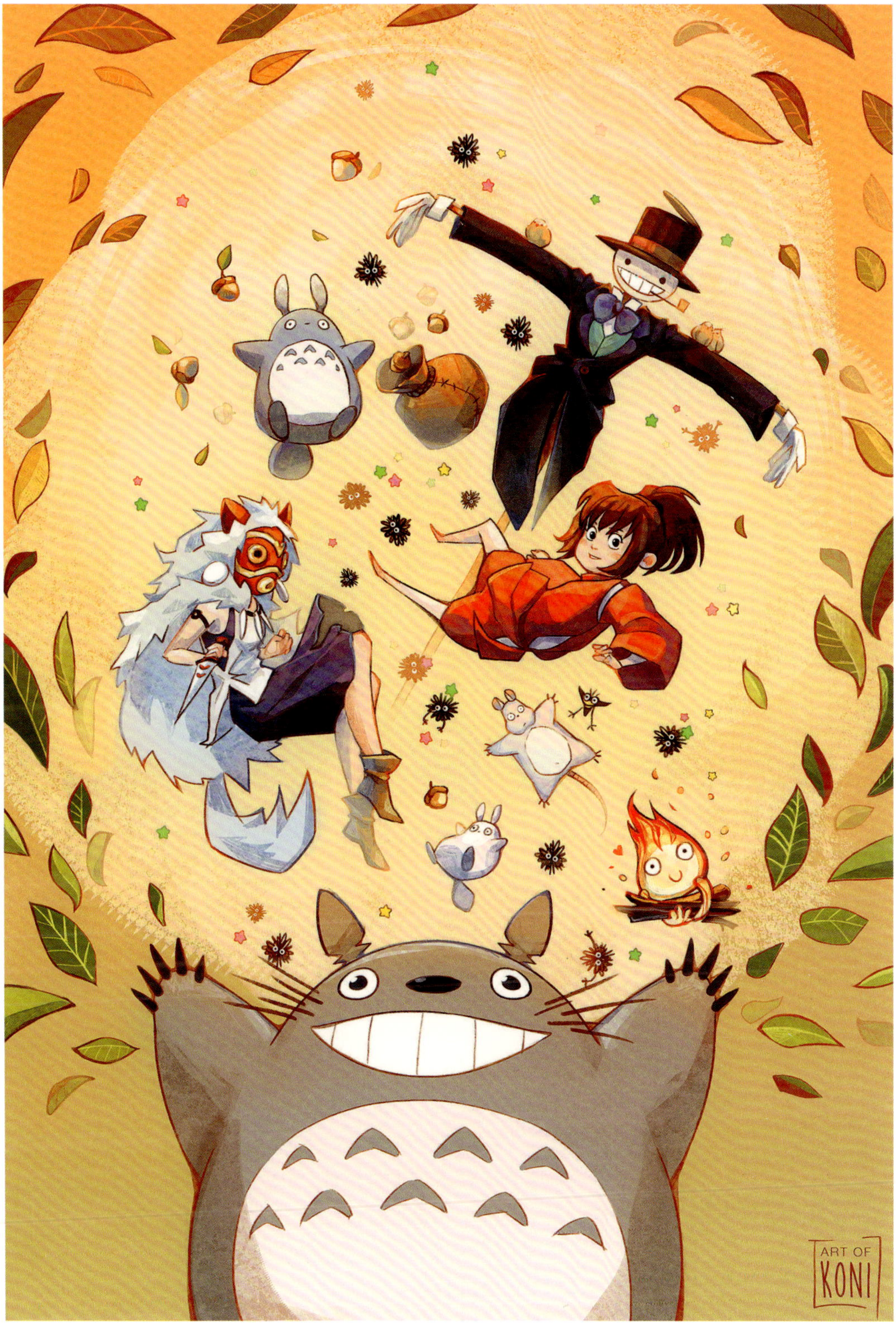

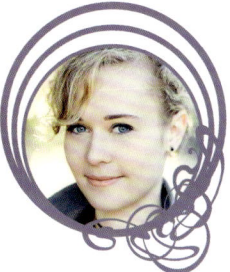

AMANDINE GIRARD (KONI)

Concept artist, illustrator

Favorite Ghibli films:
My Neighbor Totoro, *Princess Mononoke*, and *Spirited Away*

Why did you choose this drawing?
I couldn't pick just one Ghibli film as my subject, so I brought together some of my favorite characters and let Totoro dominate the illustration, because for me, he is still the best character in the Ghibli universe and represents the studio perfectly!

Titles:
Works for Ubisoft Mobile

www.facebook.com/artofkoni/

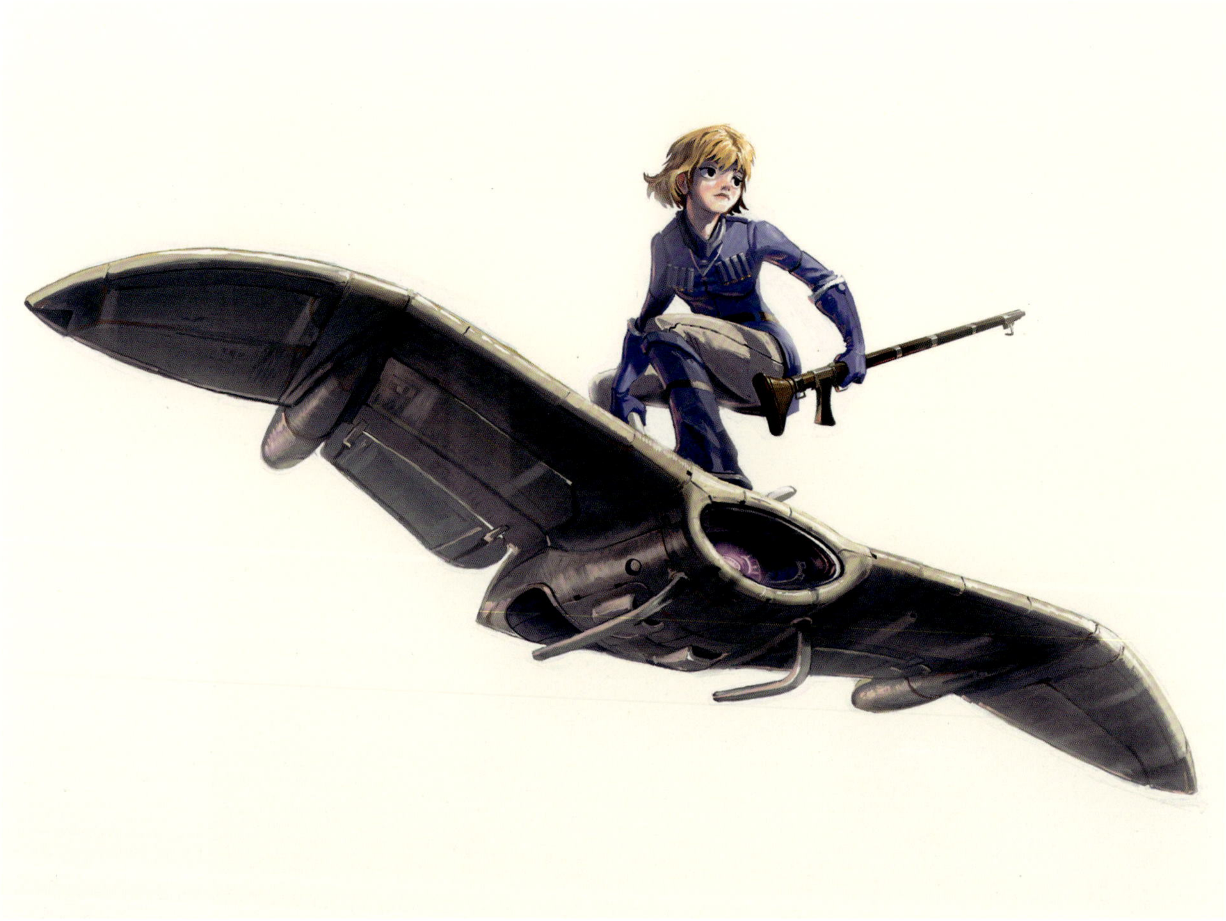

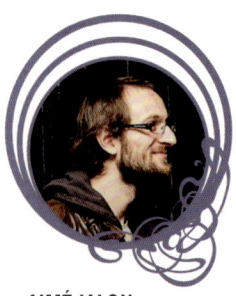

AIMÉ JALON
Video game concept
artist

Favorite Ghibli film:
Princess Mononoke

**Why did you choose
this drawing?**
I love *Nausicaä*'s
world. For me, it's
one of the best Ghibli
films. I discovered it
late in life, and it really
blew me away.

Titles:
• *Dishonored*
• *Dishonored 2*

http://jalon.ultra-book.com/

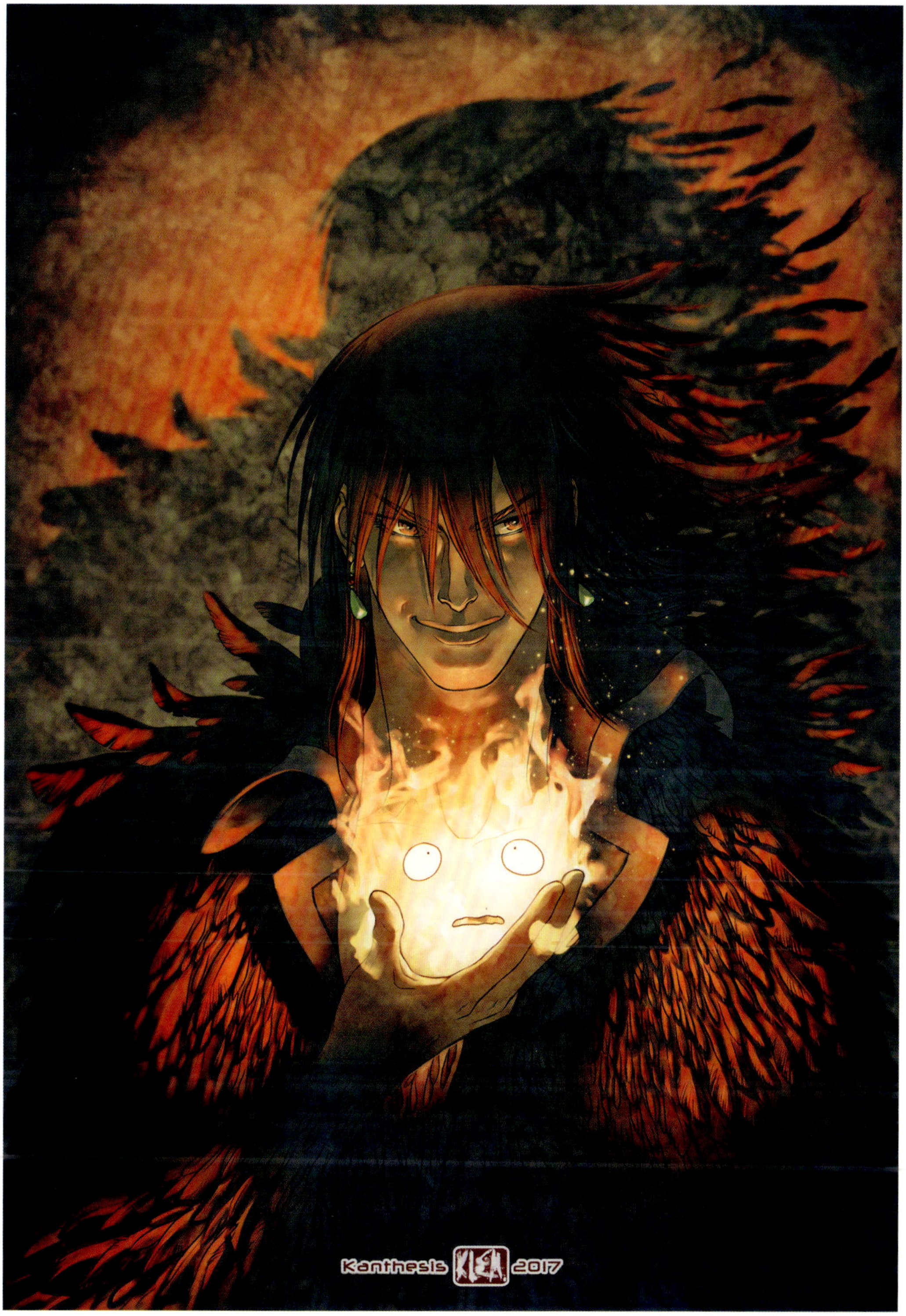

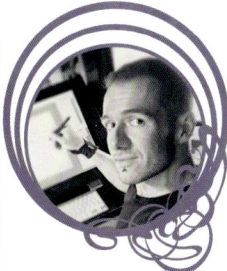

KANTHESIS

Illustrator and character designer

Favorite Ghibli film:
Howl's Moving Castle

Why did you choose this drawing?
Hauru is one of those typical Ghibli characters who is far from black-and-white. His strength and power have dark origins, and he has the character of a spoiled child, in addition to being quite charismatic.

Titles:
• *Satori* (Les Humanoïdes Associés)

• *Seigneurs de Guerre* (Glénat)

• *Art-Thérapie Star Wars* (Hachette)

www.kanthesis.deviantart.com

www.facebook.com/kanthesis.artworks/?fref=ts

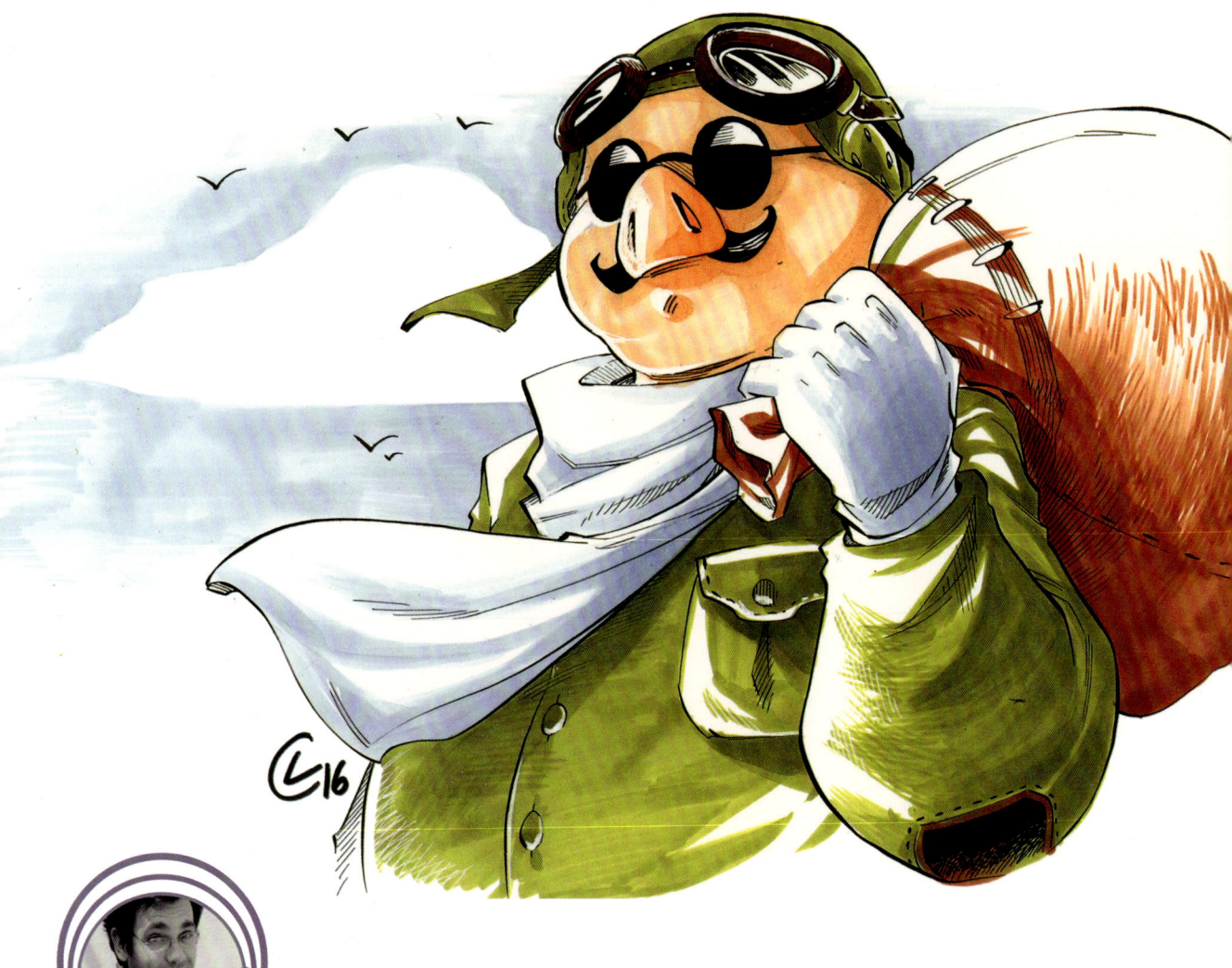

GUILLAUME LAPEYRE

Copyist monk in manga format (mainly)

Favorite Ghibli films:
ALL of them, but *Porco Rosso* put a twinkle in my eye :)

Why did you choose this drawing?
The character, the story, and the plane made a lasting impression on me!

Titles:
• *Les Chroniques de Magon* (Delcourt)
• *Ether* (Delcourt)
• *Explorers* (Soleil)
• *City Hall* (Ankama)
• *L'Intrépide* (Ankama)
• *Le Visiteur du future: La Brigade temporelle* (Ankama)
• *Booksterz* (Kana)

www.instagram.com/guillaumelapeyre_mangaka
www.twitter.com/g_lapeyre
www.twitch.tv/inthebasement_studio

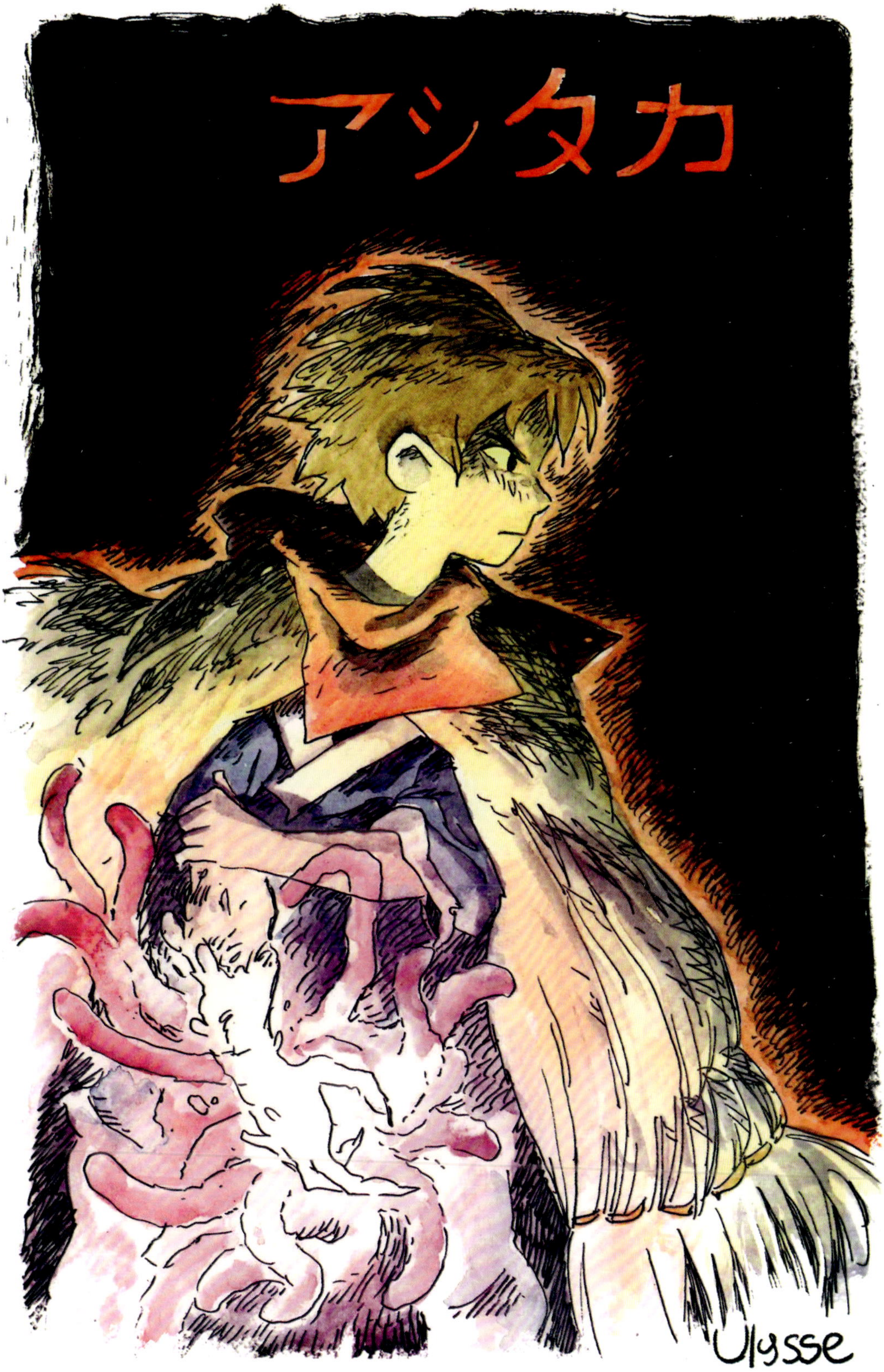

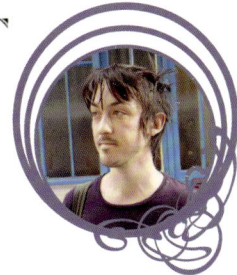

アシタカ

ULYSSE MALASSAGNE

Comic book author, animated film director

Favorite Ghibli film:
Princess Mononoke

Why did you choose this drawing?
Princess Mononoke was the first Ghibli film I ever saw, and the first animated film of such strength and maturity. Ashitaka remained one of my favorite heroes throughout my youth.

Titles:
• *Kairos* (Ankama Éditions)

• *Jade* (Glénat)

• *Kokekokkô!* (Issekinicho)

• *Le Collège noir* (Milan)

• *Mune: Guardian of the Moon* (animated film)

• *Zedd: Ignite, League of Legends* (Riot)

www.ulyssemalassagne. tumblr.com

www.studiolacachette.com

www.facebook.com/ Ulysse-Malassagne

Ulysse

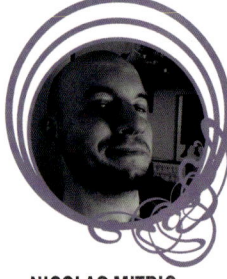

NICOLAS MITRIC

Termites Factory
creative director,
script and storyboard
instructor at École
Pivaut, comic strip
author

Favorite Ghibli film:
Princess Mononoke

**Why did you choose
this drawing?**
For the defense of the
natural environment
advocated by the
Senate, for the
incredible quality
of the character
animation, and the
beauty of the decor.
For EVERYTHING; it's
simply a masterpiece!

Titles:
• *Kookaburra* (Soleil)

• *Kookaburra Universe*
(Soleil)

• *Tessa: agent
intergalactique* (Soleil)

• *Sept dragons*
(Delcourt)

• *Arkeod* (Soleil)

• *Ultime voyage en
alchimie* (Glénat)

www.facebook.com/
nicolas.mitric

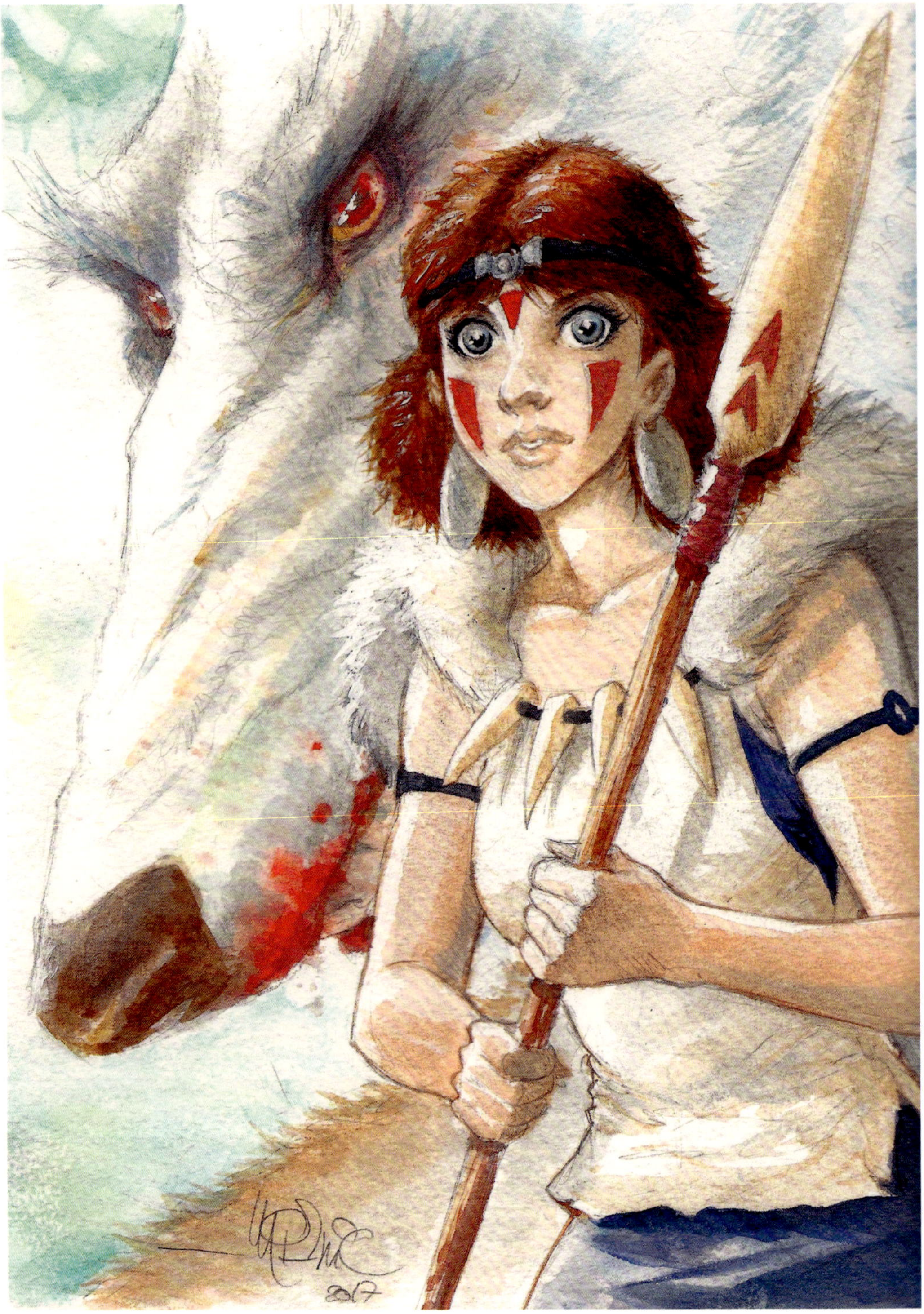

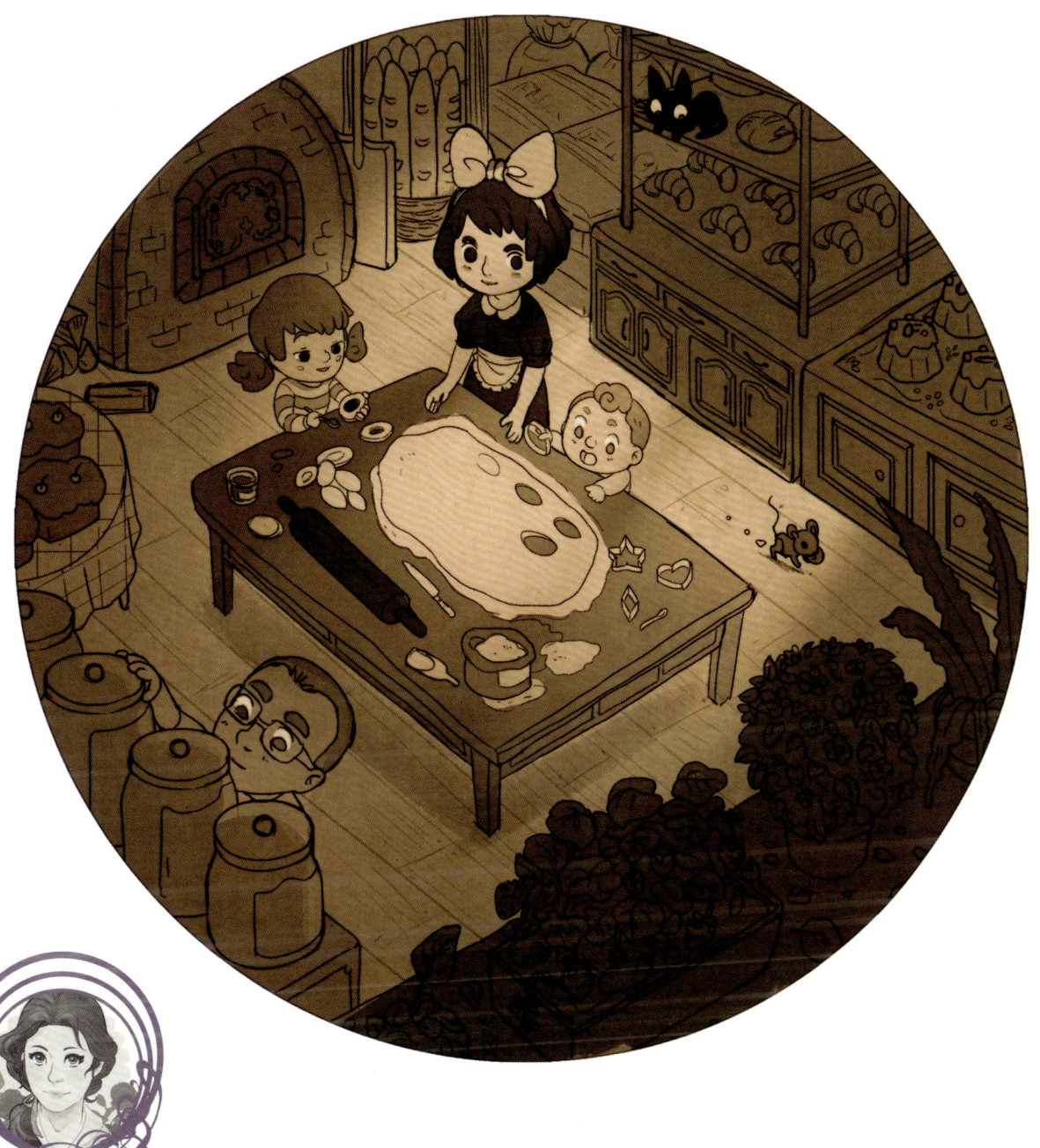

AUDREY MOLINATTI

Illustrator, comic book artist

Favorite Ghibli film:
Porco Rosso. (It was the first Ghibli film I ever saw, and I love the character Fio.)

Why did you choose this drawing?
I love witches, and graphically, I really like Kiki's world.

Title:
Le Bonheur

www.facebook.com/
audreymolinattiart

http://audrey-molinatti
-art.tumblr.com

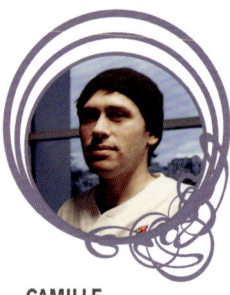

CAMILLE
MOULIN-DUPRÉ

Mangaka, writer,
director

Favorite Ghibli film:
That's a tough
question. I consider
Grave of the Fireflies
and *Spirited Away*
to be the studio's
masterpieces.

My favorite films are
Porco Rosso and *The
Tale of the Princess
Kaguya.*

**Why did you choose
this drawing?**
I have a soft spot
for *Ponyo* and the
whole marine world
it portrays. And the
growing Pop Pop
boat is absolutely
wonderful.

Titles:
• *Le Voleur
d'estampes* (Glénat)

• *Allons-y! Alonzo!*
(animated short film)

www.camille-moulin-
dupre.com

www.facebook.com/
cecharmantcamille

www.twitter.com/
Cmoulindupre

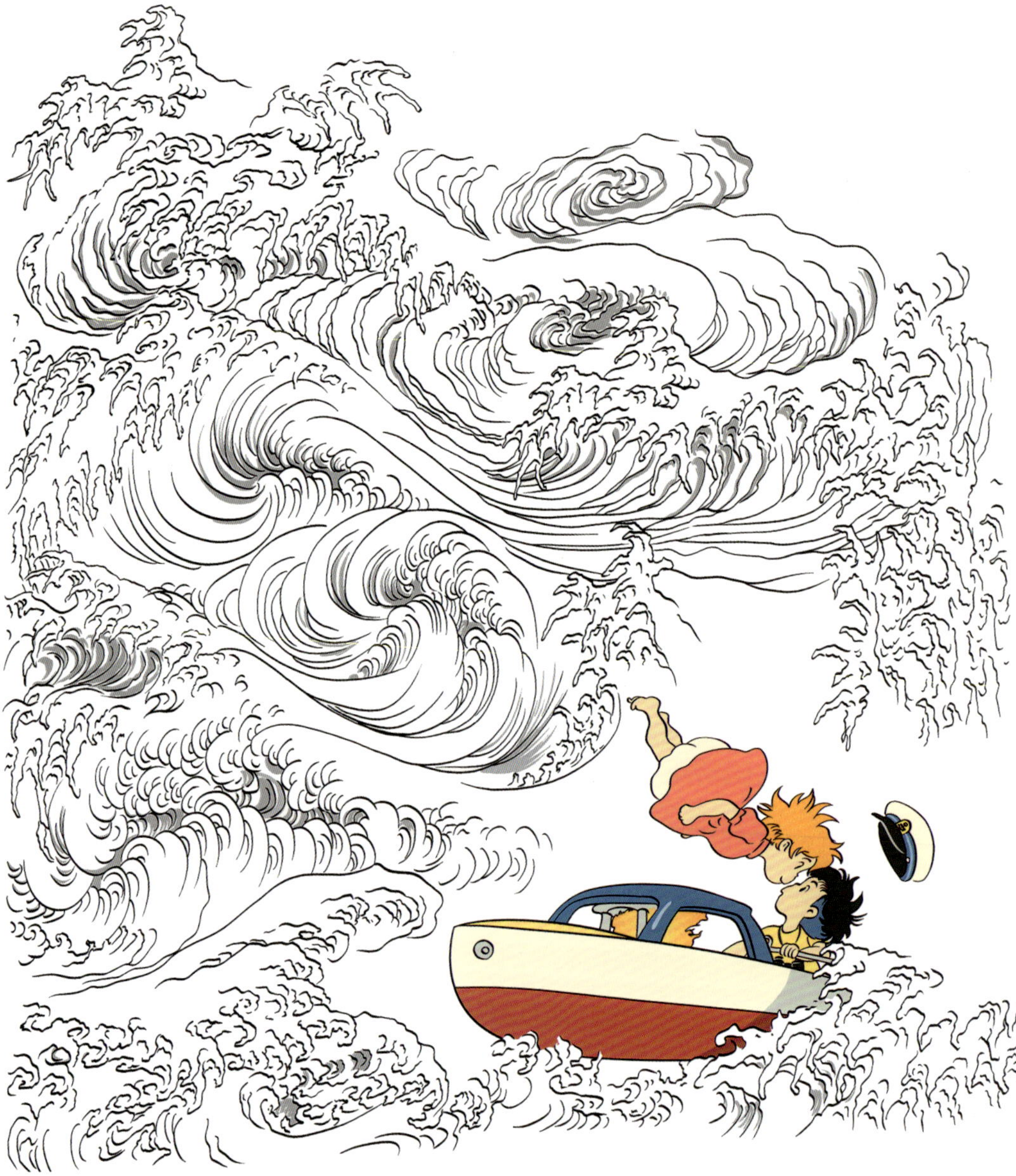

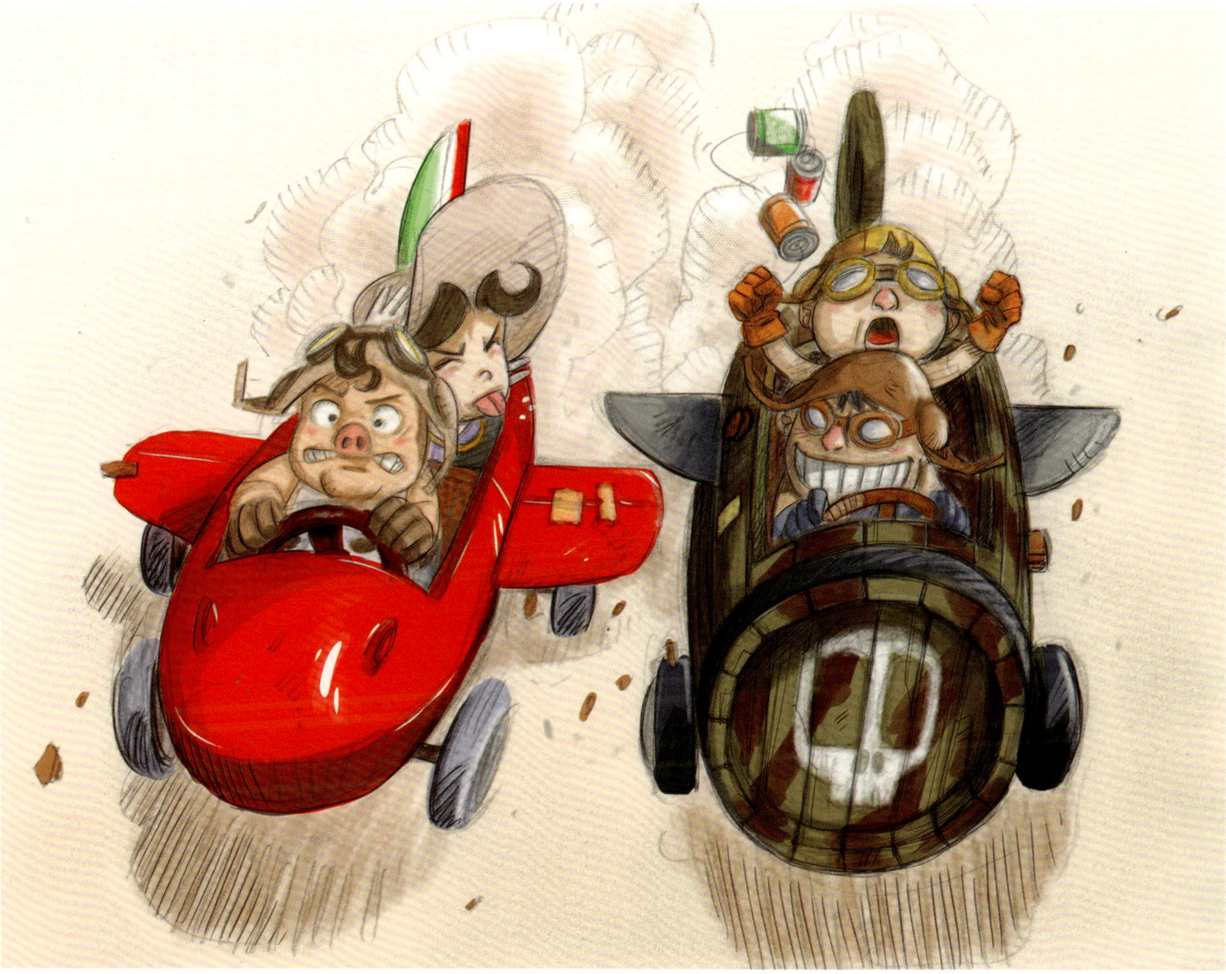

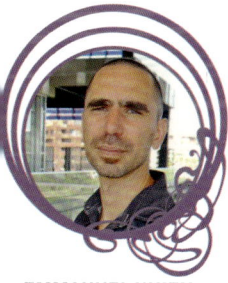

EMMANUEL NHIEU

Comic book and
manga author

Favorite Ghibli film:
Porco Rosso

**Why did you choose
this drawing?**
Because it's the first
one I ever saw, and it
just blew me away.

Titles:
• *Nocturnes rouges*
(Soleil)

• *Burning Tattoo*
(Ankama)

www.facebook.com/
manu.nhieu

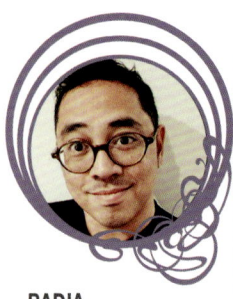

RADJA
SAUPERAMANIANE

Freelance illustrator

Favorite Ghibli film:
Spirited Away

**Why did you choose
this drawing?**
It was hard to choose
between *Mononoke*
and *Spirited Away*,
but in the end, I went
with the second
one. I loved this
character, who evolves
throughout the film.
Her delicacy and
strength of character
inspired my drawing!

Titles:
• Illustrations for the
role-playing game
INS/MV

• Illustrations for the
role-playing game
D-Start

www.radjas.over-blog.net

http://facebook.com/
RadjaIllustrateur/

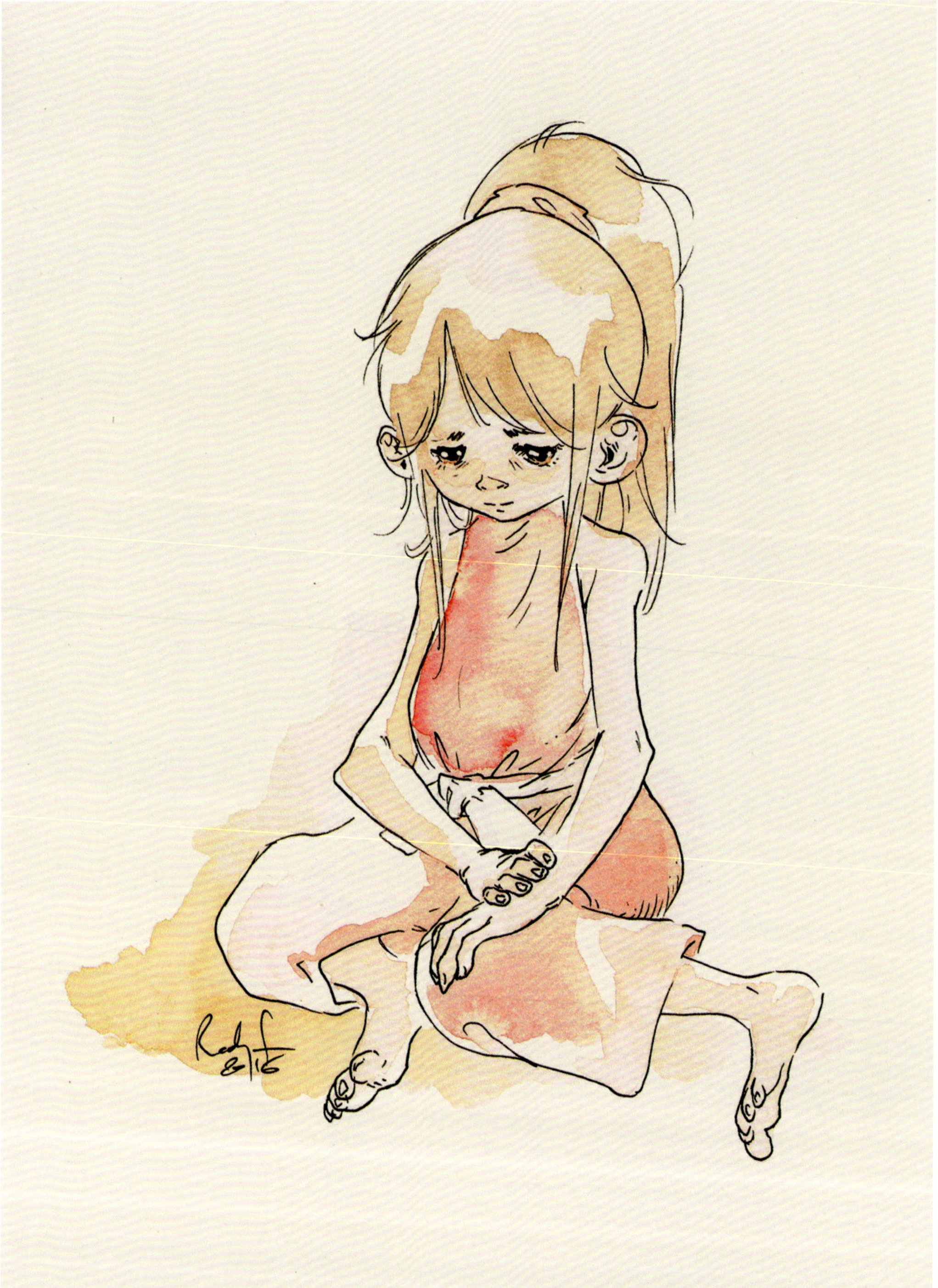

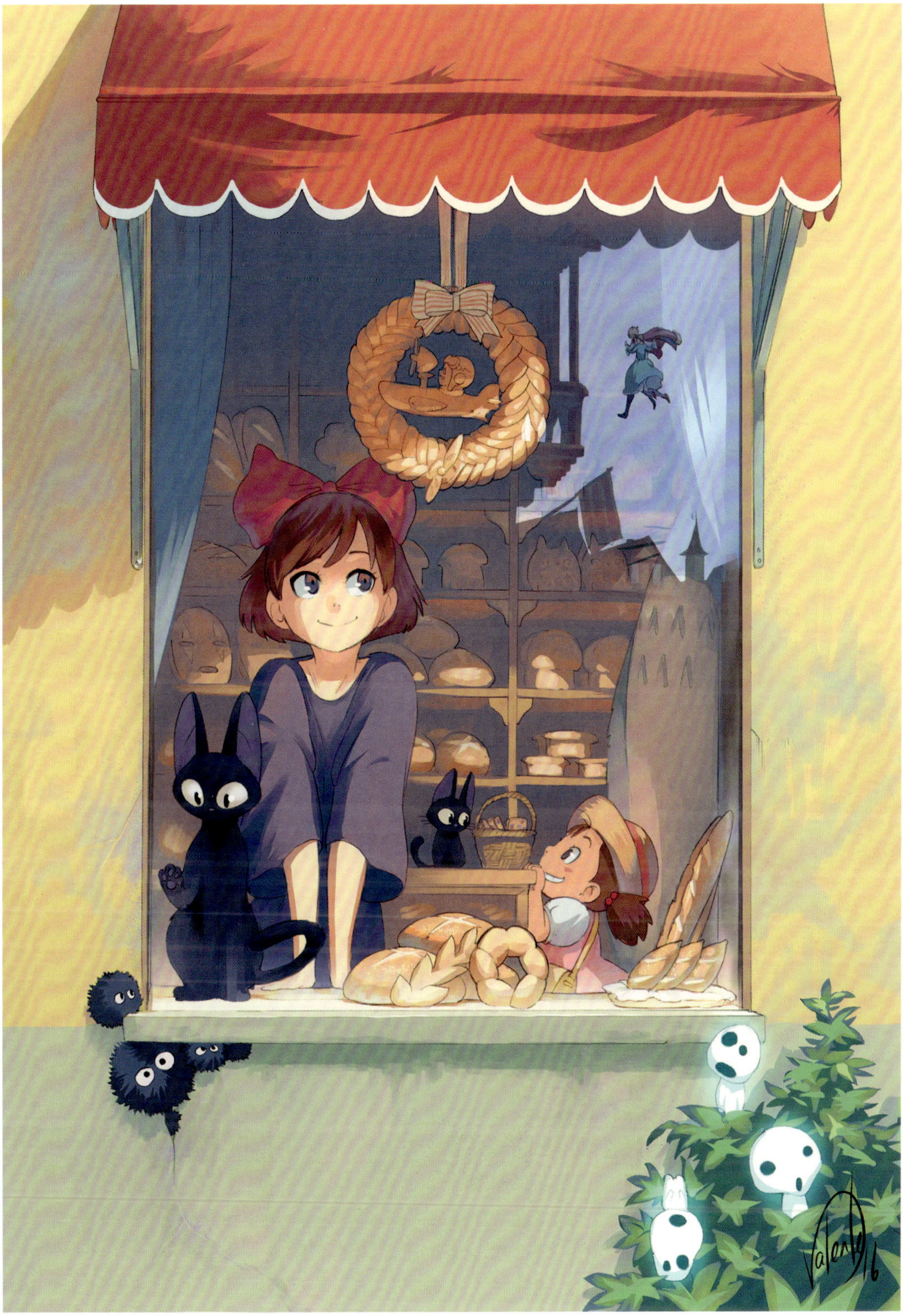

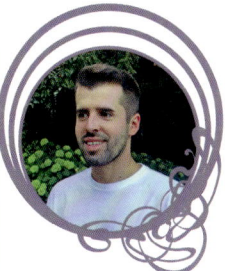

TONY VALENTE

Comic book and manga author

Favorite Ghibli films:
Howl's Moving Castle and *Princess Mononoke* (I can't decide. I could almost add *Porco Rosso*, too. ^^)

Why did you choose this drawing?
One of the things I find most touching about Ghibli, and Miyazaki's films in particular, is the relationship with the imaginary. Very often, we are shown a rather basic, routine real world, with characters firmly rooted in their everyday lives, which could almost be our own. But for those who know how to look closely (often children), fantasy and the imaginary are never far away. I've tried to capture this feeling and create a drawing with it. And I wanted to draw bread, too. I can't explain that! (-_-)

Titles:
- *Radiant* (Ankama)
- *S.P.E.E.D. Angels* (Soleil)
- *Hana Attori* (Soleil)
- *Les 4 Princes de Ganahan* (Delcourt)

www.instagram.com/tonytonyvalente

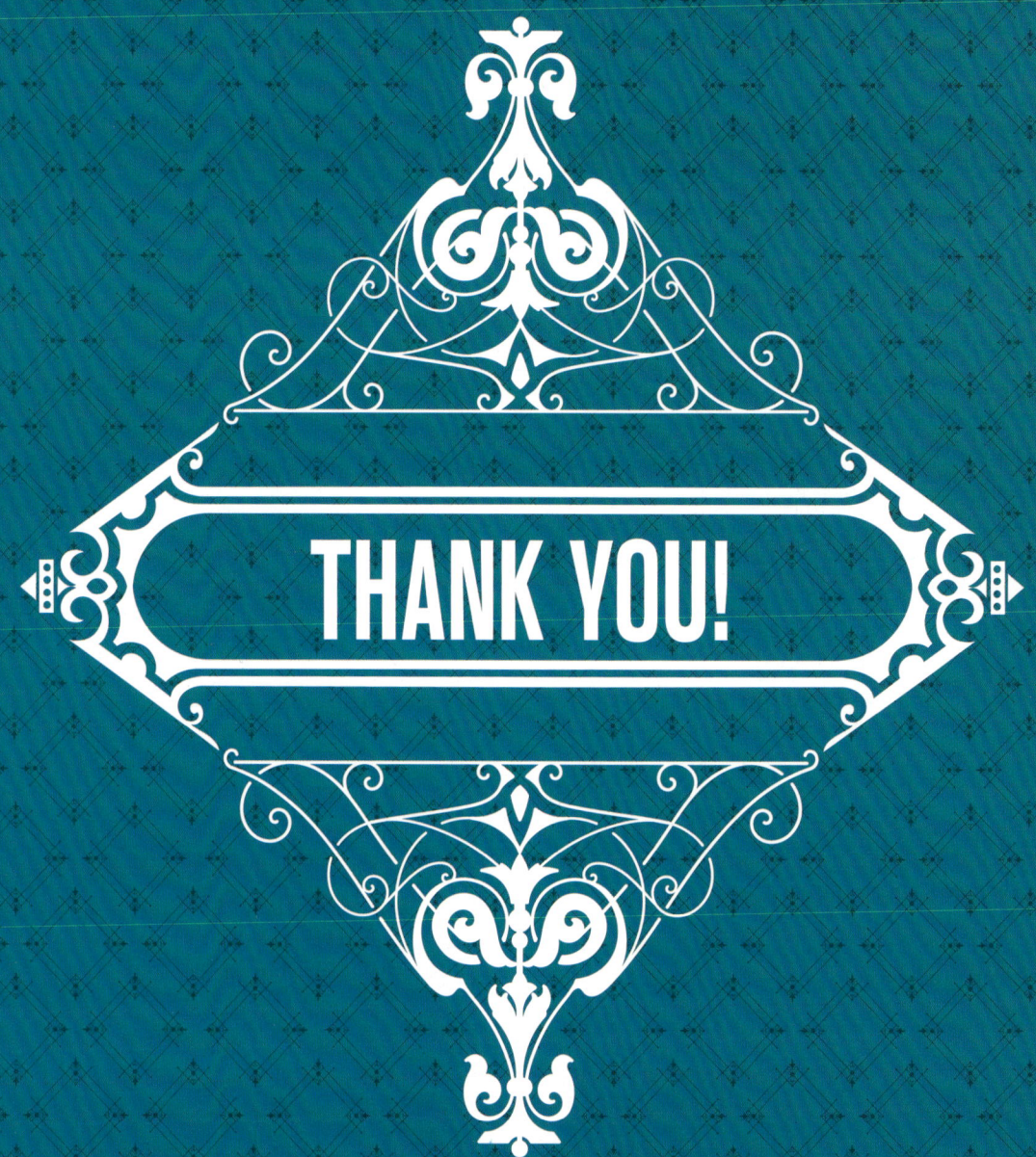

THANK YOU!

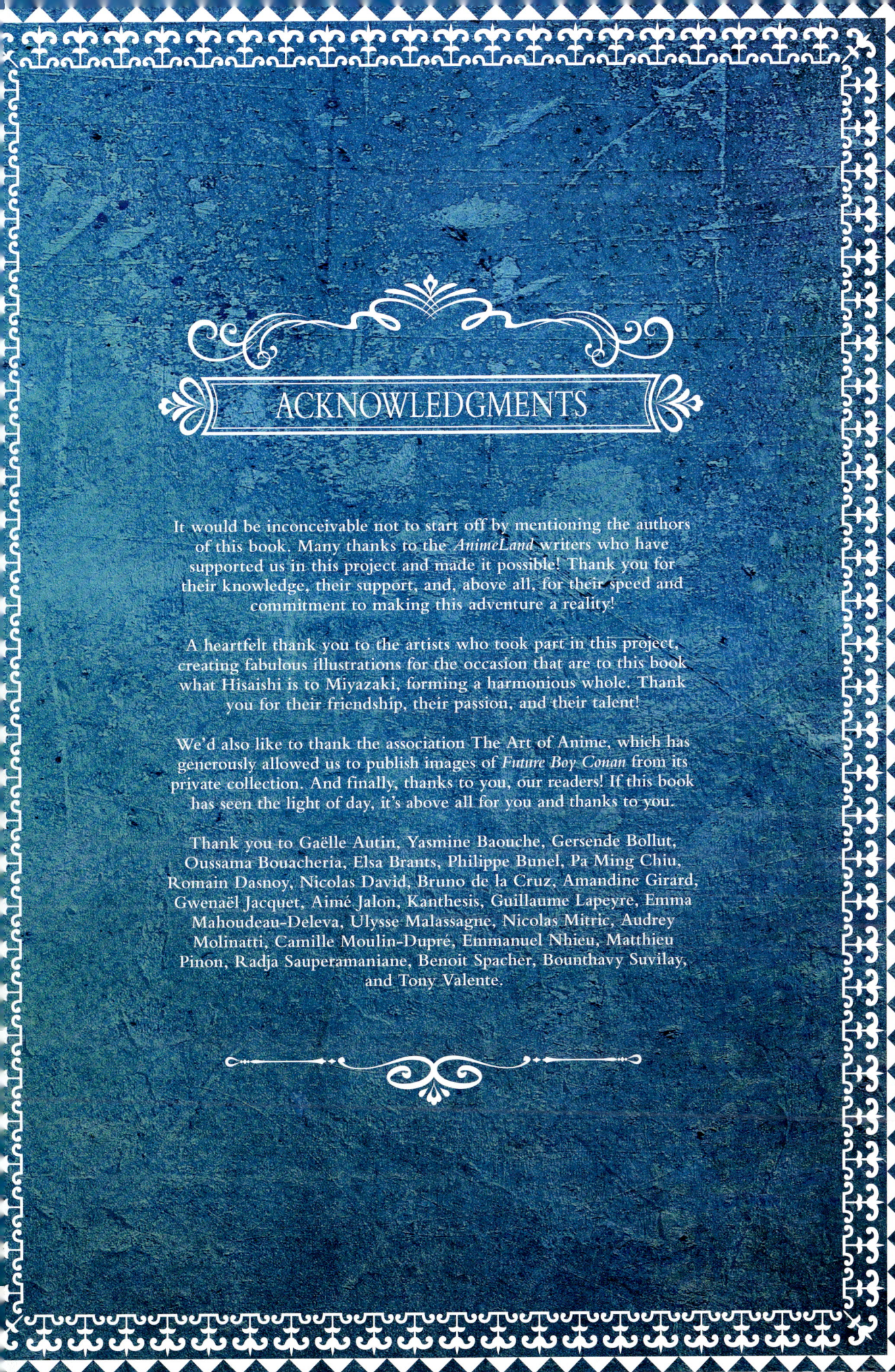

ACKNOWLEDGMENTS

It would be inconceivable not to start off by mentioning the authors of this book. Many thanks to the *AnimeLand* writers who have supported us in this project and made it possible! Thank you for their knowledge, their support, and, above all, for their speed and commitment to making this adventure a reality!

A heartfelt thank you to the artists who took part in this project, creating fabulous illustrations for the occasion that are to this book what Hisaishi is to Miyazaki, forming a harmonious whole. Thank you for their friendship, their passion, and their talent!

We'd also like to thank the association The Art of Anime, which has generously allowed us to publish images of *Future Boy Conan* from its private collection. And finally, thanks to you, our readers! If this book has seen the light of day, it's above all for you and thanks to you.

Thank you to Gaëlle Autin, Yasmine Baouche, Gersende Bollut, Oussama Bouacheria, Elsa Brants, Philippe Bunel, Pa Ming Chiu, Romain Dasnoy, Nicolas David, Bruno de la Cruz, Amandine Girard, Gwenaël Jacquet, Aimé Jalon, Kanthesis, Guillaume Lapeyre, Emma Mahoudeau-Deleva, Ulysse Malassagne, Nicolas Mitric, Audrey Molinatti, Camille Moulin-Dupré, Emmanuel Nhieu, Matthieu Pinon, Radja Sauperamaniane, Benoit Spacher, Bounthavy Suvilay, and Tony Valente.

ILLUSTRATIONS FROM FUTURE BOY CONAN

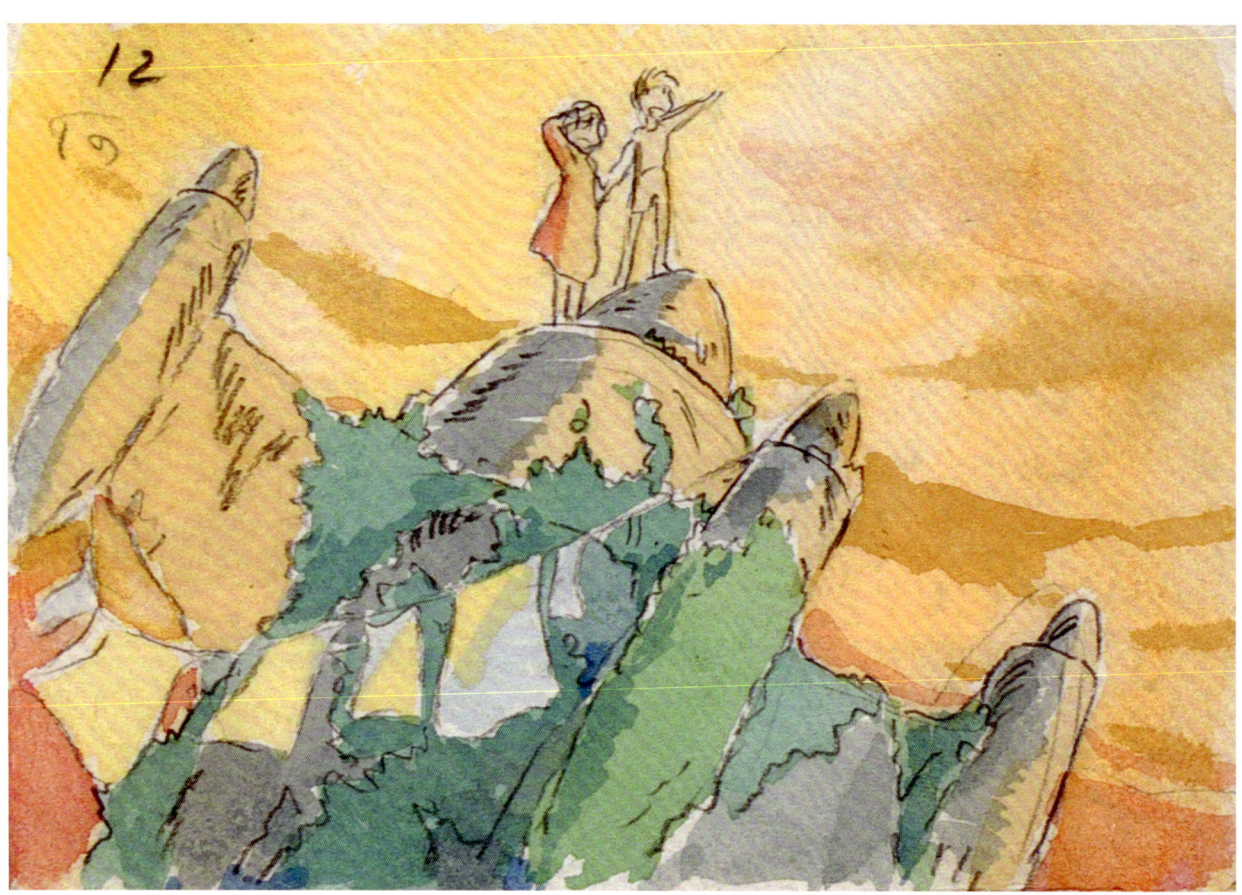

FUTURE BOY CONAN
Director: Hayao Miyazaki, Studio: Nippon Animation (1978)
THE ART OF ANIME Cultural Fund/Spacher-Vogler Collection

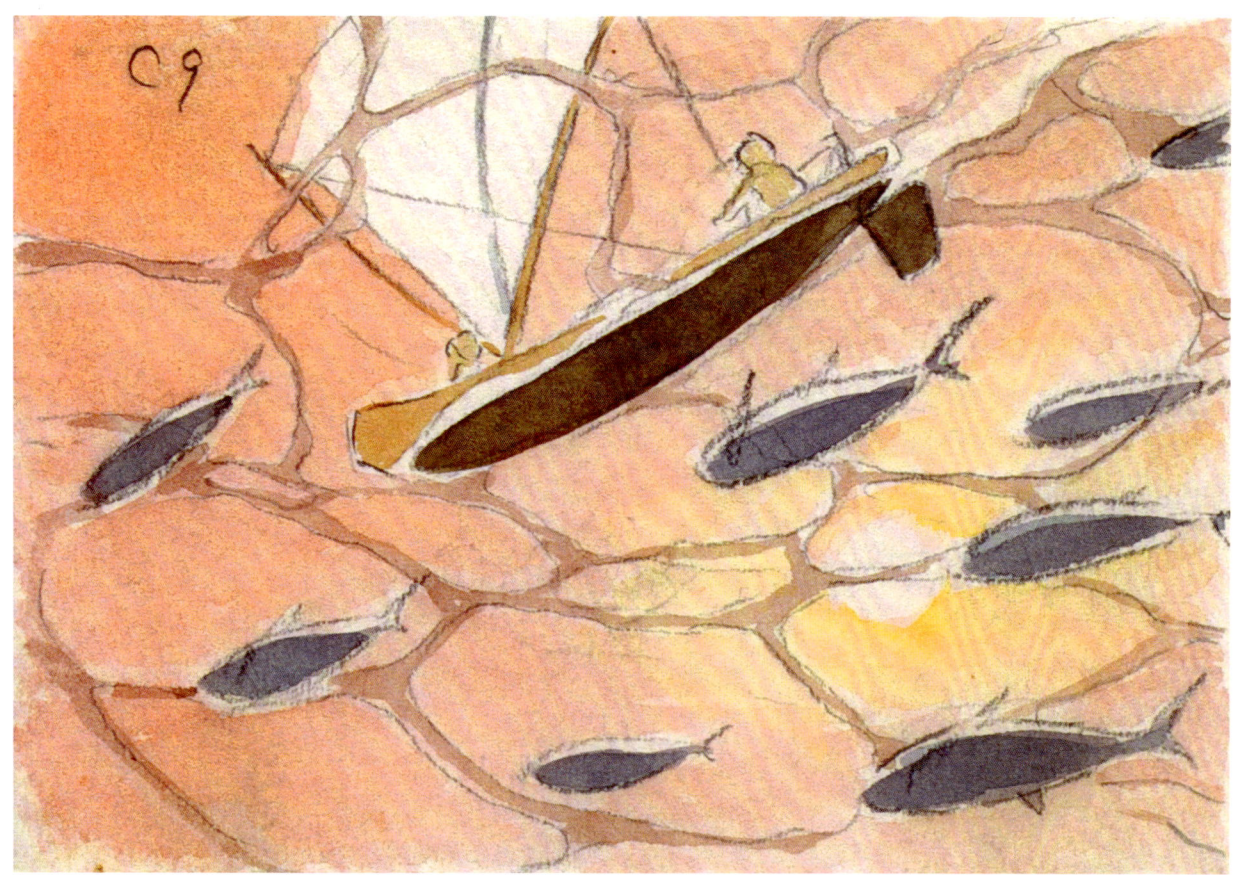

FUTURE BOY CONAN
Director: Hayao Miyazaki, Studio: Nippon Animation (1978)
THE ART OF ANIME Cultural Fund/Spacher-Vogler Collection

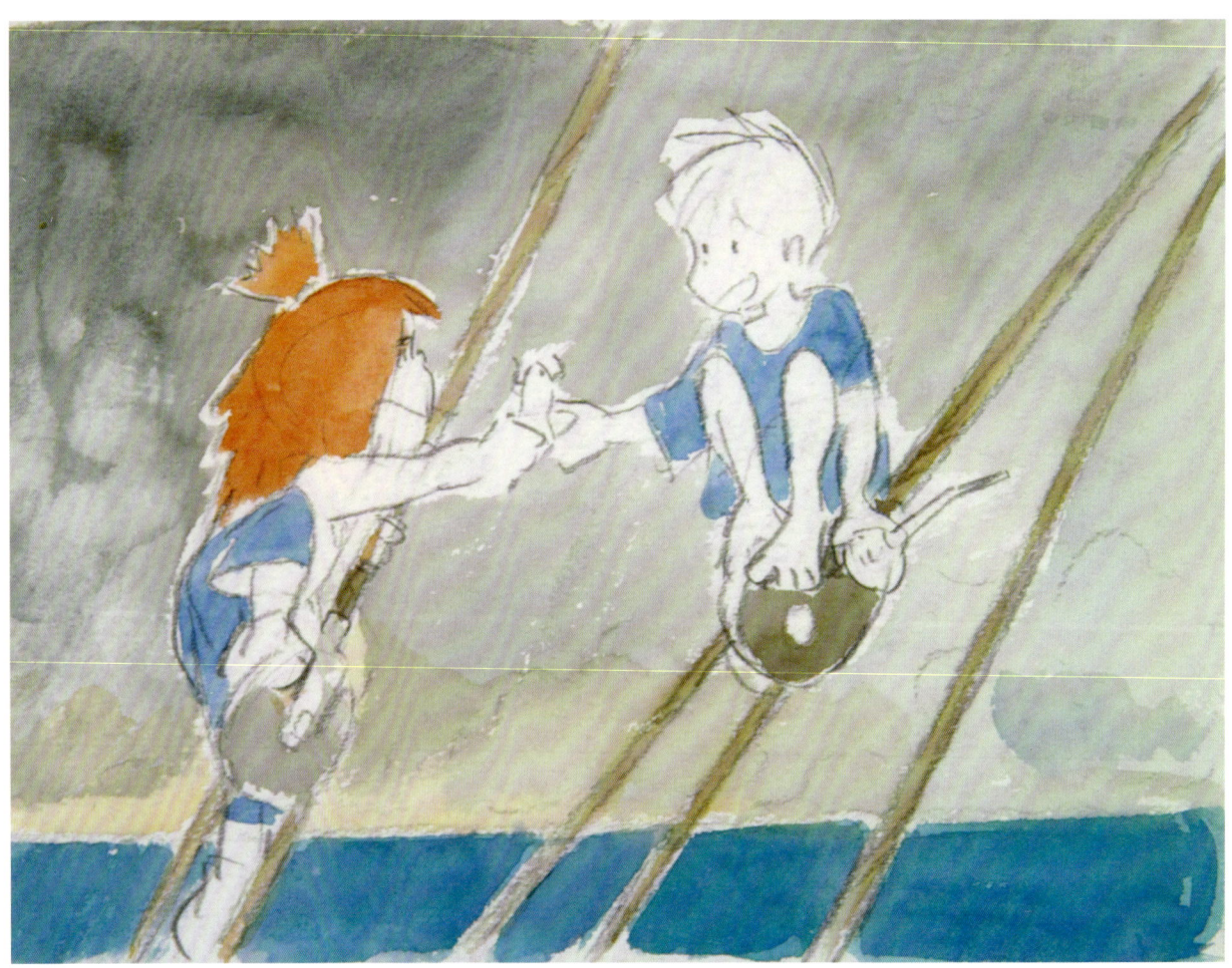

FUTURE BOY CONAN
Director: Hayao Miyazaki, Studio: Nippon Animation (1978)
THE ART OF ANIME Cultural Fund/Spacher-Vogler Collection

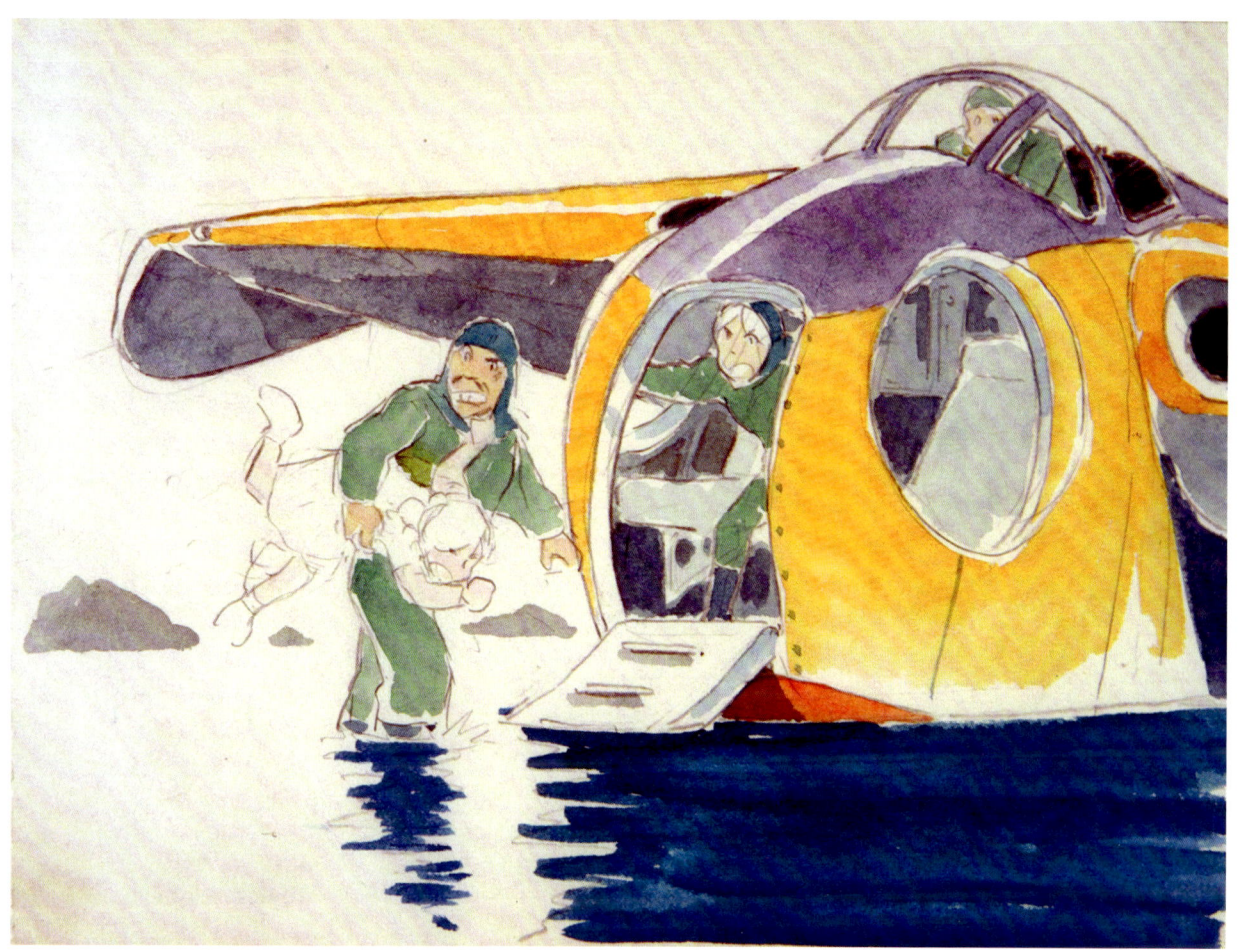

FUTURE BOY CONAN
Director: Hayao Miyazaki, Studio: Nippon Animation (1978)
THE ART OF ANIME Cultural Fund/Spacher-Vogler Collection

REFERENCES

BOOKS

In addition to all the books that inspired the films featured in this book, here are some references to help you learn more.

The Anime Art of Hayao Miyazaki by Dani Cavallaro, McFarland & Company, Inc.

Dessin du studio Ghibli – Les secrets du layout pour comprendre l'animation de Takahata & Miyazaki by multiple authors, Art Ludique (in French)

Hayao Miyazaki et l'acte créateur by Emmanuel Trouillard, L'Harmattan (in French)

Hayao Miyazaki: Cartographie d'un univers by Raphaël Colson and Gaël Régner, Les moutons électriques (in French)

Hayao Miyazaki, cinéaste en animation by Stéphane Le Roux, L'Harmattan (in French)

Hayao Miyazaki, au gré du vent by Sébastien Bénédict, Rouge Profond (in French)

Hayao Miyazaki: Master of Japanese Animation: Films, Themes, Artistry by Helen McCarthy, Stone Bridge Press

Hayao Miyazaki, nuances d'une oeuvre dirigée by Victor Lopez, Les moutons électriques (in French)

Hommage à Hayao Miyazaki: un coeur à l'ouvrage by Stéphanie Chaptal, Ynnis (in French)

Hommage à Isao Takahata: de Heidi à Ghibli by Stéphanie Chaptal, Ynnis (in French)

Isao Takahata, cineaste en animation by Stéphane Le Roux, L'Harmattan (in French)

Isao Takahata, le réel animé, revue de cinéma no. 63, Collectif Éclipses (in French)

Mixing Work with Pleasure: My Life at Studio Ghibli by Toshio Suzuki, Japan Publishing Industry Foundation for Culture

Miyazakiworld: A Life in Art by Susan Napier, Yale University Press

Nausicaä of the Valley of the Wind, Volumes 1 to 7, by Hayao Miyazaki, Viz Media

Sharing a House with the Never-Ending Man by Stephen Alpert, Stone Bridge Press

Starting Point: 1979–1996 by Hayao Miyazaki, Viz Media

Studio Ghibli: The Films of Hayao Miyazaki and Isao Takahata by Colin Odell and Michelle Le Blanc, Kamera Books

Turning Point: 1997–2008 by Hayao Miyazaki, Viz Media

ONLINE

www.ghibli.jp/
Official Studio Ghibli website (in Japanese)

www.buta-connection.net/
Unofficial French-language site on the history of Studio Ghibli, its key players, and their works (in French)

www.nausicaa.net/wiki/
Wiki on everything related to Studio Ghibli and its key players

www.bfi.org.uk/
The official website of the British Film Institute, this is a gold mine of information on film and television far beyond the UK's borders. Its online magazine, *Sight and Sound,* is particularly informative:
www.bfi.org.uk/news-opinion/sight-sound-magazine

www.imdb.com
A film directory

www.japantimes.co.jp/
The website of the *Japan Times,* which provides news about Japan in English

VIDEOS

10 Years with Hayao Miyazaki
A four-part documentary from NHK

2,399 Days with Ghibli and Miyazaki
Documentary from NHK

Ghibli: The Miyazaki Temple
French documentary by Yves Montmayeur

The Kingdom of Dreams and Madness
Cinedigm documentary on the making of Hayao Miyazaki's *The Wind Rises;* available via several streaming services in the US

The Modest Heroes of Studio Ponoc
Documentary short about the creation of Studio Ponoc and its relationship with Studio Ghibli

Never-Ending Man: Hayao Miyazaki
A follow-up documentary to *10 Years with Hayao Miyazaki;* available via several streaming services in the US

Yasuo Ôtsuka's Joy of Motion
DVD from Buena Vista Entertainment

STUDIO GHIBLI

AN ANIMATION STUDIO OF INFINITE VARIETY

Co-founded by Hayao Miyazaki and Isao Takahata on June 15, 1985, Studio Ghibli has since produced all the anime works of the two men (both feature films and shorts), as well as those of other directors. This is a list of all the works produced by Studio Ghibli, excluding those created to be shown only at the Ghibli Museum.

1986
Castle in the Sky
Written and directed by Hayao Miyazaki.
Produced by Yasuyoshi Tokuma and Isao Takahata.

1988
My Neighbor Totoro
Written and directed by Hayao Miyazaki.
Produced by Toru Hara.

Grave of the Fireflies
Written and directed by Isao Takahata.
Based on the short story "Grave of the Fireflies" by Akiyuki Nosaka. Produced by Toru Hara.

1989
Kiki's Delivery Service
Written and directed by Hayao Miyazaki.
Produced by Toru Hara and Hayao Miyazaki.

1991
Only Yesterday
Written and directed by Isao Takahata.
Based on the manga *Omoide Poroporo* by Hotaru Okatomo and Yûko Tone.
Produced by Hayao Miyazaki and Toshio Suzuki.

1992
Porco Rosso
Written and directed by Hayao Miyazaki.
Produced by Toshio Suzuki.

Sora Iro no Tane (The Sky-Colored Seed)
(Series of shorts)
Directed by Hayao Miyazaki.

1993
Ocean Waves
(TV movie broadcast by NTV)
Directed by Tomomi Mochizuki.
Written by Keiko Niwa.
Based on a novel by Saeko Himuro.
Produced by Takahashi Nozomu.

1994
Pom Poko
Written and directed by Isao Takahata.
Produced by Hayao Miyazaki and Toshio Suzuki.

1995
On Your Mark
(Music video)
Written and directed by Hayao Miyazaki.
Produced by Toshio Suzuki.

Whisper of the Heart
Directed by Yoshifumi Kondô.
Written by Hayao Miyazaki.
Produced by Hayao Miyazaki and Toshio Suzuki.

1997
Princess Mononoke
Written and directed by Hayao Miyazaki.
Produced by Toshio Suzuki.

1999
My Neighbors the Yamadas
Written and directed by Isao Takahata.
Based on the work of Hisaichi Ishii.
Produced by Toshio Suzuki.

2000
Ghiblies (Short film)
Written and directed by Yoshiyuki Momose.
Produced by Hiroyuki Watanabe.

2001
Spirited Away
Written and directed by Hayao Miyazaki.
Produced by Toshio Suzuki.

2002
Ghiblies, Episode 2
(Short film)
Written and directed by Yoshiyuki Momose.
Produced by Hiroyuki Watanabe.

The Cat Returns
Directed by Hiroyuki Morita.
Written by Reiko Yoshida.
Based on *Baron the Cat* by Aoi Hiiragi.
Produced by Toshio Suzuki and Nozomu Takahashi.

Mei and the Kittenbus
(Short film, now only shown at the Ghibli Museum after two promotional and charity screenings in the USA)
Written and directed by Hayao Miyazaki.
Produced by Toshio Suzuki.

2004
Howl's Moving Castle
Written and directed by Hayao Miyazaki.
Based on the novel by Diana Wynne Jones.
Produced by Toshio Suzuki.

2006
Tales from Earthsea
Directed by Gorô Miyazaki.
Written by Gorô Miyazaki and Keiko Niwa.
Based on *The Earthsea Cycle* by Ursula K. Le Guin.
Produced by Toshio Suzuki.

The Night of Taneyamagahara
(Short film sold on DVD in Japan)
Directed by Kazuo Oga.
Written by Kenji Miyazawa.

2007
Iblard Jikan
(Short film)
Written and directed by Naohisa Inoue.
Produced by Shinsuke Nonaka.

2008
Ponyo
Written and directed by Hayao Miyazaki.
Produced by Toshio Suzuki.

2010
The Secret World of Arrietty
Directed by Hiromasa Yonebayashi.
Written by Hayao Miyazaki and Keiko Niwa.
Based on the novel *The Borrowers* by Mary Norton.
Produced by Toshio Suzuki.

2011
Ni no Kuni: Wrath of the White Witch
(Video game co-produced with Level-5 for Nintendo DS and Sony PS3).

From Up on Poppy Hill
Directed by Gorô Miyazaki.
Written by Hayao Miyazaki and Keiko Niwa.
Based on *Kokuriko-zaka Kara* by Tetsurô Sayama and Chizuru Takahashi.

2013
The Wind Rises
Written and directed by Hayao Miyazaki.
Produced by Toshio Suzuki.

The Tale of the Princess Kaguya
Written and directed by Isao Takahata.
Produced by Yoshiaki Nishimura.

2014
When Marnie Was There
Directed by Hiromasa Yonebayashi.
Written by Keiko Niwa, Masashi Andô, and Hiromasa Yonebayashi.
Based on the novel *When Marnie Was There* by Joan G. Robinson.
Produced by Yoshiaki Nishimura and Kôji Hoshino.

Ronja, the Robber's Daughter
(Animated series for NHK)
Directed by Gorô Miyazaki.
Written by Hiroyuki Kawasaki.
Based on the novel by Astrid Lindgren.

2016
The Red Turtle
Directed by Michael Dudok de Wit.
Written by Michael Dudok de Wit and Pascale Ferran.
Produced by Isao Takahata, Toshio Suzuki, Vincent Maraval, Pascal Caucheteux, and Grégoire Sorlat.

2018
Boro the Caterpillar
(Short film)
Written and directed by Hayao Miyazaki.
Produced by Toshio Suzuki.

2020
Earwig and the Witch
Directed by Gorô Miyazaki.
Written by Keiko Niwa and Emi Gunji.
Based on the novel by Diana Wynne Jones.
Produced by Toshio Suzuki.

2022
Zen: Grogu and Dust Bunnies
(Short film)
Directed and animated by Katsuya Kondô.
Produced by Tomohiko Ishii.

2023
The Boy and the Heron
Written and directed by Hayao Miyazaki.
Based on the novel *How Do You Live?* by Genzaburô Yoshino.
Produced by Toshio Suzuki.

STUDIO GHIBLI
DREAM ARTISTS

INSIGHT
EDITIONS

PO Box 3088
San Rafael, CA 94912
www.insighteditions.com

f Find us on Facebook: www.facebook.com/InsightEditions
⊙ Follow us on Instagram: @insighteditions

Originally published in French as *Hommage au studio Ghibli: Les artisans du rêve* by Ynnis Editions, France, in 2017.

English translation by Beth Smith.
English translation © 2025 Insight Editions.

ISBN: 979-8-88663-911-7

Publisher: Raoul Goff
SVP, Co-Publisher: Vanessa Lopez
VP, Creative: Chrissy Kwasnik
VP, Manufacturing: Alix Nicholaeff
Editorial Director: Lia Brown
Art Director: Matt Girard
Designer: Leah Lauer
Senior Editor: Stephen Fall
Editorial Assistant: Alecsander Zapata
Executive Managing Editor: Maria Spano
Senior Production Manager: Greg Steffen
Strategic Production Planner: Lina s Palma-Temena

© 2024 Ynnis Éditions. All rights reserved worldwide.

CEO: Cedric Littardi
Editors: Marichka Besse, Marion Cochet-Grasset, and Mélanie Ramet
Graphic design, cover, and layout: Élise Godmuse
Shutterstock: ilolab/Digiselector/Paladin12/Mr.prasong/siam sompunya/standa_art

2024 expanded edition:
Editing: Sébastien Rost
Proofreading: Philippe Vallotti
Additional texts: Stéphanie Chaptal, Bruno de la Cruz, Mario Pasqualini
Translation from Italian: Carole Martinato (The Boy and the Heron)
Correction: Mélissa Veludo
Additional layout: Stéphanie Lairet, Sébastien Rost
Editorial coordination: Jeanne Bucher
Marketing & communication: Alexandra Sacone

The images featured on these pages are published solely to illustrate the authors'
contributions and are all © their owners (Studio Ghibli, Buena Vista Entertainment, The Walt
Disney Company, Nibariki, Tokuma Shoten, Polygon, Toei Animation, Nippon Animation,
Studio Ponoc, and TMS Entertainment).

Ynnis Éditions
38 rue Notre-Dame-De-Nazareth
75003 Paris, France
www.ynnis-editions.fr
Instagram: @ynnis_editions
Facebook: Ynnis Éditions
X: @YnnisEditions

 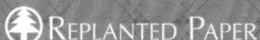

Insight Editions, in association with Roots of Peace, will plant two trees for each tree used in
the manufacturing of this book. Roots of Peace is an internationally renowned humanitarian
organization dedicated to eradicating land mines worldwide and converting war-torn lands
into productive farms and wildlife habitats. Roots of Peace will plant two million fruit and
nut trees in Afghanistan and provide farmers there with the skills and support necessary for
sustainable land use.

Manufactured in China by Insight Editions

10 9 8 7 6 5 4 3 2 1